Brother Robert Lee, fsc

MARK
Evangelist
and
Theologian

MARK
Evangelist and Theologian
Ralph Martin

Academie
Books
Grand Rapids,
Michigan
Zondervan Publishing House

CONTENTS

PREFACE

RECENT STUDY OF THE NEW TESTAMENT GOSPELS HAS GIVEN PROMINENCE to the individual message of the separate accounts of Jesus' ministry and their purpose in the early church. Until the onset of the period after World War II, it was customary to speak of the synoptic gospels in a way that showed that the assumption of a common teaching was being made. While there is an obvious truth in this blanket description, it has more recently become clear that each individual gospel must be allowed to stand on its own and its characteristic contribution to our study of the origins and development of New Testament Christianity must be allowed to stand out.

The aim of this book is to set down in some detail the fortunes and values of recent scholarly research on the Gospel according to Mark. No claim to a comprehensive coverage of the material is made, as will be obvious to anyone who knows the extent of the published literature on this theme. The bibliography has been trimmed to manageable size and kept to a minimum, consonant with the book's purpose. Nor does the book treat the entire Markan text as though it were a commentary on the gospel.

That purpose is to relate the Gospel to the General reader's understanding more than to offer another theory to the scholarly fraternity, though it so happens that for the writer the best understanding of Mark entails the possibility that a new view of the circumstances of its publication may be correct. Whether this confidence is misplaced or not is for the reader to judge.

The author's interest in this Gospel goes back to his student days and especially to classroom lectures given by the late Professor T. W. Manson at Manchester. That stimulus was further strengthened when, after several years, it fell to the author to accept responsibility, as Lecturer in New Testament Studies in the University of Manchester, for the same classes as those in which he had been Manson's student. Needless to say, the lectures were not discharged with anything like the expertise, charm and wit which characterized the earlier model; and if there was any value in the later version, it could be directly attributed to the mentor's influence and inspiration.

An opportunity to take cognizance of some trends and studies which had appeared since Manson's day came in an invitation to address the

Manson Society at Manchester in 1968 on the theme of this book. Subsequent reaction from colleagues in the Faculty and research students in the department encouraged the writing of a short resumé of the theory, which appeared in the *Expository Times* lxxx, 12, Sept. 1969, pp. 361–64. I am indebted to the editor, Dr C. Leslie Mitton for permission to use a few paragraphs from that published article.

Since then, the outline has been enlarged and with the invitation to contribute a handbook as a companion volume to I. Howard Marshall's excellent *Luke: Historian and Theologian*, further prospect of a larger book was made possible. For that invitation and for the continuing friendly interest and advice of B. Howard Mudditt of The Paternoster Press, I am deeply grateful. I am also indebted to Dr James D. G. Dunn of the University of Nottingham for several helpful suggestions designed to improve the manuscript. He, of course, is not to be held responsible for the author's argument or conclusions.

It remains for me to express renewed thanks to the Faculty secretary, Mrs. Charmian Pugh, who has typed the MS. with care and accuracy; and to a number of present colleagues and students who have reacted to the material in earlier draft.

Pasadena, California   RALPH P. MARTIN
February 1972

INTRODUCTION

SEVERAL WELL-INTENTIONED FRIENDS, ON READING THE SUBSTANCE OF what forms the following pages, have been kind enough to offer a suggestion. This is to the effect that an introductory chapter should be written in which the author sets down in some detail the main lines of his argument and says what considerations have guided him in the writing of his book. That suggestion has seemed to me to be eminently reasonable and worth acting upon.

The Gospel according to Mark holds a cherished place in the interest of the Bible-reading public. Young Christians especially are encouraged to read it because (it is promised) its language is clear, its narrative of Jesus' life swift-flowing and entertaining, and its appeal to the non-theological mind is direct. The inference is that all readers appreciate a biography simply told. Mark's Gospel is a good story, told with an economy of words and a forthrightness of style. Therefore, Mark's Gospel tops the charts in the popular ratings.

To a large measure this is true. No one can deny that there *is* an immediate appeal about this Gospel and that its message strikes home to us living as we do in a world in which we want quick answers to deep questions, a religious book which we can read in haste (if not in a hurry) and a story of a human life with which we can identify. A generation which gets action-packed drama on the TV news with on-the-spot coverage and instant news analysis is bound to be drawn to this Gospel—if it is drawn to any of the church's holy books. This is simply because Mark's Gospel is full of activity, rich in dramatic quality, and centred on a heroic figure whose master-mind controls the movement of the plot. Talking is not much in his line (in this gospel); and he strides across the chapters with a singleness of purpose and a magnetic appeal to others which identifies him as a Leader with obvious charisma.

It is an easy step from this impression to go on to conclude that Mark's Gospel appeals to us because its picture of Jesus is manageable and fits into a framework we can understand. He appears (so it seems to the rapid reader of the Gospel) essentially human and down-to-earth both in his attitudes and his actions. We are not puzzled over stories of his marvellous birth, for Mark plunges rightaway into his adult life. Equally there are no stories of his resurrection, with dead men getting up out of graves and angels speaking to distraught women, for Mark's Gospel, while it does proclaim the essential truth that he is risen (16:6), speaks of the messenger as a young man and then dramatically breaks off with the flight of the women from the tomb in great fear—a natural reaction, to be sure (16:8).

Many features of the Markan narrative are added to make up a picture of the human figure of Jesus. This evangelist does not baulk at recording items of information or narrating the stories of Jesus which present Jesus in an all-too-human light. We shall study these features in some detail. And we shall also see ample evidence for believing that this impression of a simple Galilean peasant-teacher is only part of Mark's material. Interwoven with the fabric is the apparently contrasting pattern of the enigmatic figure of the strong Son of God; the strong man who shackles Satan and neutralizes his power in order to expel the demons and release the captives; the miracle-worker whose power extends over turbulent nature (4:35–41) as well as distracted human nature; the imperious kingly figure who exercises authority as Son of man on earth and will be the final arbiter of men's destiny (8:38); and the King of Israel who entered upon his rule by the way of the cross.

The puzzle of Mark's Gospel is to be seen just here. How can the evangelist purposely allow the double image of Jesus to remain? He is true man, in the fulness of a complete empirical manhood; and he is an otherworldly being, who at times mysteriously appears on the scene and is greeted with reverence and awe, such as men adopt when they are conscious of the divine presence. It is a major part of our assignment to offer an explanation for this strange concurrence of the truly human and the fully divine elements in Mark's presentation of him whom he calls both "the carpenter" (6:3) and "the Son of God" (1:1, etc.).

It is an accepted axiom of gospel study that, in the period before the first gospel appeared in final form, the Passion narrative was put together to tell the story of the cross. As we are assuming that Mark's Gospel was the first gospel to be written in the sequence of the four gospels, we can frame our next question. Granted that, prior to Mark's work as evangelist, there were available separate, loosely-connected traditions about Jesus (especially the Passion narrative, and possibly a cluster of miracle-stories which celebrated Jesus' power as wonder-worker and charismatic figure), why did Mark choose to place these traditions into the framework of a historical saga? And why has he chosen to call his resultant work "a gospel" (both at 1:1 and at several places in the story in which he seems to be telling the reader what things to look for in the history of Jesus)? In the period before Mark's writing, "gospel" meant the oral proclamation of the good news of salvation in Christ (so Paul's usage). Mark is the first Christian of whom we know who boldly appropriated this Greek word (*euangelion*) as the description of a literary production. How is this innovation to be explained?

Our answer lies in several directions. One is to explore the obscure period of Gentile Christianity following Paul's martyrdom in the mid-60's A.D. Admittedly we know little by way of definite information. But for an earlier decade we do have evidence, notably from the Corinthian correspondence, that false ideas about Jesus were being promulgated in these Christian assemblies formed of believers only recently converted. They undoubtedly were exposed to religious notions much "in the air" in a city such as Corinth, a meeting-place of Greek philosophy, Jewish esoteric ideas and oriental mythology. To this amalgam of strange ideas the term "gnosticism" is applied, though most scholars would wish to modify it so as to distinguish it from the more developed systems of the second and third centuries.

One such bizarre "tendency" was an apparent denial of the importance of the earthly Jesus in the interest of a heavenly, cosmic figure called "Christ." To meet this situation Paul addressed his warning in 1 Corinthians 12:3, just as in 2 Corinthians 11:4f. he exposed this teaching of "another Jesus," "a different gospel," "a different spirit." Tied in with this gnosticizing depreciation of Jesus as a human being was (apparently) a heavy concentration on him as a figure of impressive power. This conclusion is borne out by what we read in 2 Corinthians 10–13 where Paul's opponents claim to share in the Lord's power and chide Paul for his finitude and frailty. It is not difficult to see how the magisterial figure of the miracle-stories in Mark 4:35–6:56 would appeal to such men, and how they would have capitalized on such a christology to bolster their own claims to be his representatives.

Against such a putative background Mark appears as the Pauline theologian of the cross. Paul had warded off the advances of heretical theology, based on an already achieved resurrection and a consequent playing-down of the cross of Jesus, in his day. The way he does it is seen in 1 Corinthians 1:18–2:16; 15:12ff.; 2 Corinthians 13:3f., and his own self-defence is a denial of the heretics' premise by an assertion that the apostle like his Lord is a man of human frailty (2 Corinthians 4:7–12, 16; 12:1–10). Mark, in the authentic Pauline succession, says the same, only in a different way. And as it turned out, his way was original and pace-setting. To this evangelist fell the task of confronting a situation made up of false notions concerning Jesus' real manhood and humiliation to death and the effect of these ideas on an understanding of Christian character and the nature of the Christian life. He responded to it by putting into the framework of a historical narration, anecdotes and stories about Jesus' earthly career which rooted him firmly in real life situations; which made it clear that his miraculous power was conditioned by a certain ambiguity which meant that he did not overwhelm people by a marvellous display of magic; and which gave the historical sequence of events by which he was condemned to death and killed, not as an unfortunate accident or a miscarriage of God's purpose but as a destiny he had long foreseen and spoken about and beyond which he promised, as a pledge of God's vindication, a victory as he came back to re-gather his disciples. Suffering, both his and theirs, is the necessary hallmark of a life of obedience to God; and the true servant must tread a path marked out by his Lord who came to his kingdom along a *via dolorosa*.

Mark's dramatization of the apostolic preaching, expressed simply as "crucified in weakness, but he lives by the power of God," is *his* answer to the same network of heretical ideas which Paul's ministry rebutted; and it is not unjustifiable that Mark should have selected Paul's favourite term "gospel" to epitomize his work.

This close connection between Paul and Mark is well-attested in Christian history. There is, however, another tradition which makes Mark the confidant and interpreter of Peter. Now it is not impossible that the same man, John Mark, shared the double privilege; and it is no part of this book to prise asunder the bond which unites Peter and "my son Mark" (1 Pet. 5:13). In another place I have tried to show that this tradition, while based on the single allusion in First Peter and given maximum credence by church father Papias in the second century, can be explained on other than historical grounds. In particular, I believe that Papias is tendentiously interested in showing the apostolic authority behind Mark because he wants to fend off the (to him) baneful influence of Marcion who championed Luke's gospel. But that is another story, details of which may be read in a short appendix in the following chapters (pp. 80–83).

However, if the link between Peter the disciple and John Mark the gospel-writer is not so tight as tradition would have us believe, it releases us from the traditional view of this gospel as a simple, uncomplicated record of "Peter's memoirs." That understanding has a respected patronage, and only with reluctance do we admit to an abandoning of it. But once we allow Mark to stand on his own feet, as it were, it becomes far more credible to see him as an independent theologian and creative Christian writer and not simply as a stenographic reporter or scissor-and-paste compiler of Petrine traditions. In effect, this is the new gain registered by the school of Redaction-criticism, about which a section (pp. 46ff.) is written.

Other motives can be seen to have entered Mark's ken as, in his desire to be faithful to the apostolic gospel he learned from his master Paul, he addressed himself to theological and pastoral problems in the church of his day. If we can see the characteristic features of his gospel—by his selective emphasis, the arrangement of the material which falls into his hands, and the structure of his entire work seen as a unity—we shall appreciate something of the historical circumstances which impelled him to write. In a word—a French word at that—we are enquiring about *le pourquoi* of this gospel.

To put our enquiry in this way is not to ascribe to John Mark a purpose and a rôle which denies his openness to divine promptings nor does it compromise his writing as holy scripture, inspired by God. The doctrine of inspiration, as classically interpreted, does not presume to say *how* God inspired the Bible writers nor does it preclude the use of their minds in research and response to historical situations (see Luke 1:1-4). In fact, we are under obligation to frame our doctrine within the boundary of all the known facts, and this includes an endeavour to place our gospel in a suggested historical and theological *milieu*, and to observe how a later writer (say, Matthew) takes over and uses the material from an earlier source (in this case, Mark). To be blind to this literary connection is to impugn the providence of God by which his word comes to us in historical dress and in the real life situations of first century Christianity.

To detach Mark from the apron-strings of Peter and set him on his own two feet is also to treat his purpose as a gospel-writer with respect. We do not expect him to answer questions which fall outside his purview. In particular, he is *not* writing a biography of Jesus or responding to a commission to compose a "Life of Jesus" to gratify the curiosity of those in his day who wanted to understand "what made Jesus tick." Such a psychologizing approach to Jesus is remarkably absent from the New Testament interest. Only within nineteenth century liberal Protestantism did this "human interest" motif get the upper-hand and the result was a crop of Lives of Jesus, made up of partly factual and partly imaginary reconstructions of "what must have gone on in Jesus' mind." But Mark is no party to this sort of inquiry, and offers no encouragement to our modern counterparts of the liberal pursuers of the "quest of the historical Jesus," for example in Dennis Potter's play *Son of Man* or in the libretto of the rock opera *Jesus Christ Superstar*.

Once again we have to be on guard against an over-reaction. To say that Mark's chief interest is in Jesus' kerygmatic value in the life of the church is not to despise the historical worth of what he writes about the Man whose feet touched the ground in Palestine in the first three decades of our era. The point at issue is Mark's ruling concern. Was he consciously setting out to "tell it like it was" by taking us back on a guided tour of where Jesus walked and seeking to awaken our interest in him as an itinerant teacher and folk hero? Almost certainly not. His primary interest centres on the living Lord as the Christians' contemporary in his own day. But, for all this preoccupation with the present reality of Christ who lives in the preaching of the gospel and the ongoing experience of the church, Mark sets out to establish a continuity of this figure with the Jesus who shared our life in Galilee and Jerusalem. To that extent he is a historian, if not a biographer.

The reason for this perspective is not hard to find. And once we have found it, it adds immeasurably to our understanding of what the gospels are all about. Too often our teaching and preaching looks back to the past as though Jesus Christ was a historical person *and no more*. Mark's gospel rebukes us for that gross error. He is saying to his contemporaries, and to us if we will but hear it, that the Galilean poet-preacher, the ex-carpenter turned prophet, the strange Man on his cross is none other than the risen Lord and a living power in his church in every age. True, the exigencies of Mark's day required that he should reverse the order of that equation. To Christians only too conscious of Christ's spiritual presence he found it needful to stress the earthly rootage of Jesus the man. And that emphasis is needed whenever there is danger of losing our grip on history and evaporating the importance of the "there-and-then" because of an over-zeal for the "here-and-now." Christian experience set up as a sole criterion of truth, a bare announcement of the kerygma without a clothing in the flesh-and-blood reality of a human existence, a sacramentalizing of the gospel which reduces it to a mystery religion—these aberrations need the corrective which the gospel according to Mark supplies for us.

Both a sentimental interpretation of the Christian story, centring on a Jesus who belongs exclusively to the past and a gnosticizing version which cuts the ties with history and allows the message to float in an existential vacuum come under the scrutiny of this gospel book. And to Mark, evangelist and theologian, the Prayer Book collect for St Mark's day rightly pays tribute:

> O Almighty God, who hast instructed
> Thy holy Church with the heavenly
> doctrine of Thy Evangelist Saint
> Mark; give us grace, that,
> being not like children carried
> away with every blast
> of vain doctrine, we may be
> established in the truth of
> Thy holy Gospel; through Jesus
> Christ our Lord.

I

READING THE GOSPELS TODAY

Why is Mark's record called a gospel? Other possibilities of description. The term "gospel" and its special nuance.

IN ONE WAY THE TASK OF READING THE GOSPELS IS EASY OF ACCOMPLISH-ment. On face-value the four records of Jesus' earthly life are both simple to understand and interesting to read. As we read the gospels, we are already on ground that is familiar, not to say well-trodden. It follows that we have formed certain impressions about these books even before we begin our reading, and this works in two ways. On the side of advantage, we are not wrestling with a subject which is completely unknown and forbidding; we can all make something of our data at first glance. But there is a serious drawback. Such ideas as we have formed over the years tend to harden and become deeply embedded, and there is resistance to change. We have to lay our account with the momentous proposition that our thinking about the gospels may need a drastic revolution. Can it be that until now we have read the gospels in the wrong way? Or at least that we have failed to grasp what the gospels are really all about? And that we have put questions to these parts of scripture which they were never intended or designed to answer? We shall see.

The first requirement is that we try to begin with a new page, as though we are coming to the gospels fresh and for the first time. Let us attempt to put ourselves back into a situation in which reading the gospels came as a new experience. Suppose we were handed a copy of Mark's gospel and were encouraged to read it for ourselves as a new book. What kind of book would it seem to be to us? And would its contents justify or disappoint the expectation aroused by our glancing first at the sentence which stands as the frontispiece: "the beginning of the gospel of Jesus Christ, the Son of God"?

We call these four books, "gospels." It is a good exercise to pause and ask the questions, What is the meaning of this title when applied to the case of literary compositions? Are the four gospels accurately described under this caption? Are they equally to be classified in this way because they are sufficiently homogeneous in their groupings, or are there distinguishing features which make the title, "gospel" more or less appropriate in the case of each individual gospel? What other designations for these booklets are possible?

We shall examine three other terms which are closely connected with what these gospels are popularly understood to be. In each instance it will be apparent that the name suggested is not too appropriate without qualification.

Other Possibilities of Description

C. F. Evans (in a chapter "What kind of a book is a gospel?" in *The New Testament Gospels* [1965], p. 7ff.) illuminates the significance of his question in an interesting way. He invites us to consider how an imaginary librarian at Alexandria in Egypt near the end of the second century A.D. would have classified a copy of Mark's gospel, had such a book been presented to the library.

(i) He might have thought of including this book, which superficially looks like an account of the life of Jesus, under the heading of "Lives of Famous Men," the Greek title for which is *βίοι*. Then, it would stand next to Plutarch's *Lives* of famous Greek and Roman statesmen, which he arranged in pairs to illustrate some moral virtue. But against this suggestion lies the fact that Mark gives no account of the birth of Jesus but plunges rightaway into the stream of his adult life. Moreover, many of the features we normally associate with a biography of a great man are singularly lacking in Mark. The evangelist has not assembled information concerning Jesus' antecedents, culture and environment. He assumes that his readers will already know that Jesus was a Jew, born to Jewish parents and living in the province of the Roman empire when Tiberius Caesar held the reins of power in the imperial city. Moreover, no attempt is made to delve into Jesus' mental or psychological development in a way which has become familiar to us in the twentieth century by modern studies of Jesus' personality such as Dennis Potter's play *Son of Man*. Jesus' response to his environment is a matter on which the evangelist is remarkably silent.

(ii) Another possibility would be the placing of the gospel-book in a section headed "Acts" (Greek *πράξεις*). Under this heading would be books containing the narratives of heroic deeds performed by some notable person like Alexander the Great. But again, the librarian may well have thought that Jesus whose life was set in a remote province of the Roman empire was too inconspicuous a person on the stage of public life to have "Acts." That word suggests movement and exploits. But there is little movement in Jesus' story and the "mighty deeds" he performed are not such as would impress a reader in a sophisticated metropolis like Rome. What would count against Jesus was simply the fact that the ending of his story is a trial scene, on a charge of sedition and revolution against the Roman *imperium*, and a state execution.

(iii) Yet another label to be suggestively affixed to Mark's story is a term translated "Memoirs" (Greek *ἀπομνημονεύματα*). These were a collection of individual anecdotes about, or sayings of, a famous figure, generally supposed to come from someone who knew him well as his disciple or chronicler. Perhaps the most celebrated documents in this category are the *Memoirs* of Socrates (469–399 B.C.) written by the historian Xenophon (c. 380 B.C.) and the *Dialogues* of Plato, Socrates' disciple (380–350 B.C.). One advantage of this pigeon-hole is that precisely this Greek term is found in a description of church worship at Rome in the mid-second century A.D.

Justin Martyr, about A.D. 150, offers the following picture of what went on when Christians assembled for worship.

> And on the day called Sunday there is a meeting in one place of those who live in cities or the country, and the memoirs of the apostles or the writings of the prophets are read as long as time permits. (*Apology* 67.3)

Helpfully Justin, in another place of his apology, tells us what the phrase "memoirs of the apostles" refers to by explaining that "the memoirs of the apostles . . . are called gospels" (*Apology* 66).

Because Justin's account is part of his apology, that is, an attempt to give a non-Christian readership as attractive a presentation of Christian belief and life as possible, we cannot be sure that he is not simply using a term which would be current coin in his readers' vocabulary; and this borrowing of a familiar term as one readily intelligible to Justin's audience is proved by the explanatory gloss which he appends, and by the fact that the title ἀπομνημονεύματα is found in no other Christian writing after Justin to designate the church's liturgical books.

It looks, then, as if this label would not exactly fit the case, either. The chief reason for the inadequacy of these descriptive titles lies in the fact that the Christian gospels are not to be understood as biographies of Jesus.

It is true that much depends on the exact sense we wish to give to the term "biography." As far back as 1915 C. W. Votaw published two essays under the title, "The Gospels and Contemporary Biographies" in the *American Journal of Theology*, 19 [1915], pp. 45–73, 217–49. These essays have recently been reprinted in booklet form as *The Gospels and Contemporary Biographies in the Greco-Roman World* [1970] as a Facet Book. To the issue, Are the gospels biographies of Jesus? Votaw returned an ambivalent reply, according to the connotation given to the term "biography."

He distinguished between biography in the "historical" sense and concluded that the gospels do not fit into this classification for the reasons mentioned above. But he argued that in the "popular" sense of the term, the title was applicable, since this genre of literature aims to make the reader acquainted with a historical person "by giving some account of his deeds and words, sketchily chosen and arranged, even when the motive of the writer is practical and hortatory rather than historical" (p. 49). The examples he drew from the ancient world were the popular biographies of Epictetus whose teaching was written by Arrian, c. A.D. 125–150, Apollonius of Tyana whose biography was recorded by Philostratus c. A.D. 217 and, above all, Socrates of whom our sources of information are the different treatments given by Xenophon c. 380 B.C. and Plato. What unites these literary works is a common effort to "eulogize and idealize their heroes . . . [to] select their best sayings and interpret them for practical use . . . [to] give the memorabilia in an atmosphere of appreciation . . . [to] commend the message to the faith and practice of all" (Votaw, p. 55).

We may question, however, whether the aim of the Christian evangelists could be adequately designated in such language; and our suspicion that Votaw is forcing the gospels into a pre-determined pattern is confirmed when we reach his conclusion, after a lengthy yet interesting comparison between the Socratic writings attributed to Plato and Xenophon and the gospels. He maintains (p. 245) that the purpose of the two groups of biographical writings was in general the same. That purpose he defines as the desire "to restore the reputation of a great and good man who had been publicly executed and defamed by the state, to re-establish his influence as a supreme teacher in respect to right living and thinking, and to render available to all the message of truth and duty which each had made it his life-work to promulgate."

This attempt to correlate the ostensible purpose of the evangelists with that of their contemporaries in antiquity in what seems to be the same literary domain must be judged a failure.

For one thing, in the history of interpretation, the search for contemporary parallels to the literary type (or *Gattung*) of "gospel" in the popular literature of the ancient world was not likely to commend itself as a fruitful enterprise at a time in the 1920's when the uniqueness of the Christian message was receiving emphasis from the Barthian revival.[1] And Votaw's plea went largely ignored.

But there is a second, more telling reason why this correlation is inadequate. For all the superficial resemblances between Socrates' or Apollonius' life-story and that of Jesus, it stands out clearly that no Christian "biographer" thought that he was preserving by his literary records the memory of Jesus, which might otherwise lapse and be forgotten. To imagine this is to overlook the Christian claim of the resurrection of Jesus Christ by which his living presence was assured to the church in every generation. It is true that Christians may well have desired a permanent acount of Jesus' earthly life, words and activity, especially since his first followers were being removed from the scene by death

---

[1] See J. M. Robinson's discussion, "On the *Gattung* of Mark (and John)," *Jesus and Man's Hope* [1970], p. 104.

with the passing of the first generation. But it still remains a conviction, shared throughout the New Testament literature, that the memory of Christ the Lord is a present reality to his people as they meet to worship in his name, to break bread "in remembrance of" him, and to realize the full extent and depth of his promise to be with them (Matt. 18:20). All that we can learn about early Christian literary techniques from the discipline of Form-criticism supports this conclusion, and shows that the thoughts and aspirations of the first disciples were not oriented to the past, as though the church was continually harking back to some "golden age" when Jesus was with them in bodily presence, or seeking to recapture a lost Camelot of spiritual life when Jesus lived on earth. On the contrary, they were conscious of his living presence in the present; and it was this reminder to us that James Denney spotlighted in his epigram, "No apostle, no New Testament writer, ever *remembered* Christ."[2]

So far we have observed the failure of any of the more obvious terms for biographical writing to convey adequately the intention of the evangelists. We have now to enquire how in fact the dilemma was met and overcome. The answer is found in the innovative practice of coining a new name for what was, in effect, a new type of literary genre.

The name Gospel

The "stories of Jesus' life" were called among Christians themselves gospels (Greek εὐαγγέλια). And in so doing they were laying claim to the appearance of a new genre of writing for which no current categories would do. Therefore they chose a new word to describe a new phenomenon, namely a type of literary composition which would not properly be called a biography of Jesus or a chronicle of his exploits or even a set of reminiscences by his friends and followers. Rather, these books were preaching materials, designed to tell the story of God's saving action in the life, ministry, death and resurrection of Jesus of Nazareth. They were called "gospels" because they gave the substance of "the gospel," declared in Romans 1:16 to be God's power to salvation to all who believe.

This is the first principle of gospel interpretation. We place such a high value on these four books of the Bible because they contain the essence of the saving events which form the bedrock of the apostolic gospel. They are kerygmatic in nature and evangelical in design. They are historical in the way in which they root the life-story of Jesus in the world of first-century Judaism and the ancient Graeco-Roman society, but it is history with a novel twist. The gospel writers were not biographers concerned to praise the personal impact made by their subject on those who came under his spell in Galilee and Jerusalem (on that showing his life's achievement was more of a disaster than a success-story). Nor were they diarists

---

[2] J. Denney, *Studies in Theology* [1895], p. 154.

who kept a day-by-day chronicle of his deeds and movements. Nor are the gospels intended to impress the reader with deeds of power and so to extol the merits of the miracle-worker as a figure of some by-gone age.[3]

The Christian writers are correctly named *evangelists*. They report the history of Jesus from a particular and individualistic perspective in order to highlight the kerygmatic (i.e. salvation-bringing) side of that history. In a word, they are men of faith who write to direct their readers' faith to a living person, once localized in Galilee and Jerusalem but now set free from all earthly limitation and exalted as Lord of heaven and the one in whom alone salvation is to be found. Yet he is accessible to those who desire him as a present, powerful reality, to be known and trusted in the worshipping congregations of his followers and in a personal faith-experience and existential commitment.

We are now ready to tackle the question of the correct nomenclature of these pieces of writing under the proposed caption of "gospel."

Why are the Gospels called Gospels?

Let us go back to our illustration of the librarian at Alexandria. He has been handed a copy of St Mark's "life of Jesus" and asked to classify it according to its contents and purpose. He has (as we have seen) no appropriate existing shelf on which to place it. So he improvises and invents and using as a clue the first phrase of the book he places it on a shelf labelled descriptively "Gospels." What led him to do this, and why?

The title "gospel" would certainly have seemed strange to him. Not because he was unused to the word εὐαγγέλιον, but rather because it was being applied to a category of literature and as such was being used without precedent. Indeed, the unheard-of manner of designating the *written* story of Jesus by the caption, "Gospel according to Mark" must have sounded strange both to Christian as well as pagan ears.

In regard to the non-Christian use of the word "gospel" the term was applied to good news, of victory in battle or of the enthronement of a Roman ruler, as in the famous calendar inscription from Priene in Asia Minor, dated 9 B.C., in which the birthday of the emperor Augustus is hailed as "joyful news (εὐαγγέλια) for the world." But it is quite different when the same word comes to be applied to a book as its title.

To Christians of the first century equally, the second century title "gospels" might have come as something of a shock. The plural form may well have seemed a contradiction of the Pauline insistence that there is, by definition, only one gospel. To proclaim any rival message is to incur the apostolic sentence of doom (Gal. 1:8), although this risk was apparently run at Corinth (2 Cor. 11:4). But it would have been just as surprising, not to say scandalous, to the early Christians to see the term

[3] The technical expression for this type of literature which aimed at recounting the miraculous deeds of a god or hero is "aretalogy." See J. M. Robinson, *loc. cit.* p. 103.

"gospel" applied to a group of written compositions. The New Testament usage invariably connects "gospel" with verbs of speaking[4] and responding, never with verbs of writing or reading.

The interesting question now is to ask why Christians in the second century felt it necessary to have recourse to a word which traditionally (to them, at least) had to do with oral communication when it came to finding a descriptive heading for the written accounts of the life of Jesus. Existing titles evidently proved inadequate to the task of conveying all that they understood these brochures to contain. They chose, therefore, a term which had strict and long associations with preaching[5] and did this because they felt that such books could be rightly called "gospels" inasmuch as they stood in close relation to the message of Jesus proclaimed by the apostles. The gospels took on this new nomenclature because the church believed that what they gave in literary form was not a life of Jesus in a biographical style; not a catalogue of his mighty deeds, composed as an aretalogy (i.e. a poem or literary piece celebrating the exploits of a god or holy man); nor even reminiscences of his contemporary followers but an account of how the good news of the church's proclamation—the Rule of God over human lives exerted through the message of a humiliated and exalted Lord—began in Galilee and Jerusalem.

The gospel writers—and the designation "evangelists" is in keeping with what has been said earlier—were not writing as detached historians to narrate "exactly what happened" in a disinterested and impartial way. They do not obtrude their own opinions by introducing a set of value judgments on the narratives or sayings they record[6] or by offering an

[4] As in the Old Testament where the Septuagint does not contain the noun form $εὐαγγέλιον$: so J. Schniewind, *Euangelion, Ursprung und erste Gestalt des Begriffs Evangelium* [i, 1927; ii, 1931] i. p. 78: "The substantive $εὐαγγέλιον$ is absent from the LXX; so is the idea of a messenger of good news. We cannot detect a religious value in the verb . . . The main result is negative: the Septuagint gives us no help in understanding the origin of the concept of 'Gospel.'" But this estimate is excessively negative in its denial that the idea of messenger of good news is lacking, and overlooks such evidence as in *Psalms of Solomon* 11:1, 2:

> "Blow ye in Zion on a trumpet
> to summon the saints;
> Proclaim ($κηρύξατε$) in Jerusalem
> the voice of him who brings good news ($εὐαγγελιζομένου$)"

This set of evidence, which follows on that in the exilic passages of Isaiah 40:9; 52:7–10; 60:6; 61:1, is equally neglected in W. Schneemelcher's discussion in *New Testament Apocrypha*, vol. i [1963], pp. 71ff. in the interest of maintaining an exclusively hellenistic origin of the terminology. But see to the contrary W. K. L. Clarke, "What is the Gospel?" *Divine Humanity* [1936], pp. 86–100.

[5] Especially because of its verbal usage in Isaiah 40:9; 52:7; 60:6; 61:1: for these verses using the verb $εὐαγγελίζομαι$, see F. F. Bruce, "When is a Gospel not a Gospel?" *Bulletin of John Rylands Library* 45 [1963], pp. 325ff.

[6] Except in the Fourth Gospel where the evangelist's rôle is certainly to do just that, e.g., Jn. 2:13–22; 11:51, 52; 12:16; 21:24; John's "threefold procedure, each part of which is characteristic of his writing: first he states what happened (factually) in the past, then he raises questions and gives hints about the significance of the event, and finally he unveils completely, for people living in the present, the positive message which is contained in the events of the past," X. Léon-Dufour, *The Gospels and the Jesus of History* [ET, 1968], pp. 86–87.

assessment of the character of Jesus, of his friends and his foes. It is remarkable how restrained the narration is, especially in the absence of any vituperative comment on those whose hostility to Jesus might well have occasioned some critical remark. The gospel writers apparently thought of their task as more objective in the sense that they did not exercise a biographer's liberty and intrude their own personal comments. Nor are they interested in assembling such information on their subject's antecedents, culture and inner mental development and response to the world around him as modern biographers deem needful to give a full-orbed presentation.

Yet there is no attempt to disguise the motives which have governed the selection of their material. Here the Fourth Evangelist speaks for all: "These are written that you may believe that Jesus the Christ is the Son of God, and that believing, you may have life in his name" (John 20:31). The story of Jesus underlies the preaching of the church, and the preaching has preserved and shaped the record of that history. In summary, the gospels may be described as theological handbooks, incorporating paradigmatic history—a history whose record is angled to set forth the fulfilment of God's redeeming motive and activity in Jesus, the Messiah of Israel and the church's Lord. That is why the gospels are so called.

Mark's use of the term "gospel"

Recent studies on the way in which the word "gospel" (Greek εὐαγγέλιον, euangelion) is used in the Synoptic gospels have yielded some interesting results.[7] These may be tabulated as follows:

(a) Mark is the creator of this term since there is no evidence that any of the pre-Markan traditions (e.g. the sayings-source Q or the hypothetical source behind Luke, so-called Proto-Luke, or putative Judaean traditions underlying the Fourth Gospel) used the noun. In fact, John's gospel lacks the noun altogether and Luke also avoids the noun εὐαγγέλιον.[8]

(b) At the points where the Synoptists diverge in their recording of sayings attributed to Jesus, it appears that Mark has inserted the noun euangelion in order to explain a tradition which was ambiguous, whereas the later evangelists have amplified the text by the addition of other terms. A case in point is Mark 8:35; 10:29 where the text reads:

Whoever loses his life for my sake and the gospel's will save it (8:35).

There is no one who has left house or brothers or sisters or mother or father or children or lands, for my sake and for the gospel . . . (10:29).

---

[7] See especially W. Marxsen, *Mark the Evangelist* [ET 1969] pp. 117-50; cf. N. Perrin, "The Literary *Gattung* 'Gospel'—Some observations," ExpT. lxxxii. 1 [Oct. 1970], 4-7.

[8] The noun does not appear in his gospel and in Acts it is rare. See H. Conzelmann, *The Theology of Saint Luke* [ET, 1961], p. 221.

Matthew 16:25 = Luke 9:24 follow Mark 8:35 with slight variation, but have no amplification of the Markan "for my sake." It is clear that Mark has elaborated the tradition[9] by the insertion of the phrase *heneka tou euangeliou* (for the sake of the gospel); and the other evangelists have chosen not to follow him in this expansion.

Mark repeats this phrase at 10:29 but Matthew 19:29 has re-cast it as "for the sake of my name" and Luke 18:29 reads "on account of the kingdom of God." The conclusion again seems clear, that Mark has expanded an original simple statement expressing heroic self-denial for Jesus' sake into a similar renunciation "for the sake of the gospel." Matthew and Luke have altered the Markan tradition, in one case by omitting the term for "gospel," in the other by re-casting the wording.[10]

(*c*) The impression to be gained from Mark's use of the word is that for him "gospel" was a favourite expression. He has inserted it into the pre-canonical tradition of which he is the first editor.[11] A similar redactional handling of the material may be detected in Mark 13:9, 10. The statement that the disciples will have to stand before governors and kings "for my sake, to bear testimony before them" has (it has been plausibly argued) been expanded to include the explanation given in verse 10 that this witness is tantamount to a preaching of the gospel to all nations.[12] The common factor is the allusion to the Gentiles, mentioned in verse 9 as "governors and kings" and in verse 10 as "the nations" (Greek ἔθνη); and the consequence follows that the evangelist may well have amplified the traditional saying of Jesus about the disciples' destiny as his witnesses in order to bring out the significance of this fact for his church and to underline the fact that faithful testimony in Roman courts (exemplified in the case of Paul who represented the Christian cause before Felix, Festus, Herod Agrippa II and Nero) was foretold by Jesus as part of the world-wide extension of the gospel ministry. Mark has utilized his favourite expression "the gospel" in this context.

(*d*) A parallel case where a world-wide proclamation of the gospel is envisaged is given in Mark 14:9. Marxsen (*loc. cit.*, p. 125) maintains that this verse too is to be assigned to the evangelist but the argument is not compelling at this point, as he admits. The most he confesses to is that

[9] Whether this is to be expressed in terms of a non-Markan Q (so C. F. Burney, *The Poetry of our Lord* [1925], pp. 74f.) or dependence on an Ur-Markus (as W. R. Farmer reasons, *The Synoptic Problem* [1964] p. 143) need not be debated for our purpose.

[10] So Marxsen, *op. cit.*, p. 121. Cf. E. C. Hoskyns and N. Davey, *The Riddle of the New Testament*[3] [1947], pp. 92–3.

[11] So G. Friedrich, TDNT, ii. p. 727 who writes: "εὐαγγέλιον was not present in these passages [where the word occurs in the gospel] in the original Mark, i.e. in the earliest stratum of the tradition."

[12] The argument for maintaining that 13:10 is an independent logion which breaks the connection between verses 9 and 11 is given by J. Jeremias, *Jesus' Promise to the Nations* [1958], pp. 22f. The verse is absent from the parallels in Matt. 10:17–22; Luke 12:11f. Cf. Matt. 24:14; Luke 21:12.

"it would be strange if it were otherwise at just this point," since the remaining instances of the use of *euangelion* are editorial. We shall revert later to this *pericope* of the anointing at Bethany.

(*e*) The two outstanding references to "gospel"—the verse given in the translations as 16:15 is non-authentic—in Mark are examples of exactly what we should expect, *viz.* Mark's use of a Greek term to denote his implicit intention as evangelist. At 1:1 he has placed the noun *euangelion* as part of the frontispiece of his entire composition; and Jesus' reported programmatic announcement at the opening of the Galilean mission is made in terms of the gospel. We may conveniently examine the latter verse now.

> Mark 1:14, 15:
> Now after John was arrested, Jesus came into Galilee, preaching the gospel of God, and saying, "The time is fulfilled, and the kingdom of God is at hand; repent, and believe in the gospel."

It is clear that Mark intends to epitomize Jesus' message as a preaching of the gospel of God. The sense of the genitive "of God" is debated, but not vitally important. Whether it means that he brought a message from God or proclaimed a message which had God as its content and subject-matter is largely an unreal issue, for the two elements of divine authority and a new teaching are not to be separated and are attested as belonging together in the subsequent section of the chapter, in Mark 1:21–28.

The announcement was in terms of a fulfilment of God's prophetic promise and the near arrival of his kingdom. In the light of this Jesus is seen to be the proclaimer of a new age in God's salvation-history, since he embodies in himself all that he announces from God and about him. The only fit response is one of turning to God in repentance and a trustful acceptance of him who thus embodies the message.

The precise form of the wording "believe in the gospel" is problematic, mainly because the verb along with the preposition "in" (Greek ἐν) is not elsewhere found in the New Testament, though it does occur in the Greek Old Testament.[13] The choice is to take the preposition as either instrumental ("believe on the basis of the gospel" or "through the gospel") or causal ("believe because of the gospel," i.e. because of the announcement which Jesus just made about God's impending Rule now at hand). W. Marxsen (*loc. cit.*, p. 135) favours the view that "believe in" should be retained and the sense given is that this is a call to faith in the proclaimer. This is an attractive possibility especially if we combine it with the idea which seems complementary to it, as Marxsen suggests. "Believe in the gospel" (i.e. in Jesus who announces it) because of the gospel, i.e. the record which tells of his proclamation. True, Marxsen has a highly individual interpretation of what "believe" means and seeks to relate

---

[13] See Arndt-Gingrich, *A Greek-English Lexicon* [ET, 1957], p. 666 for the possibilities.

faith to the returning Lord whose parousia (he holds) was awaited in Galilee by Mark's church. This specialized sense is not necessary, and we shall later have to deal critically with Marxsen's overall thesis.

For the present we will follow his lead only to this point. For Mark, Jesus' appearance in Galilee precipitated an announcement that God's Rule was imminent. A new age was breaking in,[14] since Jesus' public ministry was being inaugurated. He therefore summons his hearers to repentance and faith. Mark's record is written from the vantage-point of all that his ministry accomplished as a past fact and the evangelist, aware that Jesus as the living one was still at work in the church and the world, expresses this conviction in terms of its full Christian content by using the generally accepted term "gospel" to denote the blessings of the new age which, as Mark knows, came with Jesus. The call now addressed to readers of his work is to believe in Jesus as the bringer of the new age on the strength of what the written composition contains in its testimony to the church's Lord.

Mark 1:1
    The beginning of the gospel of Jesus Christ, the Son of God.

There are some preliminary issues to be faced before we can examine the purport of this opening verse of the Gospel of Mark. The textual question calls for resolution, and turns upon the matter whether the title "the Son of God" belongs to the original manuscript. Probably the claim that it is original and authentic is to be accepted, not least on the ground that the title "Son of God" runs through Mark's gospel and is a leading theme. With the title so amply attested (1:11; 3:11; 8:38; 9:7; 12:6; 13:32; 14:36, 61; 15:39) a scribe may well have chosen to omit the phrase here in order to allow the sentence (apparently verb-less) to read more easily and so to avoid a piling-up of genitives.

The genitive construction "of Jesus Christ" is capable of a twofold interpretation, depending on whether it means "good news brought by Jesus Christ" or "good news announced by Jesus Christ." Again, the choice is not exclusive and since either is possible and would make good sense we cannot say for sure what Mark's meaning was. The answer, if we are asked to choose, will partly depend on how the next phrase is taken.

"The beginning of the gospel." In what sense "beginning"? C. E. B. Cranfield[15] lists no fewer than ten possibilities, of which the following three seem most likely:

[14] See W. G. Kümmel, *Promise and Fulfilment* [ET, 1957], p. 19, on the verb "to be at hand" in this sense, "to denote an event which is near, but has not yet taken place." Kümmel has reinforced this conclusion in the light of recent discussion in his essay, "Eschatology and Expectation in the Proclamation of Jesus" in *The Future of our Religious Past*. Bultmann Festschrift. Edited by J. M. Robinson [1971], pp. 32–34.

[15] C. E. B. Cranfield, *The Gospel According to St. Mark* [1963], pp. 34f.

(i) By supposing that the Old Testament citation in verses 2, 3 is paren-
thetic, the predicate of the verb is John the Baptist's preaching which is
explained as being the beginning of the gospel (record). And this accords
with what we find in Acts 1:21f. 10:37; 13:24, 25 where John the Baptist's
activity was, in the apostolic preaching, the *terminus a quo*.

(ii) In a similar fashion it could be maintained that verse 1 is a sort of
title for the content of verses 2–13. This is C. E. B. Cranfield's preference.

(iii) W. Marxsen (*loc. cit.*, p. 125) has urged that the opening verse
is a title to the whole composition, and deliberately chosen by the evangelist in order to convey the sense of what he as an author is seeking to
accomplish. This makes Mark the originator of the word in the sense that
he becomes the first Christian to take a well-used word and give it a
unique connotation. Mark has transferred the noun *euangelion* from the
sphere of oral proclamation and delivery to that of literary composition.
The evangelist makes this innovative transference in full consciousness
of the momentous change in application which he is making. Therefore
he appends the term "beginning" to the dependent noun "gospel" in
order to show that he proposes to find his authority in God who is the
author of, and sanctioning power behind, the striking events which are
at the heart of the Christian proclamation. The term *arché* ($\dot{\alpha}\rho\chi\acute{\eta}$) rendered
"beginning" does not mean in this context "first part" or "opening sec-
tion" but since it covers the entire work of Mark it should be understood
as "origin" (or even "principle"). It is that to which the human author
traces back his work; and in this sense it must imply God himself, as the
author and originator of all that is, just as Genesis 1:1 opens the Bible's
story on this magisterial note.[16]

This view is to be commended, since it does justice to Mark's attested
usages of *euangelion* in his work in which he has employed the term with
deliberate intention; and his frontispiece fits into what seems to be his
carefully arranged literary plan.

We accept the proposal, therefore, that Mark's opening verse is his
chosen title embracing the subsequent narrative. His purpose is to tell
the *euangelion* as that good news (already known in his church as God's
saving power and life-giving reality) which took historical shape in Jesus
of Nazareth. As Marxsen perceptively remarks (*loc. cit.*, p. 138), it is not
that Mark has affixed the term "gospel" to the title of Jesus Christ. Quite
the opposite. The evangelist has appended the name of Jesus Christ
to the term *euangelion*. The "gospel" is the known factor. His task as the
first evangelist is to spell out the relation between the experienced good
news of God's salvation and the theologically interpreted historical facts
about Jesus of Nazareth, Messiah of Israel and Son of God. The opening
title is thus his claim to the designation, *Mark: Evangelist and Theologian*.

---

[16] So E. Lohmeyer, *Das Evangelium des Markus*[17] [1967], p. 10.

II

MARK'S GOSPEL IN THE CHURCH

Mark as Matthew's follower: a survey from Augustine to Holtzmann. The Markan hypothesis in Holtzmann and Burkitt. Form-critical attitudes in Wrede, K. L. Schmidt and Bultmann. Redaction criticism in Riesenfeld and Marxsen. How the matter stands.

From the early years to Augustine

The gospel according to Mark has had a chequered history since the time of its publication. It is apparent that the first Christian reaction to this gospel was one of acceptance and acknowledgment of its authoritativeness. The obvious proof of this fact comes in the way in which Matthew and Luke are content to follow the Markan order and to be guided by Mark's outline of the ministry of Jesus. Doubtless the close association of this gospel with Peter, referred to by Justin in his *Dial.* 106 as the "Memoirs of Peter" and in a passage making allusion to Mark 3:17, did much to commend the composition as embodying apostolic witness. In fact, the characteristic description of the evangelist in these early centuries is "Peter's interpreter," a designation which is found both in Greek as ἑρμηνευτὴς Πέτρου (Papias, c. A.D. 140, quoted in Eusebius, *HE.* iii. 39.15; Irenaeus, *Adv. Haer.* iii. 1.2) and in Latin as *interpres Petri* (Anti-Marcionite prologue, c. A.D. 160–180; Jerome) or "follower of Peter" (*sector Petri*, so Clement of Alexandria).

Further, Tatian who compiled a Harmony of the Gospels (the *Diatessaron*) c. A.D. 170 used Mark as one of his sources. In Clement of Alexandria and Origen we find a continuation of the idea first sketched by Irenaeus that Mark recorded in writing the substance not only of Peter's reminiscences of Jesus' ministry but of his public preaching at Rome. In this way, these church fathers conclude, the *evangelium secundum Marcum* was born as a response to requests that Peter's preaching should be permanently preserved in written form.

From these auspicious circumstances it might well be expected that Mark's gospel would quickly become a favourite in many Christian centres and circles. But this is not the case. That the gospel was known and highly regarded is clear; but it is a singular fact that the Apostolic Fathers and Apologists (in the second century) are reticent when it comes to actually quoting from this gospel book.[1]

---

[1] See the discussions in P. N. Harrison, *Polycarp's Two Epistles to the Philippians* [1926], pp. 285–288; and H. Köster, *Synoptische Überlieferung bei den apostolischen Vätern* [1957],

Moreover, although the gospel found a place in the canon, its position in the order of the gospels is unsettled. It is never placed first in the sequence, with the single exception of *k* (Codex Bobbiensis); and in some lists (e.g. the Old Latin, and the Greek MSS D and W) it is placed last. The reason for this uncertainty is partly a desire to give priority to those gospels thought to be directly the work of the apostolic authors (Matthew, John). We may compare the rationale for this in the dictum of Tertullian (*Adv. Marc.* iv. 2): "our faith is based on John and Matthew, it is built up on Luke and Mark, followers of the apostles." And it is partly explained by the assumption that the order which places Matthew *before* Mark thus accords with the primacy of Matthew in the order of writing. Mark was believed to be a follower of Matthew and so he is placed in a secondary position in certain lists (mainly drawn from the East).

Irenaeus in his celebrated description of the gospel writers who are likened to the four cherubim of Ezekiel 1 and the four living creatures of Revelation 4 (*Adv. Haer.* iii. 11.8) reflects the embarrassment which was evidently felt concerning the place and office of the gospel writer, Mark. Unlike the other three writers, the second evangelist is depicted as an eagle, a lion, a man and a calf in successive parts of patristic writing. This seems to show that the Fathers could not make up their mind which characterization best fitted the evangelist.[2]

No commentary on this Gospel was written before that of Victor of Antioch (in the 5th century) who complained that he could not find any treatment of this gospel comparable with expositions of Matthew and John. And there is evidence to lead to the conclusion that this gospel was neglected, mainly on the ground that its contents were embodied in the larger gospels of Matthew and Luke which incorporated much of the Markan material and, at the same time, smoothed out the rugged and unstylistic character of Mark's Greek.

There is an additional reason why Mark's gospel suffered neglect in the early centuries, already hinted at. The common view was that the gospel stood in the shadow of Matthew's work whose prestige as the first of the gospels to be written was ranked high and which became the favourite gospel both in the use which was made of its testimonies to the Christian faith (in Justin) and in the place it gained for itself in liturgical handbooks (e.g. in the Didache). E. Massaux remarks that Matthew's Gospel became "normative for the Christian life; it created the climate of ordinary Christianity."[3]

There is no reason to doubt that Mark was simply regarded as a shortened version of its illustrious predecessor; and since Matthew's Gospel contained

pp. 21f., who shows that the citation of Isaiah 29:13 in Mark 7:6 is followed by 1 Clement 15:2 (c. A.D. 96). But this is an exceptional case.

[2] See Swete, *Commentary*[3] [1927], pp. xxxvi–xxxviii.

[3] E. Massaux, *Influence de l'Évangile de saint Matthieu sur la littérature chrétienne avant saint Irénée* [1950], p. 652.

so much of the Lord's teaching in convenient blocks (like the Sermon on the Mount) which could be adapted to a catechetical purpose in the church, and yielded significant sections (*pericopae*) which had an immediate relevance to the instruction of new converts (e.g. Matt. 19:16–30) and to church leaders (e.g. Matt. 18, which P. Bonnard has aptly called "a veritable 'rule of discipline' for use in the Christian communities"[4]) it is not surprising that Mark was pushed into the backwater and virtually ignored. St Augustine c. A.D. 400 in his view of the "synoptic problem"[5] had a quick solution to hand. For him Mark was one who followed Matthew's footsteps and abridged his gospel. In this neat way he accounted for the undoubted similarities between the synoptic evangelists and did so with the simplest of all proposals. Since Matthew was generally accepted as the first of the gospels because of its proximity in thought to the Old Testament and bore the name of a member of the apostolic band, it must be that Mark copied from him and in so doing abbreviated his work. Augustine, however, never reflected that his view was really a denial of the patristic evidence according to which Mark took down the personal reminiscences of an eyewitness, for if Mark thus recorded Peter's testimony, why did he need to copy from Matthew? Nor did he pause to test this solution by making a comparison of the individual sections in which Matthew and Mark overlap. Had he done so, he would have discovered that the truth is exactly the reverse of his supposition. While Mark's Gospel as a whole is shorter than Matthew's, in virtually every instance where they tell the same story it is Mark's account which is longer and more detailed and Matthew's which is the shortened version (e.g. Mark 4:35–41 = Matt. 8:23–27). But no such objective test was applied, and there the matter rested until the rise of modern criticism. The venerable Bede composed a commentary in the 8th century and there were expositions in the Middle Ages and after the Reformation. But, in C. F. Evans's words,[6] Mark's Gospel lived on, but it lived in the shadows.

It is a direct consequence of the modern assessment of Mark as the earliest of the gospels to be written and the claim that it records an un-embellished and factual statement of Jesus' historical life—two suppositions which derive from H. J. Holtzmann's *Die synoptischen Evangelien*, 1863— that this gospel has come out of the semi-darkness. Indeed, it has been ushered into a blinding light of detailed scrutiny and painstaking examination, and the last century has seen a dramatic onset of interest in this gospel and its writer—

---

[4] P. Bonnard, *L'évangile selon Matthieu* [1963], p. 267; and his essay on "Matthieu Educateur de peuple chrétien" in *Mélanges bibliques en hommage au R. P. B. Rigaux* [1970], pp. 1–7. The adaptation of Mark 10:17–22 to fit the needs of a catechumenate in Matt. 19:16–22 is discussed in my article, "St. Matthew's Gospel in Recent Study," ExpT, lxxx. 5. [Feb. 1969], pp. 133.

[5] "Concerning the Agreement of the Evangelists," i. 2 (4).

[6] C. F. Evans, *The Beginning of the Gospel* . . . [1968], p. 3.

"The saint who first found grace to pen
The Life which was the life of men."

From Augustine to H. J. Holtzmann

For nearly fourteen centuries the literary inter-relationships of the gospels was a neglected issue, posing a situation marked by uneasy confusion. The fact is that Augustine's solution was clearly at odds with the earliest patristic evidence which made Mark's gospel the product of Peter's eyewitness testimony and preaching. Thus his rôle as an epitomizer of Matthew was hard to reconcile with this high estimate. The deadlock was partly broken by a revival of scholarly interest in the second half of the eighteenth century, which pressed back behind the patristic and early church data and judgments to the gospel texts themselves and the apostolic history in the *Acts* in order to reopen the enquiry.

It is not our intention to follow closely the course of critical debate which began with two important assumptions being made.[7] These were that an original gospel, antecedent to our written records, existed and became the prototype of the later canonical works; and, second, that the first three gospels had more in common with one another than with the fourth gospel. This gave rise to the adjective "synoptic" to denote the common relationship in which Matthew, Mark and Luke were seen to stand once their texts were printed in parallel columns and compared. This innovation, first made by J. J. Griesbach in 1789, was unlike an earlier attempt at harmonization undertaken by Tatian in his *Diatessaron* (c. A.D. 170) and showed the difficulty of fitting the gospel data together into a single, coherent record.

Our aim now is to indicate the main landmarks on this terrain of historical criticism of the gospels, with special reference to the gospel of Mark. We shall observe how the debate involved a close intertwining of literary analysis and theological motifs as men placed the church's holy books under the spotlight of studious examination and occasionally subjected them to tendentious scrutiny.

(*a*) The father of gospel criticism is usually identified as G. E. Lessing who in 1778 wrote, and in 1784 published, a discussion in the course of which he suggested that there was a putative gospel, written in Aramaic and originated soon after Jesus' death, which was based on the oral tradition of the apostles. The merit of this hypothesis was that it explained the phenomena of divergence and variation within the synoptic gospels, soon to be displayed in Griesbach's synopsis. The elements of agreement

---

[7] For the details of this debate the chapter of W. R. Farmer's *The Synoptic Problem* [1964,] ch. 1 is invaluable. Bibliographical surveys are given by W. G. Kümmel, *Introduction to the New Testament* [ET, 1966], pp. 37ff; idem, *Das neue Testament* [1958], pp. 90ff.; and W. Michaelis, *Einleitung in das neue Testament*[2] [1954], pp. 79ff. S. Neill, The *Interpretation of the New Testament, 1861–1961* [1964], ch. 4, has some illuminating discussion.

and difference among the three writers were accounted for by their following, and occasionally departing from, the original gospel or a particular version of it which each evangelist possessed.

But there was another influence at the back of Lessing. He had published the then posthumous work of H. S. Reimarus (1694–1768) who carries the distinction of being the first man to address himself to the problems of writing a life of Jesus.[8] Before him "no one had attempted to form a historical conception of the life of Jesus" (Schweitzer, *op. cit.*, p. 13). Reimarus' attitude to the gospel, however, was entirely negative and led to the conclusion that the records are historically worthless since they are the product of men guilty of manufacturing a pious fraud.

Lessing entered the discussion on the side of moderation by pointing out that Reimarus had treated all the gospels as equal in worth and had followed traditional lines in matters of authenticity and authorship. It was therefore to Lessing's advantage to be able to resort to source-analysis and to appeal to an early, pre-canonical gospel which would prove his point that the Christian religion existed prior to historical documentation in the four gospels. For the four gospels, on Reimarus' showing, contained inherent contradictions and disparities. For Lessing it was an irrefutable appeal to go back to a lost "original gospel" which by definition was self-consistent and free from historical difficulties. These difficulties only came into view once there appeared several versions of this prototype. On philosophical grounds, this manoeuvre aided Lessing's position that theology must be delivered from the clutches of historicism, since "Accidental historical truths can never become proofs for necessary truths of reason" (*Theological Writings*, iii, 12). For him the validity of the Christian faith rested on the appeal to experience (see Barth, *op. cit.*, pp. 134–137 for citations); and the hypothesis of an "original gospel" was just the supposition he needed to give evidence of "the historical truth with the power of proof *before* the Bible," as Barth remarked (*op. cit.*, p. 140).

(*b*) The name of J. B. Koppe deserves to be recovered from oblivion, since it was he who in 1782 published his dissertation in Göttingen entitled *Marcus non epitomator Matthaei*. His thesis is indicated in the title by which he sought to show that Mark does not slavishly follow Matthew as would have been the case if Augustine's dictum were true. Mark's order agrees very often with that of Luke. On the Augustinian theory, while Luke could be shown to resemble Mark by the fact that he had both Matthew and Mark before him, it became difficult to imagine why Luke should prefer Mark to Matthew if Matthew were the first and most authoritative record. Besides which, what then becomes of Papias' endorsement of the pristine apostolic testimony contained in Mark?

---

[8] See the edition of *Reimarus: Fragments*, edited by C. H. Talbert [1970], especially pp. 34ff.; the section by Albert Schweitzer in *The Quest of the Historical Jesus* [1968 edit.] ch. 2 is indispensable, along with Karl Barth, *From Rousseau to Ritschl* [1959], on Lessing (ch. 3).

These questions inevitably paved the way for an assertion that Mark is in fact the first gospel to appear in the sequence.

(c) K. Lachmann's article in 1835 prepared the ground for the rise of the so-called "Two Document Hypothesis." His chief concern and contention are indicated in the title, "The Order of the Narration of Events in the Synoptic Gospels," and it concentrated on the order of events as being the simplest, fixed point of departure in any discussion on inter-gospel relationships. He observed that when Matthew and Luke are running parallel with Mark, the order of events in the two gospels corresponds; but when there is no Markan counterpart they diverge from each other in the sequence of events. But Lachmann did not conclude that the two synoptists have drawn from Mark;[9] he simply maintained that all three gospels are derived from an "original gospel" which Mark has followed more closely than the subsequent evangelists.

(d) The case of Mark's priority was taken up and pursued by C. H. Weisse in 1838. It is worth noting that this man was primarily a philosopher, not a Bible scholar, though his observations were made on the text of the gospels. A haunting philosophical interest may be suspected, however, and this was in fact the case.

The vividness and realism of Mark's gospel had long been appreciated. In 6:39 the crowds sit down on "*green grass*"—a picturesque description not found in the parallel accounts of the feeding of the multitude stories in Matthew, Luke and John. Either this is a token of the author's artistry in supplying a vivid detail or it preserves a genuine reminiscence, traceable to an eyewitness who took note that in springtime the event occurred in the short time when the grass was green—a short period before the ground was soon baked dry by the Palestinian sun and in an age when the revitalizing properties of sulphate of ammonia had yet to be discovered!

But artistic additions of this kind are not usually supplied; and the tendency is to trim the narrative rather than embellish it. It follows, said Weisse, that the line of development more cogently runs from Mark to the other gospels which omit the detail than the reverse way. His other suggestion has to do with the bringing into this discussion of Mark's originality the notion of Schleiermacher that there was a collection of *logia*, or sayings of Jesus, mentioned by Papias, on which Matthew and Luke drew and which accounts for the common material found in these gospels.

What motivated Weisse seems to have been an ancillary interest in warding off the attacks of some new tendencies in German criticism. In 1835 D. F. Strauss published his (later notorious) *Life of Jesus* which aimed its thrust at a double front. It sought to denigrate the claims of supernaturalistic Christianity which appealed to the gospels for evidence

---

[9] As B. C. Butler has shown in *The Originality of St. Matthew* [1951], pp. 62ff.

of miracles. And it opposed the rationalists who still clung to the idea that the gospels contain factual history. Strauss tried to reduce all opposition to a vanishing point by arguing that both contenders are espousing lost causes since the gospels are mythical.[10] He treated the gospels as Reimarus had done without prior consideration of their sources, order and relative worth; and in Weisse who both expressed appreciation of Strauss's labours and then took him to task at significant points[11] we find a counter-attack well and truly launched.

Of special interest in Weisse's reconstruction of the data are his refusal to recognize the eschatological motifs in Jesus' life (which Strauss stressed) and his recourse to the two basic documents of apostolic Christianity—Mark and the *logia*—which evaded the criticism levelled at Matthew and John, documents which were highly charged with the miraculous element and so under suspicion. Further, Weisse was apparently the first "to slip unconsciously into the fallacy of thinking that Lachmann's argument from order"[12] meant that Mark was a *source* for Matthew and Luke.

The claim to fame which is linked with Weisse's name is that he was the originator of the Markan hypothesis (as Holtzmann conceded in 1863). His overall importance lies in the way he sought to erect bulwarks of historical facts in the gospels against the inroads of the mythical school. Not that he accepted all of Mark as reliably historical; his task was more modestly conceived. It was to construct an outline of the life of Jesus and assign this to history. He was less willing to grant historical value to the *pericopes* which are joined together. It became the work of the later "life-of-Jesus" school of Continental writers to fill in the *lacunae* and to reconstruct, sometimes with powerful imagination, what the full-dressed Jesus must have looked like through the eyes of a Renan and a Keim and a Farrar. At least, as Schweitzer had to admit, Renan "offered his readers a Jesus who was alive"; but his vivacity was more the work of invention than reality. Yet Renan erred less grievously than Strauss.

(*e*) The scepticism of Strauss came to full expression in Bruno Bauer whose treatise on the "Criticism of the Gospel History" (in the 1851 edition) reached the nadir of all historical assessments: there never was any historical Jesus. There were many factors which led him to this negative judgment. Ostensibly he believed that Mark's gospel was the work of an inventive genius and that it is he who has "loosed us from the theological lie" of the characterization of Jesus in dogmatic terms and of Chalcedonian proportions which we meet in the fourth gospel (cited in Schweitzer, *op. cit.*, p. 153). It was therefore in Bauer's interest to postulate

---

[10] This is not Strauss's final statement, as Barth (*op. cit.*, p. 374ff.) shows in his discussion of Strauss's later work in 1864.

[11] A. Schweitzer's chapter entitled "The Marcan Hypothesis" is mainly devoted to Weisse in his relations with Strauss's views (*op. cit.*, pp. 121–136).

[12] So W. R. Farmer, *op. cit.*, p. 23.

and supply proofs for the theory that Mark was the first gospel to be written; and he was the first to do this on the ground of the evidence of the gospel itself.

(*f*) We have now reached the terminal point in the section by arriving at the epoch which ushered in the prolific spate of "Lives of Jesus." These works were a natural reaction to the aridity and negativism of the preceding decades. And the hinge on which they turn was the appearance of H. J. Holtzmann's seminal work, *Die synoptischen Evangelien* in 1863.

The Markan Hypothesis

Holtzmann's achievement was considerable. His indebtedness to Weisse was acknowledged and the latter is credited with the designation of one "who for the first time scientifically established the Markan hypothesis." In fact, Holtzmann took Weisse's statement of the Two document hypothesis, i.e. Mark and the *logia* as foundation-documents, and pressed it into the service of a developed theory of Mark as "original document" (*Grundschrift*) on which the later gospels drew. In this way he replaced the unknown quantity of Lessing's *Urevangelium* by a known document —or rather, the antecedent (known as *Ur-Markus*, or first edition of Mark) of our canonical Mark. Just how far Holtzmann was prepared to go in attributing historical credibility to Mark is not clear. What is important is that he was seen by the composers of a succession of "Lives of Jesus" as providing a framework in Mark of a well-attested, early and reliable tradition, which could then be used to counter the extreme scepticism of Strauss and Bauer and could also yield the ground-plan for fuller descriptions of Jesus' life on earth in a way that would be uninhibited by the figure of a virgin-born, miracle-working Byzantine Christ who at length was raised from the dead by a physical reanimation (as Matthew and Luke were believed to teach).

The rôle of Holtzmann as providing just this credibility for Mark so that his work could be used to reconstruct the liberal portrait of Jesus has been clearly described by Albert Schweitzer, *op. cit.*, pp. 203f.

> What attracted these writers to the Marcan hypothesis was not so much the authenticification (*sic*) which it gave to the detail of Mark . . . but the way in which this Gospel lent itself to the *a priori* view of the course of the life of Jesus which they unconsciously brought with them. They appealed to Holtzmann because he showed such wonderful skill in extracting from the Marcan narrative the view which commended itself to the spirit of the age as manifested in the 'sixties.

That "spirit of the age" was essentially one which probed into the psychological development of Jesus' public career and suggested reasons for his actions and decisions. A Galilean success was followed by a response to political factors which in turn caused him to escape and to re-think his plan of campaign. Only then, with frustration at the impossibility of carrying out his mission in Galilee did Jesus resolve to go to Jerusalem and make his final bid for the capital. Basic to this reconstruction is a confidence that the modern interpreter can read between the lines and supply motivations in the mind of Jesus and his reactions to outward events and pressures which are otherwise lacking in the text. This is what Schweitzer calls the attempt to delineate "the inward and outward course of development in the life of Jesus" (op. cit., p. 204). At heart, it is a treatment of the gospel data as a psychological case-study, incomplete in themselves but capable, by a sympathetic drawing together of the visible threads, of forming an imaginative reconstruction and a resultant in-depth analysis.

The gospel of Mark played a decisive part in this Holtzmannian doctrine and in the use which was made of it. It had everything in its favour. Its portrait of Jesus was sufficiently ambiguous to suggest a purely human Jesus for whom no claims to divinity are made. Its outline could, with slight adaptation, be made to yield a sequential narrative with the pattern "success-retirement-failure" plainly visible. Its setting in a historical milieu shows that it was no mythical saga. And, above all, the storyline made sense, since it told of an earthly figure of flesh and blood, who shaped his destiny in response to events as he met them and who concealed his Messiahship until the psychologically critical moment when, in the last days of his life, it could be hidden no longer. Yet when it is revealed it is a spiritual secret appreciated only by the sensitive souls who discover, with Jesus, that the kingdom of God is within them and that Jesus' example of living under the Fatherhood of God is enough to encourage them to live as his children and as brothers together. This is the quintessential doctrine of the liberal theology, classically adumbrated by A. Harnack.[13]

In summary, we may state that with the "Life-of-Jesus" movement Mark's gospel came into its own, after centuries of neglect. Studies in literary criticism, gospel order and theological implicates all contrived to push this gospel into a prominent place. It found its chief niche of importance because of the decisive part it was made to play in fulfilling the aim of the liberal theology.

---

[13] No one saw more clearly or expressed more forcibly the main lineaments of theological liberalism than T. W. Manson in his essay "The Failure of Liberalism to interpret the Bible as the word of God," *The Interpretation of the Bible*, ed. C. W. Dugmore [1944], pp. 92–107. His citation of Harnack, *What is Christianity?* [ET 1950 ed.], pp. 68f. is to the point:

> The fact that the whole of Jesus' message
> may be reduced to these two heads—God as the
> Father and the human soul so ennobled that
> it can and does unite with him . . . that is
> therefore, religion itself.

The chroniclers of the "Life-of-Jesus" school had an avowed aim.

> They were eager to picture him as truly and purely human, to strip from
> him the robes of splendour with which he had been apparelled, and clothe
> him once more with the coarse garments in which he had walked in Galilee.
> (Schweitzer, *op. cit.*, p. 4).

This quotation shows that there were many motives which inspired
the writers in this era. They had a genuine devotion to the humanity
of Jesus which they felt was obscured and overlaid by the church's credal
forms and by metaphysical doctrine. The Jesus of the fourth gospel was
so obviously a transcendental figure, walking as it were with his feet two
inches off the ground. As far back as Reimarus it had been denied that
the Johannine Jesus could have spoken in Chalcedonian tones and made
breath-taking claims for himself. The liberals adopted a simple expedient
and accepted the logic of Reimarus' criticism by cutting out this body
of evidence.

But they were equally alive to the danger of a revived Monarchianism
which excluded Jesus from any relationship to God in the interests of a
stress on the unity of God. It was precisely this peril which was to appear
in the theology of Harnack for whom the pith of the Christian gospel,
the nature of Christianity, lay in the dictum:

> The gospel, as Jesus proclaimed it, has to do with the Father only and not with
> the Son.

Yet, on the whole, the results were disappointing and ephemeral.
"Those who are fond of talking about negative theology can find their
account here," wrote Albert Schweitzer at the close of his long recital
of Lives of Jesus. Already in the nineteenth century the ground was being
prepared for an assault on the Holtzmann doctrine, and more specifically
on the generally accepted notion that a portrait of Jesus as he moved
from Galilee to Jerusalem could be etched by a careful and sympathetic
drawing together on the gospel data. But before we turn to examine
these new forces of which the late nineteenth and early twentieth centuries
prepared the ground-swell, we must pause to notice the transplanted
influence of Holtzmann on to the British scene.

British New Testament scholarship in the field of gospel origins was
largely quiescent until about 1880. Then with the work of Westcott and
Hort a new era dawned. Westcott, to be sure, left a more permanent
mark on the field of textual criticism than of gospel interpretation. His
espousal of the original gospel theory was never revised to keep pace with
new chapters which were being written in Germany.

One of the first in Britain to recognize the importance of Holtzmann
was William Sanday who paid his work the tribute of the following
notice: "The year 1863 . . . might be said to mark a turning-point in the

history of Synoptic criticism."[14] The allusion is to Holtzmann's book published in that year and its statement of Mark's historical worth.

It fell to F. C. Burkitt in 1906 to utilize these results in a survey of Jesus' life. In the Jowett lectures, *The Gospel History and its Transmission* [1906] he could rest his authority for looking to the gospels for reliable history on the priority and integrity of the second gospel:

> I venture to think that what I have put before you goes far to vindicate the claim of the Gospel according to S. Mark to be a historical document, a document really in touch with the facts of history (p. 102).

He goes on in a later lecture to draw the conclusion:

> From the Gospel according to Mark, we may learn who Jesus Christ was, and what part he played on earth in human history (p. 284).

And exactly what Burkitt intended us to understand by "historical document. . . human history" is clear from the surrounding discussion. He has taken over from the nineteenth century "Lives-of-Jesus" people the notions of a flight from Herod and a failure of the Galilean mission after an initial flush of success and popularity, though his weaving together of the data into a cause-and-effect nexus is cautious and not overventure-some.[15] But the fact remains that he can cheerfully at this time expect to use Mark "if we want to begin at the beginning and reconstruct the Portrait of Christ" (*op. cit.*, p. 102). Here the Markan hypothesis is laid under tribute, and the Markan gospel climbs to a position of eminence without a peer.

The Markan Hypothesis under attack

Albert Schweitzer (*op. cit.*, p. 204) writes a perceptive section on the dominance of the Holtzmann treatment of Mark, and indicates that the Markan hypothesis possessed a sort of inevitability which could only be overcome and neutralized by a breaking of the stranglehold which a combination of psychologizing interest in Jesus' life and the liberal portrait of Jesus laid upon the interpretation of Mark. This verdict was given in 1906 when his book *Von Reimarus zu Wrede* first appeared. But several years before this, a slender volume had been released which contained all the potential to attack and disarm the Markan hypothesis.

---

[14] Article "Gospels" in Smith's *Dictionary of the Bible* [1891]. See his article, "A Survey of the Synoptic Problem," Expositor, iii, 4th series [1891], pp. 88–91 (90).

He perceived the value of the conclusion that Mark's gospel took precedence over the other synoptics, and agreed in his volume *The Life of Christ in Recent Research* [1907], p. 156, that a similar "assured" place should be given to the existence of Q as the *logia*-source in the Two Document theory.

[15] His later book, *The Earliest Sources for the Life of Jesus*[2] [1922] was written after he had come under the spell of Schweitzer's apocalyptic interpretation of gospel eschatology. He played an important rôle in reflecting Schweitzer's views and influencing British scholarship. See N. Perrin, *The Kingdom of God in the Teaching of Jesus* [1963], pp. 53f.

This was Martin Kähler's *Der sogenannte historische Jesus und der geschicht-liche, biblische Christus* (1896; ET, 1964 as *The so-called Historical Jesus and the Historic Biblical Christ*).

Kähler engaged in warm polemic against the current historicism of his day which produced the vagaries of the Life-of-Jesus portraits. He objected that inevitably such attempts at portraiture led to a false picture which obscured the transcendental qualities of the biblical Christ. The Living Lord, he averred, is essentially the Christ of apostolic proclamation, accessible to us today in a spiritual encounter and not to be dug out of historical documents as though he were "the mere object of historical research, as one can [disinter] other figures belonging to the past" (*op. cit.*, p. 92).

Many reasons are offered to account for Kähler's opposition to the historiographical methods and theological presuppositions of his day. Of central importance in our enquiry was his conviction that the gospels do not provide biographical data which would give us a window of access into the inner life of Jesus. They are—and it is apparent that in context he has his eye set primarily on Mark's gospel—"passion narratives with extended introductions" (ET, p. 80 note), containing the content of early Christian preaching and intended to awaken faith in Christ as Saviour.

The gospels, he implied, serve an exclusively religious purpose and interest: "Every detail of the apostolic recollection of Jesus can be shown to have been preserved for the sake of its religious significance" (*op. cit.*, p. 93). The Christ they portray is the Christ of faith, the proclaimed Lord whose encounter with his people is not at the mercy of historical investigation and systematic doubt. Only by insisting on the exact nature of our entrée to the "historic, biblical Christ" can we be delivered from the clutches of historical relativism (for which nothing in the past is absolutely certain) and be given an "invulnerable province" (*sturmfreies Gebiet*), unassailed and unassailable by historical, probing enquiry. The upshot of this discussion by Kähler was to place a serious question-mark against the current doctrine that Mark's gospel records plain, uninterpreted history which is capable of treatment and verification by the methods of historical science and thought to be revelatory of the secret of Jesus' person to the impartial investigator.

Other influences were at work in the early part of the twentieth century which took up and developed, if unwittingly, the historical radicalism of Kähler. These may be tabulated.

(i) W. Wrede's book on the Messianic secret in the gospels (*Das Messiasgeheimnis in den Evangelien*, 1901) addressed itself to explaining the mystery and secrecy motif in Mark. Jesus is there reported as enjoining secrecy about his miracles and Messiahship in situations where commands to silence could hardly be observed. Wrede explained that these injunctions to silence were a literary device called in by the evangelist to account for the absence of faith in Jesus' Messiahship during his life-time. That faith was born at the resurrection and formed part of the apostolic preaching, from which it was carried back into the tradition and superimposed upon it. In its pre-Markan form the tradition contained no such Messianic awareness; therefore it must have been Mark himself who devised the theory of a Messianic secret and imported it into the tradition as he took it over and edited it.

The fact that Wrede's examination of the verses yielded his particular conclusion is not, at this point, the important thing; and we shall return to Wrede later in our discussion. What Wrede succeeded in doing was to convince other interpreters that Mark's Gospel is no longer correctly assessed as a record of plain, unvarnished, and straightforward history "as it actually happened," but it is a dogmatic treatise in which the rationale of the Messianic secret is called in to account for the Markan story and imposed upon it by the evangelist himself.

(ii) K. L. Schmidt examined in *Der Rahmen der Geschichte Jesu* (1919) meaning "The Framework of Jesus' Story" the phenomena of the connecting links, the Markan seams, which join together the separate stories of the gospel and make them into a continuous narrative. His conclusion was that these notices of time-sequence and place-reference which appear to carry forward the story and make it into a coherent narrative do not rest on historical reminiscence or temporal or geographical fact but are editorial. They are additions supplied by the evangelist who often gathers his material into units on a topical basis of common subject-matter, like the collection of "controversy stories" in Mark 2, 3.

K. L. Schmidt reached the verdict that:

> As a whole there is no life of Jesus in the sense of a developing biography, no chronological sketch of Jesus' history, but only individual stories (*pericopae*) which are put into a framework (*op. cit.*, p. 317).

He elaborated by this form-critical method the idea put out first by Schweitzer that when Mark's Gospel is examined in sections not only is there no obvious psychological connection between the sections; "in almost every case there is a positive break in the connexion" (*op. cit.*, pp. 333f.). Therefore, attempts to string together the sections and read them as freely flowing narrative, suggesting events of cause and effect, are foredoomed to failure. As Schweitzer put it in a memorable metaphor:

> Formerly it was possible to book through-tickets at the supplementary-psychological-knowledge office which enabled those travelling in the interests of Life-of-Jesus construction to use express trains, thus avoiding the inconvenience of having to stop at every little station, change, and run the risk of missing their connexion. This ticket office is now closed. There is a station at the end of each section of the narrative, and the connexions are not guaranteed (*op. cit.*, p. 333).

(iii) One further factor added its weight to the crushing burden which thus destroyed the Markan hypothesis. The doctrine of *Sitz im Leben* is built on the principle that each section (*pericope*) of the gospel teaching and narrative may be suggestively placed in the setting of its historical context when we have regard to its literary form and theological context. The underlying assumption is that Mark's material in particular can be separated out into paragraphs, each of which is a self-contained unit, making its point without regard for anything which may come before it or follow after. This analysis led to a double consequence, both parts of which made the traditional view of Markan authorship difficult of credence. First, if Mark's rôle in the process of gospel-making is confined to the task of collecting and stringing together a set of independent units of narrative and sayings, he can hardly be known as the author of a life of Jesus. He is more accurately described as a compiler, an editor, a hander-on (*Tradent* was Dibelius' term[16]) of earlier traditions which he was content simply to piece together in what has been called "this curious, anecdotal, stop-go manner."[17]

Secondly, the nineteenth century understanding of Mark as the scribe of Peter's eyewitness experiences and witness vanishes before the critical assessment of these paragraphs. By literary analysis—a method which lies at the heart of the form-critical method—the units of gospel tradition were studied and placed into appropriate categories according to their literary form, stylistic features and usefulness in serving the needs of the Christian community which treasured them. They also give the impression of having been shaped by a number of hands before Mark used them and the uncomplicated picture suggested by Jerome's words (*ad Hedib.*) "Petro narrante et illo scribente" seemed, after this analytic scrutiny, to be almost ludicrous. But even worse was to follow, as the form critic proceeded to pass a judgment of the historical worth of the stories. From being regarded as straightforward, historical events of factual, episodic history in the lifetime of Jesus of Nazareth they became idealized reconstructions possessing worth mainly for the post-Easter church; the entire course of Jesus' career was seen in the gospels as it appeared when viewed through the refracting prism of the early church.

The name of Rudolf Bultmann occurs at this point. It was he who took up the protests raised by Kähler and extended the pioneering work of the earliest form critics. At the same time he added a new feature, derived from some philosophical indebtedness to Kierkegaard's type of existentialism and a Lutheran application of the dogmatic principle of justification "by faith alone." The result of a weaving together of these divergent strands of influence may be seen in Bultmann's *Jesus* [1926] and

[16] Martin Dibelius, *From Tradition to Gospel* (ET, 1935), p. 3.
[17] C. F. Evans, *The Beginning of the Gospel* . . . [1968], p. 9.

his most recent modification, "The Relationship of the Primitive Christian Gospel of Christ to the Historical Jesus" (1960).[18] Bultmann's position, both early and later, rests on two considerations. First, on form critical grounds, he avers that it is impossible to recapture Jesus as he moved in Galilee and Jerusalem and to know precisely what took place in A.D. 30–33. He does not deny some historical foundation and is willing cautiously to affirm the "having-happened-ness" of Jesus with a modest outline of his Galilean career. But he denies even to this minimum of information any real theological value because the gospels are, by definition, not concerned with "objective historicity." He stoutly denies any hint that Jesus' personality may be seen in the gospels. Thus, because there is no estimate of the "inward and outward course of development in the life of Jesus" (Schweitzer's phrase of the original Quest) we can have no sure knowledge of how Jesus anticipated his death. Mark 10:45 is a "prophecy after the event," read back into the lifetime of Jesus. It is conceivable, Bultmann still declares, that he died in utter bewilderment and abject despair, a frustrated and rejected prophet of God.

But, as we turn to the second element in Bultmann's reading of the gospels, this scepticism is not for him too great a loss. Indeed, he maintains, it is a necessary loss. For, even if it were possible to learn of the Jesus of history, it would be illegitimate so to enquire, and such knowledge as might be gained would prove a burden. For faith can never be at the mercy of historical criticism and suspend its activity while the historians debate the problematic issue, Did it happen? The person in whom the Christian faith confides is the risen Christ, living in the church and present supremely in the ministry of preaching, in the *kerygma*. The gospels perform the necessary function, not of directing faith to a past figure of whom certain historical values may be predicated with more or less certainty, but of certifying that Jesus of Nazareth once embodied the word of God in his existence in time. About this "Christ-event," i.e. the appearance of Jesus as an eschatological prophet of God who announced the imminent reign of God, nothing of *theological* significance requires to be known except *that* he once lived, taught and died. The mere *thatness, das blosse Dass* is sufficient, while all else in terms of his character and his recorded words is fraught with problems and so vulnerable to doubt. Christian faith can find no resting place in such historical uncertainties which can never be more than approximations, and must seek its point of reference in an existential encounter with the living Christ of the church's proclamation. The only "essential relationship" (*sachliche Verhältnis*) between Jesus and this kerygma on which faith builds is that continuum which is guaranteed by Jesus' existence. "It is therefore self-evident that the kerygma presupposes the historical Jesus, however much it may have mythicized him.

---

[18] This translated lecture now appears in *The Historical Jesus and the Kerygmatic Christ*, edd. C. E. Braaten and R. A. Harrisville [1964].

Without him there would have been no kerygma" (Bultmann, *loc. cit.*, p. 7).

The twin roadblocks placed by Bultmann in an attempt to offer a twentieth century version of the Life of Jesus are noted by J. M. Robinson.[19] Bultmann's "form-critical studies corroborated the view that a Life-of-Jesus research after the style of the nineteenth century is impossible, and his existential interpretation did not support the thesis that such a Life-of-Jesus research was legitimate."

At this point the history of the so-called New Quest opens; but it is not our purpose to continue the story in detail beyond this stage.[20]

Bultmann and Gospel History

It is not difficult to understand how Bultmann's proposals have proved unsatisfactory, and how his pupils have refused to remain content with their master's position. The chief reason why this was so is given in the course of Ernst Käsemann's lecture, delivered in October 1953 and which marked the beginning of the so-called "New Quest of the Historical Jesus." While sharing many of Bultmann's presuppositions about gospel criticism, Käsemann confessed himself unwilling to admit a "disengagement of interest from the earthly Jesus." In a significant statement, he proceeded: "If this were to happen, we should either be failing to grasp the nature of the primitive Christian concern with the identity between the exalted and the humiliated Lord; or else we should be emptying that concern of any real content, as did the docetists."[21]

Here Käsemann places his finger on an issue which the critics of Bultmann have always regarded as the outstanding weakness, not to say danger, in his attitude to gospel history. Although his writings are cautiously framed, they have not failed to avoid giving the impression that the human Jesus has been lost. A twentieth-century version of *docetism* means that with an over-emphasis on the "mere that-ness," the factuality of Jesus, as the chief contribution of the gospel records, the Jesus of Galilee and Jerusalem has been evaporated and his place as a historical person taken by a cipher, a symbol or ethereal idea, like a mathematical point which has position but no magnitude. The loss of the Jesus of history seems inevitably to open the road to a gnosticized version of Christianity which has severed connections with empirical history; and long before the Bultmann controversy assumed the large proportions of a public issue within the Lutheran church and across the ecumenical frontiers. T. W. Manson

---

[19] J. M. Robinson, *Kerygma und historischer Jesus* [1960], pp. 10f.

[20] See J. M. Robinson, *A New Quest of the Historical Jesus* [1959]; and more simply my essay "The New Quest of the Historical Jesus" in *Jesus of Nazareth: Saviour and Lord*, ed. C. F. H. Henry [1966], pp. 31–45. Documentation for what follows will be found in this article, as in several more recent studies.

[21] *Essays on New Testament Themes* [1964], p. 46.

perceived the warning-sign. "Bultmann undertakes to give us Christianity without tears, but what he gives us is tears without Christianity" (cited by A. M. Hunter, *Introduction to New Testament Theology* [1957], pp. 152f.).

We may press the question of Bultmann's logic here, and query with H. Zahrnt[22] whether there can ever be a historical "fact" without content; but a more effective criticism to be fastened on Bultmann's implied docetism will be to explore again why it is that he is embarrassed by a recourse to Jesus' historical person. Part of the answer comes in the way in which Bultmann's existentialism takes over from Kierkegaard a peculiar version of religious epistemology—and behind Kierkegaard we may trace the problem posed by Lessing's "ugly ditch." How can one leap over from truths of fact to truths of reason? The leap is made by these men as they are emotionally moved (Lessing), or as they exercise an irrational faith (Kierkegaard), or as they respond in a decision to the church's preaching (Bultmann). But, as ·John McIntyre has discerned, such a step must remain "non-significant without some contextual historical knowledge. It cannot take place in a vacuum, nor can a decision be made except within a framework of reference."[23]

Similarly, on theological grounds, Bultmann shies away from too close a contact with history for fear lest, if historical knowledge were to turn out to be genuine knowledge (which Kierkegaard had denied), then faith would rest on something less than Christ himself. He is driven, therefore, to dissociate faith from history; and to remove theological questions from the realm of history in the interest of securing that "invulnerable province" of which Kähler spoke. This is clearly brought out by his attitude to the question, Was Jesus the Messiah? He returns the answer: "Only the historian can answer this question . . . and faith, being a personal decision, cannot be dependent upon a historian's labor."[24]

This citation is a clear instance of Bultmann's disengagement of interest from the earthly Jesus, and shows where he wishes to place the emphasis in his understanding of Christianity, *viz.* upon a decision of faith engendered by the preaching of the risen Christ who, having lived a life whose character is concealed from us today, ascended into the kerygma!

But if this reconstruction of Christianity is true it becomes a very delicate matter to know what to do with the gospels. For they are concerned with a human figure the outlines of whose character are to be seen in his assumption of authority (Käsemann), his attitude to sinners (Bornkamm) and his conduct (Fuchs). By what he says and does he effectively communicates God's will for, as he accepts sinners and eats with them, it is implied that so God is graciously disposed to men. And this implies a way back behind the apostolic preaching to the earthly Jesus.

[22] H. Zahrnt, *The Historical Jesus* [ET, 1963], p. 93.
[23] J. McIntyre, *The Shape of Christology* [1966], pp. 119ff.
[24] R. Bultmann, *Theology of the New Testament* [ET, 1952], i. p. 26.

That way was first taken by Mark, as we have seen, the author of the first gospel writing.

A New Phase in Redaction-Criticism

Markan scholarship has moved decisively beyond form-critical evaluation with the ground-breaking proposals of W. Marxsen, *Der Evangelist Markus* [1956, ³1959; ET, *Mark the Evangelist*, 1969]. The form critics had been concerned mainly with the literary structure and "type" of the individual units (*pericopae*) which made up the gospels. Their task was one of classification and analysis. But an indirect result was to cast the evangelists in a new rôle. If the several *pericopae* were only loosely strung together and existed as independent units or blocks, the work of the evangelist was more like a compiler than a creative writer. His task was thought of more as that of a collector of traditions who put the units together into sections of teaching material rather than that of a gospel-writer who designed a work from start to finish.

Since, on this view[25] Mark is seen as an arranger of "essentially disconnected stories" which he strung together in a loose way but which in no sense formed an outline which is called the ministry of Jesus, it is not unnatural that Mark's identity should be virtually lost in a welter of separate traditions of which he is simply the purveyor. A protest made in the name of redaction-criticism is directed against this understanding of the evangelist's rôle, and represents a more constructive appreciation of what the gospel-writers were seeking to do in the arrangement of the traditions which they took over. A programmatic statement by G. Bornkamm, already foreshadowed in 1954, was given in his essay published in 1956 on the theme, "End-Expectation and Church in Matthew."[26]

Commenting on the "new direction" in which form-critical research must be continued, he expounded the meaning of "editorial criticism" in this long sentence:

> The Synoptic writers show—all three and each in his own special way—by their editing and construction, by their selection, inclusion and omission, and not least by what at first sight appears an insignificant, but on closer examination is seen to be a characteristic treatment of the traditional material, that they are by no means mere collectors and handers-on of the tradition, but are also interpreters of it.

The last few words in this citation give the clue to the new understanding of the gospel writers' rôle. Put simply, the aim and intention of a *redaktionsgeschichtlich* treatment of the gospels is concerned to upturn by

---

[25] It is represented most recently by D. E. Nineham's commentary, *Saint Mark* [1963].
[26] In German in *The Background of the New Testament and its Eschatology*. Festschrift C. H. Dodd [1956], pp. 222–69. Now it appears in translation in *Tradition and Interpretation in Matthew* [ET, 1963], pp. 15–51. Quotation from p. 11, which introduces the composite volume.

reversal the dictum of Hoskyns and Davey[27] that "the evangelists write as historians and not as theologians." The evidence adduced in support of this reversal which turns the gospel writers into theologians lies in the *Tendenz* of the gospel material, that is, in the reason why certain incidents are included in just the way they are and couched in the particular language used. Evidence is also found in the tell-tale clues of editorial redaction (hence the name) seen most obviously in the "seams" or connecting-links which the evangelists forge between the *pericopes*, and in the alterations, adaptations and emphases which the same evangelists have made to the *pericopes* they have received and then used.

On a broader front, the discipline and method of redaction-criticism[28] has addressed itself to the following issues.

(i) Attention is shifted from the small, independent units into which form-criticism had separated the gospel materials, and interest is turned to the gospels as literary wholes.

(ii) An important corollary of this change of perspective is that the evangelists emerge from the rôle of simple collectors and *Tradents* (i.e. handers-on) of the material they assemble and are re-instated in their own right as authors who by their selecting and editing the material impose on that material a distinctive theological stamp. In a phrase used by J. Rohde (*op. cit.*, p. 12; cf. p. 20), they do not simply hand on the story, but by placing it in a particular context and editing its details they become the earliest exegetes of it.

(iii) This means that we are invited to penetrate beneath the layers of the gospel data which can be identified as traditional and seek to locate the elements of the evangelist's editorializing work. We are encouraged to enter and explore the world of the evangelist himself—or more plausibly the community of which he was a member and seek to understand what the gospel sections *and the completed whole of the gospels* would have meant in those situations.

(iv) So we are bidden, at the behest of redaction-criticism, to inspect the "third life-setting"[29] of the gospels, i.e. the setting which provides explanatory contexts for the evangelist's own work. For W. Marxsen who pioneered the redactional study of Mark's gospel this entailed a study of the historical and theological background which provoked the evangelist to publish his literary work under the novel caption of "gospel." Marxsen needed to find an "occasion," called by him a catalyst which is

---

[27] E. C. Hoskyns and N. Davey, *The Riddle of the New Testament*[3] [1947], p. 147.

[28] For fuller details we may refer to J. Rohde, *Rediscovering the Teaching of the Evangelists* [ET, 1968]; R. H. Stein, "What is Redaktionsgeschichte?" JBL 88 [1969], pp. 45–56; and N. Perrin, *What is Redaction Criticism?* [1969].

[29] For this analysis, see W. Marxsen, *Mark the Evangelist* [ET, 1969], p. 23. The first and second *Sitze im Leben* are Jesus' own earthly life and that of the primitive church which transmitted the tradition.

required to cause the author to assemble, edit and then make public in written form what we know as a gospel book. Assuming that Mark had before him a collection of loosely connected sections of narrative and teaching, what impulse moved him to set them into a coherent pattern which conveyed a unified message? It cannot have been by accident that his gospel was born, for "it is not at all obvious that this totally disparate material should finally find its way into the unity of a Gospel" (op. cit. p. 17).

The precise historical event and its attendant theological ramifications which Marxsen looked to in defence of his view that Mark published his gospel at the outbreak of the Jewish war in A.D. 66 will be considered in a later section. Redaction-criticism does not stand or fall by the correctness of this part of Marxsen's thesis. His innovative work was to rescue Mark's gospel from a piecemeal form-critical dissection and, by re-instating it as the work of a theological author, enable us to stand back and see its architecture and message as a whole rather than to be minutely concerned with the structure, size and shape of each pre-Markan brick and the constituency of the cement and mortar.

In so appealing to Mark as a creative theologian in his own right, Marxsen had predecessors. In R. H. Lightfoot whose volume *History and Interpretation in the Gospels* [1934] anticipated many of the advances made in the post-war period, Mark's gospel was delivered fully from its bondage to the "Markan hypothesis" and the Life-of-Jesus research, and the theological tendencies, detected in its geographical arrangements and its centrality of the Messianic secret, were clearly brought into view. From the standpoint of the current British "Life-of-Jesus" attitude, Lightfoot's conclusion seemed to be unduly negative and out of focus; and he had later to explain what his allusion to knowing only "the whisper of his (Jesus') voice" and tracing in the gospels "but the outskirts of his ways" was really intended to convey.[30] But it remains true that he in his way, though largely unappreciated at the time, was building a more solid edifice of Markan interpretation than the contemporary form-critics would allow and offering a viable alternative to the simplistic "Life-of-Jesus" biographies which appeared in Britain between the two world wars.

Marxsen's work was almost simultaneously duplicated, though with less detail and in less spectacular manner, by H. Riesenfeld who contributed an essay on "Tradition und Redaktion im Markusevangelium."[31] He argued, in the teeth of form-criticism, that in the gospel which carries by ecclesiastical tradition the name of Mark we have the deliberately

---

[30] Namely an allusion to Job 26:14. See his book *The Gospel Message of St. Mark* [1950], p. 103 note.

[31] In the Bultmann Festschrift, *Neutestamentliche Studien für Rudolf Bultmann* [1954], pp. 157-164; there is a similar English version of this paper in Riesenfeld's volume of collected essays, *The Gospel Tradition* [ET, 1970], ch. 3.

executed work of one man and that he brought to his composition a theological purpose. That purpose is conceived to be christological and to reflect the twin aspects of Jesus' life—his preaching and his teaching—which later took their place in the church's ministry as *kerygma* and *didache*. The event of Easter naturally divides the two sets of correspondences, but the factor which runs from Jesus' ministry directly to the post-Easter church is discipleship. Mark is shown to be an author who has fashioned his materials so as to produce a model for the church of his own day. Yet he has dealt respectfully with those traditions which are not editorial inventions as K. L. Schmidt and the form-critics were in the habit of calling them. The basic outline of the ministry is sound (and is found to be epitomized in Peter's sermon in Acts 10:37–39; cf. Acts 13:31) and has provided Mark with a settled framework. Mark has edited and systematized the tradition in order to conform it to his own theological perspective, yet he has done so within the historical, geographical and temporal limits of the tradition he has received.

This sketch of the Markan problem represents a succinct and notable study. It does not try to put the clock back to the age of the original "Quest of the historical Jesus"; it takes account of form critical studies yet it is not bound to their extreme conclusions; and it points forward to Mark's new rôle as theologian and evangelist without committing itself to the excesses of Marxsen's particularistic reconstruction of a historical life-setting. Above all, it focuses attention on a burning issue which is greater than the small details of individual exegetical problems.

The germane question posed to the Markan interpreter is to know whether his story of Jesus is a loose assortment of detached *pericopae* put together in an artificial way, and partly the product of the creative imagination of the early believers in their search for "idealized situations" which they could appeal to as paradigms or teaching models. Or, whether, after all, there was interest in Jesus as a person in Galilee and Jerusalem and whether the early Christians were concerned to preserve an outline of his ministry among men.[32] The issue is between a view of Mark as a writer who bends history to his overruling purpose or freely invents his material for didactic purposes and an understanding of him as taking up a respectful

[32] The rival positions are represented in the debate between C. H. Dodd, "The Framework of the Gospel Narrative," ExpT 43 [1932], pp. 396ff. = *New Testament Studies* [1953], pp. 1ff. and D. E. Nineham, "The Order of Events in St. Mark's Gospel—an Examination of Dr. Dodd's Hypothesis," *Studies in the Gospels*, ed. D. E. Nineham [1957], pp. 223ff.; and idem, *Saint Mark*, p. 22 with the conclusion, "There would be no compelling motive for preserving, or even remembering, the order in which they [the events of Jesus' life] originally occurred during Our Lord's lifetime. The tradition about Jesus would thus assume the form of a variety of separate stories with no fixed or generally agreed order." The sequence of the passion narrative is an admitted exception to this rule which Nineham adopts. For a comment on the overall thesis, repeated in *op. cit.*, pp. 28, 29 and his later responses to critics, see later, and especially the argument of H. Sawyerr, "The Marcan framework", SJT 14 [1961], pp. 279–294, which seeks to refurbish the traditional view that "in Mark we have an expanded form of the pattern of teaching which we find in the summary of Acts 10: 37–41" (p. 283).

stance in regard to the tradition he adopts and submits to certain controls in his editorializing work.

Conclusion

We have taken notice of some of the major landmarks which stand out in the field of the interpretation of Mark's gospel. The gospel's fortunes have fluctuated from its early obscurity and neglect to its prominent place as the main platform in the "Markan hypothesis" which became the chief support of the liberal attempt to write a biographical study of Jesus' inner development and outward career. Then, with the reaction of form analysis, the gospel was fragmented and lost its character as a biographical quarry from which material for a connected, continuous and sequential narrative might be constructed. It became more a loose assemblage of individual stories and sayings, arranged for catechetical purposes in the church. More recently, the gospel has assumed a new importance as the literary effort of a theologian who in garnering the traditions has so arranged, edited and fashioned them into a unitary composition that we are asked to see the gospel as a statement of theology, with practical purpose and historicized to form a story.

Mark's gospel as a book ostensibly based on and recording historical events has suffered various ups-and-downs. The liberal estimate placed high value on its naive christology and portrayal of a human Jesus. The form-critical school saw it as a repository of church traditions cherished for teaching purposes. In the hands of redaction-criticism it is the history-writing of a creative theologian who makes history serve his purpose. No issue is more central than to ask how Mark's value will fare, either by depreciation or enhancement, in the matter of its witness to the historical Jesus.

III

MARK IN THE FRAME OF HISTORY

Traditional views of Mark's setting (Rawlinson, V. Taylor). Marxsen's theory: the outbreak of the Jewish war. Brandon's theory: the close of the Jewish war. Assessment of recent trends and detailed critique of Marxsen and Brandon.

A CONCLUSION WHICH IS AT THE SAME TIME A STARTING-POINT FOR futher inquiry was offered by J. H. Ropes in 1934. In a prescient judgment he clearly saw the way in which Markan studies could be most profitably pursued. For him (in *The Synoptic Gospels* [1934: p. 10 of 1964 reprint]) the gospel has become "a kind of theological pamphlet" with the result that the key to unlock Mark's purpose in writing is to be sought in his theological rather than historical background: "the form of the Gospel of Mark is, to be sure, that of narrative, but the important question is not of its form, but of its purpose; and that is theological."

The three terms which Ropes uses in this short statement provide us with the *leitmotif* of each of the next few chapters of this book. History, form, and theology have been fastened upon to become the ruling factor and interpretative key in the elucidation of the Gospel according to St Mark; and our task will be now to see how the composition of his work has been set within the framework of some specific historical (or set of historical) circumstances.

At its simplest this may be said to be the traditional way of evaluating Mark, and as it is usually tied in to an overall understanding of Mark as Peter's interpreter, this will be a suitable place to discuss the tradition about the relationship between apostle and evangelist. The background of this matter as of much that follows in the subsequent chapters should, however, be appreciated. S. G. F. Brandon may be reported as a recent spokesman for the general position adopted by interpreters in this area of Markan studies. He writes:[1]

> [Mark] has acquired a unique significance for the study of Christian Origins. But the key to the interpretation of that significance has remained elusive. The reason for this has been that the key lies in the date of the Gospel's publication . . . [requiring] some notable cause. However, to determine that cause no other evidence is available than that which the Gospel itself provides.

[1] S. G. F. Brandon, "The Apologetical Factor in the Markan Gospel," *Studia Evangelica* ii [1964], p. 34.

This requirement of a date of publication is a *desideratum* which has been sought in several directions. We shall survey these.

A. A Setting in the Neronian Persecution

This way of placing Mark's Gospel in the stream of early Christian history has sources which go back a long way. For convenience's sake we may separate three closely related matters:

(i) Mark's association with Peter.

(ii) Mark's identity in the early Church.

(iii) Mark's date.

(i) *Mark and Peter*. The earliest known allusion to the Gospel is that ascribed to Papias who, in turn, quotes "the Elder" (according to Eusebius, *HE*. III. 39).

> The Elder said this also: Mark who has been Peter's interpreter wrote down carefully as much as he remembered, recording both sayings and doings of Christ, not however in order. For he was not a hearer of the Lord, nor a follower, but later a follower of Peter, as I said. And he (Peter or Mark) adapted his teaching to the needs of his hearers but not as one who is engaged in making a compendium of the Lord's precepts.[2]

Modern discussion has questioned the validity of this ancient testimony, with many points raised to impugn Papias' ability and integrity as a witness;[3] but it cannot be said that the Papian tradition has been overthrown.[4]

If we accept its limited value, it says three things on the positive side. First, it traces back one of the sources which Mark used to Peter's teaching adapted to the needs of his hearers (or the needs of the moment). Then it remarks that Mark himself had no firsthand knowledge of the sayings or deeds of Jesus but was dependent on eye-witnesses. Thirdly, the information he picked up was gleaned in the course of his work as ἑρμηνευτής to the apostle Peter.

This Greek term evidently means something more than "translator" or "interpreter;" and it has been suggested by T. W. Manson that his function was more like that of a "private secretary" and *aide-de-camp*.[5]

A similar picture to that implied in Papias' words is found in the anti-Marcionite prologue to the Gospel which describes the evangelist as

---

[2] See H. E. W. Turner, "The Tradition of Mark's Dependence upon Peter," ExpT, lxxi [1960], pp. 260–63.

[3] Noted by Austin Farrer, *A Study in St. Mark* [1951], pp. 10ff.

[4] Though Papias' use of the tradition carries all the marks of his own *Tendenz*. I have suggested that he is consciously opposing Marcion's use of a truncated version of Luke by favourably contrasting Mark's claim to be recording apostolic testimony: See the Appendix to this chapter (pp. 80–83) for further discussion.

[5] T. W. Manson, *The Teaching of Jesus*[2] [1935], p. 23 note. For a view that Mark acted as "teacher" in the Pauline mission (on the basis of Acts 13:5) see now W. Barclay "A Comparison of Paul's Preaching" in *Apostolic History and the Gospel*, edd. W. W. Gasque and R. P. Martin [1970], pp. 169ff.

Peter's *interpres*.[6] The same document declares that Mark composed his Gospel in Italy after Peter's departure (*post excessionem*). There are problems with this statement but on the whole question of early attestation to Mark's relationship to Peter T. W. Manson's summing-up seems reasonable enough—at least on the assumption that early tradition is to be taken at its face value:

> If Peter had paid a visit to Rome some time between 55 and 60; if Mark had been his interpreter then; if after Peter's departure from the city Mark had taken in hand—at the request of the Roman hearers—a written record of what Peter had said; then the essential points in the evidence would all be satisfied.[7]

(ii) *Mark in the Early Church*. On the traditional understanding of the evidence, John Mark is the person known to us from references in the Acts of the Apostles (12:12, 25; 13:5, 13; 15:37, 39) and epistles (Col. 4:10; 2 Tim. 4:11; Philemon 24; 1 Peter 5:13). His close association with apostolic testimony in the person of Peter and Paul is clearly indicated in these texts. Both his home and family connections played an important part in early Christian history. His mother Mary (of sufficient importance to be named in Acts 12:12) was a member of the Jerusalem church and her home was evidently a regular venue for Christian assembly. It is sometimes thought that this was the scene of the last Supper meal referred to in Mark 14:14ff. (and parallels) and the meeting-place spoken of in Acts 1:13, 14 where certain womenfolk also gathered. To Mary's home Peter came after his escape from prison.

Then follows a period of Mark's intimate contact with Paul and his associates (Acts 13:5). With the decision to leave the apostolic group (Acts 13:13) relations with Paul were broken off, not without some bitterness of feeling (Acts 15:39). The result was that Barnabas, out of loyalty to his kinsman Mark, separated from Paul and went off independently to Cyprus. Paul gained a fresh colleague in Silas and resumed the Gentile mission in Asia Minor.

Some years later (how long depends on the dating of *Colossians*) Mark was restored to Paul's favour (Col. 4:10), though the wording of this appeal: "if he comes to you, receive him" has suggested to commentators that at this time Mark was perhaps only slowly winning back his reputation in the Pauline churches and needed the special plea put in for him by Paul: "receive him," i.e. without censure or doubt, especially since he does not seem to be widely known at this period and has to be identified as Barnabas' cousin. An even more moving display of reconciliation comes in 2 Timothy 4:11 where Mark is unhesitatingly commended as a faithful Christian worker. His restoration was now apparently complete. If Paul was a prisoner in Rome at the time of 2 Timothy,

---

[6] See W. F. Howard, "The Anti-Marcionite Prologues to the Gospels," ExpT xlvii, [1936], pp. 534-38.
[7] T. W. Manson, *Studies in the Gospels and Epistles*, ed. M. Black [1962], p. 40.

the summons to bring Mark to him at Rome since "he is very useful in serving me" would mean that Mark may well have been at Paul's side in the final days; but there is no certainty at this point since 2 Timothy 4 may belong to an earlier critical phase of the apostle's ministry.

Yet Mark's presence in Rome is attested from the association with Peter. In 1 Peter 5:13 greetings are sent from "Mark my son" and it is well supported that Peter was at Rome when 1 Peter was written. "Babylon" in the verse most naturally reads as a cryptogram for the imperial city as in Revelation 14:8; 17:5, cf. Eusebius, HE. II, 25, 5–8.[8]

The identity of the Mark to whom the second Gospel is ascribed with the John Mark of Jerusalem seems all but conclusively demonstrated by this chain of references. But there have been countervailing voices against it. They draw attention to an assortment of arguments which are offered to cast doubt on the tradition.

(a) The form-critical argument that this Gospel is an assemblage of earlier traditions handed down by a succession of nameless scribes and church leaders who used the *pericopes* in their teaching makes little room for eye-witness tradition, stemming from Peter. But, as we have observed, this argument, if taken logically, proves too much; for its conclusion would be that these handers-on and preachers invented the material *de novo* because it was convenient and necessary in their catechetical work. That the form of the *pericopes* and their inter-connections have been modified by their use in teaching is one thing; it is quite a different proposition to maintain that their *content* was the product of the fertile imagination and active construction of the preachers who, at some point in their transmission, required a suitable story from Jesus' life to illustrate or enforce a point. We may concede that the argument which builds on "Peter's reminiscences" can be overdone. But that disclaimer does not shut the door on the presence of some eye-witnesses whose personal witness set in motion the tradition which culminated in the final gospel-book. And who more than Peter could be responsible for the vivid way in which the stories are narrated?

For instance, the attitudes, the expressions and even the gestures of Jesus are reported (see 7:34; 9:36; 10:16) in such a way as an eye-witness would be likely to recall when, at a later time, he related the incidents. Special emphasis is given to Jesus' observation (5:32) and his attitude to those who came under his scrutiny (1:41, where the reading "being angry"

---

[8] On the verse in 1 Peter 5:13 see E. G. Selwyn, *First Epistle of St. Peter* [1947], pp. 60–62; and for the historical and archaeological evidence of Peter's presence in Rome the latest discussion is by D. Wm. O'Connor, *Peter in Rome* [1960]. His conclusions are that Peter's presence at Rome, probably near the end of his life, is attested as well as his martyrdom there in the Circus of Nero. A monument near the place he died memorialized the event, but his body was never recovered for burial. Later, however, in the search for relics it came to be believed that the actual grave-site could be located. See further my article, "Peter" in *International Standard Bible Encyclopaedia* (revised).

is to be preferred to the Received Text's, "being moved with compassion"). Other examples are in 3:5; 3:34; 10:21; 10:23; 11:11.

Similarly, snatches of conversation between the disciples are noted; and the remarks of the onlookers and the crowd remembered. A good illustration of this comes in 9:14–29 in which the unusual wealth of detail has convinced the form-critic K. L. Schmidt that the story "can only go back to good tradition."[9]

These facts, on a traditional view, seem clearly to point to the presence of an eye-witness who both remembered the penetrating look of Jesus and recalled that those who heard his voice and saw his mighty works reacted in a decisive way. Perhaps, the story of the rich man (10:17–22) makes this point clear and sharp, especially when we compare the absence of detail in the parallel versions in Matthew (19:16–22) and Luke (18:18–27). The Synoptists diverge from Mark in the several ways they omit such characteristic features as the trivia that the [young] man ran and knelt; and that Jesus looked upon him and loved him. And they modify the dramatic climax of the story that, when faced with Jesus' challenge, he expressed on his face profound disappointment.

Another realistic detail, peculiar to Mark, is perceived in 10:32. On the last journey to Jerusalem, Jesus walked alone, ahead of his disciples, and as they followed, fear gripped them. As B. K. Rattey comments, "Mark alone tells us all this; but who told Mark? It could only have been one of the twelve."[10]

Well, not exactly. It still remains possible to account for Mark's vivid style in writing and his concentration of detailed touches in another way. All these features may be put down to Mark's artistry as a story-teller and his bid for verisimilitude. The question is, Are these the parts of his story which he would want to embroider and dress up? What motive controlled him in making his narrative racy and breath-catching in its swiftness and his reported conversations quick-fire and staccato? There is still remaining to be explained the way in which Peter is placed centrally in this Gospel.

B. W. Bacon[11] pointed out that in the majority of references to Peter in the Gospel he is mentioned in terms of disgrace or rebuke (see, for example, 8:27ff; 9:5–6; 10:28ff.; 14:25ff.; 14:66–72). The rôle of Peter in 1:36ff. is considered later.

Two explanations are possible to account for this feature. A. E. J. Rawlinson (*Commentary* p. xxix) seeks to deduce from the candid appraisal and criticism of Peter that when the Gospel was published Peter's memory was already revered as that of a martyr and his character was already invested with an honour which no stain remaining from the record of

[9] K. L. Schmidt, *Der Rahmen der Geschichte Jesu* [1919], p. 227.
[10] B. K. Rattey, *The Making of the Synoptic Gospels* [1942], p. 32.
[11] B. W. Bacon, *The Beginnings of Gospel Story* [1909], pp. xxiv–xxvii.

his earthly life could tarnish. This may very well have been the case, but there is no proof.

The second explanation believes that Peter's own confessions of failure and disgrace account for the report of these episodes. This seems to be shown from the way in which Peter's own name is attached to certain parts of the record where the other Gospels give only a vague reference to "they" or "one of the disciples" (1:36; 11:21; 16:7). Conversely, it becomes difficult to account for the omission of the encomium of Matthew 16:17-19, "Blessed are you, Simon Bar-Jona!," if there was a desire on Mark's part to glorify Peter. Only the humbled apostle who was willing to relate, in such detail, his denial of the Lord would have left out the words of the same Lord's blessing upon him. Further, in 11:21, the notice, "Peter, calling to remembrance, says" must on its face value have come to the evangelist direct from Peter himself (cf. 14:72).

A further confirmation that Mark depends directly or indirectly upon Peter for these details is found in the traditional interpretation of the attitude to the disciples as a body of men. This evangelist spares no detail when he reports the failures and misunderstandings of the Twelve. To be sure, Mark's procedure in this kind of reporting may well have a theological motif, such as the conviction that it was from these insignificant men who offered such unpromising material that God was pleased to bring to pass the mystery of his kingdom through a hidden Messiah and his esoteric teaching communicated to them (4:11).[12] Yet this theological construction does not upset the claim that Mark's vivid language—even to the point of brusqueness and harshness as in 4:38: "Teacher, do you not care if we perish?"—came into the tradition from the one who was party to the scene and in this instance joined in the curt reproof voiced by the disciples in the storm-tossed boat. It is a stunned retort which has been softened in the corresponding incident in Matthew (8:25) and Luke (8:24).

But, once more, it is possible to offer an alternative explanation. D. E. Nineham[13] has raised a challenge to the ascription of Mark's material to his dependence on Peter. His main argument is the form-critical one, mentioned above, namely that Mark's material "bears all the signs of having been community tradition and cannot therefore be derived directly from St Peter or any other eye-witness." By way of summary, several comments may be made on this assertion. First, community tradition may well include the report of eye-witness testimony in its first stage, however much modification takes place in the subsequent history of the transmission.[14] The alternative view would leave no place for any

---

[12] See R. P. Meye, *Jesus and the Twelve* [1968], pp. 135ff.

[13] D. E. Nineham, *Commentary* [1963], p. 27. His italics.

[14] See the argument in H. Riesenfeld, "The Gospel Tradition and Its Beginnings" now reprinted in *The Gospel Tradition* [1970], pp. 1-29. Some exaggerations in the approach do not completely invalidate it.

first generation hearer of Jesus and put all the onus on that anonymous entity, the faceless "community" as the originator of the gospel tradition.[15]

Then, Nineham's subsequent statement (op. cit., p. 27) that if *some* of the Markan material is a community product (which few will deny), then "*all* of it, without exception" (my italics) is so is justified on the ground of logic. But this conclusion surely is exaggerated and in no way convincing as a logical deduction.

Third, Nineham overlooks the rôle of Mark as an evangelist and theologian in his own right, and his argument still stays within the classic framework of form criticism for which the gospel writers were scribes of the tradition[16] and not the first commentators on it. The newer appreciation of the evangelist's rôle which redaction criticism has emphasized makes it possible to argue that Mark placed the impress of his own personality on the traditions he received and fitted them into a pattern dictated by his own theological convictions. Exactly at that point he is more likely to have cherished what came to him with the hallmark of Peter's personal insignia on it and to have used what material he gleaned as part of his work as Peter's ἑρμηνευτής. This personal involvement lifts Mark above the level of a scissors-and-paste editor, content simply to shuffle traditions and stick them piecemeal into a format, and gives him a more creative part to play in which personal factors of acquaintance with the people in the tradition must have exerted some influence on him.

There is of course the possibility that the link between Peter and the gospel-writer is to be explained as a fantasy of early Christian imagination. Even if we allow that the verse in 1 Peter 5: 13 associates Peter and Mark in Rome, it says no more than that the two men were closely related in Christian service; it does not spell out the nature of that relationship in such a way that would lead us to conclude that Mark wrote down the teaching of his master. For that item of information we must go to early Christian sources, notably to Papias c. A.D. 140. And, as we have hinted, Papias may have a very definite axe to grind.

At the opposite end of the scale there is the opinion that Peter's name is introduced simply as a polemical device. J. Schreiber made this idea a ruling notion in his interpretation of Mark's gospel (see later pp. 101f.) and endeavoured to give the apostle a symbolic value as representing Jewish-Christianity which Mark wishes then to criticize. Peter is made to appear in a bad light in order to point up the gross failures of the Jewish-Christian wing of the church in the evangelist's own day. This is a very speculative theory and we will return to it by way of critical comment.

[15] In the composite volume, *Jesus of Nazareth* (ed. C. F. H. Henry) [1965] the two essays of F. F. Bruce ("History and the Gospel") and E. F. Harrison ("*Gemeindetheologie*: The Bane of Gospel Criticism") are specially germane to this issue.

[16] See his essays on "Eye-witness testimony and the Gospel Tradition", JTS, ix. 1. [1958], pp. 13–25, ix. 2 [1958], pp. 243–252; xi. 2 [1960], pp. 253–64.

(*b*) A second objection is offered in the simple reminder that "Mark (Marcus) was the commonest Latin name in the Roman Empire and that the early Church must have contained innumerable Marks"; the inference is then drawn that we should "realize how precarious any assumption of identity is in this case."[17]

There is some special pleading here, for we cannot know how many persons carried the name Marcus in Christian circles.[18] What can be maintained is that the several allusions to "John whose other name was Mark" (Acts 12:12) in both Acts and the epistles form a self-consistent picture[19] and that no other "Mark" is recognized as a candidate for the office of evangelist in the patristic period. The manner in which this man is identified suggests that while John was a common name, "John Mark" pointed to a well-known individual. If he is not the gospel-writer, we require to postulate another "Mark," associated with Peter and Paul, whom the early fathers rescued from oblivion in ascribing the second Gospel to him; or else to dismiss patristic testimony as wholly tendentious.

In parenthesis, it may be mentioned that Mark 14:51ff. with its notice of a young man in the Garden who followed Jesus and fled naked when the posse sought to arrest him contributes nothing to our knowledge. The passage may have been modelled on Amos 2:16[20]; more likely it represents a piece of individualized tradition which John Mark may well have picked up in the post-Pentecost Church when the disciples met in the upper room (Acts 1:13) which could possibly have been his mother's home in Jerusalem (Acts 12:12; cf. 1:14).[21]

(*c*) The connection of John Mark with Peter which is brought out so forcefully in 1 Peter 5:13 is threatened if the document known as First Peter is of much later, non-apostolic origin. Then (so the argument runs[22]) the collection of names in 1 Peter 5:12, 13 offers no obstacle. The men are prominent figures of the (now distant) apostolic age, known to all Christians. "It required no great effort of the imagination to place Marcus and Silvanus in the entourage of Peter at Rome." Papias (on this view) is a victim of the same illusion and because of his interest is securing attested apostolic teaching he forges the link even closer by making the author of the second gospel the personal confidant of St Peter and so the latter's trustworthy scribe and repository of his teaching.

Obviously this argument is no stronger than its initial premise, which is that 1 Peter is a pseudonymous, sub-apostolic document. That conclusion

[17] Nineham, *op. cit.*, p. 39.

[18] In the examples Nineham cites Marcus is the *praenomen*; in John Mark's case it is the *cognomen*, so the parallel is not exact.

[19] This is shown by W. Michaelis, *Einleitung in das neue Testament*[2] [1965], pp. 53–55.

[20] So Loisy: see E. C. Hoskyns and F. N. Davey, *The Riddle of the New Testament*[3] [1947], pp. 66 ff.

[21] See Michaelis, *op. cit.*, p. 55.

[22] See F. W. Beare, *Commentary on the First Epistle of Peter*[3] [1970], *ad loc.*

must be tested on the objective grounds of its historical allusions (to the persecutions described in the letter) and the type of Christianity it represents. When these criteria are applied, it is by no means certain that the setting is later than the 60's of the first century.[23]

(d) The most formidable objection to the traditional authorship of the Gospel has been isolated and enforced in a recent study.[24]

The argument builds on the form-critical foundation that a gospel which is a collection of independent *pericopae* can hardly be thought of as the deposit of an eye-witness, and that the structure of the Markan *pericopae* militates against the idea that they are recorded reminiscences. We may grant the force of this latter objection which rightly refuses to give much credibility to the older view that Mark's rugged style is explained by his faithfulness in turning Peter's first person statements into third person narrations. C. H. Turner, it seems, overplayed his hand when he appealed to this "autobiographical" trait.[25]

Turner goes on to note that on this principle he felt he could explain the vivid wording of (e.g.) 1:29, 30. Peter's original mother-tongue gave the sentence: "We came into our home with James and John; and my wife's mother was ill in bed with a fever, and at once we told him about her." Mark simply turned this direct speech into *oratio obliqua*; and there are (so Turner averred) many places where this language phenomenon is present. He instances 1:21; 5:1; 6:53, 54; 8:22; 9:14, 30, 33; 10:32, 46, 11:1, 12, 20, 27; 14:18, 22, 26, 32. And this body of material is made the ground of an appeal to Peter's apostolic testimony behind the second Gospel, written by John Mark.

But this position is difficult to maintain, however superficially attractive it seems to be. If it were true, it would lead us to expect a gospel record more sequentially tight-knit and more chronologically exact than is the case. Moreover, Papias (in Eusebius, *HE*. III. 39.15) was aware that Mark's order was open to criticism and that he made no pretence to record everything as though he were simply Peter's stenographer.

K. Niederwimmer has no difficulty in opposing this extreme view. Thereafter his positive criticisms fasten on two matters on which he believes the evangelist to be woefully in ignorance and error (*loc. cit.*, pp. 178ff.). They are (a) his geographical allusions; and (b) his reference to Jewish customs. Both sets of data are laid under tribute in order to show that the evangelist was not acquainted with Palestinian topography

---

[23] See J. N. D. Kelly, *The Epistles of Peter and of Jude* [1969], Introduction with conclusions supporting an apostolic dating (pp. 26ff.) and origin at Rome (pp. 33ff.). See too his comments on 5:13 (p. 220). Arguments for the apostolic authorship on 1 Peter are summarized in my essay, "First Peter" in *International Standard Bible Encyclopaedia* (revised).

[24] K. Niederwimmer, "Johannes Markus und die Frage nach dem Verfasser des zweiten Evangeliums", ZNTW 58 [1967], pp. 172–88.

[25] C. H. Turner in *A New Commentary on Holy Scripture*, ed. C. Gore *et al.* Part III [1928], p. 48.

and culture at firsthand; and so the writer could not have been John Mark in Jerusalem. Papias made this false identification because of apologetical interests; and his desire to claim Peter's authority behind the Markan record was motivated tendentiously in order to ward off the claims of gnostic gospels (*loc. cit.*, p. 186). But this literary and apologetic fiction has no basis in solid history, and reflects simply the dogmatic tendencies within second-century Christianity which clutched at the straws of apostolic authority, either in the living words of survivors from the apostolic age or the books which carried their authority (Eusebius, *HE*. III. 39.3–4).[26]

The Markan texts which are appealed to as the foundation of this novel hypothesis are chiefly (*a*) 5:1; 6:45; 7:24, 31; 8:22; 10:1; 11:1; and (*b*) 7:3ff.; 14:12. That there are problems associated with place-names and Palestinian geography in Mark is not to be denied, 7:24, 31 is a notorious *crux interpretum*, and it is possible that the text has suffered in transmission. The difficulty is that Jesus' movements are improbably circuitous (see Rawlinson, *Commentary*, p. 101). Some commentators note the conclusion that Mark is only vague in his geographical advice here: others follow the proposed emendation of reading "to Saidan" for Sidon, the former becoming a variant of Bethsaida. The other problem texts are concerned with place-names in Galilee and the northern parts of the province and beyond. On the supposition that Mark lived in Jerusalem with his mother (Acts 12:12) there is still nothing improbable in the idea that his geographical knowledge was not precise as we under-stand text-book accuracy, but he was content to give general descriptions of the area with which he was not personally acquainted. The same may be said on the question of Jewish rituals, though it is possible that in his description (in 7:3) of the Pharisees' practice Mark is deliberately adopting the stance of his non-Jewish readers (so Cranfield). In 14:12 this historical notice apparently confuses "the first day of Unleavened Bread" (Nisan 15) with the time when the passover lamb was slaughtered (in the preceding part of Nisan 15, i.e. Nisan 14; the date changed at 6 p.m. according to the Jewish calendar). But again there is a looseness in describing these events in Jewish sources,[27] and some textual variation caused by a trans-cription from Aramaic to Greek has been suspected.[28]

In sum, there is no compelling evidence to regard the second evangelist as a hellenist Christian, unfamiliar with Palestine or unversed in Jewish traditions, however much it is true that he belonged to the church of the later apostolic age, which was becoming increasingly Gentile. He wrote for this clientele, and explanations and asides which are added to his

---

[26] On this text see A. F. Walls, "Papias and Oral Tradition," *Vigiliae Christianae* 21 [1967], pp. 137–140.

[27] Strack-Billerbeck, *Kommentar zum NT aus Talmud und Midrasch*, vol. II. [1922], pp. 813–15.

[28] See J. Jeremias. *The Eucharistic Words of Jesus*, [ET², 1966], pp. 17ff.

story have these readers in view. He does not play fast-and-loose with geography and history—here Niederwimmer in his main contentions shows his sympathy with the ideas of Lohmeyer and Marxsen for whom geographical allusions are meant to be taken cryptically as theological ciphers. Therefore, we conclude that in Mark the evangelist we have a writer who "had considerable opportunities of gathering knowledge of the kind that would later be useful in the composition of the Gospel,"[29] through his association with the leading apostles both in Jerusalem, in Antioch and in Rome. Mark is to be credited with intimacy with both Paul on his first journey and at Rome; and also with Peter, though how he became the latter's ἑρμηνευτής is not easily determined. Whether the word means "translator" (turning Peter's Aramaic or Greek into a more acceptable form) or "interpreter" of his message to catechumens as a Christian teacher is not clear.[30] W. C. van Unnik makes a good point when he insists that, whatever the exact nuance of the word, the important thing is not the way Mark performed his rôle as interpreter but the content of his work as interpreter.[31] This suggests that Mark became Peter's ἑρμηνευτής by publishing his gospel in which he recorded Peter's teaching —or as much of it as he remembered and modified by his knowledge of Paul's gospel and of the effect of that gospel on the life of the mission churches in the Graeco-Roman world.

(iii) *The date and provenance of the Gospel.* On the traditional view of Mark's close contact and association with Peter it becomes possible to affix a fairly definite date-tag on to Mark's gospel and to place its publication in a specific situation. Not everything, however, points in favour of a publication in Rome and at a time when Nero's persecution was a recent experience, though there are several positive indications which lead to this conclusion.

(a) The external data contribute the information that Mark was Peter's interpreter; and we know that Peter was martyred at Rome. Irenaeus (*Adv. Haer.* III. 1.2) writes that "After their deaths (sc. Peter's, Paul's) Mark, the disciple and interpreter of Peter, himself also handed down to us in writing the things which Peter had proclaimed." Attempts have been made to discount the interpretation placed on Irenaeus' word by suggesting that he does not mean to give chronological information, but is concerned simply to state the continuity of Mark's writing and Peter's preaching. But this negative view (as V. Taylor grants)[32] of the evidence is far from an obvious deduction. The accuracy of Irenaeus, however, may be

---

[29] T. W. Manson, *Studies in the Gospels*, p. 37.

[30] See for the Jewish background of the word E. Stauffer, "Der Methurgeman des Petrus," *Neutestamentliche Aufsätze.* Festschrift J. Schmid [1963], pp. 282ff.

[31] W. C. van Unnik, "Zur Papias-Notiz über Markus (Eusebius *HE* III. 39. 15)" ZNTW 54, 55 [1963], 276–7.

[32] V. Taylor, *The Gospels. A Short Introduction*[5] [1945], p. 51. See idem, *Commentary*, pp. 5, 6.

impugned in the light of his earlier remark that Matthew was produced while Peter and Paul were still preaching—a historical notice which it would be difficult to maintain. Further, the witness of Clement of Alexandria (c. A.D. 200) is that Peter was still alive when Mark was written (*apud* Eusebius, *HE*. II. 15. 1,2; VI. 14. 6f. cf. VI. 25.5), but this is normally taken to be unreliable. More credence should be given to the statement in the Anti-Marcionite prologue that "after the departure of Peter himself, he (Mark) wrote down this same gospel in the regions of Italy."[33]

(b) The earliest attestation of the use of the gospel comes from 1 Clement 15:2 and Hermas *Sim.* 5:2 which are both associated with Rome.[34] The interesting thing about 1 Clement is that it quotes Isaiah 29:3 in the same form in which it is used in Mark 7:6.[35]

But not too much weight can be placed on these facts. For example, 2 Clement 7:6 cites Isaiah 61:24b in the same way as Mark 9:48[36]; and and 2 Clement has an Alexandrian background. In fact, a rival view (stated by Chrysostom, *Hom. in Matt.* 1) says that the gospel of Mark originated in Egypt. This statement is probably based on a misunderstanding of Eusebius, *HE*. II. 16.1 which remarks, "They say that Mark set out for Egypt and was first to preach [there] the gospel which he had composed."[37] We may instance also Eusebius, *HE*. II. 24 which speaks of Mark's association with the church at Alexandria. Jerome (*Vir. ill.* 8) later declared that Mark "took up the gospel which he had compiled and went to Egypt." This claim of an Alexandrian connection with Mark should not be lightly dismissed,[38] but the evidence (such as it is) seems weighted in favour of Rome.

Other hypotheses, such as the proposing of a place of origin located in Antioch or Galilee are far more insubstantial. J. V. Bartlet[39] favoured Antioch as did W. C. Allen[40] who believed (following Blass and C. C. Torrey) that the gospel was first written in Aramaic in Jerusalem and later translated into Greek at Antioch, which was a bilingual centre of early Christianity.[41] More recently, W. Marxsen has sought to uphold the view that the gospel was published in Galilee.[42] But his view is so

[33] On this text see R. M. Grant, "The Oldest Gospel Prologues," *Anglican Theological Review* xxiii [1941], pp. 231ff.

[34] On the latter text see S. E. Johnson, *Commentary on the Gospel of Mark* [1960], p. 7.

[35] H. Köster, *Synoptische Überlieferung bei den apostolischen Vätern* [1957], pp. 21ff. But he doubts whether Clement knew the gospel as such for certain.

[36] Köster, *op. cit.*, pp. 105f.

[37] So S. E. Johnson, *Commentary*, p. 15.

[38] T. W. Manson, *Studies in the Gospels*, pp. 38f. H. B. Swete, *Commentary*, pp. xviii.ff., has some interesting observations on Mark's possible connection with Egypt.

[39] *Commentary on Mark* [1922], pp. 36 f., following G. C. Storr of Tübingen.

[40] W. C. Allen, *The Gospel according to St. Mark* [1915].

[41] On Antioch as the meeting-place of Greek and semitic cultures, see G. Dix, *Jew and Greek: A Study in the Primitive Church* [1953], p. 33.

[42] W. Marxsen, *Der Evangelist Markus²* [1959], p. 41 (ET, *Mark the Evangelist* [1969], p. 66).

closely tied in to the overriding consideration that the gospel was first written to warn the community in Galilee of the imminent parousia set in the turbulent years of A.D. 66–70 that to cast doubt on the purpose of the gospel as Marxsen envisages it is to discredit all force in his argument for its locale. We shall discuss the former thesis later.

(c) We return to the tradition represented first in Papias who apparently derived it from 1 Peter 5:13, viz. that Mark published the gospel at Rome in connection with his service to St Peter. As B. W. Bacon concludes, "In the second, third, and fourth centuries all parties are agreed in making the view of Papias fundamental . . . for Papias was the fountainhead of tradition regarding Gospel origins. . . . As regards ancient testimony to the provenance of our oldest Gospel it is certainly true that 'all roads lead to Rome.'"[43]

But, Bacon is candid enough to concede that "neither the evidence of tradition nor of dissemination can be decisive of the question of provenance if unsupported by the internal evidence."[44] To that internal evidence of the gospel we may now direct attention and specifically to the two areas which are customarily appealed to in support of the claim that Mark's gospel emanated from Rome. Thereafter we must switch attention to two more individualistic theories, associated with the names of W. Marxsen and S. G. F. Brandon.

The contents of the gospel itself have two features which are germane to our enquiry: the language in which the story is told, and the interest shown in persecution and martyrdom.

(i) Mark's language

The evangelist explains Jewish customs and practices which may have been unfamiliar to his non-Palestinian readers, e.g. 7:3, 4. Pursuing the same design of intelligible communication, he has retained Aramaic expressions in his text in their Graecized form, but added an interpretative gloss for the benefit of his readers, e.g. 'Abbâ (my father) in 14:36 is translated into Greek as well as retained in the text. An identical usage occurs in Paul in Romans 8:16; Galatians 4:6. In each case, however, the addition is only approximately correct, but it is sufficiently accurate to render the sense of 'Abbâ as an invocation of God as Father. Other examples of interpretative additions to an Aramaic phrase are 5:41: t^elîtâ' qûmî: little girl, get up; 7:34: 'etpattaḥ: be opened. On the other hand, semitic words which have become habituated in the liturgical language of the church (Amen, Hosanna) are given without translation.

The presence of Latinisms poses a testy problem, to which various solutions have been given. One extreme is that Mark's gospel in its entirety is a translation from a Latin original. The Latin constructions

43 B. W. Bacon, *Is Mark a Roman Gospel?* [1919], p. 22.
44 Bacon, *op. cit.*, p. 48.

which can be seen are therefore relics or fossils left over from this imperfect rendition in Greek.[45] There is little to endorse this view, the most damaging point to the contrary being that semitic influences remain to be seen just beneath the text (e.g. 14:22ff. whose semitic background has been demonstrated by J. Jeremias[46]). It is monstrous to suppose that an editor recast a Latin original and set it into Greek but deliberately added semiticizing turns of phrase like so many fossils in the rock. By all canons of probability the work of translation proceeded the other way as Mark rendered the material of his traditions into Greek, sometimes rendering the semitic blocks of teaching in a somewhat wooden fashion and occasionally employing an expression or phrase for which a Latinism would be recognized by his bilingual readers.

In the following places the Greek of Mark's text thinly disguises the underlying Latin word or words. Modius (4:21); legio (5:9, 15); speculator (6:27); denarius (6:37); sextarius (7:4); census (12:14); quadrans (12:42); flagellare (15:15); praetorium (15:16); centurio (15:39, 44ff.). Some of these are direct loan words, i.e. Latin words written in Greek characters. It is also significant that, in the case of centurio, the parallel verses in Matthew and Luke (which do not use this word) read the Greek ἑκατοντάρχης in place of Mark's κεντυρίων. The term Ἡρῳδιανοί (Herodians) in a section (3:6) which contains another Latinism is particularly striking; we may refer to "they held a council" or "took counsel" as a Latin phrase reflected in συμβούλιον ἐδίδουν.[47] Josephus (Jewish War 1.319) regards the title Herodians as a Latinism.

Other Latin expressions are: 14:65 (verberibus eum acceperunt); 15:15 (satisfacere); 15:19 (genua ponere). It is of some importance that Mark has retained the name of Simon's family (15:21) and that these names (Alexander, Rufus) recur in Romans 16:13 as the names of church members at Rome where presumably the Latin language was current coin at that time.

The natural tendency of this argument which points to the presence of a number of Latin loan-words and Latin expressions and constructions is to lead to the conclusion that the evangelist was at Rome when he compiled his gospel and that it was for Christians in Rome that he primarily wrote. Continental scholars, however, have questioned this assumption. Ancient tradition, they maintain, is no more than guesswork and in this case Papias' statements which in a later time became the authority for the patristic testimony to the gospel, are quite likely simply deductions drawn from 1 Peter 5:13. The occurrence of Latinisms

[45] The full statement of the case returns an affirmative answer to its title question, "Was the Gospel of Mark written in Latin?" The writer is Paul-Louis Couchoud, The Crozer Quarterly, 5.1 [Jan. 1928], pp. 35–79.

[46] J. Jeremias, The Eucharistic Words of Jesus [ET², 1966], pp. 173ff.

[47] W. L. Knox, The Sources of the Synoptic Gospels, vol. i. St Mark [1953], p. 9. n. 2. But Cranfield, p. 122, disputes this.

proves nothing for two reasons. First, these terms are derived from the pre-Markan tradition,[48] so that Mark did no more than take over this material which had the Latinisms embedded in it. Secondly, the presence of Latinisms is found elsewhere in the New Testament and is not confined to literature which conceivably emanated from the imperial city.[49] To give a clear case, what is probably the most obviously identifiable Latin phrase in the gospels—δὸς ἐργασίαν in the sense of "make an effort" (da operam) is found in Luke's gospel (12:58), not in Mark. So the argument is double-edged.[50]

But Marxsen's first argument is itself open to criticism,[51] and the question remains why Mark did not eliminate the more eccentric translation-equivalents of those Latinisms that were in the text as he took it over. The argument from Mark's heavy concentration of Latin words and terms can never be more than confirmatory, but it needs to be taken in conjunction with other emphases, e.g. the reference he makes to Roman marriage law (Mark 10:12) and the orientation he displays towards a situation which was peculiar to the church at Rome in the seventh decade. This is the background of stress and fear which Nero's persecution of the Christians brought about following the fire of Rome, July A.D. 64.[52]

(ii) *Mark's gospel as a persecution tract*

The evidence of the gospel text itself endorses the supposition that *Mark* was written against the background of the incipient Roman persecution of the church in the imperial city. The data may be marshalled and evaluated.

(a) The several references to persecution are clearly to the point.

If a man would come after me, let him deny himself and take up his cross (a Roman method of execution) and follow me (8:34ff.).

For whoever is ashamed of me and of my words (or, of mine, i.e. my disciples) in this adulterous and sinful generation (by denying Christ's cause) . . . (8:38).

Compensations for present faithfulness will include "persecutions"—a Markan addition (in 10:30).

Prophecies of Jesus' death at the hands of Gentiles, with attendant disgrace (10:33).

[48] W. Marxsen, *Mark the Evangelist*, p. 66 n. 44; idem, *Introduction to the New Testament* [ET, 1968], p. 143.

[49] See Blass-Debrunner-Funk, *Grammar*, sec. 5.

[50] It is not surprising that those commentators who champion a Roman provenance of Mark (e.g. J. Schmid, "Das Evangelium nach Markus," *Regensburger NT⁵* [ET, 1968]) admit that there is no real evidence to be drawn from the presence of Latin words expressed in Greek in the text, p. 14.

[51] See J. Rohde, *Rediscovering the Teaching of the Evangelists* [ET, 1968], p. 138 n. 50.

[52] For the historical details, see F. F. Bruce, *New Testament History* [1969], pp. 378ff., with reference to the texts in Tacitus, Suetonius and the elder Pliny.

Jesus' impending death as a martyr for Israel (10:45).

The warning of forthcoming disasters as the "beginning of sufferings" (13:8).

The witness to the gospel must be borne even to the Gentiles (Romans) and be made at trial scenes and interrogations (13:10).

These texts virtually speak for themselves and take on deeper meaning when set in a background of a church which realizes its destiny as *ecclesia pressa* as the storm clouds of hostility from the Roman imperium gather. There is, moreover, a special emphasis in one detail of Mark's story which adds its confirming voice, and to which we may turn by way of a close examination of Mark's purpose concerning John the Baptist and Jesus.

(*b*) In one specific point the message of the gospel addressed to a church facing martyrdom comes through clearly. This is to do with the characterization of John the Baptist.

Recent studies on the *pericope* to do with the Baptist have exposed certain fairly settled conclusions.[53]

These are:

(i) In Mark's presentation John "has no significance in himself" (Marxsen, p. 33). The interest centres not on the teaching of John (as in Luke) nor on his independent ministry (as in John) nor on his rôle as baptizer of Jesus (as in Matthew); but all the weight of John's witness lies in what he is as the "prophesied preparer" (J. M. Robinson, p. 24) of Jesus' way. He is also the eschatological sign that in the wilderness God is about to renew his covenant with Israel (Hosea 2:14-23) and recall her to her pristine state of fidelity and obedience (Jeremiah 2:2ff.). Hence John's ministry is one of recall and a summons to repentance (Hosea 14: Jer. 3: 12, 22) followed by an outward expression in baptism (as in 1QS 5:13: "they shall not be cleansed unless they turn from their wickedness") and the promise of the holy Spirit (1QS 4:21: "He will cleanse him of all wicked deeds with this spirit of holiness": cf. Mark 1:8).

(ii) John's ministry "in the wilderness" (1:4) shows the fulfilment of Isaiah 40:3 and announces in its locale that the dawn of a new age will not be delayed. Rather, the critical time (1:15) is now at hand and God's kingdom is at hand in the greater one whom John heralded (1:7). The immediate response of "all Israel" (contained in the impressive descriptions of 1:5) indicates the nature of the divine offer which summoned all Israel to repent. Yet Mark knows, from his later perspective, that Israel failed to capitalize on the Baptist's summons to make ready a renewed people, and seems deliberately to contrast the many who come forth in verse 5 and the one who offers himself in submission to the divine will

[53] See W. Marxsen, *Mark the Evangelist* (ET, 1969], pp. 30-53; J. M. Robinson, *The Problem of History in Mark* [1957], pp. 21-32; U. W. Mauser, *Christ in the Wilderness* [1963], pp. 77-102; W. Wink, *John the Baptist in the Gospel Tradition* [1968], pp. 1-17.

in verse 9.[54] Furthermore, Judaea and Jerusalem are reputedly and inveterately hostile in Mark's gospel in contrast to Galilee whence Jesus comes, which is his land of origin and the scene of his mission to the semi-Gentiles (6:1–6; 7:24–37).

(iii) Most significantly, John's ministry is separated chronologically from Jesus' ministry. This is to be seen from the introduction of the "Passion of John" in 6:14–29. At 6:14 the rumour is that Jesus is John raised to life, an identification which could hardly have been made if John and Jesus had been seen to be active side by side (as in the fourth gospel, John 3:22–24).

The temporal successiveness of the two figures is the obvious clue to 1:14. "After John's arrest," Jesus' public work opens. But this translation veils the difficulty and quite probably mistakes the Markan sense. The time-clause requires a special comment.

μετὰ τὸ παραδοθῆναι τὸν Ἰωάννην is a Greek clause which is carefully constructed. It lacks a complementary indirect object to the verb, which is supplied by the commentators usually in the form of "when John was delivered over *to prison*" (so V. Taylor, E. Schweizer). But it is still ambiguous. Who was responsible for his arrest and detention? Furthermore, the narrative of John's prison experience and death is not picked up and continued until 6:17ff., which reverts to John's arrest by Herod and subsequent imprisonment and death.

W. Popkes[55] has rightly queried whether this exegesis can stand. Mark's interest in John is not primarily historical or biographical (nothing is told about John's deportment in prison or his courage as a martyr), but theological. It is then more to the point if the verb "to deliver, to hand over" (*paradidonai*) is taken in the sense of "delivered over *to death*" (as in 1 Sam. 24:4 [24:5 in LXX which uses the same verb]) and the hidden Agent behind the scene is God himself. This fits in with Mark's usage of the verb to denote Jesus' being committed to the betrayal, condemnation and bitterness of his Passion (3:19; 9:31; 10:33; 14:10, 11, 18, 21, 41, 42, 44). Behind the evil machinations of men we are meant to see, by the use of this Hebraic form of the passive voice, the deliberate will of God in an expression derived from Isaiah 53:6: "The Lord *delivered* him for our sins" (LXX).[56]

So Mark's intention is to make the fate of John and the fate of Jesus run parallel; and both end by their being delivered up by God to death (so Popkes, *op. cit.*, p. 144). John is thus the martyred prophet whose treatment at the hands of evil men foreshadows the end of Jesus' story

---

[54] The two sentences are structurally alike, as Lohmeyer, *Kommentar*, p. 20, observes: see U. W. Mauser, *op. cit.*, p. 93.

[55] *Christus Traditus. Eine Untersuchung zum Begriff der Dahingabe im Neuen Testament* [1967], pp. 143–5.

[56] So J. Jeremias, TDNT, v, pp. 709ff.

when as a martyr in the succession of those who yielded their lives to suffering and death in the Maccabean age[57] he gave himself an expiatory sacrifice for the many (10:45). The evangelist clearly has his eye on the end of the ministry when he composed his prologue in a way akin to the fourth evangelist's method in John 1:1–18 on which E. C. Hoskyns aptly remarked, "Not so much a preface to the gospel as a summary of it."[58] Perhaps there is a biblical precedent for this way of telling a story in the prologue and dialogue sections of the book of Job.

The upshot of this discussion leads to the conclusion expressed in Marxsen's thesis (op. cit., p. 32) that "Mark composes backward," reading back to the beginning to show that all that happened in Jesus' ministry has the cross inevitably in prospect. The practical bearing of this conclusion is seen in a message to Mark's church.

John the Baptist suffered as a victim of the wicked intentions of men who worked their malign will on him, as 9:13 recognizes. Jesus accepted this salutary lesson as part of his foretold destiny and saw in John a figure who both fulfilled an Old Testament rôle and shattered that image by having to do something no Jew expected Elijah to do—to suffer. The prospect of a dead Elijah was incredible (W. Wink, op. cit., pp. 14, 15); then, how much more unbelievable would the prediction of a suffering Son of man appear?

No vindication of the martyred prophet is given. John is consigned to his fate and to a cruel, undeserved death (as Mark 6:20 certifies in a way not found in the other Synoptists); and there is no last-minute miracle of deliverance or spectacular rescue. In parallelism, Jesus must suffer a similar fate of rejection, abandonment and cruel suffering, and there is no *deus ex machina* to relieve the tragedy and to turn the horror of his crucifixion into a surprise, happy ending by a dramatic reversal of fortune or a deliverance in the nick of time. The victory comes in defeat, with its only explanation and justification in the will of God. The Baptist goes to his fate in submission to that will; the Son of man goes as it is written of him (9:12; 14:21; 14:49), and treads a path of suffering to the end, with only the hint of vindication in the resurrection account which in Mark's account breaks off abruptly at 16:8a. There are no supernatural appearances or vindicatory episodes to give a happy ending to the story. There is only the naked promise of reappearance (see 14:28; 16:7).

The inference is that followers of Jesus in the church in Rome can expect no less. What men did to John, who out-of-character endured undeserved pain and death, and what they did to Jesus whose obedience to the divine purpose in scripture required the acceptance of the cup of woe (14:32–42), they would surely visit on the church. Nor is there any

[57] C. K. Barrett, "The Background of Mark 10:45," *New Testament Essays*. Studies in memory of T. W. Manson, ed. A. J. B. Higgins [1959], pp. 1–18.
[58] E. C. Hoskyns, *The Fourth Gospel* [1947], p. 137.

patent rationale for a Christian community in which Peter and Paul have already sealed their testimony with heroic death (1 Clement 5), and which no doubt was beginning to chafe under duress and to ask the insistent questions, How long, O Lord? Why do we see these evils coming upon us? Mark's consolatory answer is in the examples of God's theodicy which catches up the martyr's and the Son of man's suffering into his sovereign plan, at present hidden but which faith trusts the future will disclose and give meaning to. In the meantime, there are no demonstrable clues, as there are no confirming signs, that the end will reverse the tragedy of the present. "In Mark's account of the Passion, Jesus' passivity is unrelieved"[59]; and in the last chapters he played his rôle by inaction and a self-chosen silence. From the time of his arrest (14:50), Jesus speaks in this gospel only three times (14:62; 15:2, 34).

Unrelieved gloom hangs over the Markan picture of the Passion, and Jesus is the passive victim of all that is done and said. There may well be a reason for this, which is found in the prototypical character of the Markan Jesus who sets his afflicted people an example as they face their time of victimization and suffering under Nero's outburst and its aftermath. And John the Baptist foreshadowed by his undeserved death the ultimate example of Jesus himself.

Conclusion

From the evidence, both direct and inferential, the most viable conclusion to be drawn is that part at least of the historical setting of this Gospel is to be found in the conditions (both internal and outside) of the church at Rome in the middle of the seventh decade of the first century. This is the traditional way of looking at the gospel in the light of the historical evidence from early Christian sources. To be sure, it builds a great deal upon scraps of information and argues from silence. Above all, it depends on the close tie between Peter and John Mark and relates the publication of the gospel to a situation involving Mark's desire, after Peter's death as a martyr in the Neronian pogrom, to make public his reminiscences. Exactly at that point the connection is strained, as we have seen both from the standpoint of form-criticism and then from the motive of our chief witness, Papias.

The most that can be safely deduced is that, from the internal evidence, the gospel reflects a time of trial for the church. To a Christian community which had tasted the first-fruit of Roman persecution, Mark addressed his gospel book, partly in the guise of a consolatory tract, warning of the price to be paid yet assuring of the Lord's presence in time of stress. Mark's interest centres upon the interim between the resurrection and

[59] See R. A. Harrisville, *The Miracle of Mark* [1967], pp. 46ff., for a demonstration of this point.

the parousia, and his compilation of the evangelic traditions he inherited and arranged into the form of a "gospel" is partially controlled by his resolve to answer the question, What does the exalted one do in the interim-period? To that question, Mark replies: He strengthens those who confess him under persecution.[60]

This is probably as far as this line of investigation can take us. There is far more in Mark's gospel than a tract for martyrs or even a christology which promotes the exalted one's presence with his afflicted people, as though the evangelist were concerned to contemporize Jesus' presence in the present. The method of strict historical enquiry takes us so far—but not far enough to compass all that this gospel is designed to convey.

Two notable attempts to explore a more detailed historical *milieu* fall now to be considered.

(B) *A Setting in the Period of* A.D. 66–70

The work of W. Marxsen has already been noticed in connection with the approach to gospel studies known as redaction-criticism.[61] Our purpose now is to interrogate Marxsen's general thesis in respect to a historical setting which he proposes for the Markan record.

He borrows the hypothesis of the evangelist's geographical interest from Lohmeyer and R. H. Lightfoot, and turns it to his own purpose.[62] In particular, Mark is believed to show a proclivity towards Galilee throughout his gospel, with the references to this area carrying the signs that it belongs to Mark's redaction of the tradition.[63] But these geographical allusions to Galilee are for Mark no simple historical reminiscence. Rather their use is an assertion that Jesus "made Galilee the home of his gospel and his community" (Lohmeyer[64]); and more, the region is invested with theological significance by Mark because it speaks of the area to which Mark's gospel has special appeal. Behind Mark is a Galilean community which in turn is being addressed by the evangelist in the form of a published appeal, *eine Programmschrift*, as H. Conzelmann labels it.[65]

The historical setting to match this geographical orientation is the outbreak of the Jewish War in A.D. 66, an event which served a double purpose as far as Jerusalem Christians were concerned. They heeded an oracle which bade them flee from Jerusalem to Pella in Transjordan; and the onset of political trouble aroused a fever of apocalyptic hope that the end was near at hand. The oracle which called them to leave is described in Eusebius, *HE*. III. 5.3:

---

[60] So H. Conzelmann, *An Outline of the Theology of the New Testament* [ET, 1969], p. 141.
[61] See above pp. 46ff.
[62] *Mark the Evangelist*, pp. 102ff.
[63] Marxsen, *Introduction*, p. 138.
[64] E. Lohmeyer, *Das Evangelium des Markus*, p. 29.
[65] H. Conzelmann, *Grundriss der Theologie des NT* [1967], p. 163 [ET, *An Outline*, p. 144].

Moreover, the people of the church in Jerusalem were commanded by an oracle given by revelation to men worthy of it, before the war, to depart from the city and to dwell in a certain city of Peraea, namely Pella.

Among this emigrant community Mark is seen to have his place, for his gospel was composed as an encouragement to the church in Jerusalem to make its flight to Pella which Marxsen locates in the geographical region of Galilee (*op. cit.*, p. 107). Chapter 13 is an eschatological address written to dampen the apocalyptic frenzy caused by the outbreak of the Jewish War. It is also a *Flugblatt*, urging the church to forsake Jerusalem and migrate to Pella where, according to the promise of 16:7 (cf. 14:28), the prospect will be realized that the returning Lord will appear in his parousia and greet his people. Mark, of course, wrote this in anticipation of the eschatological event and with the parousia still awaited. He then had no choice but to conclude at 16:8a where his gospel breaks off. And he did so somewhere between A.D. 67 and 69.

It is not difficult to pick holes in Marxsen's thesis; and he has commanded very sparse agreement with his endeavour to find a definite historical occasion for the gospel's publication.

(*a*) Some interpreters take a position of historical scepticism in regard to Eusebius' description of the Pella flight, which is also attested in the slightly later work of Epiphanius (*De mens. et pond.* 15). This reads:

> For when the city was about to be conquered by the Romans, all the disciples were warned by an angel to leave the city, since it was about to be destroyed completely. Becoming migrants, they dwelt in Pella (cf. Epiphanius, *haer.* 29:7).

These historical notices were written in the fourth century, and earlier attestation is not absolutely certain. S. G. F. Brandon who opened a period of criticism directed at the Pella-story remarks that the supposed flight is passed over in the earliest Christian literature until we come to the time of Eusebius and Epiphanius, [66] and can only be regarded as a later fabrication. But these historians are evidently not creating their material *de novo*, and it is Zahn's suggestion that Hegesippus in the second century is the source.[67] Moreover, a much wider attestation has been sought by S. Sowers who offers a full defence of the tradition[68] in opposition to the negative positions adopted by Brandon, G. Strecker,[69] W. R. Farmer[70]

[66] S. G. F. Brandon, *The Fall of Jerusalem and the Christian Church*[2] [1957], pp. 168–173, 263–4; idem, *Jesus and the Zealots* [1967], pp. 208ff.

[67] So also E. M. Yamauchi, "Historical Notes on the Trial and Crucifixion of Jesus Christ." *Christianity Today* xv. 14. April 9, 1971, p. 636.

[68] S. Sowers, "The Circumstances and Recollection of the Pella Flight," *Theologische Zeitschrift* 26. 5. [1970], pp. 305–20.

[69] G. Strecker, *Das Judenchristentum in den Pseudoklementinen* [1958], pp. 229–31; idem, "Besprechung von W. Marxsen *Der Evangelist Markus* 1959[2]," ZKG 72 [1961], pp. 145, who dubs the Pella tradition "one without historical value."

[70] W. R. Farmer, *Maccabees, Zealots, and Josephus* [1957], p. 128 n. 2.

and L. E. Keck.[71] Literary allusions in earlier writers and some possible archaeological data in the excavation of the site of Pella are brought into the discussion to counteract the rival views of Brandon who explains the flight as a piece of church legend which originated from the claim made by the church at Aelia Capitolina in the second century.[72]

So far Marxsen may be on good ground in appealing to the synoptic *logion* of Mark 13:14f. which warns of a desecration of the Temple as in Josephus (*Jewish War* 4.388). But there is not much compulsion in Marxsen's further argument that Mark 14:28 and 16:7 refer to a flight of Christians or in the lexical point that the verbs rendered "to see, be seen" (ὁρᾶν, ὀφθῆναι) are used exclusively in reference to the parousia. In fact, the verbs are used indiscriminately.[73]

Moreover, the appeal to a Christian community in Galilee (where Pella is conveniently located for Marxsen's hypothesis, *op. cit.*, pp. 115f. n. 176) is an example of explaining *ignotum per ignotius*, for there is no independent witness to this Galilean church in the 60's of the first century. Finally, we may wonder whether Marxsen has misappropriated the Galilean tradition behind Mark and turned it into a datum for his theory of a putative community in that district. The interpretation which makes Galilee the land of eschatological fulfilment and reunion between the returning Lord and the church has been justly criticized by M. Karnetzki[74] who offers a much more reasonable view. This is that Galilee plays a prominent rôle in Mark as the land of Jesus' preaching and indicates the success it encountered there with the result that a "community" (Gemeinde) of faith was formed; and it was from Galilee that the Gentile mission was to be inaugurated, according to Mark 14:28.

A more speculative extension of this view is given by J. Schreiber[75] that the call to mission from Galilee is a polemic aimed at the Palestinian Jewish Christian church who rejected the kerygma of hellenistic Christianity and its missionary zeal. The verses 14:28; 16:7 are attributed to the exalted Lord as a side-glance at Peter's failure to recognize the validity of the Gentile mission. The apostle was blind and did not go to Galilee, the springboard of that mission; hence in 16:7 the risen Christ is depicted as himself engaged in that work as a tacit rebuke for Jewish Christians and a further summons to them.

This interpretation can hardly be sustained in view of what we know of Peter's attitude from the Acts of the Apostles and Galatians, and savours

---

[71] L. E. Keck, "The Poor among the Saints in Jewish Christianity and Qumran," ZNTW 57 [1966], p. 65 n. 36.

[72] See Sowers, *loc. cit.*, pp. 307ff., for a sound critique of Brandon's theory.

[73] "Promiscue" is Strecker's word, *loc. cit.*, p. 145, ὁρᾶν is used for a vision of the *risen* Christ in Matthew 28:7, 10: John 20:18, 20.

[74] M. Karnetzki, "Die galiläische Redaktion im Markusevangelium," ZNTW 52 [1961], pp. 228–272 (256).

[75] J. Schreiber, "Die Christologie des Markusevangeliums," ZThK 58 [1961], pp. 154–183 (176f.).

of the old Tübingen hypothesis with its sharp cleavage between Peter and Paul representing two types of Christianity.[76] We are drawn back to a position which may be stated rather naively in the form of a question. Does not Mark emphasize Galilee as the area of Jesus' activity because it was the *terminus a quo* of the apostolic kerygma in the earliest preaching according to Acts (1:8-11; 13:13; cf. Luke 23:5) and because in the outline of Peter's sermons (Acts 10:36ff.) the ministry of Jesus is anchored in Galilee (10:37)?

(*b*) H. Conzelmann[77] makes a valid criticism when he writes that Marxsen's use of Mark 13:41 "overlooks the improbability that anyone who saw the catastrophe (in A.D. 66) rushing towards him would write a book with complete composure in order to summon (his readers) to a flight which brooks no delay." The point is that if Mark were concerned to centre his message on a single theme, viz. the imminent invasion of Palestine as a harbinger of an eschatological fulfilment, it is passing strange that he should publish a "gospel" with a story of Jesus' activity and not be content to emphasize his main message by releasing just an apocalyptic fly-sheet with imperious tones of warning and exhortation. One possible way in which Marxsen's view could be made intelligible is to adopt E. Trocmé's theorizing[78] and contend that the original draft of Mark's gospel ended on the climactic note of chapter 13, with chapters 14-16 regarded as additions of a later, non-apocalyptically motivated reviser. But this is to build one hypothesis on top of another like a house of cards.

The question emerges here, What value does Marxsen give to the history Mark purportedly writes about in his "life of Jesus"? If all is directed to a single end, viz. the parousia in Galilee, why did Mark trouble to write a full length "gospel"? To this we now turn.

(*c*) In his section devoted to Mark's gospel in his *Introduction to the New Testament*, Marxsen offers a fuller statement of the case presented at the close of his earlier book on *Mark the Evangelist*. This statement relates Mark's purpose exclusively to a preaching of Christ ($εὐαγγέλιον$ and $Χριστός$ are treated by him as equivalent terms) as part of the evangelist's desire to ward off a process of "historicizing" in which "salvation comes to be presented as something belonging to the past" (*op. cit.*, p. 144). Mark's aim is "to preserve the character of the work as proclamation—it is meant to remain *kerygma*" (*op. cit.*, p. 144, cf. pp. 133, 137).

But this is a doubtful contention, and it is seemingly contradicted by Marxsen's earlier dismissal of any dichtomy between "kerygmatic" and "historical" (*op. cit.*, p. 128). Paul's *kerygma* never lost contact with events which he believed had happened on earth, and Marxsen's acceptance of

[76] J. Munck, *Paul and the Salvation of Mankind* [ET, 1959] has as its express purpose a refutation of the Tübingen school's understanding of early Christianity.

[77] H. Conzelmann, *Grundriss der Theologie des NT*, p. 163 f. (ET, p. 144). My translation.

[78] E. Trocmé, *La formation de l'évangile selon Marc* [1963], pp. 176ff.

the statement that Mark writes "an illustrative commentary on the concept of *evangelion* as it is used—for the most part without explanation —by Paul" (*op. cit.*, p. 138) makes his later statements hard to piece together into a coherent whole. At all events, on the showing of his final remarks, he runs against the critique levelled by L. E. Keck[79] that on Marxsen's view Mark has evacuated his gospel of any historical substance by telling stories which are "almost accidental" (fast zufällig, *Der Evangelist Markus*, p. 87), and treated simply as material used for the sake of announcing the parousia.[80] Even what appear to be stories of Jesus firmly set in history are problematical, and in particular "Galilee" has lost its character as a topological reference and become a symbol of theological interest as the locale of the imminent parousia.[81]

The final verdict to be registered is undeniable. "On the strength of Mark's contemporizing of Jesus, Marxsen has simply modernized Mark's theology into Marxsen's!"[82] And, we may add as a summary statement, Marxsen's admirable determination to preserve the kerygmatic value of the gospel is carried through—but at too high a cost. For what Mark is apparently not willing to do is to surrender the historical at the expense of the kerygmatic. Nor is there need to set these two emphases as alternatives. The kerygmatic message is conveyed through historical report, but historical report is not self-contained or self-validating however much it is needed to provide a foundation. The gospel as history does not dispense with its call to faith, for faith is engendered through the historical document and is finally directed to the person whose story Mark tells. So we may conclude against Marxsen that Mark is attempting to write the life of Jesus from a historical viewpoint; and thereby to present the kerygmatic message as report.[83]

Marxsen's systematic attempt—on form-critical, historical and theological grounds—to give this gospel a setting-in-life as an exercise in topical eschatology must be judged a failure. Seen as a warning message to Jerusalem Christians to leave the city in the course of the Jewish War of A.D. 66–70 and to escape to Galilee where the imminent parousia of Jesus is expected and as a bid to give existential depth to a story in danger of being caught in the toils of historicism, this gospel takes on a character it is hard to recognize as Marxsen so views it. If these had been Mark's motives in writing a new literary form, known as "gospel," he has gone about his task in an incredibly cumbrous fashion and produced a type of writing which has all the tokens of the opposite kind of literature from

[79] L. E. Keck, "The Introduction to Mark's Gospel," NTS 12 [1965–6], pp. 357f.

[80] Proof of this assertion comes in his book, *Mark the Evangelist*, p. 134: "Briefly put the gospel [of Mark] declares: I am coming soon."

[81] *Op. cit.*, p. 92.

[82] Keck, *loc. cit.*, p. 358.

[83] So G. Strecker, "Zur Messiasgeheimnistheorie im Markusevangelium" in his contribution to *Studia Evangelica* iii [1964], 87–104 (103f.).

that which he was intending to produce. Marxsen's overall construction is too ingenious to be true, and too lop-sided (in its concentration on a single historical situation and its eschatological challenge) to be convincing.[84]

(C) A Setting in the Close of the Jewish War (A.D. 71–72)

S. G. F. Brandon has expressed himself in many places on the subject of the "Date of the Markan Gospel"[85]; his latest and fullest presentation appears as chapter 5 in *Jesus and the Zealots* [1967].[86] He opens his case for regarding Mark's gospel as an *apologia ad christianos romanos*, that is, a tendentious document designed to clear the name of the church at Rome in the eyes of the imperial authorities, with a statement of certain assumptions. These are three in number:

(*a*) that Mark is the first gospel to appear;

(*b*) that its place of composition and publication is Rome;

(*c*) and that the key to interpret its message is the contemporary historical background in the months immediately following the end of the Jewish War, A.D. 71–72.

The last-named assumption depends on the political colouring of certain narratives and dialogues, notably the discussion on the Tribute money (Mark 12:13–17); the cryptic allusion to the "desolating scourge" which defiles the Jerusalem Temple, 13:14; and the Trial scenes which Brandon believes show evidence of redaction in the interest of charging the Jews with the prime responsibility for Jesus' crucifixion.

This approach to the internal evidence of the gospel is taken with a view to discovering a suitable life-setting of the book as a whole. Brandon's critical concern to offer a *Sitz im Leben* of Mark, which he discovers to "correspond exactly to that of the Christian community at Rome in the years immediately following the Flavian triumph in A.D. 71 over insurgent Judaea" (*op. cit.*, p. 242).

To endorse this conclusion the following items in a series of cumulative arguments are deduced. We may tabulate some of these which are germane to our study to gain an overview of Brandon's line of reasoning. First, it is concluded from a study of Mark 12:13–17 that in its revised (Markan) form Jesus is made to endorse the Jewish obligation to pay taxes to Caesar. Second, Mark shows an observable interest in the significance of the Temple veil, set in the context of the profanation and destruction of the

---

[84] See for a further critique J. Rohde, *Rediscovering the Teaching of the Evangelists* [ET, 1968], pp. 113–140; H.-D. Knigge, "The Meaning of Mark," *Interpretation*, 22 [1968], pp. 53–70.

[85] The title of his essay, NTS 7 [1960–61], pp. 126–41.

[86] With a more popular sketch in *The Trial of Jesus of Nazareth* [1968], ch. 4. Pagination in the section which follows below is in reference to the earlier book.

Temple by the Romans in A.D. 70, and with the relation of these events to the parousia. Thirdly, the Barabbas episode (Mark 15:6ff.) is utilized by Mark to explain how the long-standing intention of the Jewish leaders to destroy Jesus actually took the form of a Roman execution for sedition.[87] This death by Roman crucifixion is the primary datum of the New Testament story of the historical Jesus. Brandon is concerned to ask how it came about that a Jewish preacher ended his days on the Roman gibbet.

Mark the gospel-writer is seen to be an apologist all along the line. By shifting the responsibility for the crucifixion from the Roman governor to the Jewish leaders, he has overcome the most embarrassing problem of all for the Christians of Rome at that time. He has adroitly deflected the blame to the Jews who were increasingly in bad odour in Rome's esteem at the end of the punitive war which was fought to put down a Jewish insurrection. Mark as a Christian rushed to dissociate the church from its Jewish connections—hence his anti-Jewish polemic throughout the gospel[88] and equally his pro-Roman attitudes which culminate in the praise of a Gentile centurion who at the climax of the narrative gives expression to the faith (15:39) which opens the gospel (1:1) and which the Jewish people, in Mark's day, were bitterly opposing.

One of the impressive features of S. G. F. Brandon's hypothesis is the close-knit structure of the argument, with recourse made to several interlocking pieces. How far he has been irresponsibly selective in the use of the evidence is an open question, and critics have not withheld the charge of *Tendenz* which governs his choice of convenient data and leads to a refusal to consider the total picture. But even his main contentions based on the evidence he selects are not free from criticism, and it is easy to attack his thesis on the principle, Divide and conquer.

(a) The Roman origin of the gospel forms for him an assumption that several scholars have questioned. This has been already discussed and support has been offered for the view that, of all the possibilities, Rome is the most likely place of origin. But this does not include the setting in Rome in the early eighth decade, which is a separate item in the case.

(b) The Tribute money incident is something of a linchpin in Brandon's argumentation (*op. cit.*, pp. 345ff.) and recurs in his many essays on this general theme. He approaches the text, however, with some conclusions already wrapped up in his presuppositions, viz. "Since Mark's purpose was to present Jesus as innocent of the charge of sedition on which he was condemned, the answer he represents Jesus as making is evidently intended

---

[87] That there are historical problems associated with the Barabbas story is clear, but it is equally clear that Pilate was a man under unusual pressure at the time of Jesus' trial, in fact, in the period after October A.D. 31 when Sejanus' conspiracy was discovered and Tiberius took up a pro-semitic line. See P. L. Maier, "The Episode of the Golden Roman Shields at Jerusalem," HTR 62 [1969], pp. 109–21.

[88] Cf. T. A. Burkill, "Anti-Semitism in St. Mark's Gospel," NovT 3 [1959], pp. 34–53.

to be understood as refuting such a charge; in other words, the answer of Jesus is meant to prove that he agreed that the Jews should pay the Roman tribute" (*op. cit.*, p. 345). If that were the evangelist's purpose, he has left the text of Jesus' pronouncement very ambiguous; and the very vagueness of Jesus' reported reply is consonant with what we know elsewhere of the way Jesus dealt with trick questions (e.g. Mark 11:27–33). The ambiguity, then, lies in the original dialogue and not in Mark's editorialized version which (on Brandon's view) covers over a plain statement that Jesus refused the claim of Roman taxation as a Zealot sympathizer or "fellow-traveller."

An alternative proposal (rejected by Brandon, *loc. cit.*, n. 3) that Jesus saw no necessary opposition between the claims of Rome and the Jewish religion (expressed by Mark in the slightly changed nuance of the verbs, "to give" [δοῦναι—δῶμεν] and "pay" [ἀπόδοτε[89]]) therefore commends itself as of a piece with Jesus' attested habit of leaving his hearers to interpret his message in the way they preferred. He will not be impaled on the horns of a false dilemma, for the issue is not "giving" in a voluntaristic way but of "paying" what is due. Romans 13:1ff. echoes the same teaching.[90]

We conclude that Jesus' answer was purposely ambiguous, since either direct statement would fail to convey exactly the impression he wished to make: to say "Yes" and accept the legitimacy of Roman taxation would be to align himself with the Herodian party and place an imprimatur on the existing political order. To reply "No" would be to accept a Zealot portfolio and countenance violent revolt. To do what he did was to run the risk of misunderstanding and distortion—and this is precisely how it turned out at the time of his arraignment on a political charge (Luke 23:2).[91]

(c) The argument based on Mark's adaptation of the Passion narrative rests on a prior assumption of a pre-Markan Jewish-Christian account which the evangelist took over and edited.[92] The nice question is, How did these Jewish Christians view the execution of Jesus by the Romans? Brandon's response runs: "That they would have regarded it with grief and horror is certain; but would they have been embarrassed, as Mark evidently was, by the fact that the Romans had executed Jesus as a rebel against their government?"[93]

[89] ἀποδίδωμι, as Swete observes, *Commentary*, p. 276, implies that the tribute is a debt; cf. Rom. 13:7; Matt. 5:26.

[90] See L. Goppelt, "The Freedom to Pay the Imperial Tax (Mark 12, 17)," in *Studia Evangelica* ii [1964], pp. 183–194. Cf. J. Schmid, *Regensburger NT ad loc.*, pp. 220, 221, citing Dibelius: "One is justified in seeing a sort of ironic parallelism between the two statements, *viz.* 'Render to Caesar . . . and to God.'"

[91] So O. Cullmann, *Jesus and the Revolutionaries* [1970], pp. 45–7.

[92] See Brandon's article, "Jesus and the Zealots," in *Studia Evangelica* iv [1968], p. 16, where this assumption is made in a single sentence.

[93] "Jesus and the Zealots," *Studia Evangelica*, *loc. cit.*, p. 16.

But to pose the issue like this is to miss the point, and the matter is further confused by Brandon's discussion in *Jesus and the Zealots*, p. 255 (cf. pp. 177ff.) that these Jewish Christian believers would have deemed Jesus as a noble martyr for the freedom of Israel.[94] But he had made messianic pretensions and a death on a Roman cross (the attested alternative to other [Jewish] forms of capital punishment, e.g. stoning) would perforce rule out these claims, in accordance with the rubric of Deuteronomy 21:23. That Paul had to wrestle with this obvious objection to Jesus' messianic claim and his ignominious death on a cross is clear from Galatians 3:13.[95] Brandon's earlier attempt to overcome this objection shows how early preachers explained the apparent contradiction, but it leaves untouched the problem of a pre-Markan passion narrative which was allowed to remain in circulation and in which no such theodicy for the messianic death on a cross is found. "Christ crucified" was bound to prove a *skandalon* to Jewish Christians no less than to the Jews (1 Cor. 1:23), and this failure to give a *raison d'être* for a Jewish-Christian passion document which held out no justification for Messiah's accursed death calls in question the existence of the document itself. For all its supposed concern to repudiate the accusation that Jesus had spoken against the Temple, it could not deny his death on a Roman gallows. If the Jews had tried and sentenced Jesus to death by stoning according to their Law (in the Old Testament and Mishnah), this putative pre-Markan passion story might have had relevance. But not otherwise.

Conclusion

When examined at the points of its greatest claims, Brandon's reconstruction of historical circumstances surrounding the publication of Mark's gospel hardly proves cogent. As with Marxsen's theory, full marks must be given for an imaginative—if implausible—theory. Doubtless there was need for some rationale of the Christian story when Christians at Rome felt it important to dissociate themselves from the rebellious nation of Israel. Doubtless parts of the New Testament do reflect the momentous consequence of the Fall of Jerusalem in A.D. 70 and make urgent the dis-

---

[94] This recovery of the "historical Jesus" as an essentially patriotic freedom-fighter and martyr is a conclusion emerging from Brandon's work, reviving the old theories of Reimarus but with a contemporary relevance in a time of Israeli nationalism. See W. Wink, "Jesus and Revolution: Reflections on S. G. F. Brandon's *Jesus and the Zealots*," *Union Seminary Quarterly Review* 25. 1. [1969], pp. 37–59, who perceptively notes that Brandon's thesis gains in plausibility because it is an idea (Jesus as a loyalist revolutionary) whose time has come. S. G. F. Brandon has replied to Wink's article in "Jesus and the Zealots: Aftermath," BJRL 54. 1 [1971], pp. 47–66.

[95] As a factor in his conversion-experience leading to a reversal of understanding of how the blessed one could endure the curse and be approved by God in that deed. The study of J. Dupont, "The Conversion of Paul, and its Influence on his Understanding of Salvation by Faith," *Apostolic History and the Gospel*, eds. W. W. Gasque and R. P. Martin [1970], pp. 176–194, is most illuminating.

cussion of the continuing place of Israel in salvation-history. But on Brandon's showing Mark's gospel in its main emphasis is not that rationale nor does its most obvious *Sitz im Leben* fall in the days of the Flavian triumph along the streets of Rome in A.D. 71 and following.

Indeed, we can go further, and say that in respect of both Marxsen's and Brandon's individualistic and original attempts to squeeze the historical data to the last ounce, neither argument is convincing for the sole reason that the key to Mark lies not solely in the historical setting of Mark's community, whether in Galilee or Rome. Rather theological considerations have to be taken into view; and as we shall maintain, they should be given first preference in elucidating this story of Jesus addressed to Christians in the Graeco-Roman world.

A NOTE ON PAPIAS' WITNESS TO MARK
(Eusebius, HE, III. 39)*

Ταῦτα μὲν οὖν ἱστόρηται τῷ Παπίᾳ περὶ τοῦ Μάρκου. "Such then is Papias' account of Mark."

Eusebius' record of these words and their preceding statement has engendered a considerable volume of discussion.[1] The focus of interest has been on some of the specific terms which Papias uses in this fragment, whether he is quoting what "John the elder used to say" or adding his own comment to the way in which he envisages the origin of Mark's gospel. The key terms of this order are: Mark as Peter's ἑρμηνευτής; the admission that Mark wrote οὐ μέντοι τάξει; the explanation that Peter used to adapt his lessons πρὸς τὰς χρείας and did not intend to produce a σύνταξις of the Lord's oracles; and the assumption that the evangelist knew what he was doing and is therefore to be exonerated of any charge that he made a mistake, or was guilty of a sin of omission.

It is not the purpose of this *opusculum* to survey the many possibilities of interpretation regarding these controverted words, terms and phrases, though personal preferences will be registered as our argument unfolds. Rather, the aim is to ask about Papias' intention in what he says here concerning the provenance of the second gospel.

1. There is a consensus regarding the general purpose of this fragment. It is fairly clear, from the tone and tenor of Papias' statement, that he is offering in a roundabout way a defence of Mark's gospel. "It is clear from the words of John [the elder], as well as from the explanation which Papias adds, that unfavourable opinions had been expressed concerning Mark's book in the circle to which Papias and John belonged. Only the purpose to counteract such opinions enables us to understand John's ἀκριβῶς ἔγραψεν and Papias' οὐδὲν ἥμαρτεν[2]." In this appraisal Th. Zahn speaks for most commentators on the Eusebian text.

The precise nature of the attack on Mark's gospel is less clear. The main objection underlying the text would appear to be that Mark was not a personal witness to the events which he records, nor did he hear the Lord's words at first hand. But he is not a writer of fiction (Papias infers) because he did faithfully record the witness of a person who was an eye-witness, viz. St Peter, though Mark was able to recall

---

* This appendix contains the substance of a paper given at the International Patristics Conference in Oxford, September 1971.

[1] Recent surveys of the problem include the following: J. V. Barlet, "'Papias's Exposition': Its Date and Contents" in *Amicitiae Corolla*: Festschrift J. Rendel Harris, ed. H. G. Wood, London, 1933, 15–44; A. Farrer, *A Study in St. Mark*, London, 1951, 10ff., concluding that "'the Papian tradition must be simply given up as someone's ingenious but false construction" (20); H. A. Rigg, Jr., "Papias on Mark," NovT 1, 1956, 161–183; H. E. W. Turner, "The Tradition of Mark's Dependence upon Peter," ExpT 71, 1960, 260–263; T. Y. Mullins, "Papias on Mark's Gospel," *Vigiliae Christianae* 14, 1960, 216–224; K. Beyschlag, "Herkunft und Eigenart der Papiasfragmente" in *Studia Patristica* iv: TU 79, 1961, 268–280.

[2] Th. Zahn, *Introduction to the New Testament*, Vol. ii [Edinburgh, 1909], 439.

only *some* of what Peter in turn remembered. Mark's lack of order (τάξις) is explained on the single ground that Peter's original preaching was *ad hoc* (if this is what πρὸς τὰς χρείας means) and not arranged to form a σύνταξις of dominical oracles, as Matthew had done in his gospel (Ματθαῖος ... τὰ λόγια συνετάξατο).

Mark's aim was more narrowly conceived than Matthew's. He was content simply to reproduce Peter's teaching as accurately as he could from memory. This points to a composition of the gospel after Peter's death and encourages us to follow the tradition in Irenaeus (*Adv. Haer.* iii, 1.2) and the so-termed Anti-Marcionite Prologue, which place the writing of the gospel after the death of Peter rather than in Peter's lifetime (so Clement of Alex. *apud* Eusebius, HE. II. 15.1, 2; VI. 14. 6f.; cf. VI. 25.5).

2. Papias' own interests are set out in Eusebius, III. 39.3, 4. Here he is expressing his concern to learn all he could from "the elders." They are looked upon as guardians of apostolic teaching which in turn derives from the Lord himself.[3] Papias was fascinated by the possibility of overhearing in the speech of the elders (apparently this term covers both the collegiate members of the apostolate and their disciples) the "words" or "instructions" of the Lord. Papias was eager to search out all the sources available whether in "the traditions" (III. 39.7, 11, 14) or in the spoken words uttered by those who were in direct or penultimate contact with the events of the gospel tradition (III. 39.4 *ad finem*).

This confidence in hearing the voice of those who were alive as survivors of the apostolic age (in contrast to dependence on "books") is an important part of Papias' witness, for it indicates that his primary interest was to be assured of apostolic authority, whether conveyed through the *viva vox* or through written sources.[4]

3. If we assume that Papias is imposing his own convictions on the wording of the *testimonium*,[5] it is remarkable how closely his choice of words follows the prologue of Luke's gospel. The terms common or similar in both documents are: ἀνατάξασθαι, παρέδοσαν, παρηκολουθηκότι, ἀκριβῶς, καθεξῆς. This correspondence raises the question whether Luke is indebted to Papias or Papias is consciously drawing upon the evangelist.[6] The latter explanation is altogether preferable,[7] though Papias does not otherwise show any evidence of Luke's writing in his gospel (but see HE. III. 39.9, 10 for Papias' evident knowledge of incidents in the Acts of the Apostles).

This striking agreement in terminology and *Tendenz* invites the suggestion that Papias is thereby consciously paying tribute to Mark as a gospel-writer who, in spite of well-known deficiencies, could lay claim to an authority which matched that of Luke.

Papias' appeal to apostolic authority is somewhat curious, since he apparently knows little (if Eusebius is not quoting him selectively) of the Twelve, and relates

---

[3] Cf. R. P. C. Hanson, *Tradition in the Early Church*, London, 1962, 35–39.
[4] See A. F. Walls, "Papias and Oral Tradition," *Vigiliae Christianae* 21, 1967, 137–140.
[5] A. Farrer, *op. cit.*, 15ff.
[6] Cf. W. R. Schoedel, *The Apostolic Fathers*. A new Translation and Commentary, Vol. 5, London 1967, 105.
[7] So R. M. Grant, "Papias and the Gospels," *Anglican Theological Review* 25, 1943, 219, against the alternative proposal argued by R. Annard, "Papias and the Four Gospels," SJT, 9, 1956, 46–62 (50, 51).

only scraps of information which reached him by way of tradition. In particular, Paul the apostle to the Gentiles is completely passed over in silence.

The close association of Luke and Paul reaches back, in Christian literature, to an early source in the New Testament itself and the fathers. It has been asked whether Papias' "ignorance" of Luke-Paul is deliberate and whether he was anti-Pauline.[8] But we do know that he set his face against the man who professed to be the true exponent of Paul and who published a truncated version of Luke's gospel, Marcion. To this possible link we shall return.

4. Papias' fragment serves a controlling purpose which is not free from *Tendenz*. He is anxious to claim Mark's gospel as a source of apostolic authority. But to do so he must rebut implicit charges against this evangelist's qualifications, both personal and literary. He does so by a series of counter-statements:

(*a*) He will emphasize on John's authority that Mark has the most intimate association with Peter, the apostle *par excellence*. Mark was Peter's ἑρμηνευτής, his right-hand man, who was his personal assistant on his missionary tours and served as a trusted associate by putting the apostle's language (whether Aramaic or Greek) into serviceable and acceptable form. He was thus qualified in every way to publish Peter's "memoirs" in a manner which would inspire confidence that he was correctly reproducing the apostle's unique teaching.[9]

(*b*) Peter's own peculiar way of giving instruction was either by using a highly functional method and speaking *ad hoc* or (as recent discussion proposes) offering a set of *chreia*-forms, which in Greek rhetoric were brief statements, too unconnected to make a story-narrative or a compendium of teaching.[10] The latter explanaton of πρὸς τὰς χρείας helps to elucidate the subsequent admission that Peter was not making a compilation (σύνταξις) of the dominical oracles and that Mark did no wrong in writing down single items in the form of ἀπομνημονεύματα ὡς ἀπεμνημόνευσεν. In fact, Mark is exonerated in Papias' "final" sentence of the twin charges which Theon brings against a χρεία, viz. it leaves out material and it tells what is false.[11]

Papias draws upon an explanation involving specialized literary usages in order to show how Mark's gospel faithfully contains Peter's original deposit of witness, and thus it is an accurate source of apostolic teaching.

(*c*) As a final tribute Papias remarks that while Mark's gospel is short, it is not truncated nor does it contain false teaching.[12] This may suggest that Papias has

---

[8] See W. Bauer's discussion of the reasons why Papias regarded Luke (and John and Paul) with suspicion, *Orthodoxy and Heresy in Earliest Christianity*, ed. R. A. Kraft and G. Krodel, Philadelphia, 1971, 184f., 186f., 214f. (ET of *Rechtgläubigkeit und Ketzerei im ältesten Christentum*, Tübingen, 1934, 187, 189, 217f.).

[9] In the debate on the precise meaning of ἑρμηνευτής, W. C. van Unnik, "Zur Papias-Notiz über Markus (Eusebius, HE. III. 39, 15)," ZNTW 54/55, 1963, 276–7 correctly emphasizes that what is important is not the way Mark performed his rôle as interpreter but the content of his work as interpreter.

[10] See the ground-breaking discussion of χρεία-forms by R. O. P. Taylor, *The Groundwork of the Gospels*, Oxford, 1946, 75–90.

[11] Theon in *Progymnasmata* (cited in L. Spengel, *Rhetores Graeci*, Vol. ii, Leipzig, 1853–6), p. 104. 15–18. Cf. R. M. Grant, *The Earliest Lives of Jesus*, New York, 1961, 14–18.

[12] The meaning of τάξις as "completeness" rather than "order" is offered and defended by J. A. Kleist, "Rereading the Papias Fragment on St. Mark," *Saint Louis University Studies*, Series A, Humanities, Vol. 1, no. 1, March 1945, 1–17 (13).

his eye on a document which while purportedly apostolic was abbreviated and was being employed for the purpose of false teaching. Earlier Eusebius had recorded that Papias deliberately turned away from "those who relate alien commands" (III. 39.3) in his adherence to those who taught the Truth itself, i.e. Jesus Christ portrayed in the fourth gospel.

Can we submit an identification of what Papias may have had in mind by those who taught "alien commands"? Luke's gospel was cut short by Marcion; it became by his critical surgery less than three-quarters of its original length and it formed the substance of his "canonical" *Euangelion*. His teaching was known in the Asian province after he left Pontus and before he came to Rome in A.D. 138.[13] Papias had collided with him in person, if we are correct in so interpreting the so-called Anti-Marcionite prologue to the gospel of John.[14] This tribute to Mark's gospel may plausibly have been written in conscious opposition to the use made by Marcion of Luke's gospel.

5. Papias says that Mark had all the credentials which Luke could claim. If Luke's gospel carried the authoritative impress of Paul as Luke's mentor, Mark no less was Peter's $\dot{\epsilon}\rho\mu\eta\nu\epsilon\upsilon\tau\dot{\eta}\varsigma$. If Luke wrote $\dot{\alpha}\kappa\rho\iota\beta\tilde{\omega}\varsigma$, so did Mark (Papias had both items of information on John the elder's word). If Luke claimed to "follow" ($\pi\alpha\rho\alpha\kappa\omega\lambda\omega\upsilon\theta\epsilon\tilde{\imath}\nu$) the sequence of gospel events, Mark was known to have shared Peter's company (cf. Acts 12:12; 1 Pet. 5:13). If Luke had access to eye-witness traditions, Mark had personal ties with Peter himself. If Luke professed to write in strict chronological order ($\kappa\alpha\theta\epsilon\xi\tilde{\eta}\varsigma$), Mark's seeming lack of $\tau\acute{\alpha}\xi\iota\varsigma$ can be understood once the background of his connexion with Peter is explained.

So Mark's non-membership of the apostolic circle is no disadvantage nor does this shortened account of Jesus' life disqualify him from serious regard. For his abbreviated gospel is not like Marcion's abbreviated version of Luke. The latter was a torso;[15] Mark's gospel is intentionally short, since he reproduces only what he had heard from Peter's lips even if he could recall only a portion of this teaching. Above all, Mark stands for apostolic truth, verified by his close tie with Peter. This is Papias' chief *desideratum*. He asks no more than to be in touch with apostolic Christianity; he will tolerate no less when Marcion proposes to be the authentic exponent of a Pauline gospel.

[13] For this conclusion see A. Harnack, *Marcion*[2] [Leipzig, 1924], 26.

[14] There is some uncertainty here voiced by B. W. Bacon, "The Latin Prologues of John," JBL 32, 1913, 194–217; id. "Marcion, Papias and the 'Elders,'" JTS 23, 1922, 134–160; id. "The Anti-Marcionite Prologue to John," JBL 49, 1930, 43–54.

[15] This way of putting it, which is the traditional way, is opposed by J. Knox, *Marcion and the New Testament*, Chicago, 1942, who maintains that we should assume that the catholic churches "enlarged Marcion's Gospel (or, rather, a Gospel roughly equivalent to it) rather than that Marcion abridged the catholic Gospel of Luke" (162). This a novel theory but it is in danger of being built on insufficient evidence, as Knox himself concedes (*op. cit.*, 97) and as E. C. Blackman, *Marcion and his influence*, London, 1948, 38–41, has noted. In any case, to Papias Marcion's *Euangelion* must have seemed less than complete, if we assume he possessed the full version of canonical Luke.

IV

MARK AS A THEOLOGICAL DOCUMENT

A new beginning: the rise of patternism (e.g. Carrington, Farrer, Bowman and Schille). The originality of Wrede: truth and falsity of the "Messianic secret" idea. Jesus as Son of God (Vielhauer) and "divine man" (Schreiber). Jesus as "redeemed-Redeemer" (Harrisville). Evaluation.

1. *The Rise of Patternism*

THE TERM "PATTERNISM" IS INTENDED IN THIS CONTEXT TO DENOTE A method of gospel elucidation which finds in the arrangement of the text and the flow of the narrative and teaching sections a discernible pattern which conforms to the author's set purpose. There are at least two antecedents to this discipline.

(*a*) The puzzle of Mark's order of events has been recognized since the time of Papias' observation in Eusebius *HE*. III. 39. He writes to the effect that, while the evangelist wrote down accurately all that he heard and remembered of Peter, he did not record "in order, however" (οὐ μέντοι τάξει). The simplest meaning to be drawn from this disclaimer is that Mark's order is not chronologically precise and the impression Papias gained was that there were parts of the Markan account (σύνταξις) which did not seem to be in their right place. Evidence for the "disorder" of the gospel has been collected by H. A. Guy[1] under the sectional headings of (i) interruptions in the narrative (e.g. 3:22–30; 4:10–25; 5:25, 34; 11:18–27a; 14:27–31), (ii) repetitions, especially the doublets of 6:34–7:37 and 8:1–26; haphazard arrangement (e.g 7:31 which describes the route of Jesus as "from the borders of Tyre and [passing] through Sidon to the sea of Galilee, through the midst of the borders of Decapolis"—an almost unbelievably circuitous route); and lack of connection in those places where there seems to be no topical or logical connection between successive statements, e.g. 2:28; 11:23–25.

These phenomena pose the question, Was Mark consciously conforming his existing material to fit a pattern which was *not* the arrangement of a freely flowing chronological scheme, where events are held together in perceptible sequence? Perhaps it was not historical or topical but calendrical order that interested Mark.[2]

---

[1] H. A. Guy, *The Origin of the Gospel of Mark* [1954], ch. 3.
[2] So P. Carrington, *The Primitive Christian Calendar* [1952], p. 58. But see Guy, *op. cit.*, p. 19.

(b) The second way in which the ground was prepared for the rise of patternism was the form-critical experiment in which the unity of the gospel was destroyed by the dissecting of Mark into its component parts, consisting of small units of narrative or teaching. Each unit was shown to have an independent life and to serve a particular purpose of teaching. Mark's task as an evangelist was that of putting together the dismembered pieces, which he knew only as isolated units; and this prompts the question. According to what kind of plan did Mark assemble his pre-canonical material and fit it together into what we know as his gospel? The answer was returned: according to a predetermined pattern which was expressive of conformity to a calendar known in his church (so P. Carrington). Or he wrote because he was artistically governed by Old Testament examples of typology and prefigurations (so A. M. Farrer) or because he wished to compose his gospel as a Christianized version of the Passover *haggadah* in the Jewish festival (so J. Bowman) or because he sought to convey through a dramatized "life of Jesus" the steps of catechetical instruction and training for new converts on the road to church membership (so G. Schille).

The immediate presupposition on which all these theories are based is that Mark has put together a loose assemblage of *pericopae* or gospel sections into a connected form of narrative. The results of Form criticism are taken for granted and it is assumed that these pre-Markan units were to hand when the evangelist set about his task. But whereas even for moderate form critics such as V. Taylor[3] the evangelist had only a limited objective in that task, namely, to be a systematizer of earlier traditions, the proponents of the newer criticism see him as a literary artist whose "gospel is beautifully constructed, delicately balanced, and intricately woven together" (Carrington, *op. cit.*, p. 15).

These newer theories of Markan structure may be sub-divided according to their special interest.

(i) *Calendrical Hypothesis*

P. Carrington's interest in the gospel of Mark arises directly out of the reason he is led to give for Form criticism's success in being able to isolate the individual *pericopae*. The reason is simply that these units were first used as lectionary sections in the services of the church. This view of the Markan gospel as the distillation of lectionary material is true, however, only of a pre-canonical version of Mark (so called Mark I). The evangelist has adapted and updated this original form of the gospel patterned on the

---

[3] V. Taylor, *Commentary*, pp. 90–104, for his view that the evangelist has utilized a series of what he calls "complexes" which he regards as small groups of narrative or sayings which belong together. Mark, according to Taylor, took over these complexes which had an independent existence, added his own comments and connected them with some simple literary ligatures. On this view Mark's rôle is strictly that of an editor and compiler.

Hebrew calendar of agricultural festivals to fit in with the Julianic calendar at Rome. The starting-point is the discovery[4] of the arrangement of Mark's narrative to include both a Passover celebration (in the Feeding of the Five Thousand) and a Pentecost allusion in the Feeding of the Four Thousand. These stories are not to be regarded as duplicate narratives, but carefully set in the narrative framework to show Mark's adherence to the Jewish calendar. With this discovery as a ground-plan "the various points in the Gospel [begin] to fall into their calendrical places with the precision of a jig-saw puzzle" (*loc. cit.*, p. 100).

Additional material in this gospel is held to support this interpretation, in particular what he calls the "major triads" in Mark (*op. cit.*, pp. 94ff.), and specifically the three-mountain-triad in 3:13ff., 6:30f.; 9:2f. On a different level Carrington argued that the earliest chapter divisions of the gospel manuscript endorse his findings. He champions the earlier dating of the chapter divisions in B (Codex Vaticanus) which has sixty-two sections. He argues that these are lectionary divisions and that by a literary analysis of Mark it is possible to demonstrate how the earlier portions of the gospel fall into forty-eight sections (which is the number of divisions in Codex Alexandrinus). The Passion narrative yields an additional fourteen sections, and this brings the total to sixty-two, the tally in the fourth-century family. Carrington offers these facts as proof of "external mathematical confirmation" of his theory (*op. cit.*, p. xiii).

At each point the theory has been attacked and its weak points exposed. W. D. Davies[5] has challenged the first principle of this reconstruction, viz. that the early church took over the lectionary practice of the Jewish synagogue. R. P. Casey[6] raised serious objection to both Carrington's appeal to the divisions in the leading uncial authorities and his reliance on a hypothetical Markan "triadic structure." Apart from the arrangement of the Passion narrative there is no evidence that these chapter-divisions had anything to do with liturgical usage; and as for Carrington's argument which appeals to the three mountains "the second mountain is unhappily missing from Mark, though Carrington fails to note this interesting omission and supplies it in the story of the feeding of the five thousand from John 6:3" (*loc. cit.*, pp. 368f.).

On a broader front, a damaging weakness of this theory—which his later commentary *According to Mark* [1961] has not succeeded in repairing, though at significant points it represents a reconsidered apportionment of the so-called lections (e.g. *op. cit.*, p. 349)—is seen in the need to suppose

---

[4] P. Carrington, "The Calendrical Hypothesis of the Origin of Mark," ExpT, lxvii [1956], pp. 100–103.

[5] In an extended review article, "Reflections on Archbishop Carrington's 'The Primitive Christian Calendar'" in the C. H. Dodd volume *The Background of the New Testament and its Eschatology*, eds. W. D. Davies and D. Daube [1956], pp. 124–152, and reprinted in his *Christian Origins and Judaism* [1962], pp. 67ff.

[6] R. P. Casey, "St. Mark's Gospel," *Theology*, lv [1952], pp. 362–370.

that the gospel material has been "doctored" to conform to a supposed liturgical pattern, and that there are some verses which do not fit in and therefore need to be ironed out.

The main value of this elaborate exercise is to call attention to the transmission of the gospels *via* the worshipping life of the early churches.[7] But it is one thing to believe that Christians used these stories for purpose of edification, teaching and catechesis. It is a different proposition to maintain, as Carrington does, that Mark deliberately so composed his gospel "as to be read through in sequence Sunday by Sunday in accordance with the Jewish calendar" suitably modified to conform to the Christian liturgical counterparts.

(ii) *Passover Haggadah theory*

J. Bowman[8] recognizes that an objection to be brought against calendrical hypotheses is that while they seek to explain some elements in the overall gospel form, they do not convincingly provide a *raison d'être* for the gospel as a whole and in its published form. These theories overplay the evidence and are guilty of reading back from later church practice a system of lectionary usage which is anachronistic in the mid-first century. Mark's gospel must be evaluated by its internal data, and the question is raised, Granted it is not a piece of biographical literature but "highly stylized and rigorously subordinated to a certain pattern. But what pattern?" (p. xiv).

The needs of the entire liturgical year are too strung-out to account for the highly concentrated structure and closely-knit texture of the gospel. We should therefore look to one specific festival, on its Jewish background and its Christian counterpart, to provide the occasion; and this is discovered in the festival of Passover with its past and future aspects, celebrating an age-old redemption and providing an archetype for Israel's future deliverances.

At Passover there is the re-telling of the story of redemption[9] in the Haggadah, or Passover narration. Bowman's contention is that this "Passover haggadah with all its diversity but underlying unity provided the pattern not merely for the Last Supper, but for the whole of Mark's Gospel form."

One of the most interesting features in this highly individualistic work is the way it tries to relate Mark to a Hebraic background and to clarify the relation between Mark's written form of a gospel and Peter's oral

---

[7] See, for example, the short discussion which considers how far this statement is true by C. F. D. Moule, "The Intention of the Evangelists," *New Testament Essays*. Studies in memory of T. W. Manson, ed. A. J. B. Higgins [1959], pp. 165–177.

[8] J. Bowman, *The Gospel of Mark* [1965].

[9] For a recent discussion, see G. J. Bahr, "The Seder of Passover and the Eucharistic Words," NovT, xii. 2 [1970], pp. 181–202.

preaching (*op. cit.*, p. 312). He accounts also for the heavy emphasis on Jesus' passion and explains much of Mark's episodic narrative-writing as being in conscious imitation of Jewish haggadah (a noun drawn from Exod. 13:8: "And you shall *tell* (Heb. causative verb *h-g-d*) your son on that day").

But certain reservations must be entered. To suppose that Mark's gospel was composed in the literary style of a midrash presupposes a Jewish readership who would be familiar with these methods of Bible interpretation and application. To attempt to get back to the original setting of Mark and his audience is laudable, as Bowman desiderates (*op. cit.*, p. 125 note), but all our evidence points in the direction of Mark's concern to make the story of Jesus intelligible to a Gentile constituency on whom much of the subtlety of Jewish hermeneutical methods would be lost. Otherwise, it is very difficult to explain why Mark adds interpretative comment on Jewish customs (7:3f.; 14:12; 15:42) and translates Hebrew and Aramaic terms for his readers' benefit (3:17, 22; 5:41; 7:11; 7:34; 10:46; 14:36; 15:22, 34).

(iii) Markan "Prefigurations"

The same judgment must inevitably be passed on Austin Farrer's exercise in typological theory. On this theory,[10] even the simplest gospel story becomes invested with cryptic significance and esoteric meaning, especially in regard to the employment of numbers. For Farrer, the ruling principle in Mark's composition is his consciously artistic and poetic style by which the narratives are put together in a series of cycles and epicycles. Therefore, the interpreter must try to "seize the actual cyclic movement of the Evangelist's thought" (p. 35) and tune his ear to catch the accents of "Marcan rhythm" (p. 33).

The fact that this method of biblical criticism is so self-consciously subjective and inferential is its greatest weakness. Nor does the elaborateness of Farrer's reconstruction of the Markan enterprise argue in its favour. Rather its over-subtlety is an added liability.

In a penetrating survey of Farrer's ideas, Helen Gardner places her finger upon the real point at issue.[11] She writes this estimate, after a section in which she considers the propriety of calling Mark a poet who, though recording history, is so under debt to the idea of prefiguration that his his historical testimony is governed by his powerfully imaginative methods of writing.

> But my difficulty does not lie here. I am dissatisfied because this method does nothing to illuminate, and indeed evaporates, St. Mark's sense of what we

[10] A. M. Farrer, *A Study in St. Mark* [1951]; his thesis is somewhat modified in his later work, *St. Matthew and St. Mark* [1954].

[11] H. Gardner, "The Poetry of St. Mark," *The Limits of Literary Criticism* [1956], pp. 20–39.

mean by historical reality, the "Here and Now" of our daily experience, the "Then and There" of memory, by which I do not mean detailed precision of testimony, but the deep sense of "happening" (p. 33).

The methods employed in this interpretation of Mark's gospel tell us more of the interpreter's mind than the evangelist's; and the conclusion cannot be evaded that the patterns are read out of the gospel simply because they have first been read into the text by the erudite scholar. And since it was Farrer's intent to bring us into "touch with St. Mark, a living Christian mind, a mind of great power" (*op. cit.*, p. 7), his endeavour must be judged a failure and his ambition unachieved.

On another level, Farrer's appeal to this method of understanding Mark's gospel has been rigorously scrutinized. This is concerned with the inter-relation of history and theology. According to T. A. Roberts[12] who brings this criticism, Farrer wishes to place Mark's worth as a historical testimony beyond the range of critical examination by making its final value to be expressed in terms of its theological truth. Because that theological truth is conveyed not in the history *per se* but in its symbolism, Farrer believes that he has successfully rehabilitated Mark as an important witness, overcome the probing attacks of the Form critics who have adjudged Mark's history to be defective, and set the gospel in an invulnerable area where historical criticism cannot touch it.[13]

Roberts will have none of this effort to gain a sanctuary for Mark's theology by way of attributing symbolic interest to the evangelist. He questions the fundamental philosophical assumption of Farrer's historical method which is asked to do far more than it can do. "The fact that people in the past believed or disbelieved theological propositions can be inferred from historical data. But all that can be based upon historical data is the fact, if it be a fact, that certain historical beliefs have been held in the past. The truth of those theological beliefs cannot be proved from purely historical data" (*op. cit.*, p. 139).

For a final judgment on the foregoing, we will appeal once more to T. A. Roberts who asks the pertinent question, Is Gospel history true?[14] This issue can only be faced if there is an agreed technique or method by which the historical claims of the Christian faith can be tested. This statement need not be pressed to include a belief that the truth of Christianity can be proved by these methods, but it does show that no esoteric appeal to some way of looking at history which is available only to the initiates will suffice. Mark's Gospel reads like an account of historical events. The evangelist may well have intended a theological purpose in so narrating the deeds and words of Jesus, but it remains a fact that Christian

[12] T. A. Roberts, *History and Christian Apologetic* [1960], pp. 114–143.
[13] Kähler's wish to find an "invulnerable province" free from such exposure to historical scrutiny will be recalled here. See earlier p. 40.
[14] T. A. Roberts, *op. cit.*, p. 146.

conviction has been based on the "having-happenedness" of these events and not on some hidden sense to be read out of them.

(iv) Catechetical Structure

The needs of the early Christians to provide instruction for the training and edification of new converts to the faith are recognized as a factor in the analytical study of the New Testament.[15] It is a type of study which arises directly out of Form criticism and concerns the possibility of discovering in the background and structure of the evangelic *pericopae* material that took shape in the training and care of those newly won to the Christian faith. Matthew's Gospel has been treated in this way, notably in the study of K. Stendahl, *The School of St. Matthew* [1954,[2] 1968].

Attention has been drawn to Mark's gospel in this way by G. Schille[16] who puts forth the view that the composition of the gospel is so arranged as to indicate an elaborate parallel between the life of our Lord and the experience of catechumens who came into the church's fellowship and membership through the gateway of baptism, instruction, the holy supper, and were given as a salutary admonition the prospect of temptation and a martyr's crown. Schille holds that this sequence is reflected in the chapters of the gospel as in other parts of early Christian literature (Heb. 6:1ff. and the Didache).

Mark's interest in pedagogy which Schille concludes (*loc. cit.*, pp. 23f.) to be his chief work in his rôle as catechist does make sense of one meaning of the phrase "interpreter of Peter" in the Papias *testimonium*; and there are undeniable traits of Jesus' mission which have to do with his rôle as Teacher of the Twelve and Revealer of the secrets of the kingdom of God (Mk. 4:10, 11, 34). But to argue that the entire gospel is patterned along these lines is to exaggerate such allusions and hints, and turn them into guiding principles of gospel composition. The earthly course of Jesus' life may well have formed a ground-plan for the instruction of believers, though it is an emphasis which is singularly lacking in Paul who makes the essence of his "imitation"-appeal the christological events of the incarnation and Jesus' obedience unto death and his own example as apostle (1 Cor. 11:1; 2 Cor. 8:9; Phil. 2:5-11, 12f.) rather than incidents taken from Jesus' Galilean ministry and their influence upon his disciples.

(v) Geographical Emphases

R. H. Lightfoot switched his attention in his book *Locality and Doctrine in the Gospels* [1938] from a messianic interpretation of the gospels to an

[15] Pioneering work in this field was done by A. Seeberg, *Der Katechismus der Urchristenheit* [1903] and P. Carrington, *A Primitive Christian Catechism* [1940].
[16] G. Schille, "Bermerkungen zur Formgeschichte des Evangeliums. Rahmen und Aufbau des Markus-evangelium," NTS iv. 1 [1957–58], pp. 1–24.

intention to find Mark's purpose in hypothetically significant geographical allusions. In this move he was reflecting the influence of E. Lohmeyer's *Galiläa und Jerusalem* [1936][17] which maintained that there were two main centres of early Christianity, quite distinct from each other and located in Galilee and Jerusalem. As far as Mark is concerned, the dominant motif, according to Lohmeyer, is the importance of Galilee as the locus of divine revelation and the place to which the apocalyptic Son of man will return as a prelude to the parousia (see 14:28 and 16:7 on which Lohmeyer builds a great deal). These notions were picked up by W. Marxsen in *Der Evangelist Markus* [1956] as we have seen, and much importance is attached in these reconstructions of Jesus' mission (as understood by the later church whose theology is reflected in the way the gospel's geographical notices are given) to what takes place in specific areas and in certain locations (e.g. on mountains). But for all the ingenuity and suggestiveness there is no abiding certainty in these appeals to locality for the determining of Mark's doctrine, for the reasons we have suggested earlier (see pp. 72f.).

Finally, the verdict passed on all these patternistic analyses of Mark by J. M. Robinson[18] is apposite. He finds fault with the methodological assumptions of all such enterprises whose "argument is not built upon what Mark clearly and repeatedly has to say, but upon inferences as to the basis of the Marcan order, a subject upon which Mark is silent."

At the conclusion of a survey of these somewhat eccentric studies of the format of Mark's gospel we feel justified in endorsing the opinion of the majority of scholars that the key to the elucidation of the gospel is not to be found in some hidden secret known only to the evangelist and his enlightened readers, whether in the first or the twentieth century. First impressions of Mark's gospel as the reader today comes to it are that it is not a book belonging to the genre of apocalyptic mysticism, like the book of Revelation, nor does it draw special attention to items of place, date or number which would suggest that these pieces of information held a cryptic meaning which reveals to the initiate the profundity of the gospel. Whatever Mark's deep meaning is—and that it has a significance deeper than a surface impression suggests will be clear as we proceed—it does not lie in the solving of a conundrum or the unravelling of a tangled skein of scattered hints or mysterious allusions. Patternism as a method of gospel study must be pronounced a brilliant, but unachieved, endeavour to read into Mark what is not there.

2. *The Originality of Wrede*

With the epoch-making work of Wilhelm Wrede, *Das Messiasgeheimnis*

---

[17] An English version of this theory appears in L. E. Elliott-Binns, *Galilean Christianity* [1956], and it is sympathetically treated in F. C. Grant, *The Earliest Gospel* [1943].
[18] *The Problem of History in Mark* [1957], p. 12.

in den Evangelien, published in 1901, Markan studies were turned in a new direction from which the more recent attempts in patternism have failed to distract them. In a word, the indispensable key to unlock the secret of Mark's gospel story is the secret of Messiahship which this gospel contains. Up to the time of the nineteenth century, as we have seen, Mark's record was accepted by mainline interpreters as historical, and an impressive body of evidence was adduced in support of the claim that this gospel's realism, vividness and piece-meal arrangement—in an expressive term, its *actualité*[19]—all contributed to endorse this conclusion.

Wrede's importance lies in his challenge to this simplistic conclusion. So far from being an uninterpreted record of factual history, the gospel of Mark was for him a piece of tendentious writing by a man who had a theological purpose to accomplish and whose motives and interests must be inspected and evaluated before we can reach the figure of Jesus whose image is refracted through the Markan prism.

This judgment meant the virtual death-knell to all historical and psychologizing studies which were optimistic in their confidence in Mark as a quarry of factual materials, and which imagined that theology was a later accretion from whose presence Mark as a basic document (unlike Matthew and John) was free. Wrede brought Mark's gospel within the orbit of Christian theologizing and saw it as a specimen of reflective thought, not straightforward reportage.

The originality of Wrede consisted in his calling attention to a group of facts which had never, up to that point, been set in a distinctive context.[20] These facts to which Wrede drew attention were related to the way Jesus consciously silenced those who confessed his Messiahship:

(*a*) The demoniacs cry out and are rebuked to silence (1:25, 34; 3:12; 5:6f; 9:20).

(*b*) Miracles of healing contain the injunctions of Jesus that the persons healed must not make him known (1:43–45; 5:43; 7:36; 8:26).

(*c*) There are those occasions when Jesus retired from public view as though to conceal himself (1:35–38; 7:24; 9:30f.).

These three motifs are regarded as unhistorical since they plainly deal with matters on which silence could not be observed and retirement was an impractical course. The conclusion is that they are Mark's own creation (Wrede, *op. cit.*, p. 54).

---

[19] This term is used by X. Léon-Dufour in reference to the structure, style and contents of John's gospel: "Actualité du quatrième Evangile," *Nouvelle Revue Théologique* 76 [1954], pp. 449–68.

[20] As William Sanday recognized in his comments, *The Life of Christ in Recent Research* [1907], p. 71. Not that Sanday was in the least sympathetic to this new approach, as may be gauged from his now famous dictum: "I consider it [Wrede's book] to be not only very wrong but also distinctly wrong-headed" (p. 70).

(d) Mark 4:11–13 is a puzzling paragraph. Jesus is described as gathering his disciples into a secret conclave, distinguishing his teaching to "those outside" from a private teaching to the disciples and revealing some esoteric truth to his own. After Peter's confession, the disciples are enjoined to secrecy (8:30), which suggests to Wrede that the secret truth revealed to the Twelve was his Messiahship, as Mark imagined it. In a preview of the resurrection of Jesus (9:9) the truth is again guarded, with the idea that it will become public property in the Easter message of the church.

In later phases of the ministry Jesus has private instruction for the disciples (9:28f.; 10:32–34; 13:3ff.), but they are dull-witted and so obtuse that they do not catch the implications of what he says and does. In this way Wrede explains how it was that the Messiahship of Jesus was never made explicit during Jesus' ministry. Mark has accounted for it by these episodes which both describe how the secret was covered up by Jesus and how the disciples were so lacking in comprehension as to be unable to put it together. Wrede accounts for it by another route. Jesus was never confessed as Messiah in his lifetime because he never was Messiah; and Mark's elaborate attempt at story-writing is a mammoth enterprise to show by these stories and silences how his theological point of view can be justified. He did so as a member of the post-Easter community who were wrestling with a problem of the non-Messianic character of Jesus' life in the light of their sure article of preaching that the exalted Lord *was* Messiah (Acts 2:36; Rom. 1:4; Phil. 2:6–11).

The three principal elements in Wrede's reconstruction, most recently discussed by J. D. G. Dunn,[21] may be mentioned in summary as we try to give some positive evaluation.

(i) Wrede did a service in drawing attention to those parts of Mark's gospel where "commands to silence" are found, and (ii) in contexts in which their success could hardly be given much of a chance (e.g. 5:43; 10:48); (iii) he posed again the problem of the historical value to be attributed to these stories. Wrede faced the issue of the *character* of Jesus' ministry by asking some radical questions, If he was conscious of his Messianic office and proclaimed it, how did it come about that there was such a singular lack of response? Is it not simpler to believe that the Messianic dignity of Jesus awaited the resurrection, and that only then was it revealed in the glory that became his? Mark (Wrede implied) was not content with this but had to invest his earthly career with a veiled Messianic authority, which Wrede could not find in the pre-resurrection period. For him the resurrection was all-determinative. Indeed, Sanday finds fault at a most unexpected place:

---

[21] J. D. G. Dunn, "The Messianic Secret in Mark," *Tyndale Bulletin* 21 [1970], pp. 92–117. His conclusion follows that of V. Taylor, "The Messianic Secret in Mark," ExpT lix [1947–48], p. 149: "Far from being an editorial device imposed upon tradition, it [the secret] is an integral part of the material itself."

It is true enough that the belief in the Resurrection bore a great weight of superstructure in apostolic times. But I doubt if at any time, from the first century to the twentieth, it has ever had so much weight thrown upon it as in this theory of Wrede's (*op. cit.*, p. 75).

Criticisms of Wrede have not been lacking. Sanday thought (*op. cit.*, pp. 75f.) that an appeal to the argument from logic would be sufficient to refute him. This raises the incongruity that the belief in the Messiahship should have originated after the resurrection of Jesus if the evidence for it had been lacking in the pre-Easter character and ministry of Jesus. But this cavalier retort hardly does justice to the facts of Wrede's case and fails to appreciate the tremendous significance of the resurrection in the experience of the disciples which gave them an understanding of Messianic prophecy (especially Psalm 110:1) which in turn may well have been read back into Jesus' time. *On logical grounds* there is no way of refuting this; on strictly *form-critical grounds* there is much to argue in its favour, with the belief that all gospel-writing reflects the standpoint of the post-Easter church. The issue must be faced and fought out on an exegetical level.[22]

(*a*) It is true that there are significant places where Jesus commands silence. Both demons and men are bidden to keep quiet—but about what? In a number of cases the point in question is not his claim to be Messiah or a discovery that he is such, but rather a confession of him as wonder-worker and thaumaturge. This explains why Jesus enjoins to silence and it is not that his Messiahship shall not be made public but that a false impression about his mighty deeds may not be gained and he will avoid appearing in the rôle of a "divine man," a type of magician-philosopher familiar in the hellenistic world of antiquity.[23] Or else the appeal for secrecy may more naturally be explained as expressions of regard for those lives were affected and of a desire to secure for them some privacy from public attention (as Dunn notes; compare 5:40–43; 7:33, 36a; 8:26).

(*b*) Wrede's assertion that it was Mark who first turned a non-Messianic body of material into a Messianic story by his use of the "secret" has been challenged on the ground that the pre-Markan tradition itself contains evidence of the "secret," and that Mark's real problem was to know what to do with this Messianic emphasis.[24]

---

[22] A useful critical discussion of Wrede's several positions is given by A. E. J. Rawlinson, *Commentary* [1925], pp. 258–62; and V. Taylor, "W. Wrede's The Messianic Secret in the Gospels," ExpT lxv [1953–54], pp. 248–50.

[23] U. Luz, "Das Geheimnismotiv und die markinische Christologie," ZNTW 56 [1965], pp. 9–30.

[24] H. Conzelmann, "Present and Future in the Synoptic Tradition," *God and Christ*, vol. 5 of *Journal for Theology and the Church* [1968], pp. 42f., writes: "It was not the non-messianic character of the units in the tradition which causes the evangelist trouble, but rather their messianic character." Mark's contribution is depicted as not consisting "in his forcing non-messianic elements into a framework of christological belief, but rather in his putting

It is clear too that in the pre-Markan tradition there is also an emphatic declaration of Messianic revelation, i.e. on occasions when the sequel is exactly the opposite of what the "Messianic secret" purported to achieve. These are the times when the obverse command is given and those healed and blessed are bidden (or at least permitted) to blazon the news. The two notable cases are 5:19, 20 and 10:47–52, though there are other incidental notices to the same effect (1:28, 45; 6:31; 7:24).

Wrede (op. cit., pp. 278–8) in a Detached Note on Mark 10:47, 48 argues that this cry, "Jesus, Son of David, have mercy on me!" and its rebuke has nothing to do with the Messianic secret but that the rebuke is similar to that administered to the mothers in Mark 10:13. But, as J. D. G. Dunn insists, the Messianic character of the title, "Son of David" is proved from 12:35–37a, and this is the sense in 10:47f.

There can be no reason why Mark allowed the text to retain traits of Messianic publicity if he was determined to insist that the Messianic secret was observed throughout the ministry and only made public at the resurrection. Nor is G. Strecker's expedient[25] of conceding the existence of a publicity motif and yet arguing for the simultaneity of both revelation and secrecy motifs as part of Mark's theology any real solution since on Wrede's original thesis the one would cancel out the other.

(c) The real question, however, turns upon the nature of Jesus' ministry. Wrede denied to it any Messianic significance except what may be inferred from the secret which was imposed upon the record of the ministry by Mark the theologian. The negative reply to the question, Did Jesus know himself to be the Messiah? has been a commonplace ever since Wrede's book appeared, and represents a judgment shared by a considerable body of opinion.[26] But the case cannot be regarded as foreclosed. In fact, recent discussions have re-opened the matter of Jesus' Messianic claim which in its ostensible nature was ambiguous and so capable of misunderstanding. For that reason Jesus' attitude to the title "Christ" can be regarded as ambivalent and reserved.[27] The exegetical test-cases are found in the Feeding of the Five Thousand and its sequel (in the light of John 6:1–15); Peter's confession (Mark 8:27–33); the

together a mass of materials already understood christologically in such a way as to conform to the kerygma" (loc. cit., p. 42) and so to produce the literary genre of "gospel" (loc. cit., p. 43). See B. G. Powley "The Purpose of the Messianic Secret: A Brief Survey," ExpT lxxx [1968–69], p. 310.

[25] G. Strecker, "Zur Messiasgeheimnistheorie im Markusevangelium," Studia Evangelica iii [1964], pp. 93 f.

[26] Examples include R. Bultmann, Theology of the New Testament i [1952], pp. 26ff., who re-phrases Wrede's theory to give it a more cautious formulation (op. cit., p. 32); E. Stauffer, "Messias oder Menschensohn?" NovT i. [1950], pp. 81 ff.; J. Héring, Le Royaume du Dieu et sa venue [1937], pp. 96 ff.; F. Hahn, The Titles of Jesus in Christology [ET, 1969], pp. 148–161, 171.

[27] O. Cullmann's classic presentation of this idea of "reserve, not rejection" may be mentioned: The Christology of the New Testament [ET, 1959], pp. 117 ff.

entry into Jerusalem (11:1–11); the Trial scene (14:61, 62); and the self-designation of Son of man as a cryptogram which both concealed and defined his true self-understanding in the light of Daniel 7:13. The debate here turns less on the formal claiming of a titular office or function than on a datum of Jesus' self-awareness that he stood in a special relation to God[28] which needed to be sharply defined and set over against popular misconceptions of what Messiahship meant. That he did not publicly state "I am the Messiah" need occasion no surprise in view of the whole tenor of his ministry among men and as the choice presented in the Temptations was repeated and re-enacted throughout his life. But that he did not disown the title out of a sense of denial of its applicability or a refusal to acknowledge it for himself is clear from his strangely para-doxical attitude to its use, whether as "Christ" or "Son of David" or "Son of the Blessed."

J. D. G. Dunn writes:

> He did not take what might appear the easiest course—that of completely renouncing the title. He did not deny his right to the title, but attempted to re-educate his hearers in the significance of it for him [and for them, we may add]. And the claims he made to Messiahship and Messianic authority were of a parabolic sort whose significance was there, plain for all to see whose eyes were not blinded and whose ears were not clogged by misconceptions (8:17–21). (*loc. cit.*, p. 112).

All that needs to be added is that Jesus' whole ministry was such as to encourage a response and an allegiance. Yet his coolness and indifference to the honorific titles and enthusiastic gestures tells us that he came to be a sort of Messiah no one would suspect. The secret lies in his own person and ministry and as such could be penetrated only by insight, sympathy, faith and a commitment to following him. Where these responses were present even in embryo Jesus sends off his new disciples with a charge to confess him; but in cases of delicacy and where misunderstanding and popular acclaim would follow as an inevitable consequence of his wonder-ful works, he counsels silence. The "Messianic secret" is not thus a theo-logical construction or doctrinal straitjacket into which the Markan Jesus and his contemporaries are put. It is the inevitable consequence of the type of "Messiah" Jesus came to be, whose "secret" is not heard by open claims and loud shouts but in the intimate atmosphere of a home and among men who are on his side, at least in being committed to him even if their understanding is woefully defective. And it was a secret which could not

---

[28] A partial parallel between Jesus' attitude to Messianic titles and yet a consciousness in deed and gesture of an indirect claim to be God's special agent, and other Jewish Messianic figures is now possible in the light of Simon ben Kosebah's bid to Messianic dignity at the time of the Second Jewish revolt. The precedent was set by the Teacher of Righteousness at Qumran where the Nathan prophecy in 2 Samuel 7 was applied to the Messiah. See O. Betz, *What do we Know about Jesus?* [1968], pp. 88ff., and R. N. Longenecker, *The Christology of Early Jewish Christianity* [1970], pp. 66–74.

be disclosed until after his destiny was fulfilled in the Passion. "In truth the Messiah, he would not be the Messiah until his task was accomplished" (V. Taylor, *loc. cit.*, p. 151). To this conclusion the latest study[29] points with the affirmation that the secret is bound up with the Passion, accepted as part of the divine will by Jesus but known only *after the event*. Therefore demons are silenced and men are rebuked, for there can be no real understanding of Jesus' mysterious person until it is disclosed in his freely embracing God's will to suffer.

Mark's purpose in relating the secret to the suffering Messiah was calculated to answer Jewish objections that Messiah cannot die so unthinkable a death as a Roman crucifixion and so Jesus cannot be the Messiah. Mark responds: he is Messiah because his death is God's plan for redemption.

There is another explanation of the data to which we will refer in a later section. Not necessarily in conflict with the foregoing, it will argue that Mark did have a purpose in phrasing the Messianic secret, which inheres in the historical texture of Jesus' ministry. The history is assumed; Mark's theological purpose is an extra dimension. By this we will contend that he is endeavouring to show that even those nearest Jesus' person and specially favoured as recipients of Jesus' private instruction failed to grasp his teaching and his significance and remained dull and misguided. Yet unlikely characters on the stage, the demoniacs, a semi-Gentile mute in Decapolis, a blind beggar were quick to discern him. They even disobeyed his orders to silence in order to proclaim their discovery. Mark uses this material to do two things: to indicate how closeness to Jesus on earth was no guarantee of spiritual discernment and knowledge, and to show that unexpected persons were both blessed and became missionaries of their benefactor.

Wrede's survey of the Markan texts and his reconstruction by way of the Messianic secret theory have value in pinpointing the issues of Jesus' Messiahship-rôle. His complex solution is hardly feasible as it stands, though later supporters have tried to refine and modify its precise outline. Nevertheless, Wrede did achieve one important result in the history of Markan interpretation: he showed how theologically oriented the evangelist was. And while we must dispute the exact way in which Wrede called him a theologian, we cannot go back on Wrede's work and forget that the evangelist's rôle was one of writing history-and-theology.

The inter-relation of history and theology is still the vital issue. We move on to consider some summaries of Mark's message as theological constructs before returning to a consideration of how this gospel correlates historical fact and theological meaning.

---

[29] G. Minette de Tillesse, *Le secret messianique dans l'évangile de Marc* [1968], pp. 321ff. A similar conclusion is reached by D. E. Aune "The Problem of the Messianic Secret," NovT xi [1969], 1–31 (31).

3. *Mark's Hellenistic Theology*

As a point to be registered against Wrede's hypothesis of an unmessianic life of Jesus which Mark has transformed by reading back the so-called "Messianic secret," we may make one simple observation. This is that the actual term "Christ" (a Greek form of the Hebrew "Messiah" = the anointed one) is found only rarely in significant passages. The cases are:

(i) In the title (1:1): the editorial context is plain.

(ii) Peter's confession (8:29); but the meaning of the title is not found. Jesus proceeds to speak about the Son of man (8:31)

(iii) The Temple debate on the Messiah as David's Son (12:35–37).

(iv) "See, here is the Christ" (13:21).

(v) The high priest's interrogation, Are you the Messiah, the Son of the Blessed? To which Jesus replied in terms of the Son of man (14:61, 62).

(vi) The taunt of the crucified (15:32), recalling the title on the Roman superscription (15:26).

(vii) 9:41 stands apart as a use of *Christos* without the definite article, and clearly in an editorial part of the verse. It is also textually uncertain.[30]

The evidence leads to the conclusion, voiced by E. Best[31]: "Mark leaves the title, so far as we know, in the material as it comes to him; he does not deny that Jesus is the Christ, nor does he stress it. In itself the title tells us nothing about the achievement of Jesus; it may even suggest a false conception of the central figure of Mark's Gospel."

To this conclusion may be added by way of confirmation the fact that Mark has not chosen to emphasize the Messianic office of Jesus even when he might be expected to do so. He does not supply the Old Testament prophecy from Zechariah 9:9 to his account of the entry into Jerusalem (11:1–11) and, while the underlying motif may well be a tacit assumption of authority as Lord of the Temple which Lohmeyer[32] detected in verse 11, there is a conscious playing down of Jesus as Davidic King and political Messiah by a transference of the cry Hosanna to a coming kingdom and an omission of the title "Son of David" which could carry political overtones.[33]

---

30 See V. Taylor, *The Text of the New Testament* [1961], pp. 85f.

31 E. Best, *The Temptation and the Passion* [1965], pp. 165f.

32 E. Lohmeyer, *Lord of the Temple* [ET, 1961], pp. 34f.

33 Contrast E. Lohse, "Hosanna," Nov.T, vi [1963], pp. 113–119, who argues from an implicit reference to Psalm 118:25f. that a Messianic identity is meant; and J. S. Kennard "'Hosanna' and the Purpose of Jesus" JBL 67 [1948], pp. 171–176, who maintains that the exclamation is drawn from a Maccabean setting and has explicit Messianic and political motives. See for the view accepted above B. Lindars, *New Testament Apologetic* [1961], pp. 111f.

It is therefore extremely unlikely that the Messiah-rôle formed for Mark a question of vital importance, except that his conscious de-emphasis of the title is an indirect witness to the fact that, in his view, Jesus attached little importance to it and saw its sole value in a re-interpreted content. Hence the substitution of "Son of Man" at the critical passages of 8:27–33 and 14:61, 62.

At the opposite end of the scale of interest the appellative "Son of God" carries a much more central significance in this gospel. And it is small wonder that Mark's intention to portray Jesus as divine Son has been recently exploited. The three main contributions to this theme may be examined now: they are united by a common desire to see Mark as theology in narrative form with the accent heavily falling on the depicting of a hellenistic Son-of-God figure which is interpreted in the story of the quasi-earthly life of Jesus. All three writers acknowledge their debt to R. Bultmann's thesis[34] that in the Markan gospel we have the combination of the hellenistic kerygma of Christ (expressed as a *mythos*, i.e. a story of a heavenly being told in earthly terms) and the tradition of the story of Jesus as a figure of history. There are divergent emphases but it is remarkable how the pattern set in Philippians 2:6–11 (noted by Bultmann) should play the part of providing a ground-plan for Mark's gospel in these theories. It is accepted that the Christ-hymn in the Philippians passage is couched in mythological language and tells the story of Christ's threefold existence as heavenly being, quasi-human figure and exalted world-ruler.[35]

(a) To be sure, Ph. Vielhauer[36] objects that Philippians 2:6–11 can hardly have been a normative type of teaching for Mark since the death of the cross in Mark is set in a context of fulfilled prophecy—an emphasis lacking in the hellenistic framework of the Christ-hymn. Nonetheless we feel at liberty to question his disclaimer since his main interpretative key to Mark in terms of an enthronement pattern matches exactly the format of the finale of Philippians 2:9–11 with its stresses on kingly power, bestowal of a name, and exercise of world-lordship.

Vielhauer examines the various christological titles in Mark and gives pride of place to υἱός θεοῦ (Son of God). He observes that at three crucial points in the story the title is proclaimed: 1:11 (baptism); 9:7 (transfiguration) and 15:39 (enthronement and acclamation). These are the chief nodal points where the title gains meaning; the other places (i.e.

---

[34] R. Bultmann, *The History of the Synoptic Tradition* [ET 1963], pp. 347f.

[35] These characterizations are believed to have been shown by E. Käsemann in his ground-breaking essay on Phil. 2, now in translation as "A Critical Analysis of Philippians 2:5–11," *God and Christ, Journal for Theology and the Church*, vol. 5 [1968], pp. 45–88. The influence of Käsemann in the exegesis of this passage is noted in my *Carmen Christi: Philippians 2:5–11* [1967], pp. 89ff. and passim.

[36] Ph. Vielhauer, "Erwägungen zur Christologie des Markusevangeliums," *Zeit und Geschichte*, Bultmann Festschrift [1964], pp. 155–169.

1:24; 3:11; 5:7) where demons confess him in similar terms are the subject of rebuke since they do not represent a Christian sentiment.

What unites these three verses into a drama, is, for Vielhauer, the use made of an ancient Egyptian enthronement ritual by which the king is adopted as divine son, presented and acknowledge before the gods, and enthroned.[37] The Markan counterparts of this ritual are in Jesus' baptism, transfiguration and crucifixion when he is made Son of God in the fullest sense. Hence 1:1 can be written as a superscription over the entire narrative which binds together these three "moments." It is only at the crucifixion, however, that he becomes eschatological king; and he enters the heavenly realm to become world-ruler from the resurrection. The fact that his kingly power was kept in the dark up till then is Mark's Messianic secret, which is only made known by the centurion's cry (15:39).

It is a strange interpretation of the grim scene of Golgotha to see it as part of the enthronement-scene by which Jesus enters upon his rule, subsequently to pass into the heavenly world (loc. cit., pp. 167, 168). This gospel trails off into silence at 16:8 with no proof of his resurrection or kingly authority provided. If 16:19, 20 (in AV-KJV) were an authentic part of Mark's εὐαγγέλιον, Vielhauer's theory would have more credibility; and J. Schreiber's expedient (loc. cit. in the next section, pp. 167f.) of regarding 16:7 as referring to the exaltation is a desperate one.

In Vielhauer's hands, the story of the Markan Jesus is to be read as an incognito mission of a divine Son who passes through the world of time and space as one unrecognized. The demonic world, however, does admit to his real being but is rebuked. The three "moments of revelation" show the progress of his journey from veiledness to acknowledgment as the baptism and glorification on the mount prepare for his recognition as divine Son by the centurion (loc. cit., pp. 166-7). Wrede was correct to describe the events as a "secret" but it is not one of Messianic destiny. Rather it is Markan theology of the cross read back into Jesus' existence on earth (loc. cit., p. 169) as the myth is "historized."

(b) For Vielhauer, the crucifixion was the occasion "by which Jesus became eschatological king and was installed as kosmokrat (world-ruler) in heaven" (loc. cit., p. 168). The moment of the cross became the moment of his exaltation.

The same idea is seized upon and used in the reconstruction of J. Schreiber.[38] In his view Mark's gospel is the re-casting of hellenistic theology in the light of the centrality of the cross (loc. cit., p. 183).

---

[37] For details of this ceremony, see O. Michel, Hebräerbrief [1960], p. 54; and Carmen Christi, p. 242.

[38] J. Schreiber, "Die Christologie des Markusevangeliums—Beobachtungen zur Theologie und Komposition des zweiten Evangeliums," ZThK 58 [1961], pp. 154-183. His later book Theologische Erkenntnis und unterrichtlicher Vollzug [1966] represents a different line of approach as he uses Mark's gospel as a model in early Christian pedagogy and draws lessons for today.

Philippians 2:6–11 provides the model with its teaching of a divine being who accepts a human existence while at the same time remaining divine (*loc. cit.*, p. 156). He passes through this world—as the Markan Jesus journeys on the road to Jerusalem. He consents to be victimized by evil powers and (in the Christianized version of the gnostic myth) to die as a divine Redeemer. So Jesus in Mark's account goes to his fate, after a series of conflicts with demons. Yet the moment of his outward defeat is his triumph, as God exalts and instals him in the heavenly sphere as world-ruler and judge over all now-subjugated evil forces. Mark makes the terminal point of his story the confession in 15:39: "Truly this man was a divine Son."

But what becomes of the resurrection? The promise of 16:7 is taken to refer to the exalted Lord whom the church will see in the land of its mission, namely Galilee. But Peter and the other disciples did not in the event go to Galilee but chose, out of culpable blindness (9:6), to remain in Jerusalem. In this way Mark plays down the Jewish-Christian church and extols the Gentile missionaries and their evangelistic enterprise. Reflecting on the pattern of humiliation-exaltation in Jesus' earthly life, couched as an example of a "divine-man" experience, Mark drives home the point that the Christian is called to follow the Redeemer from this world to the heavenly realm. The Redeemer thus blazes the trail by overcoming death and emerging triumphantly after conflict and suffering. The disciple can expect no less in his passage from earth to heaven.

Two matters in this reconstruction call for some comment.[39]

(i) He parts company with Wrede whose "Messianic secret" idea he accepts only to modify it substantially by insisting that the pre-Markan tradition already portrayed Jesus' life in Messianic terms. Yet this characterization was (to Mark's mind) a distortion because it left the main impression of Jesus' mighty works being performed as by a hellenistic θεῖος ἀνήρ or divine man (*loc. cit.*, pp. 158, 163, 173). This picture of Jesus as an exorcist and miracle-worker who overcame satanic powers and displayed his prowess and fame needed to be held under control; and Mark achieved that control by his use of the secret, not of Jesus' messiahship but of his office as Son of God. The commands to silence and the rebukes administered to demons are proof of his divine authority and a sign of his destiny to remain on earth as an unrecognized, unacclaimed Redeemer-figure. Mark has run these two presentations together—one of a gnostic Redeemer belonging to hellenistic theology and the other of the θεῖος ἀνήρ miracle-worker (*loc. cit.*, p. 158); and he has done it in such a way by his use of the υἱὸς θεοῦ title as to modify the latter by his employment of the redeemed Redeemer christology (*loc. cit.*, p. 163).

[39] For a further critique, see E. Best, *The Temptation and the Passion* [1965], pp. 125–133.

(ii) The hiddenness and ultimate vindication of the Markan Jesus, along with his victory over demonic forces, are all part of the gnostic stock-in-trade which Mark has used for Christian purposes. The Redeemer's achievement is set in a cosmic dimension and his final triumph and heavenly exaltation are cast in transcendental terms. For Mark the imagery of Jesus' death is that of 1 Corinthians 2:8, interpreted to mean that the "rulers of this age" are the demonic princes who crucified Christ, yet were deceived as to his true identity. Hence their seeming triumph is their defeat since it was the glorious Lord that they tried to overcome; and they were abashed by his vindication by the Most High God.

The cosmic setting of the crucifixion is one way of looking at Mark's passion story. But only one way. For example, the tearing of the Temple veil (15:38) as a prelude to the centurion's cry (15:39) is far more likely to refer to the curtain in the Jerusalem sanctuary than to some gnostic idea of a breaking down of a barrier between heaven and earth in the *pleroma*[40]; and the cry springs from the human lips of a man before the cross and is not, in the first instance, an acknowledgment of the Redeemer's cosmic authority, as Schreiber wishes to interpret it (*loc. cit.*, p. 176).

The lack of any finale by which the victory of the aeon-Christ is proclaimed in his heavenly journey back to God and the absence of resurrection appearances which would corroborate his celestial person are both remarkable in a reconstruction which sees this gospel as portraying a gnostic Saviour who is eventually saved (*salvator salvandus*). The only way to explain this omission is to read 9:2–8 as a post-resurrection story (*loc. cit.*, pp. 173f.) and to take the promise of 16:7 as applicable to the glorified Christ. The Jesus of Mark has his feet firmly on the ground and, while there is a numinous quality about his person and a secret which only faith can pierce, there is a factualness and a reality which makes this theological construct very difficult to credit.

(c) A much more reasonable attempt to square a theory with the totality of Mark's witness to Christ comes in R. A. Harrisville's book.[41] For him Mark can only be properly understood as a sermon, which is the essential meaning of εὐαγγέλιον in the frontispiece (1:1).

But good sermons have a structure and a purpose. The scheme to which the gospel conforms is found in Philippians 2:6–11 with its motif of humiliation-enthronement. This is Mark's model, and his gospel aims to express in narrative form the theology of the hellenistic church, encapsulated in the Christ-hymn.

---

[40] The same problem is found in Ephesians 2:14 with reference to the "dividing wall." See my commentary on *Ephesians* (Broadman Bible Commentary [1971] *ad loc.*) with reference to H. Schlier, *Christus und die Kirche im Epheserbrief* [1930], pp. 18ff.; and F. F. Bruce "St. Paul in Rome 4. The Epistle to the Ephesians," BJRL 49 [1967], p. 316.

[41] R. A. Harrisville, *The Miracle of Mark* [1967].

While there is much that is suggestive in this approach, the parallelism is by no means exact or explicit. Only by moving around the Markan units of material and exploiting them to find therein a superhuman Jesus on earth can anything in the first chapters be categorized under the title, "He was in the form of God" (Phil. 2:6). Harrisville is prepared for this expedient, because he has already concluded that Mark has no interest in chronological sequence. But this is to run wild over the Markan territory and believe that Mark had no idea of order but was content simply to put panels of narrative side-by-side in incomprehensible disarray. It is one thing to say that Mark does not have a sequential pattern recording Jesus' life on a day-to-day basis; it is quite otherwise to believe that he did not know where the starting-point and the onward progress of Jesus' ministry were to be located on the chart of history. To impute this carefree abandon is to imply that Mark is flying in the face of such a rough outline as in Acts 10:37–39; 13:31 and to divorce the gospel from any semblance of history.

The middle section of the Christ-hymn is arguably cast in the mould of the pattern of the Servant of God; and undoubtedly there are motifs in Mark which fit this scheme of salvation-history.[42]

The test-issue comes in the attempts to find in Mark anything to correspond to Philippians 2:9–11. Absence of any resurrection story is again a weak link in this chain; and Mark's christology does not emphasize the title "Lord." The closest we get to a parallel is the submission of demons in the earlier part of the gospel, though these episodes fall out of place by being read back from the post-resurrection period, according to Harrisville's theory.

Mark's focus on the secret of Jesus' person lines up with the incognito-pattern in the pre-Pauline hymn. But there are outstanding features which set the two christologies apart. There is in Mark no pre-existence teaching, no incarnational motif and no cosmic dramatization of enthronement and world-rulership. Indeed, the heavy emphasis on Jesus' sonship, earthly finiteness and the use of the promise-fulfilment nexus taken from the Old Testament thought-world are all pointers in the opposite direction.[43]

Evaluation

The essays we have surveyed share in common at least one conviction in regard to the significance of the second gospel. While it is a record of history in its literary form, its chief characteristic is that it is theology cast in a narrative style of writing. With that initial conclusion we shall proceed to express agreement in subsequent sections.

[42] Though this is challenged by E. Best, *The Temptation and the Passion* [1968], p. 151.
[43] The *carmen Christi* in Philippians 2 is best taken as a species of hellenistic christology adapted for missionary purposes, as I have tried to argue in *op. cit.*, pp. 297ff. The more this understanding may gain in feasibility, the less correspondence there is between the hymn and Mark's gospel and its message. It is the measure of distinction between a pre-Pauline and post-Pauline construction.

But in the further definitions of the way in which theology and history are related there is room for debate and dissension. For these interpreters who follow in the wake of Wrede's footsteps it is the theology which mattered supremely to Mark. They all concur in and build upon the conclusion of Wrede (*op. cit.*,[44] p. 131): "Only pale remnants [of historical evidence for the actual life of Jesus] survive in what is a suprahistorical interpretation based on faith. In that sense Mark's gospel belongs to the history of dogma." For Vielhauer and Schreiber Mark's main work was that of a theologian who laid under tribute the form of a gnostic myth of the redeemed Redeemer in order to convey a message to the hellenistic church of his day. This is the picture of a gnostic revealer who communicates esoteric truth to his devotees and a Saviour who pioneers a path from this world of fallen matter to the celestial region from which he has come. He calls his followers to take the road he has opened up.

For Mark who has christianized this story it becomes a narrative of a Son of God, declared to be such by a heavenly voice who treads a lonely path fraught with misunderstanding, conflict and rejection, eventually to be put to death. Death is not the end since he is taken up to God and acclaimed as divine Son.

For these interpretations of Mark as a Gentile Christian capitalizing on a myth to make the Christian salvation-drama intelligible much importance lies in the title "Son of God." It is accepted ever since W. Bousset's discussion in *Kyrios Christos* in 1913 [ET, 1970, pp. 92–98] that this term finds its origin in the hellenistic church which derived it from the contemporary idea of the "divine man" figure. Recent study has questioned such a connection in view of the possibility that "Son of God" was a term just coming into use as an element in Jewish Messianic expectation.[45]

The Messianic picture in *The Psalms of Solomon* 17, 18 (c. 50 B.C.) and the fate of the righteous sufferer as a son of God in the book of Wisdom 2–5 as well as the use made of the Nathan-oracle in 2 Samuel 7 (with its assurance, "I will be his father, and he shall be my son") at Qumran are very much germane to the study of the title in the New Testament. Nor should the adoption-formula of Psalm 2:7 be left out of consideration, since it clearly holds the potential for explaining the filial relationship to God which the resurrection of Jesus made necessary for the early church (e.g. Rom. 1:3f.; Heb. 1:5).

But even at the back of these uses of the title which are mainly descriptive of a function there is the notion of the divine Son as a title betokening a personal, filial consciousness. Mark's gospel is not too expressive in its witness to this but the places to which appeal may be made are all the more significant, even though there is not the clear affirmation of the "Cry of delight" in Matt. 11:27 = Luke 10:22.

44 W. Wrede, *Das Messiasgeheimnis in den Evangelien* [1901].
45 R. H. Fuller's description: *The Foundations of New Testament Christology* [1965], p. 164.

The following may be mentioned here, and will be the subject of our exegetical study in a later section.

1:1 In the title (if we accept the reading) Mark's emphasis on "Jesus Christ, the Son of God" is made.

1:11 The voice at his baptism certifies, Thou art my Son, the Beloved (in a direct form of address).

9:7 The theophany at the Transfiguration repeats the witness to "My Son, the Beloved."

12:6 In the parable-allegory Jesus is the "beloved Son."

13:32 Even "the Son" does not know the day or the hour of the future.

14:61
62 The high priest's question is: Are you the Messiah, the Son of the Blessed [God]? To which Jesus responded: I am. Or, if we follow the longer reading on the principle of the "harder reading" given in the Caesarean text (cf. Matt. 26:64; Luke 22:70) his reply was a non-committal: "It is your way of putting it, not mine." The preference for the latter is that it makes sense of an evasive reply since the point at issue in the question was his Messianic pretensions, not divine Sonship.[46]

15:39 The centurion's cry.

At least one interesting result emerges from these data. Leaving aside the indirect attestation of 1:1; 14:61, 62 and 15:39, we observe the close association of the epithet "beloved" (ἀγαπητός) with Jesus' Sonship, and note that this has suggested to recent writers that Jesus' Sonship "goes beyond a purely functional or messianic use of the title by the use of the qualifying adjective ἀγαπητός which indicates the unique relationship of Jesus to his Father."[47]

While there is no sure argument for a uniqueness in this filial relationship, since in the gnostic story the Redeemer is loved by God as his "form" (μορφή) or "image,"[48] nothing can exactly parallel the closeness of the bond that unites Jesus and God in these Markan texts. This suggests that the presentation of Jesus moves in a different world from that the gnostic Saviour or the hellenistic "divine man." There may be hints of Jesus' activity in exorcism and healings which are set in the framework of the divine man portrayal. But it is questionable whether Mark intended

[46] See for this accepted reading B. H. Streeter, *The Four Gospels* [1924], p. 322; and E. Lohmeyer, *Kommentar*, p. 328, note 2.

[47] I. H. Marshall, "Son of God or Servant of Yahweh? A Reconsideration of Mark i. 11," NTS 15 [1969], pp. 326-36 (336), referring to his article "The Divine Sonship of Jesus," *Interpretation* 21 [1967], pp. 87-103.

[48] In the *Poimandres* tract of the Hermetic literature, printed in translation in R. M. Grant *Gnosticism: An Anthology* [1961], pp. 213f.

to draw a parallel; rather he may well have wanted to indicate a contrast (see later, pp. 146ff.).

In summary, the theology in Mark's christological title (clearly his favourite) of "Son of God" owes little to the Greek ideas of gods and heroes in the surrounding pagan world. He is harking back to the Old Testament-Jewish tradition by which "Son of God" denoted a special agent, chosen and invested with a mission, offering obedience even to the point of suffering and humiliation, and vindicated at length by God. In Mark's hands the figure is enriched by the personal element of a unique relationship in which Jesus stands to God as his beloved one, the Son par excellence.[49]

---

[49] On "'The Beloved' as a Messianic Title" see J. A. Robinson, *St. Paul's Epistle to the Ephesians* [1904], pp. 229–233. Perhaps more suggestive in the background of Markan usage is the description of Isaac as the beloved son of Abraham: cf. Gen. 22:2 (LXX) Λαβὲ τὸν υἱόν σου τὸν ἀγαπητόν, ὃν ἠγάπησας; 22:16 οὐκ ἐφείσω τοῦ υἱοῦ σου τοῦ ἀγαπητοῦ. See E. Best, *op. cit., pp.* 169–173, 177; and N. Hillyer, "The Servant of God," EQ 41 [1969], pp. 143–60.

The origin of Mark and the rise of the *Gattung* "gospel" are rightly traced to a historical, not mythical, christology which centres in Jesus as Son of God, in an article by Lewis S. Hay, "The Son-of-God Christology in Mark," *The Journal of Bible and Religion*, 32 [1964], pp. 106–114. But his attempt to find that sonship exclusively explained by Jesus' obedience inverts what is surely the correct order. Jesus obeyed *because* he was God's Son (as in Heb. 5:8), not vice versa.

V

SPECIAL EMPHASES IN MARK'S CHRISTOLOGY

The Jesus of history and Mark's factualness: (a) prominence of human faith; (b) Jesus as teacher of the Twelve (R. P. Meye); (c) interest in the Passion; (d) human traits in the gospel. The Christ of faith and Mark's numinous christology: (a) Mark—"a book of secret epiphanies" (Dibelius, Vielhauer); (b) Mark's "high christology" of the Son of God and risen Lord.

I N MARK'S PRESENTATION OF JESUS CHRIST THERE IS A PARADOXICAL BLEND of what seem, at first glance, to be contradictory motifs. It is the purpose of this chapter to investigate the data which bear upon the twin ideas of (i) the evangelist's picture of Jesus as a man and (ii) his conviction expressed in several christological passages that Jesus laid claim to a dignity which placed him on God's side as a divine being. These are indeed paradoxical strands which are woven together to make the composite thread which runs through Mark's chapters. Our task is to unwind the cord and separate out the various parts.

I. The Jesus of History and Mark's Factualness

Quite obviously the evangelist intended his readers to understand that his "gospel" was centred on a man who lived a human life. To be sure, as we have already seen, there is little to suggest that Mark was consciously interested in writing Jesus' life-story. But he does write with a historical person in his mind's eye. Though he is concerned to begin Jesus' story without introduction or apology—and with no nativity story as preamble—nonetheless there is no mistaking that for him Jesus walked with his feet firmly set on Palestinian soil. He was moved with anger (1:41, if this is the true reading; 3:5; 10:14) and acted in a forthright way (11:14). He was disturbed by human unbelief (6:6; 9:19), yet was anxious to promote faith where a trustful attitude was present if only in embryo (9:23). He could deal sternly with a favourite disciple (8:33), yet his heart went out in love to another man at the crossroads of decision (10:21). He spoke out against the religious leaders of his day (12:12), but he had time for the sick and needy (10:46–52) and expressed a deep interest in children by welcoming them in a tender manner (10:14–16). He was touchingly appreciative of human kindness (14:6), yet a note of disappointment over his friends who were only weakly loyal is also heard (14:37, 41). He foretells that one of his band will turn traitor (14:18) and that a trusted disciple will disown him at the last (14:30), but in the end he pledges his forgiveness and hope for that forlorn disciple (16:7). He anticipates the prospect of death with great agitation and emotion (14:33) and cries out in spiritual anguish in the hour of his bitterest need (15:34), yet he adds an *au revoir* to his leave-taking of the disciples (14:28).

This random sampling of the evidence confirms the verdict. The Markan Jesus possessed the traits and qualities of a human figure; and his life's course ran in channels of emotion, purpose, response and hopefulness that we can recognize as belonging to what we know of life's demands, opportunities and challenges. Indeed, Mark's record gives the impression of accentuating just those human traits which stamp his life as akin to ours. To these particular features we now turn, as we pick out evidences of Mark's factualness, to use E. Schweizer's term.[1]

(a) *The prominence of human faith*

Mark's Gospel is rich in the importance it gives to faith. It is a religious attitude which Jesus calls forth and praises.[2] Negatively this is shown by Jesus' rebuke of "unbelief" in 4:40; 6:6; 9:19 as much as by his encouragements to faith (5:36; 11:22). Moreover, whenever human faith is present, he attaches a special importance to it as the key to release God's power in healing (5:34; 10:52) as well as in the divine prerogative of forgiveness (2:5) which he claims to exercise.

Three passages are particularly to be noted, in illustration of the general theme.

(i) The story of the woman's healing (5:25–34) is intercalated within the framework of the *pericope* of the raising of Jairus' daughter (5:22–43). Both sections emphasize the place of faith. The woman's touching his garments is a hesitant venture (v. 28) which is immediately rewarded by her healing and recognized and applauded by Jesus as an act of faith (v. 34).

As the journey of Jesus proceeds after interruption to Jairus' home and the news comes that all human hope of recovery is gone (v. 35), Jesus follows through on his tribute to the woman by encouraging Jairus to maintain his expectancy of faith (v. 36: "Cease to be afraid; only continue to trust" brings out the nuance of Mark's Greek).

(ii) In 9:14–29 the scene is set in immediate sequence with the Transfiguration story. During the absence of Jews and the three disciples on the mountain, the nine disciples are confronted with a situation which outstrips their ability to cope (v. 18). The epileptic's father simply states the

---

[1] E. Schweizer, *Das Evangelium des Markus*, NT Deutsch [1967], pp. 220–224. His term is "Nüchternheit," which the ET does not sufficiently bring out.
[2] J. M. Robinson, *The Problem of History in Mark* [1957], p. 74.

case, with only an unspoken request for help at this stage. The poignancy of Jesus' retort, "O faithless generation, how long am I to be with you? How long am I to bear with you? Bring him to me" is probably the most forthright declaration of Jesus' emotional response to human need in all the gospels and provides a window of access into the inner life of Jesus which is without parallel. Critical suspicion (voiced by Dibelius, *From Tradition to Gospel*, p. 95 and Bultmann, *History of the Synoptic Tradition*, p. 157) has been raised against verse 19 as an authentic logion of Jesus. These writers conclude that the saying expresses a homelessness which a divine being felt whilst he was on earth and yearned to return to his native home in heaven. Thus, in their view, the saying is set on a mythological background.

But this conclusion is not compelling for the reason that the language of Jesus here has a nearer parallel than that in the world of contemporary religions. In the Old Testament, both God himself (Num. 14:27) and his prophets (Isa. 6:11) express in emotional terms a sense of disappointment over a wayward people (Deut. 32:5; Isa. 65:2). And it has even been suggested that the use of the verb "to bear" ($\dot{\alpha}\nu\acute{\epsilon}\chi\epsilon\sigma\theta\alpha\iota$), reflects the same idea as in Isaiah 46:4 where Yahweh bears his people in their infirmity (cf. Isa. 40:11). So H. E. Tödt, *The Son of Man in the Synoptic Tradition* [ET, 1965] p. 179.

The saying may be seen as Jesus' self-awareness that the mission he had come to fulfil has met with little response, and the prospect of his death is in his sights. His task is a thankless one (so Lagrange) and he gives vent to his deep sentiment in this outburst in which tenderness and frustration mingle.

The subsequent dialogue between the father and Jesus ends on the note of the plea, "If you have the ability, have pity on us and help us" (v. 22). Jesus' response picks up the implied doubt: "Did you say ability? Why all things are within the ability of him who has faith!" (v. 23). With the father's confidence restored (v. 24) and under the pressure of a turbulent crowd now gathering, Jesus exorcizes the spirit and the boy is restored to mental health and wholeness. The reason for Jesus' success (in contrast to the disciples' failure) is given as a sort of punchline of the episode: "This kind cannot be driven out by anything but prayer." The inference is that Jesus healed and exorcized by *his* confidence in God's power working through him and this required a sympathetic and expectant atmosphere in which that power could be released. If this is so, verse 23 may well be a self-reference as Jesus retorts that ability to invade and spoil Satan's domain (3:22–27) and to expel demons from their human tenement (5:9–13) is granted to the obedient Son of the Father who maintains an ever-trustful attitude of dependence on God his Father and provides a channel through which this power of God can flow. Jesus as the archetypal believer may well be in Mark's thought in this section.

(iii) That conclusion seems required by the wording on the fig tree incident in 11:12–14, 20–25. Peter's remark, "Master, look! The fig tree which you cursed has withered" is met with Jesus' rejoinder: "Have faith in God" (v. 22). This general statement leads into a more expanded discussion on the efficacy of faith and the nature of prayer (vv. 23–25), though the connection is only a loose one.[3] Evidently Mark felt that the consideration of the fig tree's fate, denoting the impending judgment on Israel in the fall of Jerusalem, required some explanation in terms of Jesus' confidence that what he had predicted would inevitably if sorrowfully come to pass. So the *logion* on faith in God is added,[4] with its undertone that Jesus' words will be fulfilled because he acts in obedience to God and in dependence on his working in history. The opposite of faith in this section is doubt (v. 23); and Jesus is presented as superbly confident that his prophetic words will be realized. The "absolute simplicity" of faith is the teaching here (re-echoed in James 1:6–8)[5]

Mark's teaching on faith centres on the example of Jesus who was supremely aware and confident of God's purpose in his life. He acted with authority as one who was conscious that divine power flowed through him to heal the sick, expel the demons and to change the course of history. He exemplified faith in the whole range of his dealings with men and the disciples and in his attitude to his Father. It would be equally true to say that he elicited faith both by his call (1:15; 4:40; 5:36; 11:22) and by his claim to be God's special emissary. He can therefore speak of those "who believe in me" (9:42) and Mark drives the point home by closely associating faith with discipleship. Those who hear and respond to Jesus' summons are invariably described as "following" him (1:18; 2:14f.; 3:7; 5:24; 6:1; 10:52; 14:54; 15:41) and even the term "those who followed" has become something of a technical term for the disciples[6], both actual (10:28, 32; cf. 9:38) and would-be (8:34; 10:21).

The object of this faith is given in only the most general way, with no content similar to a credal statement or confession of faith. The nearest Mark gets to defining the object of faith is in 1:15: "believe in the gospel." Mark seems far more concerned to relate faith to active discipleship as a continuing experience, though it "never loses its concrete relation to the history of Jesus."[7] It is tied to the term "understanding" in Mark, and has its logical outcome in a maintained attitude which embraces the total response to a given situation (5:36; 11:22) as distinct from a single

---

[3] D. E. Nineham, *St. Mark* [1963], p. 298.
[4] On its authenticity, see G. Ebeling, "Jesus and Faith" in *Word and Faith* [ET, 1963], p. 227 n. 9.
[5] E. Schweizer, *Commentary*, pp. 234f.
[6] J. M. Robinson, *op. cit.*, p. 75.
[7] J. M. Robinson, *op. cit.*, p. 75, referring to G. Kittel's observation on the use of the verbal noun "followers" of Jesus. The verb ἀκολουθεῖν is used only in the gospels which restrict the relationship signified by it to the historical Jesus: see TDNT i, p. 214.

act once-for-all accomplished. Also its opposite is often described as fear, since Jesus' encouragements to faith are occasionally prefaced by the admonition, "Fear not" (5:36 cf. 4:40). In this latter case, Mark's intention in showing how Jesus slept amid the raging storm on the lake clearly indicates that his trust in God was his secret. In the biblical tradition, the mark of the trusting man whose confidence reposes in God is that he sleeps in the midst of peril because he is sure of the sustaining and protecting care of God (Ps. 4:8; Prov. 3:23–24; Job 11: 18–19; Lev. 26:6). So he whose heart is unafraid in the storm both dispels fear and calls for faith. And it is faith such as he exemplifies (v. 40).

This leads us to a conclusion. While Mark does not explicitly comment on Jesus' personal faith—only the saying in 9:23 comes near to that—it remains very probable that the evangelist does picture him as sharing in the attitude of faith which he encourages others to adopt. "Jesus himself is not to be dissociated from the faith of which he testifies, but rather identified himself so closely with it that he very properly did not speak of his own faith but devoted himself to awakening faith. For whoever is concerned to awaken faith will have to bring his faith into play without speaking of his faith."[8]

(b) Jesus as teacher of the Twelve

Jesus' rôle in this gospel includes a part cast for him as teacher. Against the popular idea that the Markan Jesus is ceaselessly on the move and active as healer and worker on behalf of God's kingdom we must set the counter-balancing view that considerable attention is given to Jesus as teacher. The verb "to teach" ($\delta\iota\delta\acute{\alpha}\sigma\kappa\epsilon\iota\nu$) is found 15 times, and the noun used of Jesus as "teacher" ($\delta\iota\delta\acute{\alpha}\sigma\kappa\alpha\lambda o\varsigma$) occurs 12 times. Rabbi, an equivalent term used of Jewish teachers, is found 3 times. The general word "teaching" ($\delta\iota\delta\alpha\chi\acute{\eta}$) is used 5 times.[9] The significance of this word-count is drawn out by C. F. Evans in his observation that the verb "to teach" is "found more often in Mark's Gospel than in any other New Testament book."[10] In Mark it is used as an inclusive term for Jesus' activity in the synagogue or temple court (1:21; 6:2; 11:17; 12:35; 14:49), for his instruction of the crowds (2:13; 4:1f; 6:34; 10:1) as well as of the disciples (8:31; 9:31). Just occasionally the verb is employed of the disciples' instruction of others (6:30) in obedience to his commission.

But these figures also do not tell the full story. Often the verb used is imperfect in its tense or is a present participle in form, denoting a continuous action of teaching; and Mark employs an auxiliary verb, "he began to teach," so suggesting that this was his habitual practice.[11] Some

---

[8] G. Ebeling, loc. cit., p. 234.

[9] See E. Schweizer, "Anmerkungen zur Theologie des Markus," *Neotestamentica et Patristica.* Festschrift O. Cullmann [1962], p. 37.

[10] C. F. Evans, *The Beginning of the Gospel* . . . [1968], p. 47.

[11] The auxiliary verb ἤρξατο may be non-significant, if this construction is a semitic one.

synonymous terms, e.g. "he was preaching the word to them" (2:2) or "speaking the word" (4:33) increase the list, and endorse the impression that Mark has gone out of his way to stress the activity of Jesus as a Palestinian rabbinic teacher,[12] engaged in a ministry of instructing by means of parables (4:33, 34) and followed by a group of disciples (3:13, 14). But that description left by itself would give a wrong impression, for the following reasons:

(1) The call addressed to the disciples was a summons to turn one's back on an existing way of life and to become attached to Jesus in a totally new situation of obedience and service (1:16ff.; 2:13, 14; 3:13ff.). Its radical nature went far beyond what the rabbis expected of their pupils.[13]

(2) Jesus' disciples were not students in a rabbinic school or followers of a new rabbi. T. W. Manson's discussion[14] of the most likely term in Aramaic (underlying Mark's Greek for "disciple") leads to the view that they were learner-apprentices whose education was practical and not book-ish, and it was gained above all in the company of Jesus (3:14: "to be with him"), and in everyday contact with people in real life situations.

(3) The secret of Jesus' person was known only to the disciples and this was revealed to them, not as a formula to be learned and repeated but as a privilege which came as they accepted his way and followed him in obedience to his mission. The teaching in 4:11, 34 makes this clear; and it lies behind the narrative in 8:27ff.[15]

(4) The heart of Jesus' instruction was centred in the Passion and from 8:27ff. onwards the shadow of the cross falls ever more darkly over the Markan narrative. Jesus' teaching is expressed in the sombre tones of warning and prediction that he and the Twelve are on the road which leads inevitably to a violent end. He calls them to share with him that bitter experience and be prepared for what lies before them (8:34ff.; 9:31; 10:32ff.).[16]

(5) The attentive reader of this gospel cannot fail to observe a surprising thing in regard to Jesus as teacher in direct contrast to the Jewish rabbis. In the latter case their name is appended to the collection of their teaching and far more weight is given to its content than to the rabbis themselves, as for example in the Mishnah, a codification of rabbinic *halakah* or "specific and authoritative direction for the life of Jewish obedience."[17] In the case of the Markan Jesus, while there are these various allusions to

12 So C. F. Evans, *op. cit.*, p. 48.
13 E. Schweizer, *Lordship and Discipleship* [1960], p. 20.
14 T. W. Manson, *The Teaching of Jesus*[2] [1935], pp. 237ff.
15 So E. Schweizer, *Lordship and Discipleship*, p. 21.
16 We discuss these so-called Passion sayings later, pp. 188ff.
17 C. K. Barrett's definition in his *The New Testament Background: Selected Documents* [1956], p. 145. He prints a varied selection from the rabbinic literature.

his teaching, very little is actually given of the substance of that instruction. If, following C. F. Evans,[18] we divide the sections of teaching into five groups, we see how Mark has arranged what small amount of didactic material he had at his disposal.

A. 2:1–3:6   Controversy stories and debates with the Jewish leaders.

B. 4:1–34   A long section on parables, beginning with a parable on parables, and ending on a note which assures the reader that Jesus interpreted his parables to the disciples.

C. 7:1–23   Another conflict section, in which matters of Jewish custom are the subject of debate between Jesus and the Jewish authorities.

D. 9:33–10:31   Aspects of discipleship are brought together here, and arranged into a pattern by link-terms or catch-phrases, which suggest a catechetical arrangement. Additionally, themes such as divorce, true greatness and true wealth are assembled into a block of teaching.

E. 11:27–12:44   Set in Jerusalem these narratives are teaching vehicles which tell how Jesus confronted his enemies and responded to their charges and questions. Pharisees, Herodians, Sadducees, a single scribe are introduced as interlocutors, after which it is Jesus himself who poses the question of Davidic messiahship based on Psalm 110:1.

From this cursory survey it is reasonably clear that there is no interest in reproducing anything like a corpus of Jesus' teachings (similar to Matt. 5–7).[19] There is no attempt at systematization or orderly sequence. Instead, Mark's design is to offer "a succession of single authoritative sentences, each bringing to an end a dispute over some issue raised by opponents with hostile intent" (C. F. Evans, *op. cit.*, p. 54). Mark's record of Jesus' teaching is similar to the form of the pronouncement-story where the narrative or drama is told for the sake of the climactic punch-line. And it is interesting that what impressed the hearers, according to 1:22,27, was not the artistic detail or telling stylistic features but the note of compelling authority which characterized his teaching. That authority resounds in the anecdotal sections of Mark and the aphoristic sayings which his record of the Lord's teaching contains. This feature of immediacy and directness marked Jesus' teaching off from the rabbinic pedagogy

---

18 C. F. Evans, *op. cit.*, pp. 49ff.
19 Ch. 13 is an obvious exception, but even that section is usually regarded as a compilation. See later, pp. 135ff.

in which precedents and legal judgments hedged about their opinion and produced an indecisiveness which was frustrating. The scribes taught with the "authorities"—previous rabbis and their rulings were cited, qualified and debated; Jesus taught with authority, which went straight to the heart of the issue.

Mark's account of Jesus the teacher is not like that of Matthew's. Nevertheless, even if with these qualifications, it does remain that he has shown interest in presenting Jesus as above all the teacher of his disciples. Three comments may be offered on this general theme.

First, this emphasis is a needed corrective of the view which sees Mark as a gospel of action and which places all the weight of the evangelist's purpose on the Passion story. To be sure, there is no denying the heavy concentration of interest on the Passion in Mark, but it still remains that Mark is "also concerned to show that the Messiah *teaches* the Twelve regarding this all-important fact."[20] R. P. Meye also concludes from the investigation of his study that "even the deeds of Jesus were recounted by Mark from the point of view of their parabolic function."[21] This adds an extra dimension to Mark's overall purpose, for it is shown how he wished to convey the fulness of Messianic revelation in Jesus, and this was done as much by a recital of Jesus' mighty deeds as by his actual words. In anchoring this deposit of Messianic revelation in the combined action and effect of Jesus' words plus deeds, the evangelist has ensured that Jesus' authority remains in the life of the church, even after the original eye-witnesses are no longer present. And he further seems intent on showing that the revelation of Messiah's passion and victory was confirmed by the turn of events which is promised in 16:7: "There you will see him, *as he told you.*" The authority of Jesus in word and deed is thus shown to be validated by the promise and prospect that beyond the crucifixion and its seeming defeat he would fulfil his pledge to regather his own; and that this was done in accordance with what he had assured them would happen (14:28).

Secondly, the issue of whether Mark turns Jesus into an esoteric instructor of a select group of men and offers them a predestinarian teaching is a question provoked by what he reports in 4:11, 33-34 on the one side and 4:12 on the other. In the first set of texts, the disciples appear as a specially select and privileged group to whom the secret of the kingdom is revealed. "Those outside" are not so fortunate, since they are given the teaching in parables, but without the benefit of Jesus' explanation. The disciples are initiated into the secret because to them he adds the interpretation of the parables (4:34).

---

[20] R. P. Meye, *Jesus and the Twelve* [1968], p. 214. See too the same author's essay, "Messianic Secret and Messianic Didache in Mark's Gospel" in *Oikonomia*. Festschrift O. Cullmann [1967], pp. 57-68.
[21] R. P. Meye, *op. cit.*, p. 214.

On the other side, the use of Isaiah 6:9–10 in the form in which Mark quotes the passage in 4:12 has given rise to the opinion that Messiah's mission is to blind the eyes of those to whom he is sent as part of the theological determinism which decrees that God withholds his revelation from sinners. In this instance it seems part of Mark's anti-Jewish polemic, since the phrase "those outside" would refer to the Jews.[22]

It may be that Mark's purpose in this passage is different, whatever the original intention of the tradition that Jesus spoke in parables may have been; and if he chose this method of teaching in order to illumine the spiritually sensitive and conceal the truth of the kingdom from casual or careless hearers who would have leapt to wrong conclusions about the nature of that kingdom if Jesus had spoken plainly (as in 1:15), it would appear that Mark saw another meaning. His use of this section may be to direct attention to the disciples' failure to understand even when they are given special instruction.[23]

For those outside, the parabolic teaching about the mystery of the kingdom of God in Jesus' person is nonsense; and even the disciples cannot understand at this stage of Mark's story the hidden nature of that kingdom or divine the secret of who Jesus is. Not until Caesarea Philippi (8:31) and the sequel in the Transfiguration of Jesus do they begin to glimpse the deep truth; and even then their understanding is partial and perverted (10:35ff.).

Not much, therefore, can be said for the view which makes Jesus a gnostic revealer who reserves his teaching for the elect and consigns the rest of mankind to their fate. In Mark's redaction the Twelve are not narrowly conceived as a select group. In this passage a large circle is already envisaged in verse 10, described as "those who were about him." They are apparently distinguished from the Twelve[24]; and the plain meaning of the little episode in 9:38–41 is to administer a rebuke to the Twelve who so restricted discipleship to their own company.

Decisively the purport of Jesus' training of the Twelve is to initiate them into the suffering which awaits him *and them* as they go up to Jerusalem. "The main purpose of his teaching is to bring his followers to an understanding of his own Cross, not only as redemptive, but also as a way of life for themselves; they must take up their crosses as he did and serve as he served."[25] The entire tenor of this messianic *didache* spelled out in

---

[22] On the question of what the underlying semitic form of Mark's ἵνα clause (expressing purpose, or possibly result, as in RSV) might have been, see T. W. Manson's discussion in which he raises the possibility of a mistranslation of the Aramaic relative pronoun *de*. Then the citation would read smoothly, with no difficulty or a predestinarian intention behind the use of parables. See *The Teaching of Jesus*[2] [1935], pp. 75ff.

[23] So E. Schweizer, *Commentary*, p. 95.

[24] R. P. Meye, *op. cit.*, pp. 152ff. argues to the contrary but the verse reads more naturally of a larger group, even if 4:34 speaks only of Jesus' explanation to the disciples themselves. Cannot "his own disciples" include the wider number, including but larger than the Twelve?

[25] E. Best, *The Temptation and the Passion* [1963], p. 190.

terms of Jesus' foretold sufferings and death is counter to any understanding of him as a gnosticizing revealer of secrets who gathered around
him a group of would-be *illuminati* and promised them a share in his
heavenly destiny.

Thirdly, Mark's picture shows up the disciples in a very human light.
To say more, e.g. that Mark positively hated the Twelve, is probably to
go too far.[26] Yet it does remain that consistently the disciples are shown
to be dull-witted and uncomprehending when the teaching of Jesus is
directed to them (7:18; 8:21). When they *do* understand, they oppose
Jesus and reject his warning that the Son of man must suffer (8:32; 9:10,
32; 10:28, 35-45). In the end they abandon him to his lonely fate (14:49),
but not before one of the Twelve has betrayed him (14:17-21, 42) and
one of the inner group has disowned him (14:66-72).

The evangelist's purpose is not immediately clear. Why should he lose
no opportunity in his editorial work of selective emphasis and descriptive
writing of showing up the faults and failings of these men who had the
inestimably great gift of receiving Messiah's *didache* at first hand? Several
reasons can be given. E. Lohmeyer[27] relates this purpose to Mark's pastoral
care for a persecuted church facing martyrdom. The point of connection
is that if there was hope for the disciples in spite of their disloyalties and
fears there must be hope for a church undergoing trial and facing temptations to unfaithfulness under that trial.

R. P. Meye emphasizes that the humanness of the Twelve does not
invalidate their high place as the chosen company of the Messiah.[28]
E. Schweizer's discussion emphasizes that Jesus' secret remains hidden
even from the Twelve in order to make it plain that throughout the
story there was a painful inability on the part of men to understand Jesus.
Those closest to Jesus who might have been expected to understand him
because they observed him at short range failed to comprehend; and for
Mark this implies the divine gift of perception and faith, which is granted
to those whom God chooses to enlighten.

This last interpretation seems plausible since it coheres with other
evidence drawn from the Gospel itself. The evangelist makes it plain that
ties of human kinship (3:20, 21: in the latter verse the Greek οἱ παρ'
αὐτοῦ means not "his friends" but "his relatives"; cf. v. 31) are no guarantee of sympathy with Jesus' mission. Quite the contrary. In Mark the
immediate family of Jesus is hostile (3:31-35).[29] In his native place (6:1-6)
he encounters offence and unbelief. The religious leaders of the nation
are implacably opposed to him, from start to finish (3:6; 15:32). And, of
a piece with this insistence that little or no recognition of Jesus was found

---

[26] As R. P. Meye (*op. cit.*, pp. 222ff.) has remarked: "It is simply impossible to believe that
the Marcan Church did or could have loved the Messiah and hated the Twelve" (p. 224).

[27] E. Lohmeyer, *Das Evangelium des Markus* [1955], pp. 170-72.

[28] R. P. Meye, *op. cit.*, p. 224.

[29] On the verb "seeking" in 3:32 used in this gospel as a term of reproach, see later pp. 168f.

in those who stood nearest to him as a figure of past history is Mark's use of the tradition about the Twelve. They do have the advantage of proximity to Jesus (3:13, 14) and are the favoured recipients of his instruction, but they remain hardened (6:52)[30] in their refusal to see who he is and to follow him with full acceptance of what he has come to accomplish. Not surprisingly at the time of crisis they fail and fall away; and they are restored only by Jesus' steadfast desire to reunite them to himself.

(c) The interest in the Passion[31]

One of the most generally accepted axioms in the modern study of Mark's Gospel is that this evangelist is pre-eminently interested in Jesus' Passion. We may go further and claim that, in the light of a *redaktionsgeschichtlich* approach to Mark, this evangelist has imposed upon a mass of materials at his disposal a theological understanding of Jesus' ministry in terms of a preaching of the cross.[32] He "has brought the announcement of suffering into the center of the text" by "working over traditions from which the passion motif is relatively absent, and which proclaim the authority of Jesus apart from the cross."[33] This is his greatest theological achievement, to be the first theologian of the cross to make use of the literary vehicle of a gospel narrative. An incidental ramification of his major purpose is that he puts the figure of the human Jesus in the framework of suffering; and so he powerfully conveys to his readers the vividness of the anguish and bitter grief which were involved in an acceptance of the cross as Jesus' destiny. The Markan Jesus knows well what that destiny will entail, but Mark adds in his "human" touches to show that he was no Olympian figure untouched by human emotion and natural shrinking from what lay before him. Several indications of this Markan feature may be noticed.

(a) 6:1–6: his rejection at Nazareth is so written as to bring out the sense of pathos. The townsfolk cannot deny his credentials and fame (v. 2). But they find fault with a teacher and healer whose family connections are only too well-known (v. 3). Jesus sums up this bitter

---

[30] It is the single thesis of Q. Quesnell's *tour de force*, *The Mind of Mark* [1969] that Mark's gospel is a sustained commentary, with the use of eucharistic symbolism, on the disciples' failure to appreciate the meaning and mystery of the bread-motif. The justification for viewing the entire gospel and its message through the prism of a single verse (6:52) is never proven by this author, whose method is thereby placed under suspicion. A similar attempt to see Mark's purpose through a single item of his gospel is made by Karl-Georg Reploh, *Markus—Lehrer der Gemeinde* [1969]. For him Mark's redaction of the *pericopes* relative to the disciples shows his chief interest, viz., to lead to true faith in the church of his own day.

[31] For a recent, full study of Mark's Passion teaching see G. Strecker, "The Passion and Resurrection Predictions in Mark's Gospel" *Interpretation* 21 [1968], pp. 421–42.

[32] See pp. 154ff.

[33] H.-D. Knigge, "The Meaning of Mark," *Interpretation* 22.1 [1968], pp. 69f.

contempt by a proverbial retort[34] that a prophet has no honour in his native place. It is part of his total destiny that his mission to the nation at large will meet with indifference and disregard (12:6–8).

(b) 9:19: his *cri de coeur*, "O faithless generation, how long am I to be with you? How long am I to bear with you?", rings true to what we learn of Mark's purpose in conveying the reality of Jesus' manhood, though the utterance at the same time places him on the divine side of the issue which has prompted this reaction. Jesus does not belong to the faithless generation he castigates. He stands over against it and sees it from God's viewpoint, in reminiscence of the divine indictment of Deuteronomy 32:5, 6, 20. Yet there is no petulance in the cry nor indignation untempered by sympathy and fellow-feeling. Above all, there is the deep suggestiveness that his stay on earth is fast running out as he moves irresistibly to the cross and to an acceptance of his destined lot.

(c) 10:39: his future will involve an acceptance of God's will in terms of human suffering and woe. This is the meaning of the metaphors, cup and baptism. Set on an unmistakable Old Testament canvas, these descriptive terms are powerful reminders of all the pain and sorrow of the human condition. Cf. Psalm 75:8: "For in the hand of the Lord there is a cup with foaming wine, well mixed . . . all the wicked of the earth shall drain it down to the dregs"; Isaiah 51:17ff.: "You who have drunk at the hand of the Lord the cup of his wrath, who have drunk to the dregs of the bowl of staggering"; Jeremiah 49:12: "If those who did not deserve to drink the cup must drink it, will you go unpunished?"; Ezekiel 23:31, 32: "You shall drink your sister's cup . . . . A cup of horror and desolation is the cup of your sister Samaria"; Psalms of Solomon 8:14: "He gives them to drink a cup of wine for drunkenness."

These verses tell their own tale; it is one of grief undergone as a judgment from God and a sorrow over sin.[35]

It is similar with the imagery of water as a symbol of overwhelming calamity in Psalms 42:7: "All thy waves . . . have gone over me"; 69:2: "I have come into deep waters," v. 15: "Let not the flood sweep over me."

These two metaphorical expressions relate to Jesus' forthcoming death. "He was thinking of his Passion when he used these metaphors,"[36] though it is also true that the whole of his messianic life was an acceptance of the human state, with the death at its climax.

---

[34] Cf. Gospel of Thomas, logion 31:

> No prophet is well received in his own town.
> The doctor does not cure those who know him.

For the second line, we may compare Luke 4:23.

[35] Not necessarily one of divine wrath. See M. Black, "The Cup Metaphor in Mark xiv 36" ExpT lix [1947–8], p. 195.

[36] V. Taylor, *Jesus and His Sacrifice* [1937], p. 98.

(d) 14:32–42: in the Gethsemane narrative the metaphor of the cup reappears with the background of his final refusal to tread any other path save that of complete filial obedience to God's plan. In his true human experience the "flesh" i.e. his human nature is weak and open to Satanic attack (v. 38). Hence the counsel to watchfulness and prayer in order that this may be repelled. But he will emerge as victorious, yet not without a struggle against this temptation. The concepts here are parallel with those features of the christology in the epistle to the Hebrews, especially 5:7f. If there is this link, we may recall how in that document much stress is laid on the frail humanity of Jesus and his exposure to temptation (2:14, 17–18; 4:14–16) as an encouragement to God's pilgrim people, the church.

The depth of the conflict in the garden is plumbed in the Markan version in one special way. Mark records the poignancy and realism of Jesus' agitation in the vivid language in 14:33: "He began to be greatly distressed and troubled." These two Greek verbs are strongly emphatic. "To be greatly distressed" (ἐκθαμβεῖσθαι) is peculiar to Mark (1:27; 9:15; 16:5f.). It is "suggestive of shuddering awe" (Rawlinson, *Commentary*, p. 211) or "terrified surprise" (Swete, *Commentary*, p. 342).[37] An adequate translation is hard to seek, as V. Taylor observes, for the word denotes "amazement amounting to consternation" (Taylor on 9:15).

The second verb (ἀδημονεῖν) describes "the distress which follows a great shock" (Swete, p. 342), and once more translation is not easy. The word has an original meaning in the sense of bewilderment.[38] Moffatt's rendering of "agitated" is the strongest to be observed.

The impact of the two verbs combined is incalculable and carries its own power to stab the reader wide awake. Having been led along the path to the Lord's final destiny, he is now forcefully reminded that Jesus faced the ordeal in full human consciousness of what it would cost in terms of his suffering and woe. The emotional quality of the words is considerable, as the NEB brings out: "He said to them, 'My heart is ready to break with grief'."

But something more than grief is involved. Lohmeyer's comment catches another dimension to the Gethsemane preview of the cross: "The Greek words depict the utmost degree of unbounded horror and suffering." V. Taylor rightly remarks on the insight the reader gains here into Mark's christology which is blocked by the absence of the terms from Luke and their modification and weakening in Matthew's version.[39]

---

[37] Swete explains: "Long as he had foreseen the Passion, when it came clearly into view its terrors exceeded his anticipations." But this psychologizing estimate goes beyond the evidence.

[38] W. Grundmann (*Kommentar* [1971], p. 291) however derives the verb from the component parts, meaning to be away from one's own home, to be lonely.

[39] V. Taylor, *Commentary*, p. 552. E. Lohmeyer, *op. cit.*, p. 314 is cited according to Taylor's

It is Jesus' human grief which weighs down his spirit, yet at a deeper level there is a truly human revulsion at the prospect of being implicated in human sin. And from that bitter experience he naturally recoils.

(e) In a final utterance "My God, my God, Why hast thou forsaken me?" (15:34) with the opening lines of Psalm 22 on his lips Jesus expired. This is a cry of spiritual anguish the depths of which may not be known. Not surprisingly some commentators shy away from an attempted interpretation and are silent on its meaning (e.g. Swete). This attitude is preferable to a rationalizing of the words as though Jesus were just beginning to recite the entire psalm and died before he got past the first verse. Equally to be refused is a minimizing exegesis which implies that Jesus only *felt* forsaken in a moment of extreme anguish.

V. Taylor candidly admits that "it is hard to see how the question (of whether the words imply a sense of abandonment) can be answered otherwise than by saying that they do involve that inference."[40] He goes on guardedly to insist that that sense of abandonment was real, without committing himself to any transactional theory of atonement read out of these awe-ful words. Whatever the dogmatic significance of these considerations may be, for Mark's purpose the application of Psalm 22:1 seems clear. Jesus' cry of forsakenness certifies the closeness of his identification with sinners as he is committed into their hands (14:41) and the reality of his destiny as one appointed by God to give his life a ransom for many (10:45). In all this horror of desolation Jesus is really man and cries out in momentary anguish.

From the standpoint of a strictly historical perspective it is possible to see yet another significance in these words from the cross. Admittedly Jesus dies as a man torn with anguish and immersed under a tide of separation from God. At the same time he clings to God and calls upon him in the darkness. The language, albeit borrowed from Psalm 22, is "*my God*," and professes a belief in God who is hidden in darkness. It may well be that the Markan church cherished this hard saying for precisely that reason. In the grim scene of the crucifixion, when Jesus was left alone by his friends and was given over to the cruelty and mockery of his tormentors he still retained his faith and made his appeal to God. though with a question and an anguished cry. To a church facing the darkness of persecution and loss this model of the Lord who still prayed and called upon God would bring a salutary comfort and hope.

(d) Human traits in the Gospel

Commentators are in the habit of referring to Mark's gospel as the

translation. There is a paraenetic application of these words of emotional perturbation aimed at showing Jesus' humanity and sympathy with a Christian community facing sudden persecution. So W. Grundmann, *Kommentar*, p. 292.

[40] V. Taylor, *Jesus and His Sacrifice*, p. 162; idem, *Commentary*, p. 594.

most realistic and vividly narrated of all the evangelical records. This estimate is true. With a working hypothesis of Mark's priority it becomes possible to demonstrate this feature of Markan style and content by a simple comparison with the corresponding versions in Matthew and Luke. If this is done, it is evident that the later writers have softened Mark's rugged manner of writing and have altered those parts of Mark which could be misunderstood because they describe too realistically a situation or sequence of events. An obvious example comes in the heart-cry of the disciples in the storm-tossed boat, "Teacher, do you not care if we perish?" (4:38). Matthew (8:25) has modified this cry which attributed an indifference to Jesus. It then becomes a plain statement of fact with no imputation of neglect: "Save, Lord; we are perishing"; similarly in Luke (8:24), "Master, Master, we are perishing!"[41]

We now draw attention to other passages in Mark where possibly the same process of embellishment has occurred in the later re-writing of the narrative by Matthew and Luke. These have to do with Mark's christology, and they are adduced as evidence that his christology is written in terms of the stark lineaments of Jesus' humanity.

(a) Human emotions are ascribed to Jesus, chiefly anger and indignation. The original reading at 1:41 was very probably "being angry" ($\dot{o}\rho\gamma\iota\sigma\theta\epsilon\dot{\iota}\varsigma$ attested in D a d ff^2 r^1)[42] which later scribes found embarrassing and so altered to "being compassionate" ($\sigma\pi\lambda\alpha\gamma\chi\nu\iota\sigma\theta\epsilon\dot{\iota}\varsigma$). Only on this supposition can the harder reading be explained, though strong emotion is attributed to Jesus in verse 43 and apparently this found an outlet in an explosive command to the leper.[43]

At 3:5 Jesus is described as looking round on the carping scribes who challenged his actions as a violation of the sabbath laws, and doing so "with anger" ($\mu\epsilon\tau'\dot{o}\rho\gamma\tilde{\eta}\varsigma$ a word used of the divine wrath expressed in opposition to evil), though tempered by his being grieved at their hardness of heart. These interfacing emotions—wrath at the scribes' judgmental attitude, yet sorrow over their hard hearts[44]—are peculiar to the Markan

---

[41] Mark's boldness is well brought out in Moffatt's translation: "Teacher, are we to drown, for all you care?" An indignant statement like this is either an instance of Mark's story-telling ability (to add verisimilitude to the tale) or more likely a genuine eyewitness reminiscence (so E. Schweizer, Commentary, p. 109). The querulousness of the cry would answer to a situation within a persecuted church when the storm of cruelty and savage treatment swept upon it. Then the issue of God's providence and care would be raised in the face of contradictory circumstances.

[42] V. Taylor, The Text of the New Testament [1961], pp. 82f.

[43] See V. Taylor, Commentary, p. 188 for a full discussion of translation problems over the verb $\dot{\epsilon}\mu\beta\rho\iota\mu\tilde{\alpha}\sigma\theta\alpha\iota$. He quotes J. H. Bernard's comment (ICC John, pp. 392f.) that the verb "represents the inarticulate sounds which escape men when they are physically overwhelmed by a great wave of emotion. And Jesus, the Perfect Man, experienced this as he experienced all else that is human and not sinful."

[44] Thus insensibility or obtuseness (Greek $\pi\dot{\omega}\rho\omega\sigma\iota\varsigma$) is characteristic of Israel's rejection of the Pauline mission, according to Romans 11:25.

record. Matthew and Luke both omit the two references, probably from an unwillingness to ascribe these emotions to Jesus (so V. Taylor).

And, still remarking on the vivid descriptions of Jesus' negative emotions in this gospel, we note 10:14: Jesus is indignant at the disciples for their rebuke of the mothers who brought their children for his blessing. The verb used is ἀγανακτεῖν = to be displeased to the point of anger. Only here in the gospel is the trait ascribed to Jesus, though the verb is found elsewhere of other people being roused to indignation. The reason for the indignation, of course, varies with the context, and it is noteworthy that, according to Mark, Jesus was moved to acute displeasure at the disciples' narrow thinking. "The disciples were busy men, who did not like to have their time wasted on receptions for children, when they and their Master should be getting on with the important business of the Kingdom of God (by which they meant high politics). Jesus tells them that they can learn the real nature of the Kingdom of God from these very children;"[45] and that they deserve a stinging rebuke for their pettiness and false notions about what really matters in life.

One other passage should be included in this short list. At 8:12 we have another inner revelation of Jesus' emotional life. Faced with the demand for a sign, he "sighed deeply in spirit," more in sorrow than in anger at the perversity of the Pharisees who tried to trap him in an argument and to force him to show his hand.[46] Again, the other synoptists omit this description in their versions.

(b) The rejection at Nazareth (6:1–6) is a section full of instruction for our purpose,[47] especially when set along the parallel accounts in Matthew (13:53–58) and Luke (4:16–30). The objection raised against Jesus by his townsfolk is expressed in the pointed question, "Is not this the carpenter, the son of Mary?" etc. Only here in the gospels is Jesus called ὁ τέκτων, a craftsman in wood, stone or metal. Later writers (e.g. Justin, Dial. 88) speak of him at work in the Nazareth workshop-home, making ploughs and oxen-yokes; and Hilary of Poitiers calls him a smith.

But these are romantic embellishments, presumably based on this verse or inferred from Matthew's parallel (13:55) which however calls him only "the carpenter's son." And it is interesting that Matthew's reading ὁ τοῦ τέκτονος υἱός is supported by the Chester Beatty papyrus P. 45 and family 13 as well as Origen who declares roundly that nowhere in the gospels current in his day is Jesus spoken of as a carpenter (Contra Celsum, vi. 36).[48]

---

[45] T. W. Manson, The Beginning of the Gospel [1950], p. 68.
[46] On this pericope, see later, pp. 165ff.
[47] Cf. R. H. Lightfoot, History and Interpretation in the Gospels [1935], pp. 182–205; T. A. Burkill, Mysterious Revelation [1963], pp. 137–40.
[48] C. S. C. Williams, Alterations to the Text of the Synoptic Gospels and Acts [1951], p. 30.

The matter is further complicated by the reading which omits the reference to Mary as Jesus' mother (so P. 45), probably in assimilation to Matthew 13:55. An easy solution[49] is to accept Origen's reading as the most primitive, "the son of the carpenter and Mary" and to explain the alteration which gives our present text as due to dogmatic tendencies which wanted to insert the idea of the virgin birth of Jesus. So only his Mother is mentioned, on that understanding. However, there are objections to this explanation. More likely is the suggestion that Origen deliberately preferred Matthew's version and championed the variant reading ὁ τοῦ τέκτονος υἱός—the carpenter's son—which he found in some Caesarean manuscripts. This would have in every way been acceptable to him over the Markan text which suggested that Jesus soiled his hands with manual labour as an artisan. It looks also as if the evangelist Matthew too was scandalized by this stark statement which he found in Mark and was the first commentator to do what Origen did later in the third century.

For a second reason the existing text in Mark would be a cause of offence. As it stands, it makes Jesus illegitimate. For to call someone the son of his mother in Eastern lands is to cast a slur on his true sonship. Ordinarily a person is known as the son of his father unless this stigma is intended.[50] And it is Tatian in his second-century Harmony of the Gospels who prefers the reading in Matthew on that account. As a semi-oriental he would be familiar with the Eastern suspicion of Jesus' paternity contained in Mark's account. Once Tatian had preferred Matthew, it would be natural for some later Markan MSS. to follow suit and become assimilated to the Matthean reading.

Our conclusion, therefore, is to maintain the primitiveness of Mark's text with its bold assertion that Jesus was a carpenter, and the scurrilous rumour put out by the Nazareth populace did cast an ugly slur at his origin. As a calculated insult—that he was base-born—it would damage his reputation, which otherwise they were compelled to admit (v. 2).

In such an atmosphere of suspicion and enmity it is not surprising that Jesus' mission was foredoomed to failure. But only Mark has the boldness to write up this failure in the language of verses 5, 6:

> He was not able to perform any mighty work there, except that he placed his hands on a few sick people and healed them. He was astonished at their unbelief.

It is indeed "one of the boldest statements in the Gospels, since it mentions something that Jesus could not do" (V. Taylor, op. cit., p. 301). Luke has left it out altogether (in Lk. 4:16–30) and Matthew (13:58) has re-cast

---

[49] Adopted by E. Klostermann, Das Markusevangelium [1950], p. 55.
[50] See E. Stauffer, "Jeschu ben Mirjam" in Neotestamentica et Semitica. Festschrift Matthew Black [1969], pp. 119ff.

the statement in such a way as to rob it of its forcefulness: "He did not do many mighty works there, because of their unbelief." His inability is omitted and the blanket declaration that Jesus performed no mighty work (δύναμις) is modified to remark only that he had a limited success at Nazareth.[51] In the face of a total lack of response it is small wonder that, in the Markan story, Jesus reacted with great astonishment. The counterpart of this reaction is the unmeasured enthusiasm at the Gentile's faith (Matt. 8:10, which has the same verb). Just as he appeared startled at the faith shown outside of Israel, so here at Nazareth and among his own people he is taken aback by their complete unresponsiveness and unbelief.

(c) The puzzle of the question, "Why do you call me good?" (10:18) has plagued many thoughtful readers of this gospel. Is Jesus dissociating himself from any claim to moral perfection? Is his statement, "No one is good but God alone" a tacit refusal to rank himself equal with God and so an admission that he is inferior? Neither question, provoked in some modern readers' minds, is really germane to Mark's purpose. Mark is not interested in discussing such Trinitarian questions nor does he record this question to teach about Jesus' person as a lesson in systematic theology. Probably the setting of the saying is a mild rebuke of the questioner who came up to Jesus hastily and tried to flatter him with a fulsome tribute: "Good Teacher . . ." Jesus calls him to sober reflection. What does the epithet "good" mean? It belongs to God who is good; and it should not be used unthinkingly or as a flippant gesture of praise.

Matthew in his account (19:16–17) evidently had problems with this retort, and has modified the entire dialogue by transposing the epithet into the theme of the questioner's search: "Teacher, what good deed must I do? . . . And he said to him, Why do you ask me about what is good?" Here I think we learn more about Matthew's redactional interest than about his embarrassment with Mark's problematic record;[52] and Luke has chosen to retain the Markan wording. Nonetheless Mark's account remains in its realistic assessment of Jesus on whose lips there may be put an apparent disavowal of goodness.

(d) The admission, attributed to Jesus (in 13:32), that "about that day or that hour no one except the Father knows, neither the angels in heaven nor the Son" has been an exegetical embarrassment from the beginning. Its trustworthiness as part of Jesus' teaching has been impeached partly on the ground that it seems to betray the very truth which an orthodox christology championed. So the phrase "not the Son" was dismissed

[51] E. C. Hoskyns and F. N. Davey, The Riddle of the New Testament [1931], p. 100.
[52] See R. P. Martin, "St. Matthew's Gospel in Recent Study," ExpT lxxx [1969],p.133 note. N. B. Stonehouse's full study of "The Rich Young Ruler" section in his book, Origins of the Synoptic Gospels [1963], pp. 93–112, concedes the point that Matthew has utilized Mark and has done so with considerable editorial freedom (p. 108).

as an interpolation inserted by the Arians to justify their position.[53] Or else the ignorance ascribed to the Son was explained away as a piece of make-believe. "He usefully pretended not to know";[54] or (more reasonably) it was contended that the text said no more than that the Son depended for his knowledge upon the Father's will.[55] A different line of interpretation was taken by Hilary of Poitiers[56] who ingeniously argued that the verse is really an indirect tribute to his divine knowledge, for he claims to know that no one else knows except God, and that claim puts him in a unique category.

But these examples are really vain efforts to avoid the obvious meaning of the text. Still less is to be said in favour of the view[57] that the *logion* was originally a Jewish proverb added at the end of a Jewish apocalypse (thought to close at 13:27). A Christian editor has supplied the words "neither the Son nor the Father."

The chief critical problem of 13:32, as W. G. Kümmel has noted[58] is not to be found in the statement that even Jesus does not know the time set for "the day," but in the mention of the "Son" alongside the "Father." The issue whether Jesus ever referred to himself as "the Son"—the word is also found in 12:6 but in a slightly different sense—must be postponed until a later section (p. 194; cf. p. 106). For our immediate purpose it is enough to direct attention to what the Markan verse says in the setting of chapter 13. The most straightforward reading of the text suggests that, for Mark, it means that, while the parousia is close at hand, its precise time is not known.[59] This concession is that "the Son" (an incontrovertible reference to Jesus, in Mark's mind; no other possibility is viable) does not know the item of information in question—with a probable reference back to the question of 13:4.[60] Mark has allowed this statement to stand in his redaction of the Little Apocalypse, and it is a tribute to his historical sense that he has so incorporated it; for it is part of his overall concern to emphasize the reality of the Lord's manhood. The corresponding verse in Matthew (24:36) probably omits the offensive term οὐδὲ ὁ υἱός (neither the Son);[61]

[53] So Ambrose, *De Fide* v. 16.

[54] Cyril of Alexandria, *Adv. Anthr.* xiv.

[55] Basil, *Ep.* 236.2 (cited by Swete, p. 316).

[56] Hilary, *De Trinit.* 356.9.9 (cited by C. E. Raven, *Apollinarianism* [1923], p. 96).

[57] R. Bultmann, *The History of the Synoptic Tradition* [ET, 1963], pp. 123, 125.

[58] W. G. Kümmel, *Promise and Fulfilment* [ET, 1957], p. 40.

[59] V. Taylor, *Commentary*, p. 523.

[60] So T. W. Manson, *The Teaching of Jesus*[2] [1935], p. 262 note 1.

[61] The textual evidence is divided. The preponderance of the testimony favours the inclusion of the words. But, as V. Taylor (*The Text of the New Testament*, p. 80) observes, the phrase is omitted in most Syriac MSS., i.e. in MSS. from the region in which Matthew was probably written. Also Matthew, in other places of his gospel, often avoids words which imply a limitation of Jesus' knowledge (e.g. Matt. 8:29) and would be the more likely to avoid a plain statement of it here, at 24:36. So A. H. McNeile, *St. Matthew* [1915], (p. 113, 356). Further, if Matthew himself omitted the phrase, his addition of μόνος to εἰ μὴ ὁ πατήρ may be intentional agreeing with Mark but not saying so explicitly. This is a cogent argument, and all but convinces that Matthew has dealt editorially with Mark in a way which

and it is not represented in Luke's version of the eschatological discourse. That leaves only Mark with the unmistakable statement of Jesus' ignorance, and it is further evidence of his endeavour to set before his readers a figure whose feet touched the ground and whose life shared human experience in a concrete historical setting.

But is that all? Is Mark's presentation given solely in terms of the historical man Jesus? It remains now for us to see the other side of the coin, and to lay our account with the paradox that this human figure is also a divine being, according to the full Markan testimony.

II. *The Christ of Faith and Mark's Numinous Christology*

Whatever the main thrust of the traditions which Mark the evangelist has taken over, there is no disputing the use to which he has put them in terms of his christological teaching. If one theme runs through his gospel from its initial title (1:1) to the declaration of the Roman centurion (15:39), that theme is concerned to promote the majesty and power of Jesus Christ the Son of God. The sonship of Jesus is "the inner guiding-line in Mark's presentation."[62]

Mark has arranged his material in such a way as to accentuate the hidden glory of Jesus, and at special points in his story he has made it clear to his readers that the otherwise human figure of Jesus is also and equally an other-wordly person whose "secret" is unshared and who is the object of heavenly revelations and more-than-human confessions. Mark's redactional principle is a thoroughly christological one, as the title-piece of his book makes clear.[63] It is time now to pass the major texts under review.

(*a*) 1:1 The textual question is open to discussion, but on balance the wide attestation of the full title, "Beginning of the gospel of Jesus Christ, *Son of God*" is a pointer in the direction of its originality. The omission of the last words (υἱοῦ θεοῦ) can most easily be explained by the accidental passing over of the scribe's eye from the similar-sounding endings of the previous two words ('Ιησοῦ Χριστοῦ). Moreover, with so many later references to the title in the gospel, it is not unexpected that Mark should

---

indicates he was not happy with Markan's realistic statement, found it embarrassing and dropped it, while wishing to conserve the truth that God alone has preserved the secret of the eschatological dénouement. *Per contra*, C. S. C. Williams (*Alterations to the Text of the Synoptic Gospels and Acts* [1951], p. 30) argues for the originality of Matthew's full text, submitting that later scribes deleted the difficult phrase out of reverential motives. What these motives were is discussed by B. H. Streeter, *The Four Gospels* [1924], pp. 594–97.

[62] So M. Albertz, *Die Botschaft des Neuen Testamentes* [i, 1947], p. 129; V. Taylor, *Commentary* p. 120: "Beyond question this title [Son of God] represents the most fundamental element in Mark's Christology."

[63] W. Grundmann, *Das Evangelium nach Markus* [1971], p. 11.

wish to place the full ascription of divine sonship as a frontispiece to his work.[64]

But the Markan doctrine of Jesus' heavenly origin is seen as much by the earlier part of his opening (verbless) title. To write the opening phrase as "beginning of" ($\dot{\alpha}\rho\chi\dot{\eta}$) is to strike a "miraculous note"[65] in conscious imitation of the sonorous opening of Genesis 1:1 in the Greek Bible ($\dot{\varepsilon}\nu$ $\dot{\alpha}\rho\chi\tilde{\eta}$). Mark, it is clear, is modelling his work on the Old Testament precedent, and intends the reader to catch the profound thought that *his* book is a new Genesis with a declaration of good news now to be told with the advent of God's Son. The opening verse is Mark's *confessio fidei*.

At special points the historical narrative is punctuated with transcendental messages which are introduced unmistakably to convey to the reader the evidence of Jesus' supernatural origin. E. Lohmeyer writes of the total effect of these episodes: "The Son of God is not primarily a human but a divine figure . . . he is not merely endowed with the power of God, but is himself divine as to his nature; not only are his word and work divine, but his essence also."[66]

The chief points in the story where this divine intervention occurs are as follows:

(*b*) 1:11

"And a voice came from heaven,
'Thou art my beloved Son; with Thee
I am well pleased'."

Though as to its *form*, this short section is to be classified as a biographical story or "story about Christ" (Bornkamm's nomenclature),[67] the categories used in the story of the baptism are taken from the world of Hebraic thought. The mode of religious initiation through the use of water, the opening of the heavens (Isa. 64:1), the descent of the Spirit as the accompaniment of Jesus' emergence from the water (cf. Isa. 63:11, 14)[68] and the symbolism of the dove (referring to Israel in the Old Testament; Hos. 11:11; Pss. 68:13; 74:19; 54:7 (LXX) and rabbinic literature)[69] —all these features are understandable only on a Jewish background. The mention of the heavenly voice (in verse 11) takes us back to the Jewish

---

[64] See some judicious discussion of the evidence in C. E. B. Cranfield, *Commentary*, p. 38; also N. B. Stonehouse, *The Witness of Matthew and Mark to Christ* [1944], pp. 13f. who cites Lohmeyer, C. H. Turner and R. H. Lightfoot as all accepting the longer reading, attested in Alexandrian and Western authorities as by important Caesarean manuscripts. V. Taylor, *The Text of the New Testament* [1961], p. 82 prints the evidence.

[65] Lohmeyer's term, *Kommentar*, p. 10.

[66] Lohmeyer, *Kommentar*, p. 10 (as quoted by Stonehouse, *op. cit.*, p. 13).

[67] Bultmann uses the category "biographical or faith legend" but this is objectionable as pre-judging the question of historicity. See *History of the Synoptic Tradition*, pp. 247ff.

[68] See I. Buse, "The Markan Account of the Baptism of Jesus and Isaiah LXIII," JTS 7 [1956], pp. 74f.

[69] Midr. *Cant.* 1:15 (93b); 2:14 (101a).

idea that when God speaks in heaven, his voice—the daughter of a voice, the rabbis said—is heard on earth.[70] Some solemn announcement is anticipated as the content of the heavenly voice; here the Father's witness to the Son is clear: "Thou art my beloved Son: with thee I am well pleased." The theophany is a striking concurrence of Old Testament terms. The royal son of the coronation psalm (Ps. 2:7) is combined with Isaiah's servant (Isa. 42:1)[71] and a third element is introduced if those interpreters are correct who see in the ascription "My beloved (ἀγαπητός) Son" a veiled designation of Jesus as the second Isaac, since the language recalls the description of Abraham's son in Genesis 22:2.[72] The exalted background of these titles and the way in which Mark is able to run them together into a pattern which dazzles and excites us (as it must have done his first readers whose close acquaintance with the Old Testament scripture he presupposes from start to finish of his gospel)[73] are tokens of his purpose to present Jesus as the heavenly Man on earth. But the vision is limited to Jesus alone (cf. Luke 3:21, 22; John 1:32–34); only he hears the voice. So we should more correctly say that in Mark's presentation Jesus is the *God-man incognito*.[74] His baptism marks the inauguration of his office.

(c) 1:12, 13. Two verses emphasize Jesus' office as a Man possessed by the Spirit and victor over Satan. Mark knows no explicit detail of the Temptation story such as Matthew and Luke record in full. He gives the bare facts, but his interest lies elsewhere in remaining content with the minimum of narrative.[75] He stresses that Jesus is impelled by the Spirit to the place of testing and (by inference) that he emerged victorious

---

[70] For the rabbinic teaching on *bath qol* see I. Abraham, *Studies in Pharisaism and the Gospels*: First series [1917], pp. 47f. Two examples of Jewish ideas are interesting. *Sanhedrin* 11a explains the idea in terms of an echo: "as when a man strikes a powerful blow and a second sound is heard." In *Berakoth* 3a it is compared to the moaning of a dove.

[71] See W. Zimmerli and J. Jeremias, *The Servant of God* [ET, 1957], pp. 80ff.

[72] See G. Vermes, *Scripture and Tradition in Judaism* [1961], pp. 222f. Recent studies have capitalized on this element, e.g. N. Hillyer, "The Servant of God," EQ 41 [1969], pp. 143–160 and I. H. Marshall, "Son of God or Servant of Yahweh? A Reconsideration of Mark i. 11," NTS 15 [1965], pp. 326–36 who forcefully maintains that the language of the heavenly proclamation addressed to God's Son "goes beyond a purely functional or messianic use of the title by the use of the qualifying adjective ἀγαπητός which indicates the unique relationship of Jesus to his Father" (p. 336). See also J. E. Wood, "Isaac Typology in the New Testament", NTS 14 [1968], pp. 583–9.

[73] See A. Suhl, *Die Function der alttestamentlichen Zitate und Anspielungen im Markusevangelium* [1965] who discusses the purpose of Mark's use of the Old Testament in his prologue and shows how Mark sees its purport as a prophecy of the Baptist, the herald of Jesus (*op. cit.*, pp. 133–37).

[74] To use S. Schulz's term, *Die Stunde der Botschaft*[2] [1970], p. 46.

[75] Possibly Mark wished to show how Jesus faced satanic temptation (the verb πειράζειν meaning to "test" is frequent in Mark) throughout his ministry and so passes over the critical nature of the initial testing and victory. See further on his use of verb "to test," pp. 168f. and B. Gerhardsson, *The Testing of God's Son (Matt. 4, 1–11 par)* [1966]. H. D. Betz, "Jesus as Divine Man," *Jesus and the Historian*, ed. F. T. Trotter [1968], p. 119 sees in Mark's abbreviated version a polemic against the understanding of the "Son of God" as *theios aner* (divine man) exempted from trial and suffering.

because Satan is powerless before the royal Man. In words which recall Adam as king of paradise Jesus is in the company of the wild beasts and served by the attendance of angels.[76]

The demonic world is stirred to frenzied activity and opposition as it encounters the presence of Jesus the exorcist and liberator (1:23–28; 5:1–20; 7:24–31; 9:14–29). Yet there is no open acknowledgment of him as heavenly Man since this "confession" in 3:11 and 5:7 is checked as part of the Markan messianic secret. The demons which recognize that he is none other than God's holy one (1:24)[77] are cautioned to silence (1:34; 3:11). The disciples fail to recognize who he is—at least until the Markan watershed of 8:27ff. Then a glimmer of light breaks and the complementary narrative of the transfiguration shows Jesus in his full radiance. But the real meaning of both stories, the confession of Peter at Caesarea Philippi (8:27ff.) and the Transfiguration (9:1–8), is closely related and can only be seen in the light of the continuing misunderstanding of the disciples and the ongoing satanic struggle.

(d) At Caesarea Philippi (8:27–33)[78] Peter utters the confession, You are the Messiah, and is enjoined to silence. If an explanation is sought for this command, the simplest expedient will be to suggest that Peter like the demons in the earlier part of the story has no understanding of what Jesus' true office is. "Holy one of God" suggests a charismatic figure (so F. Hahn); Peter's mind is filled with ideas which refuse to include Jesus' call to suffering and by inference, we may conclude that his notion of Messiahship was one about which Jesus entertained the utmost reserve. Hence the episode of 8:32–34, which sets Peter's understanding of Jesus the Messiah on the side of Satan who seeks to sidetrack Jesus (Matt. 4:8–10; Lk. 4:5–8) and of men who think of authority in terms of earthly power and lordship (10:42), is a necessary part of the whole incident.

Nor is the situation much improved as far as the clearing away of misunderstanding is concerned when Mark goes on to relate the Transfiguration story (9:1–8). Again, it is Peter who perceives that Jesus is worthy to be revered and placed in an exalted position alongside the two patriarchs both of whom escaped to the heavenly world in a glorious manner.[79] If the setting of the Transfiguration scene is laid near the celebration of the feast of Tabernacles,[80] it may be supposed that nationalist feelings were running high and that implied in Peter's remark is the

---

[76] F. H. Borsch, *The Son of Man in Myth and History* [1967], p. 279.

[77] For this title, see F. Hahn, *The Titles of Jesus in Christology* [ET, 1969], pp. 231–4 who cites and criticizes G. Friedrich's view (ZThK 53 [1956], pp. 265–311) that Jesus as vanquisher of demons is performing a rôle expected of the messianic high priest (Test. Levi 18:12 etc.).

[78] A recent but radical attempt to solve some of the problems in this *pericope* is that by E. Dinkler, "Peter's Confession and the 'Satan' Saying," *The Future of our Religious Past. Essays in honour of Rudolf Bultmann* ed. J. M. Robinson [1971], pp. 169–202.

[79] See later pp. 171ff.

[80] This is H. Baltensweiler's thesis, based on his interpretation of the dating (rare in Mark) of verse 1 and the imagery of verse 3: see *Die Verklärung Jesu* [1959].

Zealot call to lead God's people against their enemies (so Elijah) and to freedom (as Moses had done). Then it is possible to make some sense of Mark's strange wording in verse 6: "For he did not know what he should answer" (τί ἀποκριθῇ). Strictly taken, this statement suggests that there was a rebuke implied in the narrative, and Peter is dumbfounded and unable to respond. Could it be that Jesus once more rebuked him for his crassly worldly ideas and a Satanically-inspired summons that he should lead an army to battle and so gain his glory *in that way*? If so, the implied rebuke would agree with Mark's general style of writing which "never introduces the Apostle to the circumcision for any individual part without making him the target for severe reproof and condemnation."[81] At all events, the sentence is puzzling and is omitted by Matthew (17:4) and altered by Luke (9:33).

As though to raise the disciples' thoughts to a higher level, the divine voice is heard out of the cloud, "This is my beloved Son; listen to him" (9:7) and Jesus is seen to hold the stage in solitary splendour (verse 8). But the close proximity of the following *pericope* is important (9:9ff.), for it shows that in Mark's mind Jesus the heavenly Son was not only unpersuaded by Peter's remonstrance to accept a road to earthly glory; he was equally unwilling to step up to an immediate acclaim by having the disciples proclaim what they had seen—at least until the Son of man were risen, a terminal point in Mark which is unique. This has suggested to some interpreters that the Transfiguration is a story re-told in the light of the Easter glory in which the risen Lord was bathed. But this latter suggestion is unnecessary, once it is seen that for Mark there could be no true glory for Christ the Lord except he first tread the pathway of obedience. And that obedience as God's loyal Son and faithful servant would entail an acceptance of the road down from the mountain and on towards Jerusalem. The destiny of the Son of man at the end of that road is no secret; already Elijah, his precursor, had met his fate in the person of John. The Son of man can expect no less (9:11–13).

(e) 15:39. The centurion who was standing in front of him, seeing that he expired thus, said, Truly this man was the son of God!

The sequence of the section which records this cry should be noted. The Roman authorities, in Mark's account of the trial and execution of Jesus, are presented in a neutral light. Pilate, in particular, is viewed as a man caught in a very difficult position. The Jews, on the other hand, are the villains (15:11, 13, 15) and represent a pressure group which exerts a baneful influence on the procurator, who knows full well how they are motivated (15:10, 14).

The tragedy, painted in sombre colours by this evangelist, moves to its close with the chief theme—that Jesus is the royal Messiah, incriminated

---

[81] B. W. Bacon, *Is Mark a Roman Gospel?* [1919], p. 76.

by the Jewish leaders and so branded as a rebel against the empire—picked up in the soldiers' mockery (15:16–20).

At the scene of the cross, the same charge is levelled at him as that which had been brought against him in Caiaphas' court (14:61, 64). Only now it is couched in the form of a mocking taunt: "Let the Messiah, Israel's King, come down from the cross, that we may see and believe him" (15:32) The Jews are hostile to the last, while the Romans maintain a reserved impartiality, passively acquiescing in an ugly situation.

In fact, passivity turns to a more positive attitude as Mark records the interlude of the kindly centurion. Some anticipation of a friendly Roman gesture may be seen in verse 36 if the drink of "vinegar" offered to Jesus was really the soldiers' *posca*, a mixture of sour wine and egg with water drunk by Roman soldiers on duty. But the centurion's rôle goes much further, as part of Mark's overall intention to present the Romans in a uniformly good light.

On this soldier's lips is placed the early Christian confession, hailing Jesus as God's Son (cf. Rom. 1:4; 1 Thess 1:10; Acts 8:37 in the Western text; 1 John 5:5: these are all credal passages). To be sure, the Greek of Mark's text lacks the definite article, but the absence of the article before the word rendered "son" is no proof that the statement should be understood in an indefinite sense.[82] The evangelist evidently intended that the confession on the soldier's lips should represent the first fruits of Gentile Christianity,[83] and sought to offset the total Jewish rejection of the Messiah by the hint and promise that the outlook for Gentile evangelism in the Roman world is full of hope and prospect.

These are the several places where the honorific title "Son of God" or its equivalent as royal Man or heavenly King occurs in the Markan text. A good case could be made out for the belief that they are all editorially significant and are placed by the evangelist at crucial points in his story. Obviously 1:1 stands at the important place of his title to the ensuing book, and is meant to describe the contents of what follows. The Markan version of the ministry emphasizes Jesus as a Man of the Spirit, possessed with charismatic power ($\delta\acute{v}\nu\alpha\mu\iota\varsigma$, though $\grave{\epsilon}\xi o v\sigma\acute{\iota}\alpha$ is Mark's more characteristic term—1:22, 27; 2:10; 3:15; 6:7; 11:28–33[84]) and a claimant to messianic dignity.

[82] See E. C. Colwell, "A Definite Rule for the Use of the Article in the Greek New Testament," JBL 52 [1933], pp. 12–21, for the rule that "definite predicate nouns which precede the verb usually lack the article" (p. 20).

[83] So M. Dibelius, *From Tradition to Gospel* [ET, 1935], p. 195: "The first Gentile was converted and in his word the Gentiles give their answer to the death of Jesus." But there have been anticipations of Gentile conversion earlier in Mark (5:20; 7:26–30, 31–36).

[84] For that reason, viz. that in Mark's presentation Jesus' authority ($\grave{\epsilon}\xi o v\sigma\acute{\iota}\alpha$ Heb. *rešut*) is more related to his messianic work than to a characterization of him a hellenistic "divine man" ($\theta\epsilon\~\iota o\varsigma$ $\grave{\alpha}\nu\acute{\eta}\rho$), H. D. Betz's summing up of the pre-Markan tradition as containing a "Divine Man Christology" in which Jesus does superhuman feats by reason of his $\delta\acute{v}\nu\alpha\mu\iota\varsigma$ may be questioned; and with this questioning would go a doubt as to Mark's revision of a Divine Man christology. See Betz, *loc. cit.*, pp. 116, 122, 123.

His teaching carries the ring of authority, as Mark makes clear by such indications as Jesus' right to displace the Torah of Moses and to act unilaterally (1:27; 2:28; 3:4; 10:5-12). He invests his own death with an atoning significance (10:45) and promises that the sacrifice of his life will seal a covenant between God and man (14:22). The inference is that he has come to replace the Sinaitic compact with a new order to be celebrated at a new Passover. Moreover, he looks beyond death to a resumption of relations with his own in a perfected kingdom of God (14:25; 28:16:7). That death and its vindication by God will not be forgotten (14:9).

In these specific areas the Markan Jesus carries a numinous aura.

(a) *He calls men to follow him*. It is a well-known feature of the gospel tradition that in the opening of Jesus' public work he summoned disciples to leave all and to attach themselves to him (1:16ff., 2:13ff.). He appointed twelve to be with him as his companions (3:14);[85] to them he delegated his authority—a trait which is unique to Mark,[86] as though he wished to emphasize the originality and importance of this creation of the Twelve who became an extension of Jesus' messianic work as they perform exorcisms in his name (9:38). Jesus calls them "my disciples" (14:14) and the Twelve are recognized as having a distinct (9:18) if not exclusive (9:38–40) attachment to Jesus.

The closeness of the bond between Jesus and his chosen followers is a matter of unusual significance. Attention is called to it by E. Schweizer[87] who writes, "This concept of discipleship is Jesus' own creation . . . . The primary difference is that the rabbi does not call his disciples—he is sought by them . . . . Above all, the rabbis never could have conceived of a call so radical as to make clear that being with Jesus is more important than all of God's commandments . . . . A disciple of a rabbi might dream of some day becoming even better, if possible, than his master; but a disciple of Jesus could never expect that some day he himself might be the 'Son of Man.' Jesus never debates with his disciples as a rabbi would have done. Thus the word 'follow' received a new sound when Jesus said it" since it is a call comparable with the summons, Follow Yahweh, in the Old Testament (1 Kings 18:21). To this may be added one additional feature,[88] viz. that Jesus imperiously decides who shall and shall not be called to follow him, even to the point of refusing (5:19) as well as claiming men for his service (10:21).

[85] On the significance of the verb "appointed" (ἐποίησεν) Lohmeyer's comment (*Kommentar*, p. 74) that the sense is "he created" by doing this new thing is important. The verb is also used in LXX for the appointment of men to God's service; here it is envisaged that Jesus is creating a nucleus of a new community of Israel.

[86] "Mark alone mentions in this context that Jesus was to confer upon the Twelve his own Messianic powers", E. J. Mally in *The Jerome Biblical Commentary* [1968], §42.22).

[87] *The Good News according to Mark = Commentary* [ET, 1970], p. 49.

[88] It is hinted at in Schweizer's commentary (German edit. p. 26 in a reference which is not represented in the ET).

This total attitude certifies Jesus' authority. He boldly innovates a new type of relationship, of which the rabbinic "master-pupil" model is only dimly adequate as a precedent. Rather, in his way of calling men, what he pledged to make them and his expectation of them, he showed that he is their Lord who can command them to follow him even to the point of suffering, shame and death (8:34–9:1; 10:29, 30, 35–40; 13:9–13; 14:27). In a phrase which almost all commentators recognize as editorial Jesus is made to refer to these men as "belonging to the Messiah" (9:41), that is, men over whom the Messiah extends his control and who represent him.

The disciples respond to this relationship by their acceptance of his sovereign call and their yielding to his claims. But the response is limited by their ignorance, blindness and fickle obedience. Nonetheless they are shown to be at least partially aware of the true stature of Jesus, especially in such a section as 4:35–41. Their fear at the perilous storm is replaced by a different kind of fear which seizes them once the waves and wind have abated. Then they exchange the question, Who then is this, for even wind and sea obey him? This is the fear of the divine presence, the realization on man' part that he is a finite creature confronted by his creator. Jesus' control of the unruly elements betokens his victory—which is God's victory—over all hostile, demonic forces in the universe; and the disciples shrink back before this Man in whose presence and authoritative word they instinctively recognize the *mysterium tremendum* of Yahweh, Lord of creation.[89]

Of more significant interest to Mark's first readers would be the Old Testament picture of sleep in the midst of upheaval as a token of perfect trust in the sustaining and protective care of God (as we have noted earlier, p. 111). And when Yahweh seemed to be "asleep" i.e. inactive, in the face of his people's danger, he would be invoked to "awake" (Pss. 44:23f.; 35:23; 59:4 and Isa. 51:9). To the church in Mark's day, threatened by persecution and fearful of the outcome, the reassuring and commanding word of its unseen Lord (given in full in Mark, 'Peace be still') would come home with special relevance. See P. J. Achtemeier, "Person and Deed. Jesus and the Storm-tossed Sea," *Interpretation* 16 [1962], pp. 169–176.

(b) Jesus is *portrayed as the possessor of supernatural knowledge* and gifted with perception which enabled him to read the secrets of men and demons. The material in question is:

[89] Ability to control the sea and subdue tempests is a characteristic sign of divine power (Pss. 89:8, 9; 93:3, 4; 106:8, 9; Isa. 51:9, 10). The nearest parallel to the Markan text is Psalm 107:23–30. In the background of these O.T. texts lies the imagery of the monster "chaos" (Heb. $t^e h \hat{o}m$: for this background see G. von Rad, *Theology of the Old Testament* i [ET, 1962], pp. 150ff.) subdued by the powerful God, in near eastern thought. For the adaptation of this piece of cosmology made by the writers of the Old Testament, see F. F

(i) 2:8   Then Jesus perceived in/by his spirit that they were debating like this within/among themselves, and said to them . . .

(ii) 5:32   He looked about to see [the woman] who had done this, i.e. touched him and received the healing virtue which, he knew, had flowed from him (v. 30).

(iii) 5:39   "The girl has not died, she is asleep," and may be awakened from the state of death which she has entered according to the report of the synogogue officers (v. 35).

(iv) 6:48   The language of Jesus' coming to the disciples in the boat is that of a divine epiphany. He sees their distress and comes to their aid; but this is described in such a way by Mark that the advent of divine presence is unmistakably suggestive of God's drawing near to men in numinous power (Job 9:8, 11; cf. Ps. 77:19; Job 38:16; Isa. 43:16; Ecclus. 24:5). Not unnaturally the disciples react in terror at what they think to be an other-worldly spectre (v. 49).

(v) 8:16   Jesus is aware that the disciples are discussing together the problem of their forgetfulness to take provisions on board, before they tell him.

(vi) 9:4   The appearances of Elijah and Moses on the mountain cause no problem for Jesus who converses with them.

(vii) 9:33   His question concerning the reason for the disciples' debate on the road is meant to lead to a teaching on the meaning of greatness. He knows already that they are confused over this question.

(viii) 11:2, 3, 6   Jesus has foreknowledge of the availability of the colt and of how the disciples are to explain his need of the animal.

(ix) 11:14   His prophecy of the fig-tree is best interpreted as a veiled personal statement with the word of Jesus meaning, "I will not eat fruit from the tree," i.e. the *eschaton* will have occurred before the harvest[90] and my life will not survive until them. If this is correct, it is a mark of Jesus' prescience about his own future.

(x) 12:9   This gives another example of how Jesus foresaw the future. This time it is the more distant scene, as in

Bruce, "'Our God and Saviour': A Recurring Biblical Pattern" in *The Saviour God*. E. O. James Festschrift, ed. S. G. F. Brandon [1963], pp. 53ff.
    [90] So H.-W. Bartsch, "Die 'Verfluchung' des Feigenbaums," ZNTW 53 [1962], pp. 256–60.

parabolic-allegorical fashion, he warns that rejection of the vineyard owner's claims will bring disasters in its train and the owner "will come and destroy the farmers and will give the vineyard to others" (v. 9). Judgment upon faithless Israel is the theme here, with a clear (if unspecified) prediction that Israel's ruin will follow in the wake of her rejection of God's overtures and the sending of his son.

(xi) 13:1ff. The same theme is elaborated in much fuller detail and with greater scope in the Markan apocalypse.[91] The evangelist's evident purpose in this chapter is to depict Jesus as cognizant of apocalyptic events. The setting of verses 3–8 deepens the reader's interest in Jesus' office as *Apokalyptiker*. The earlier verses (1, 2) are more in the prophetic tradition as Jesus foretells the destruction of the Temple, even if that event is a token of the nation's collapse and the Parousia.[92]

At verse 3, however, the scene changes and Jesus is found seated (in the posture of a teacher)[93] on the Mount of Olives—not surely only a geographical detail but a traditional place (Zech. 14) from which the secrets of the end-time will be disclosed.[94] Moreover, the disclosure is made to a select group of disciples (v. 3) and proceeds by the use of terms which are drawn from the technical vocabulary of apocalyptic literature, e.g. "to be accomplished" [v. 4];[95] "the beginning of woes" [v. 8].

Verses 5–23 are a catalogue of signs which will presage the end-time, with a heavy concentration on the theme of the church's sufferings and persecution. The critical time of opposition, however, gives unprecedented opportunity for the church to be faithful and active in witness (v. 10); for in the interim before the Parousia there is a call to patience and to fidelity (v. 13). A pastoral purpose runs through this section, for as Cranfield remarks, "the purpose (of Jesus' words) is not to pass on esoteric information but to strengthen and sustain faith".[96]

---

[91] The use by Mark of an apocalyptic source is shown in R. Pesch's *Naherwartungen. Tradition und Redaktion in Mk* 13 [1968]. A pre-Markan exposition of Daniel which the evangelist has drawn upon is postulated by L. Hartman, *Prophecy Interpreted* [1966]. The history of interpretation prior to the advent of Redaction-criticism is given by G. R. Beasley-Murray, *Jesus and the Future* [1954].

[92] So G. Schrenk, TDNT iii p. 245 (I owe this reference as well as much that follows to the illuminating articles by C. E. B. Cranfield, "St. Mark 13," SJT 6 [1953], pp. 189–96, 287–303, 7 [1954], pp. 284–303).

[93] See C. Schneider, TDNT iii, pp. 443–7.

[94] Lohmeyer, *Kommentar*, p. 268.

[95] συντελεῖσθαι is "almost a technical term for the happenings of the end-time" (Lohmeyer, *op. cit.*, p. 269).

[96] C. E. B. Cranfield, *art. cit.*, p. 196.

Verses 24–27 talk of cosmic signs which portend the Parousia of the Son of man, and the language and imagery are drawn from the Old Testament. The main point of this section is to stress that *then*—at the Parousia—what has been hidden will be openly revealed. The Son of man who is at present an incognito, veiled figure will be shown to be one full of power as he comes to gather his chosen.

The final section (verses 28–37) is couched in the form of *Mahnrede*, i.e. warnings and instructions to maintain the watchful spirit lest the Parousia comes to surprise those who should be ready to greet it. The purpose of the premonitory signs is that the disciples will not be caught unawares but rather be ready to expect an imminent Parousia of the Son of man.

Throughout this entire block which is the longest section of Jesus' teaching in this gospel the stress falls on Jesus' concern to prepare his disciples, to forewarn them of what lies ahead, and to encourage them not to lose heart (over their sufferings) or to become lax (because of a delay in the return of their Lord). The exact hour of that return is a secret to which even the Son has no access (v. 32), but he knows *that* fact and can thereby warn his own that, once the signs begin to appear, then they should be ready to welcome the returning Son of man (vv. 35–37). Above all, there is a call to faithfulness to present tasks (v. 10) and duties (v. 34). Aside from the practical intent of Mark's transmission of these apocalyptic words there is his great objective (which in turn would inspire his readers, whom he has his eye on directly, v. 14). This is to present Jesus as Lord of history and as one in control of all events which may bring trouble to the church. Believers should in no way be startled or dispirited by what they see and have to endure. Their Lord has foretold these things. Better still, he will be with them in the Holy Spirit (v. 11). "What does the Exalted One do in the intermediate period? He strengthens those who confess him under persecution."[97]

(c) The third sector of Markan interest in which he displays Jesus as possessing superhuman powers is, of course, *in his transmission of the miracle-stories*.

It is customary in recent discussion to classify these stories as pre-Markan *pericopes* in which Jesus is depicted after the model of a hellenistic divine man.[98] The evangelist is thought to have taken over these stories which proclaim Jesus as a wonderworking hero, with their emphasis on his impressive presence and power to exorcize and heal. In their pre-Markan form they function as proofs of his divine nature which is seen by his

[97] H. Conzelmann, *An Outline of the Theology of the New Testament* [ET, 1969], p. 141.
[98] See one notable treatment in H. D. Betz, *loc. cit.*, pp. 120ff. and now T. J. Weeden, *Mark—Traditions in Conflict* [1971], passim.

performing miracles.[99] Not willing to accept this characterization of Jesus Mark is imagined to have edited the stories chiefly by showing how ambiguous this presentation of Jesus as the miracle-monger was (and is); and by placing all the weight of his emphasis on the kerygma of the death and resurrection of Jesus as the only legitimate route by which he could be exalted in power Mark has subtly modified the purpose of the miracle-stories.

An alternative proposal to this bisecting of Mark's material into a pre-Markan segment (which then becomes anti-Markan because it is thought to contain a false theology from the evangelist's viewpoint, against which he then polemicizes) and a Markan editing and adaptation, may be offered. The evangelist's purpose may be conceived more in terms of demonstrating how Jesus' true being and nature were recognized by demonic powers (but with no hint of their allegiance) and, at another end of the scale, by unlikely characters in the drama. Most poignantly the very persons nearest to Jesus in the family circle (3:31–35; 6:1–6), by ethnic grouping and religious affiliation (the Pharisees, 3:6; 7:1–13; 12:1–12, etc.) and by his own choosing and design (the disciples) were uncomprehending and hostile. Jesus' secret remains undisclosed save to sympathetic perceptiveness and genuine interest born of real need. The demons react forcefully—and are rebuked. The disciples blunder into a confession of his messiahship which has connotations he does not own. But to a wayside beggar (10:46–52), a troubled woman (7:24–30) and a rough Roman soldier (15:39) the secret is partially made known. It remains now to consider the miracle-stories.

He performs deeds of power by overcoming disease, demons and death (1:29–31, 40–45; 2:1–12; 3:1–6; 5:25–34; 7:31–37; 8:22–26; 10:46–52 for Jesus' power over human infirmity and disease. He exorcizes and expels demons—1:23–28; 5:1–20; 7:24–31; 9:14–29. He conquers death—5:21–24, 35–43).[100] And these mighty acts elicit a tribute to who he is, notably at

3:11 "When the unclean spirits saw him they prostrated themselves before him and cried out, 'You are the Son of God'"; and

5:7 The Gerasene demoniac "shouting in a loud voice said, Why are you interfering with me, Jesus, Son of the Most High God?"

Both incidents are better interpreted as a recognition of Jesus' power as hidden Messiah who "binds the strong man" (3:27)[101] than as the work of

---

[99] For a recent example of a strictly literary analysis see P. J. Achtemeier, "Toward the isolation of pre-Markan miracle catenae," JBL 89 [1970], pp. 265–291. And on the deeper issue of the type of theology represented in such a putative "miracle-source," see K. Kertelge, Die Wundergeschichte im Markusevangelium [1971], pp. 170ff.

[100] Betz, loc. cit., pp. 117f.; S. Schulz, Die Stunde der Botschaft, pp. 64ff.

[101] L. E. Keck, "Mark 3:7–12 and Mark's Christology," JBL 84 [1965], pp. 341–58.

a hellenistic wonder-worker. The Jewish Messiah fulfils his rôle as vanquisher of Satan and destroyer of demonic power which holds the Gentiles captive (1 Kings 18:40).[102] But in neither case is there general recognition, and the confession of Jesus' person is concealed from public notice. The disciples who stand closer to Jesus are impressed by his wonderful works (4:41) and raise the question, Who then is this? But no explicit answer is forthcoming until Caesarea Philippi when again elements of misunderstanding enter into Peter's response (8:32, 33). Not even the final entry into Jerusalem (11:1-10) gives away the secret of Jesus' person, since in Mark's version the cry of Hosanna is related to the coming kingdom and does not directly designate Jesus as Davidic King (verse 9; cf. Luke 11:38; Matt. 21:9; John 12:13).

The mystery of Jesus' person remains up to the end. A partial glimpse is seen in the record of the centurion's cry, but this is no more than a token and a promise of greater things to come. In any case it coheres with Mark's concern to show how Israel failed to perceive the Messiah as God's Son and the disciples remain blind and misguided in their understanding of Jesus' messiahship. Unlikely people, such as the woman at Bethany (14:3-9), Bartimaeus the beggar (10:46-52), the Gentiles (7:24-37) achieve an anticipated understanding of Jesus and his mission,[103] but the full revelation awaits the resurrection and the return of Jesus to his own (16:7). Significantly this gospel ends on a note which has characterized it throughout—the element of uncertainty and trembling in the presence of the numinous. The women at the tomb (16:8) are gripped by an emotion of quaking and panic as they leave the tomb in great fear.[104]

In summary, Dibelius' famous expression that Mark has written "a book of the secret epiphanies of Jesus" is amply justified.[105] If this body of data were alone characteristic of Mark's gospel and remained uncomplemented by all that we have tried to show as equally characteristic in terms of Jesus' earthliness and the *bruta facta* of his humanity, then there would be some ground for E. Käsemann's conclusion that for Mark "the life history of Jesus becomes almost the subject of a mystery play."[106] As it is, the counterpoise of Jesus' earthly existence which Mark witnesses

[102] H. Sahlin, "Die Perikope vom gerasenischen Besessenen und der Plan des Markusevangeliums," *Studia Theologica* 18 [1964], pp. 159-172. He holds the story to be a midrash on Isaiah 65:1-5 offered for the sake of depicting Jesus as the Saviour and Deliverer of the Gentiles.

[103] See later pp. 206ff.

[104] If 16:8a: "for they were afraid" (ἐφοβοῦντο γάρ) is the intended ending of the gospel as many think, it closes on a climactic note, emphasizing the same numinous quality which has characterized Mark's presentation of the person of Jesus. The strong language of verse 8 ("quaking and panic seized them") as well as Mark's characteristic word ("fear", φόβος) suggests that this may well be so. See R. H. Lightfoot, *The Gospel Message of St. Mark* [1950], pp. 90ff.

[105] M. Dibelius, *Die Formgeschichte des Evangeliums*[4] [1961], p. 232 (= *From Tradition to Gospel* p. 230).

[106] E. Käsemann, "The Problem of the historical Jesus," *Essays on New Testament Themes* [ET, 1964], p. 22.

to precludes our acceptance of Käsemann's view that "the historical life of Jesus is no longer the focus of Mark's attention. It merely provides the stage on which the God-man enters the lists against his enemies. The history of Jesus has become mythicized." Quite the contrary, we submit. Mark paradoxically stresses *both* the human *and* divine, and neither is allowed to displace the other. The resultant picture of a human Jesus who at the same time as revealing his frailty in embarrassing realism also exercises supernatural powers and strides majestically through the Markan stories poses our problem. Why does Mark allow the paradox to remain? What is his intention in permitting his material to lie cheek-by-jowl and unsynthesized into a coherent picture? Is it his way of saying to his first readers that the one whom they worshipped as risen Lord came to that lordship along a road of weakness, humiliation and death? And that behind the present status of the exalted Christ is the fully human life of Jesus the carpenter?

Mark is at once evangelist and theologian. If we may, for the sake of argument, separate these distinctive rôles in which he is cast, we may say that as evangelist he is concerned to set out the evidence that Jesus was an empirical figure in history, and his putting together of traditions to do with the earthly life of Jesus has a design to set him firmly on Palestinian soil as teacher and man. In his capacity as theologian Mark wishes to convey the teaching that he is also none other than the church's Lord who, looked at from the evangelist's standpoint, is now exalted and worthy of the highest honours. It is faith which glimpses the true worthiness of Jesus and appreciates his true stature. Partial recognition of who he is was found in the days of his ministry, but in its fulness the evaluation awaits the resurrection. It is only in the light of his post-Easter vindication and glory that he can be adequately known for what he is—Son of God and Lord. Mark writes from that perspective, and in so doing inevitably sees the human Jesus as a figure who is both man and more-than-man since what he was incognito and known only to percipient faith in the days of his flesh has become plainly visible since his enthronement, and is the accepted article of the church's confession.

VI

WHY MARK WROTE HIS GOSPEL

The correcting of false Messianic notions (Schulz, Luz). The opposing of heretical christological beliefs (T. J. Weeden). An antidote to docetic tendencies (E. Schweizer). A supplement to Paul's kerygma.

AN UPSHOT OF OUR PREVIOUS SECTION IS THAT, WITH THE RECOGNITION of Mark's subtle concurrence of history and theology, it becomes necessary to ask about the purpose of his writing. The issue may be formulated by looking closely at a maxim which is in danger of becoming a scholarly say-so and therefore of being accepted without a second thought. Martin Kähler wrote, with a clear allusion to Mark, that the gospels are "passion narratives with extended introductions."[1]

There is a good deal to be said in favour of this way of summarizing Mark's gospel. The most assured result of Form criticism is that the Passion story was written and preserved as a connected sequence at a time before the canonical gospels were composed as literary wholes. Mark's deployment of material in regard to John the Baptist is, as we have shown,[2] so arranged as to produce a parallelism between John and Jesus and to make John's fate as a martyred prophet a prototype of what will befall Jesus. Parts of the earlier sections of the narrative clearly point forward to the impending turn of events in which Jesus will have to suffer and be rejected.

"Why does this man speak thus? It is blasphemy!" (2:7).
The last verb could be translated, he is blaspheming. Either way the remark foreshadows the Trial scene and the accusation of blasphemy (14:60–64).

The days will come, *when the bridegroom is taken away* from them, and then they will fast in that day (2:20).

The Pharisees went out, and immediately held counsel with the Herodians against him, how to destroy him (3:6).
(This is a somewhat unexpected collaboration which united Pharisees with sympathizers of a political group who favoured the rule of Herod Antipas the tetrarch of Galilee;[3] and it recurs in 12:13, as a prelude to the Passion.)

---

[1] M. Kähler, *The So-Called Historical Jesus and the Historic Biblical Christ* [ET, 1964], p. 80 note.

[2] See earlier pp. 66ff.

[3] See H. H. Rowley's study of the Herodians in JTS 41 o.s. [1940], pp. 14–27.

Judas Iscariot, who betrayed him (3:19): παρέδωκεν: another instance of the Markan key-verb of the Passion, παραδιδόναι.

"He is beside himself" [i.e., deranged] (3:21).
"He has an unclean spirit" (3:30).
"They took offence at him" (6:3).
These indications of hostility on the part of Jesus' family and kinsfolk foreshadow the rejection of the nation as a whole.

The majority of interpreters see 8:27ff. as constituting something of a watershed in Mark's narrative. This paragraph, which focuses on the confession of Peter, You are the Christ, is attached to the subsequent announcement that the Son of man must suffer and be vindicated, with the details of the Passion spelled out by references to "the elders and the chief priests and the scribes" (8:31). The statement which immediately follows: "And this he said plainly" (παρρησίᾳ, as opposed to "in secret" or "in parables") is invested with significance, as though to draw explicit attention to a clear announcement of the fate of the Son of man. Thereafter the prediction is renewed twice (9:30–32; 10:33, 34), and the direction of the narrative is set in a conscious march on Jerusalem (10:32; 11:1) where the Passion drama unfolds.

It seems pretty clear that Mark's intention is to lay heavy stress on the Passion story by working backwards from the event to embrace the Baptist's destiny as being handed over by God to his death; by making the *pericope* of 8:27–9:1 the central section; by the insertion of three explicit passion prophecies; and by so constructing his whole gospel that a topheavy weight falls on the end-section.[4]

So much is obvious whether we calculate statistically or leave the decision to the judgment of our impression. The shadow of the cross falls across the Markan story at an early point, and the finale of chapters 14:1–16:8 is written in sombre, tragic terms, with scarcely a glimmer of hope to brighten the dark scene.

Kähler's designation, then, looks to be accurate. It is faithful to what we observe from the structure of the gospel of Mark. But it is defective at a *crucial* point. By its very emphasis on the cross and Passion of Jesus it fails to account for the need of a "rather long introduction" (*mit ausführlicher Einleitung* was Kähler's expression [1956 edit. p. 60]) to preface the Passion story. And this omission has been remarked upon by subsequent scholars.[5]

---

[4] It has been assessed that three-eighths of Mark is given over to the Passion story: cf. J. Bowman, *The Gospel of Mark* [1965], p. 312.
[5] H. J. Ebeling, *Das Messiasgeheimnis und Botschaft des Marcusevangelisten* [1939], pp. 8–18; J. M. Robinson, "The Problem of History in Mark Reconsidered," *Union Seminary Quarterly Review*, 20 [1956], p. 137; H. Conzelmann, "Historie und Theologie in den synoptischen Passionsberichten," in *Zur Bedeutung des Todes Jesu*, ed. F. Viering [1967], pp. 35–53 (p. 39); C. F. Evans, *The Beginning of the Gospel . . .* [1968], pp. 63f.

The main difficulty with an easy acceptance of Kähler's dictum is that "it fails to do justice to the traditions of the acts and the teaching of Jesus in their own right, and seeks to arrive too easily at a unity both of the gospels in themselves, and of the gospels with the rest of the New Testament, by bringing them within a Pauline formula" (Evans, *op. cit.*, p. 64). On a more technical level, the problem is to know why Mark chose to preface a passion narrative with a lengthy introduction and so to produce the literary form (or *Gattung*) of "gospel" (Robinson, Conzelmann) or, more specifically, why Mark found it needful to utilize collections of miracle-stories and controversy-narratives (in which Jesus is in dispute with his opponents over his words and actions) as the main body of the preparatory material. It has been calculated that the miracle-stories represent some two hundred verses out of a total of Mark's 661 verses. Why did the evangelist have recourse to this type of material which he used to prepare the ground for his passion narrative (Ebeling)?

Before we address our enquiry to these questions, we must face another matter which has played an important part in recent Markan research. This is described under the title of Tradition and Redaction, and arises directly out of the chief assumption of redaction-criticism. It will be recalled that a fundamental idea in this newer discipline of gospel study is to maintain that the evangelist inherited traditional sections of gospel material which he then editorialized and conformed to his own theological bent. He played the rôle of a creative writer who adapted and fitted the existing units of tradition into a pattern in such a way as to produce a composition which would both reflect his own theology and convey that theology to his constituency in his church.

If this way of looking at Mark is at all feasible, it raises a deeper question than the one just formulated, Why did Mark embody narratives of healing and other miracles into his gospel? The prior question should be framed. As Mark took over these extant units of (pre-canonical) tradition, what has he done with them, either by way of modification or adaptation in order to fit them into the total picture of his understanding of Jesus' activity and mission? Admittedly this is a speculative exercise and requires a great deal of cautious handling. For we have no certainty over the precise limits of the pre-Markan tradition, and can only know this stratum by critical examination in which the subjective element plays an inevitable part. Nonetheless, where there are controls (e.g. linguistic and stylistic usages [such as Mark's preference for connectives like καὶ εὐθύς, πάλιν] which betray either a non-Markan or a Markan segment) or where Mark's redactional enterprise is to be seen in the re-modelling of the narrative by his inserting his own theological evaluation, it becomes an important contribution to enable us to press behind Mark to the pre-evangelic layer of tradition. It also opens a new window of access into the evangelist's situation which his gospel was designed, by human exigency and providential circumstance, to meet. These two factors are worth pursuing on their own account.[6]

The former matter will occupy our attention in the next chapter when we take a closer look at some exegetical passages; the latter is more germane to our present purpose, which is to ask about the intention of Mark in writing a "gospel" in the context of his church situation. The heart of this issue lies in the nature of Mark's work which was published under the self-chosen literary genre of "gospel." When we ask for the reason for the evangelist's use of this term, both in his title (1:1) and in his singular addition of the word in those verses where we may justifiably suspect his own editorial hand at work (see earlier, pp. 24ff.), it is not adequate to reply that he was composing a tract for the encouragement of Christian martyrs at Rome (though this may be one of several ancillary reasons), or that he was promoting by his book a flight into Galilee (as Marxsen thought, on the basis of 13:14, as we noted earlier, pp. 70ff.), or that he wished to preserve the records of Jesus' earthly life for posterity because they were in danger of being forgotten with the death of the apostles, though this again may be a secondary intention (as R. S. Barbour describes the situation).[7]

The tide of Markan studies is flowing in the direction of a new wave altogether. Mark the evangelist is seen as a church teacher who is engaged in a struggle with false doctrine and who by this publication to which he gives the innovative name of "gospel" seeks to enter the lists on behalf of an apostolic understanding of the gospel message. It is nothing less than the apostolic *kerygma* which is at stake, and he boldly appropriates the term which was taken in current parlance to refer to the apostles' preaching ministry and applies it to his own literary creation in order to set out the antidote to heresy in his day.

That species of false teaching centred in the person of Jesus Christ. The evangelist's purpose was "to teach the Christians of his day a true Christology in place of the false Christology that he felt they were in danger of accepting."[8] It is at this point that the value of a redactional study of the gospel enters into the picture, for on this showing the *pre*-Markan layer of the material is likely to be the *anti*-Markan source against which the evangelist is contending. And the chief burden of the book is christological through and through, since Mark is concerned to bring repeatedly before his first readers' notice the claims of Jesus and to raise some fundamental issues. If the gospel whose "origin" ($\dot{\alpha}\rho\chi\dot{\eta}$, 1:1) Mark purposes to relate

[6] Recent studies in this field are: Karl Kertelge, *Die Wunder Jesu im Markusevangelium* [1970]; and R. Pesch, *Jesu ureigene Taten?* [1970]. W. Schmithals, *Wunder und Glaube* [1970] deals with Mark 4:35—6:6a in a popular way.

[7] R. S. Barbour, "Recent Study of the Gospel according to St. Mark," ExpT lxxix. 11 [1968], p. 324.

[8] N. Perrin, "The Creative Use of the Son of man Traditions by Mark," *Union Seminary Quarterly Review* 23 [1968], p. 357.

finds its centre and substance in "Jesus Christ, the Son of God," exactly who and what is the central character who comes to inaugurate the reign of God on earth? He appears "out of the blue," unheralded by any pre-natal or nativity or infancy story, and is witnessed to by the lonely voice of John the Baptist; and the gospel record is narrated with such a swift-flowing succession of events that we are hurried along to a climax, prefaced by solemn announcements of Jesus' Passion and vindication. Moreover, the appearances of Jesus are so tantalizingly brief and so crisply narrated and so half-veiled in details of mystery and movement that Dibelius can speak of "a book of secret epiphanies"[9] in which the revela-tion of Jesus' person is both half-displayed and half-concealed. The extreme to which this notion has been pushed is indicated in the treatment of Siegfried Schulz.[10] He can epitomize Mark's christology as concerned with a figure of Jesus portrayed as "a divine man, indeed God himself in human form." This is surely an exaggeration since Mark is at obvious pains to accentuate the humanity of Jesus, as we have seen, and the sheer earthiness and factualness of Mark's Jesus are too well attested to destroy this part of the total picture, however much he may want also to convey impressions of mystery and other-worldliness in Jesus' secret.

Schulz is on more secure ground when he describes the evangelist's purpose in more general terms (*op. cit.*, p. 36). This he does by maintaining that Mark's interest is kerygmatic and that his task is not to record history but to proclaim a message. That message is related to the life of the con-gregation. "The gospel—and this is true of the gospels generally—is a book which edifies. What is contained in Mark's gospel is not history pure and simple, but interpreted history. That is why the record [of Jesus' life] becomes the centre of the preaching" (*op. cit.*, p. 36).

These two emphases—of the stories of the earthly Jesus and of his death and saving work—are brought together in Mark's account. And it was Mark who first so united the verbal kerygma of apostolic proclamation (epitomized in 1 Cor. 15:3ff.) with the stories of Jesus' Galilean ministry. One problem is to know why he did this. Another fruitful question is to ask about his dual presentation of Jesus' person as a human figure.

Mark's gospel is a strange blend of a characterization of Jesus in his human finiteness and weakness, and a portrayal of a strong Son of God, healing, exorcizing demons and teaching with authority. How are these two sets of data to be brought together? Do they lie unrelated cheek-by-jowl? Or has the evangelist a purpose in so weaving them into a single pattern, though with so many loose threads that we can disentangle them and see what the individual patterns looked like before the separate pieces were stitched together to make the completed garment? Several attempts

---

[9] See earlier p. 138, with reference to Dibelius' *Die Formgeschichte des Evangeliums*[4] [1961], p. 232.
[10] S. Schulz, *Die Stunde der Botschaft*[2] [1970], p. 46.

have been made to explain this phenomenon. We begin with an earlier contribution of Siegfried Schulz[11] and categorize it as an attempt to depict Mark's intention as follows:

I. *The Correcting of False Messianic Notions*

(a) He begins with an observation which draws attention to the key term εὐαγγέλιον for an understanding of this gospel. And, he avers, to understand Mark is to have a key to unlock the history of the theology in the early church. So the root matter is not one of setting Mark in a correct historical or liturgical or cultic frame, but of discovering what *theological* problems this gospel was designed to confront. We recall at this juncture J. H. Ropes's seminal dictum which has been a fertilizing agent in recent discussions: "The important question is not of [Mark's] form, but of its purpose; and that is theological."[12]

Faced with the significance of this question, Schulz finds the motif of Mark above all in the fact that Mark was the first and only person [so far as we know, we should add] to have written a *gospel*. The term εὐαγγέλιον before Mark meant a message of "good news" in oral or epistolary form; and after him Matthew and Luke set about to compose "Lives of Jesus," more conformable to the pattern of *βίοι* than is true of Mark. So Mark is uniquely placed as the inaugurator of the written "gospel."

The only person of whom we have certain knowledge in the pre-Markan period is Paul. It is remarkable that Paul makes no significant appeal to the traditions of the Galilean ministry, though we should not overpress this point to the exclusion of all knowledge of or interest in the Jesus of the gospel tradition.[13] Something of his earthly life is reflected in such statements as:

"born of the family of David on his human side" (Rom. 1:3).
"born of a woman" and "born under the [Jewish] law" (Gal. 4:4).
He was "made a minister of the circumcision" i.e., undertook his ministry to the Jewish people, by confirming God's [Messianic] promises to them (Rom. 15:8).

[11] S. Schulz, "Die Bedeutung des Markus für die Theologiegeschichte des Urchristentums," *Studia Evangelica* ii [1964], pp. 134–45.

[12] J. H. Ropes, *The Synoptic Gospels* [1964 impression], p. 10; cited and approved by D. E. Nineham, *Commentary*, p. 37.

[13] Continental scholars tend to gloss over the extent of this knowledge on the assumption that 2 Corinthians 5:16 forecloses the issue with its (apparent) disavowal of interest on Paul's part in knowing "Christ after the flesh." Part of the reason for this denial seems to be that in the search for the historical Paul exaggerated claims have been made to forge a personal and immediate link between the earthly Jesus and the future apostle, e.g., by C. A. A. Scott who argues [*Christianity according to St. Paul* (1927), p. 11] that Saul of Tarsus may actually have seen Jesus in the flesh, witnessed the crucifixion and at least have learned something of his teaching. He cites Continental interpreters who share his opinions, viz. J. Weiss, W. Bousset and H. Lietzmann (*op. cit.*, p. 12).

(Cont'd. on p. 146)

But, all in all, there is nothing substantial which would permit us to believe that Paul consciously utilized an outline of the Galilean ministry in his preaching ministry. And he makes no appeal to Messianic features in Jesus' life; indeed he seems disinclined to stress the entire question of Jesus' Messianic office. He gives a personal connotation to the name "Christ" rather than a functional or national one. In his concern for Gentile Christians this perhaps is not surprising.[14]

In default of any recourse to available gospel traditions which were not part of the missionary kerygma handed on to him at Antioch (Acts 11:26), Paul was bound to appeal to the only argument for Jesus' authority he had available. This was the Old Testament scripture, with its witness to the office of the divinely appointed agent in God's saving purposes and in particular to a divine Son, humbled in death yet now exalted as heavenly Lord. In those places where Paul is consciously indebted to and is drawing upon pre-Pauline formulas (e.g. 1 Cor. 15:3f.) he expresses this in terms of the Messiah[15] who died and was raised "according to the scriptures." His appeal to the Old Testament is much more variegated than would appear from a list of the instances where he prefaces his citations with "as it is written," which is his customary procedure to introduce an explicit quotation. Deeply embedded in his theological discussions is an implicit concern to find his teaching both attested in and supported by the Old Testament salvation-history prefigurations.

One example of his practice will suffice. In Romans 15:1ff., he introduces a discussion in which he is advocating the concern of the Christian for his neighbour and fellow-believer. One trait of this solicitude is shown in a willingness to forgo personal preferences and subject personal convictions to the overall good and well-being of the community. He then endorses this teaching with an example of Christ.[16]

This "example" of a Christ who refused to please himself and endured rejection by his own people as a consequence is buttressed by a citation

Cont'd. from previous page:
For a recent discussion of the extent of Paul's knowledge of the earthly Jesus, see C. F. D. Moule's essay, "Jesus in New Testament Kerygma," *Verborum Veritas*. Festschrift G. Stählin [1970], pp. 15–26.

[14] So N. A. Dahl, "Die Messianität Jesu bei Paulus," in *Studia Paulina*, eds. J. N. Sevenster and W. C. van Unnik [1953], p. 94. But this is challenged by G. Bornkamm, "Baptism and New Life in Paul," *Early Christian Experience* [ET, 1969], p. 76, who argues that Paul uses Χριστός in kerygmatic contexts to explain the soteriology of his death.

[15] Assuming that here Χριστός is a title, not a personal name. See F. Hahn, *The Titles of Jesus in Christology* [ET, 1969], pp. 182ff.

[16] The description "ein Vorbild ad imitandum" is certainly applicable in the context of Romans 15:1–7, as used by E. Larsson, *Christus als Vorbild* [1962], p. 234. But his attempt to find exact parallels with the thought and terminology of Philippians 2:1–12 fails on at least two counts. More importantly there is no appeal to an incarnational motif in Romans 15; and the apostle's use of the "as it is written" formula (v. 3) is noticeably absent in the Christ-hymn, even if we grant (as most commentators apart from E. Lohmeyer who first proposed the idea do not) that the introductory "which was in Christ Jesus" (Phil. 2:5) is a "kind of formula of citation." See my remarks in *Carmen Christi: Philippians ii:5–11* [1967], p. 26.

from Psalm 68 (69):10 in agreement with both the Hebrew and LXX. But no allusion is made to the Jesus-tradition in either the pre-canonical materials or what later became the gospel tradition. Instead, the appeal to scripture is enforced by a tribute to the encouragement which the scripture affords (v. 4), as though Paul were saying that this *testimonium* of Christ, drawn from the prototype of the Israelite king, should be sufficient to ensure acceptance of his plea for a harmonious settlement of disputes (vv. 5, 6).

But what pre-Markan tradition was available on which Paul might have drawn? Very little is known of the sources and experiments in gospel composition to which Luke refers (Luke 1:1, 2). But one such source is inferentially attested. This is the hypothetical sayings-source, underlying Matthew and Luke, known by the cipher Q. The Q-stratum of tradition offers a picture of Jesus[17] as a present and coming Son of man, whose word was authoritative for the community which assembled these logia and appealed to them. They awaited the *parousia* of an eschatological figure who would vindicate them before God as they were faithful in their present allegiance to him. In this compressed sentence what is omitted is perhaps more germane to our present task than what is included. For, on this showing, Q's "kerygma" is a passion-less story of Jesus, who is "not . . . the redeemer who gives his blood for many but . . . the authoritative teacher who by means of his word summons men to follow him" (Tödt, *op. cit.*, p. 266).

For Tödt, this collection of Jesus-traditions stands over against Mark's gospel which is dominated by the drama of the Lord's Passion, which is invested with redemptive value. Whether we accept Tödt's estimate of Q's place in early christology or prefer to believe, with T. W. Manson, that Q was by design a manual of teaching in which the kerygma of the cross found no explicit place because it presupposed an acceptance of the message of the Passion of Jesus,[18] is an issue we need not linger to settle.[19] The vital point is that Mark's originality as the evangelist of the cross-kerygma is thrown into relief by our admission that no pre-Markan tradition which united both Jesus' words and Jesus' Passion is attested.

Mark's supreme achievement, according to Schulz, is seen in his work of uniting, for the first time, the Jesus-traditions of the Palestinian community and the hellenistic Christian materials which he inherited from

[17] I draw here on H. E. Tödt's conclusions, *The Son of Man in the Synoptic Tradition* [ET, 1965], ch. 5.

[18] T. W. Manson, *The Sayings of Jesus* [1949], pp. 15f.: "Q . . . a book of instruction for people who are already Christians and know the story of the Cross by heart" (p. 16).

[19] My inclination is to believe with T. W. Manson that Q existed as a para-evangelic source, not a rival christological statement which emanated from a non-Pauline wing of the church. The earliest Palestinian community from which the pre-Pauline 1 Corinthians 11:25, 15:3f. emanated, is hardly the community to have assembled Q, thought of as containing a non-soteriological christology, as W. G. Kümmel has noted (*Introduction to the New Testament* [1965], pp. 56f.).

Paul's kerygma of the cross. The result is that the centre of gravity is re-located in the passion story and the Q version of a future Son of man is radically reinterpreted through a hellenistic epiphany christology (*loc. cit.*, p. 144) based on a Son of God eschatology. Underlying this reconstruction is the same thesis which undergirds Tödt's dichotomy of Q and the Pauline gospel. If the Jesus-traditions of the pre-Markan story were preserved not in isolation from the message of the cross but for a separate purpose (e.g. as catechesis and for instructional purposes), Schulz's proposal collapses, for he has offered no motivation on Mark's part why he should have wished to reinterpret in a new way the early Palestinian traditions apart from the problematic reason that he found the Q kerygma enshrined in these stories of Jesus defective and wished to orient them in a new way to the gospel of a suffering Saviour.

(b) It is the merit of Ulrich Luz's study[20] that he does reach a conclusion which satisfies the requirement he has set for an understanding of Mark as the first evangelist. His theological accomplishment is to be sought not in the use to which he has put the pre-Easter traditions about Jesus nor in the selection of the material he has made but in the way he has produced a complete sketch incorporating both the Messianic secret theory and at the same time a significant theological construction (*loc. cit.*, p. 10, note 7). In other words, both the separate parts of the gospel and the putting together of these parts to form a completed whole are Mark's concern, and his achievement is seen in what he has done to produce a theological writing.

Luz's opening dictum shows the direction in which his contribution will be set: "Messianic secret remains still a secret." Following Wrede he proceeds to divide the material in Mark into the three customary sections: healing stories, accounts of exorcism, and instructions to the disciples. In each case Wrede had sought to show that these injunctions to secrecy were Mark's way of explaining the apparent non-messianic life of Jesus in view of the post-Easter faith that he was, since the resurrection, the proclaimed Messiah. But we are faced with the question of why this harmonization of Jesus' life and the post-Easter faith in Christ would be needed—part of the critique brought against Wrede by H. J. Ebeling.[21] The latter moves on in his critique to maintain that there is no secrecy motif in Mark's gospel. What Wrede imagined were efforts to conceal Jesus' person (in the commands to silence, the disciples' misunderstanding and the interpretation of parables to the initiated in 4:11–13) are in fact revelations. But the injunctions to keep his "secret" dark are intended to heighten the dramatic effect *for the reader* by showing that they were in fact disobeyed. It is clear that Mark's intention is seen not in the secret but in its violation since it cannot be concealed that Jesus is the glorious

---

[20] U. Luz, "Das Geheimnismotiv und die markinische Christologie," ZNTW 56 [1965], pp. 9–30.
[21] H. J. Ebeling, *Das Messiasgeheimnis und die Botschaft des Marcusevangelisten* [1939].

Son of God whose epiphany shines forth in spite of attempts to hide it.[22] Mark's literary device gives his reader a sense of the preciousness of the mystery which *he* has been permitted to understand. In this way Mark's readers may congratulate themselves that what the disciples did not appreciate is now their prized possession. In sum, Mark's gospel for Ebeling was designed to clarify for the Christian community the meaning of the kerygma and to enhance its value in their eyes as they sense their privilege in being numbered among the chosen ones who see Jesus as "the secret of God made known in Christ"[23] expressed in a Johannine idiom.

U. Luz takes over and adapts from Ebeling the idea that the injunctions to silence in the miracle stories are placed in the Markan narrative in order to show how they were disobeyed; hence the purpose of what Wrede called the "Messianic secret" is in fact to proclaim the way in which Jesus' miracles were not-able-to-remain-hidden (Nicht-verborgen-bleiben-können, *loc. cit.*, p. 17). Only in the exorcisms and Peter's confession is there a command to preserve Jesus' Messiahship in secrecy. Luz thus distinguishes between "Miracle secret" (Wundergeheimnis) and "Messianic secret" (Messiasgeheimnis).

With this distinction in mind, he argues that the "Messianic secret" acts as a corrective, its secrecy being required because in Jesus' lifetime (for Mark) it could not be fully understood, and needed a content derived only from the experience of the Passion. So "the Messianic secret describes the nature of Jesus' messiahship which must be understood kerygmatically, i.e. in the light of the cross and resurrection" (*loc. cit.*, p. 28). Then, the Messiahship-in-the-light-of-the-Passion is used by Mark to re-interpret the miracle stories which portray Jesus as a hellenistic $\theta\epsilon\tilde{\iota}o\varsigma\ \dot{\alpha}v\acute{\eta}\rho$. The way Mark does this is to run together the two sets of data—a picture of a "divine-man" wonder-worker who mysteriously appears on the scene and effects miraculous cures and is acknowledged as such, and a corpus of Messianic material subordinate to the theology of the cross (*loc. cit.*, p. 29); and his purpose is to preserve the kerygmatic witness of both parts. In the first half of the gospel (1:16–8:26) the nearness of God's kingdom is shown in Jesus' mighty works; in the second half (8:27–10:52 [13:37A]) the heavenly kingdom is peopled by those who follow a way of life which is a path of suffering, first trodden by Jesus.

Mark has chosen by this conflation to make the $\theta\epsilon\tilde{\iota}o\varsigma$-$\dot{\alpha}v\acute{\eta}\rho$ christology which was current coin in hellenistic congregations meaningful when related to the kerygma-of-the-cross, since the former is for him a type of christology which leads only to unbelief as the effect of Jesus' miracles led only to incredulous amazement (*loc. cit.*, pp. 28f.). Rather, however,

[22] G. Minette de Tillesse, *Le secret messianique dans l'évangile de Marc* [1968], pp. 26f.
[23] Ebeling, *op. cit.*, p. 96, cited by H.-D. Knigge, "The Meaning of Mark," *Interpretation* 22 [1968], p. 59, who offers some critical comments on Ebeling's book.

than eliminate this "divine man" christology and epiphany pattern of a wonder-worker (*loc. cit.*, p. 30), Mark has subjected it to the kerygma by making the road to the cross the chief element of his "gospel."

II. *The Opposing of Heretical Christological Beliefs*

With the assumption made that Mark is working with at least two sets of material and using his own tradition to correct an existing christology—not by cancelling out the earlier one but rather by superimposing his strand—T. J. Weeden offers the most imaginative dissection and rationale of the Markan gospel to date.[24]

He makes his starting-point in two conclusions already believed to be established, viz. that Mark conducts a polemic against the Twelve disciples and that two opposing christologies are discernible within the few chapters of the final edition of the gospel. One doctrine of Christ proposes a figure of Jesus as a θεῖος ἀνήρ, or mighty healer and miracle-performer, the other has a doctrine of a suffering Messiah. Weeden's thesis is an attempt to bring together these presupposed ideas into the pattern of a coherent whole.

He achieves this by pairing the θεῖος ἀνήρ christology with the disciples (whom, he thinks, Mark positively hated) and the suffering Messiahship belief with Mark's own theological stance. Thus, "Mark has cast the disciples as advocates of a θεῖος ἀνήρ christology which is pitted against the suffering messiahship of Jesus" (*loc. cit.*, p. 150).

Why was this correction needed and what was the exact heresy which Mark felt obliged to rebut? The answer lies in the nature of the church situation which spawned this false teaching. Weeden envisages the Markan church as a community of Christians all agog with eschatological excitement, eagerly and anxiously awaiting the End. Their golden text which fills them with impatience as they wait on tip-toe is 13:30: "Truly I say to you, this generation shall not pass away before all these things take place." But they are caught in a tension because the End is not yet and is unaccountably delayed; they are compelled to live out their days in a *Zwischenzeit*, an in-between time when the Lord is absent, yet is fervently expected at any moment.

In this void teachers who appear on the scene appeal to a picture of Jesus as wonder-worker since they claim to be performing miracles and reproducing what he did in his ministry. These teachers capitalize on the

---

[24] T. J. Weeden, "The Heresy that Necessitated Mark's Gospel," ZNTW 59 [1968], pp. 145–158. Less far ranging and more concerned to investigate one single issue (namely, Mark's use of the title Son of man) is N. Perrin's article, "The Creative Use of the Son of Man by Mark," *Union Seminary Quarterly Review* 23 [1968], pp. 357ff. He follows closely Weeden's method and reaches his conclusion in regard to Mark's chief christological concern though without specifying exact circumstances.

(Since the manuscript of this book was completed, T. J. Weeden has published a full study of his earlier position regarding "the Heresy that necessitated Mark's Gospel." See his *Mark—Traditions in Conflict* [1971] for a fuller elaboration of his essential thesis contained in the article noted above.)

unbearable disappointment known in Mark's church over the delay of the returning Lord. They make out that they are his representatives, duly accredited by miracles. They awaken strong feelings of identity with this type of pneumatic Christianity.

Mark senses the imminent danger of this type of enthusiasm and rebukes their pretensions by his use of such warnings as 13:6: "Many will come in my name, saying, I am he!"; and offers in 13:22 a foretelling of their appearance on the scene as "false Messiahs and false prophets" who work wonders and perform signs to accredit themselves. As they place reliance on Jesus as "divine man", it may be inferred that they purported to be "divine men." In so doing they by-passed the message of the cross, claiming that "authentic Christian existence finds meaning and fulfilment not in the humiliation of suffering servanthood (8:34f.; 10:43f.; 13:9–13), but in the pneumatic glory of $\theta\varepsilon\tilde{\iota}o\varsigma$ $\dot{\alpha}v\acute{\eta}\rho$ existence" (loc. cit., p. 155).

Mark's answer to this incipient heresy lies in a threefold emphasis: (i) he makes central the picture of Jesus as a suffering figure, both positively by demarcating the way to the cross as a theologia crucis, and negatively by having Peter's confession of a $\theta\varepsilon\tilde{\iota}o\varsigma$ $\dot{\alpha}v\acute{\eta}\rho$ Christ duly rebuked. (ii) He equates Jesus and the gospel, thus insisting that there is no other authentic message save that which Jesus began to preach (1:15) and commissioned to the church (13:9–10). (iii) The third contribution of Mark is the way he addresses himself to the immediate situation in his church which was facing problems over the deferment of the End. False prophets claimed to be extensions of Messiah's person in their midst. This claim Mark regards as bogus and argues that it is the Holy Spirit who provides true continuity between the earthly Jesus and the Lord of the church (13:11), and it is the Spirit who authorizes those who claim to speak for God and work in his name. Yet the Spirit came upon Jesus to commission him to the task of suffering Messiahship (1:10) and there can be no denying that he directs the community to follow in this way and no other.

Mark sees his current opponents typified in the disciples whose heirs they are. So he makes out that the disciples are not Spirit-directed (14:38) nor are they spiritually sensitive to see who Jesus is. When he goes to his destiny, they are ashamed and faithless (14:43–45, 50, 66–71), and of their successors, the heretical leaders in Mark's day, Jesus will be ashamed when he comes again (8:38f.; 13:26).

There is no disputing the originality and power of this presentation which incidentally casts Mark in the rôle of a combative theologian of no mean stature. Nor do we wish to dispute the underlying conflict between a false christology and Mark's own preaching conveyed through the historical narration. Our difficulty lies mainly with Weeden's analysis[25] of the gospel as proceeding in orderly stages which are held to reflect an

[25] Which is based on A. Kuby, "Zur Konzeption des Markus-Evangeliums," ZNTW 49 [1958], pp. 52–64.

evolution (or rather devolution) in the disciples' relationship to Jesus. Weeden traces three stages, which form the structure of the gospel:

1:16—8:26	They are imperceptible to Jesus
8:27—14:9	They misconceive his person
14:10–72	They reject him

To argue that this is not historical but "a polemical device created by the evangelist to disgrace and debunk the disciples" (*loc. cit.*, p. 147) is to say too much. For the sections are not so tightly structured. The Twelve are perceptive enough to ask about the parables and are given instruction (4:10, 11). Jesus has confidence in them as he chooses them and sends them out to preach (3:13; 6:7, 12). The misconception of who Jesus is, voiced by Peter (8:29) and associated by Weeden with the θεῖος ἀνήρ Messiahship is (he argues) the inevitable conclusion to be drawn from the Markan picture in 1:1–8:29.[26] Peter is rebuked as Satan's mouthpiece (8:33) since he has confessed to a θεῖος ἀνήρ Christ. But the *pericope* in 9:38–41 presents a difficulty since it has Jesus finding no incompatibility in the fact that a man (reproached by the disciple John for being an exorcist and yet not one of the Twelve) can be both an exorcist and "on our side." Peter was earlier rebuked for expressing this view of Jesus in precisely this way (on Weeden's hypothesis), and is classified as "on the side of men" (8:33).

The various ways in which the disciples failed to comprehend the nature of Jesus' person and mission are, to be sure, a ruling motif in Mark's story. But because their misunderstandings go from bad to worse is no sign that this is Mark's "polemical device." They may well have been initially impressed with his mighty acts and have paid tribute to him as an accredited Messianic figure. Their expectations of earthly power and glory would be raised to a fever pitch en route to Jerusalem and they would grow deaf to all warnings of what Jesus anticipated for himself (and for them as they remained loyal, 10:32–40). It is small wonder, therefore, that with their hopes dashed to the ground, they should desert him and run away (14:49), with even Peter's loud protestations of loyalty (14:29) turning to hollow sounds. That there is this noticeable downward progression and deterioration in their attitude to Jesus is plain for Mark's readers to see; but it is not fictitious on that account.

When Weeden tries to identify Mark's opponents as charismatic leaders who claimed to be following the earthly Jesus' example as a thaumaturge and miracle-worker, he is necessarily speculative, though there is evidence in other parts of the New Testament of the presence of such figures, e.g. Matthew 7:21–23 and 2 Corinthians 11:13–15 (cf. 12:12)[27] as well

---

[26] This way of describing the impression made by Jesus on both the demonic world and the human bystanders in the miracle-stories is shared by A. Kuby, *loc. cit.*, pp. 148f. We revert to it in a subsequent chapter.

[27] See D. Georgi, *Die Gegner des Paulus im 2. Korintherbrief* [1964], pp. 220ff.

as the examples in Acts 8:9ff.; 19:13–16. But to attribute the prototype of this false teaching to the Twelve disciples is unwarranted, for there is no evidence that they claimed a divine man status in the days of his ministry or later. If recourse is had to the way in which Peter acts in such situations as Acts 5:3ff.;[28] it must equally be conceded that Paul, exponent par excellence of the theology of the cross, is made to appear in a similar light (Acts 19:11ff.; 28:1–6, 8, 9; 2 Cor. 12:1, 12). And to argue[29] that the Twelve appear as men lacking in the Holy Spirit, on the basis of a single text in 14:38, is precarious indeed.

We conclude that Weeden has correctly identified Mark's theological interest in contrasting two rival christologies—one of power, the other of suffering—but his further endeavour to place the disciples and their successors in Mark's church (seen as a group of *illuminati* who pretended to be Jesus' personal envoys on earth) on the one side rests on a fragile base.[30] Moreover, not necessary to his reconstruction is his scepticism about the historical worth of Mark's presentation. He may be using historical materials for his own purpose, and proclaiming a message of the true kerygma by so utilizing traditions of what he believed to be true in the earthly life of Jesus. It is not impossible that he should be *both* sensitive to the historical traditions he has received *and* concerned so to interpret and angle these traditions as to bring home to the Christians of his day the meaning of Christ. Thus, his setting as a controversialist, opposing a dangerous trend in christological belief and practice in his own church situation, need not incapacitate him from being a faithful narrator of gospel history.

III. *An Antidote to Docetic Tendencies*

A less speculative reconstruction of Mark's background and purpose in writing, which does not pretend to be able to identify the exact nature of the heresy which prompted his composition, is given by E. Schweizer.[31]

---

[28] Peter is called "der Wundermann" who knows all secrets of the human heart and his character is described as that of a θεῖος ἀνήρ by H. Conzelmann, *Die Apostelgeschichte* [1963], p. 39.

[29] Based on E. Schweizer, TDNT vi, pp. 396f.

[30] At this point T. J. Weeden is anticipated by R. Bultmann (*History of the Synoptic Tradition* [ET, 1963], p. 258) and J. Schreiber (ZThK 58 [1961], pp. 154–183) in the view that Mark's gospel uses the Twelve as a target for attack as representing Jewish Christians. See for a reply R. P. Meye "Messianic Secret and Messianic Didache in Mark's Gospel," *Oikonomia*. O. Cullmann Festschrift, ed. F. Christ [1967], pp. 65ff.

[31] E. Schweizer, *Das Evangelium nach Markus* [Das NT Deutsch, 1, 1967], pp. 220–224; ET, *The Good News According to Mark* [1970], pp. 380–386. References are given to the ET. This writer has contributed several studies to the theme of Mark's purpose; among them we note: "Anmerkungen zur Theologie des Markus," in *Neotestamentica et Patristica*. O. Cullmann Festschrift [1962], pp. 35–46 (pp. 42ff.); "Die theologische Leistung des Markus," *Evangelische Theologie* 24 [1964], pp. 337–355; "Mark's Contribution to the Quest of the historical Jesus," NTS 10 [1963–64], pp. 421–32.

In response to the question, What is the theological achievement of Mark? Schweizer relates his answer to the dangers posed by a docetic tendency within post-Pauline Christianity. He offers in an Epilogue to his commentary a description of the way in which Mark's gospel seems to him to have emerged.

Three phases of development are traced. First, the Jewish-Christian community was primarily interested in Jesus' words (preserved in the sayings-source Q) which gave guidance in ethical instruction and prepared the congregation for the approaching End-time. Secondly, the Pauline churches placed the cross and the resurrection at the centre of their confessions (e.g. 1 Cor. 15:3-5) and paid little attention to the traditions about the earthly life of Jesus. At Corinth we have the case of a tendency represented by enthusiasts who based everything on the resurrection and excluded the human Jesus by their exaggerated emphasis on the heavenly Christ. It was to check such fanaticism and incipient gnosticism that Paul found it needful to stress the message of the cross in 1 Corinthians 1-2. Thirdly, hellenistic communities (perhaps in Syria?) championed a "divine man" thaumaturgy based on the use of magic and expressed in a personality-cult which centred in a wonder-worker, familiar in contemporary society in Greece, Asia Minor and Syria. The focal point was the mighty deeds performed by a religious teacher who was "looked upon as some sort of incarnation of divine powers" (*op. cit.* p. 382). Apparently Jesus was placed in this category, and hailed as a divine being by virtue of his miracles. Here is a tradition behind Mark's gospel with his earthly life made central, but knowing his death only as an unintelligible and tragic end, a piece of misfortune caused by the folly of men who failed to recognize him.

Now Mark's emergence signalized a new understanding. And its token is the creation of a new literary form, called a "gospel" (1:1). He had already to hand available materials in a compendium of sayings and an assortment of miracle-stories, but he chose to ignore much of the former and to refuse the model which the miracle-stories may have offered him. Instead, he concentrated on the passion narrative and its antecedents, since this was for him the centre of gravity. At a time when Jesus' shameful death was in danger of being pushed into the background, Mark boldly accentuated this part as pivotal in his story of Jesus and set the announcement of the Passion and resurrection of the Son of man at "the heart of the Gospel (8:27-9:1)" (*op. cit.* p. 384).

But it was not enough simply to tell the facts of Jesus' death, as some of the pre-Pauline creeds and hymns had done, as solely an item in a series of theological statements. Mark[32] must draw upon the traditions of Jesus' human life and ministry in order to ward off the dangerous possibility that

---

[32] This part of Schweizer's contribution is taken from his other articles as cited.

Jesus as man might fade into a "mere symbol or cipher which says noth-ing"[33] about a real incarnation and so this lack of interest in him as a figure of empirical history might become an expression of "a theology of the kerygma which has lost all roots in history."

Yet in his meeting the challenge of an implicit docetic tendency which would deny significant interest in the historical figure of Jesus, Mark was not able to offer a simple "biography" or life-story; otherwise his gospel would have contained more of a transcript of Jesus' actual teaching than it does.[34] Instead Mark is remarkable in passing over the substance of Jesus' teaching, though he does refer often to Jesus as "teaching." In fact, his description of Jesus as "teaching with authority" (1:22, 27) plays a decisive rôle; it signifies for Mark the intervention of God in his authorita-tive person, even though he does not spell out the content of that teaching.

The reason for this fact is clear. Mark is guarding against the possibility that Jesus can be "historicized," as though a mere repetition of his sayings or a report of his deeds would be the same as a proclamation (in the kerygma) of the Christ of faith, i.e. a Christ who is known not at the end of an exercise in historical enquiry, but in the immediacy of the church's proclamation to be received by faith.[35]

In other words, the evangelist is seeking to make room for "faith" in an "existential" sense, and is thereby avoiding the twin dangers of (a) a docetic attitude which cuts the message of Christ loose from its historical moorings and (b) a false reliance on history as when Christians believe that historical facts can in themselves prove the claims of the kerygma.

Mark's overarching purposes are above all apologetic. That is, he is concerned to defend the true nature of the church's faith by his presenta-tion of a gospel of the "unbelievable condescension and love of God who, in Jesus, seeks the world."[36] That world is not the world of Jewish privi-lege but the Gentile world where recognition of the hidden God is made by those who take the centurion's place at the foot of the cross (15:39) and marvel at the crucified who cries out in despair (15:34, 37). So it is perceptive faith which discerns who the sufferer is—this is the meaning of the so-called Messianic secret, as Mark indicates with his weighty expres-sion διαστέλλεσθαι [to command] (loc. cit., p. 431; p. 355)—and a willing-ness to follow in faithful discipleship; for Mark "faith always means discipleship, following Jesus" (loc. cit., p. 432). Mark's insistence on the

[33] E. Schweizer, "Die theologische Leistung des Markus," loc. cit., p. 338: "So drohte Jesus zu einem blossen Symbol oder einer nichtssagenden Chiffre zu verblassen . . . eine Kerygmatheologie sichtbar, die alle Wurzeln in der Geschichte verloren hatte."

[34] NTS 10 [1963–64], p. 422; Evangelische Theologie, 24 [1964], p. 340; "Anmerkungen," loc. cit., pp. 44f.

[35] NTS, loc. cit., p. 423: "The so-called Messianic Secret of Jesus is actually a No-trespassing sign for all handing down of the 'historical Jesus,' namely for all mere repetition of his sayings or of reports of his deeds which would not be, at the same time, the proclamation of the Christ of faith."

[36] NTS, loc. cit., p. 431: Evangelische Theologie, loc. cit., p. 355.

historical Jesus is not given with any supposed idea of convincing his readers, ancient or modern, that faith can be awakened by a study of history—that would be to resort to illegitimate methods of historical enquiry for the Christian. Rather, the Jesus of Mark's history "keeps our faith from becoming unfaith or distorted faith" (loc. cit., p. 432), as it most certainly would become if it lost touch with historical reality and were absorbed in an other-worldly docetic figure, as in gnostic religion.

IV. A Supplement to Paul's Kerygma

The following section is indebted to much of what E. Schweizer has contributed to an elucidation of Mark's purpose as a gospel writer. It aims at expanding the author's sketch in the Expository Times[37] though the exegetical justification must await the subsequent chapter of the present book. The plan is to offer a suitable background in early Christianity for Mark's publication and to place it in an appropriate Sitz im Leben.

(1) A background in Paul's churches

We may begin with some indisputable facts, which speak of a situation in one of the Pauline mission churches. At Corinth, itinerant preachers had appeared in the scene, offering a version of the Christian message at odds with the message which Paul maintained and proclaimed. One aspect of the debate turns on the question whether Paul had to encounter the same group in Corinth as in Galatia and Philippi. W. Schmithals[38] has argued that Paul's enemies were the same in each place and that he was required to defend his gospel against a single foe who appeared on different fronts. In each case they were gnostic opponents; the variation within Paul's reply is explained by his coming only slowly to realize the nature and gravity of the menace they represented.

Schmithals's position has been challenged, partly on the ground that the variation within Paul's exposition of and response to the heresy mentioned in the several epistles suggests that he was answering different opponents in each case (so H. Köster[39]), and partly on the score that his Galatian opponents are more probably to be identified with a Judaizing group, so that it is wrong to assume "that Paul had to deal simply and solely throughout his career with one type of problem and one variety of opposition" (so R. McL. Wilson[40]).

[37] R. P. Martin, "A Gospel in Search of a Life-Setting," ExpT lxxx. 12 [1969], pp. 361–64.

[38] W. Schmithals in his book, Paulus und die Gnostiker [1965], pp. 175ff.

[39] H. Köster, "Häretiker im Urchristentum" Religion in Geschichte und Gegenwart³ III [1959], pp. 17–21; idem "The Purpose of the Polemic of a Pauline Fragment," NTS 8 [1961–62], pp. 317–32; idem, "GNŌMAI DIAPHOROI: The Origin and Nature of Diversification in the History of Early Christianity," HTR 58 [1965], pp. 279–318.

[40] R. McL. Wilson, "Gnostics—in Galatia?" Studia Evangelica iv [1968], pp. 358–367 (p. 367).

The extreme in another direction is taken by D. W. Oostendorp[41] who argues that there was one single type of false teaching Paul had to combat and that this was advocated by Jewish-Christians who stressed the supremacy of Israel and advocated the "Jewish-Christian superiority" of the original apostles, the Law and the Jewish heritage of the gospel at Corinth as in Galatia and at Philippi.

For our purpose we need not decide this question. What is more interesting is the explicit allusion contained in 2 Corinthians 11:4:

> If some one comes and preaches another Jesus than the one we preached, or if you receive a different spirit from the one you received, or if you accept a different gospel from the one you accepted, you submit to it readily enough (cf. Gal. 1:8, 9).

Quite clearly this was no imaginary danger;[42] nor was it to do with a marginal element in the Christian message as Paul understood it. Some christological heresy was being propounded; and propounded with success.

The linking of "another Jesus" and "another spirit" recalls a similar contrast in 1 Corinthians 12:3 where Paul is concerned to check the aberration of those in the same Corinthian church who uttered the cry, Jesus is damned, and professed to be inspired by the Holy Spirit. The Holy Spirit, Paul insists, is the author and inspirer of the confession, Jesus is Lord.

It is not certain whether these two statements (in 1 Corinthians 12:3 and 2 Corinthians 11:4) of an unPauline christology do really belong together; and even if they do, we know very little about its precise nature.[43] The chief differences of interpretation are seen at the point where we ask about the meaning of the curse, Jesus is *anathema*. Of the many possibilities of understanding this text in its Corinthian situation,[44] the most imaginative reconstruction is that it refers to Corinthian gnostics who were dissociating the human Jesus from the heavenly Christ, even to the extent of denying the manhood of Jesus altogether.[45] For them the focus of interest lay in the risen Lord whose resurrection life they claimed to share

[41] Derk William Oostendorp, *Another Jesus: A Gospel of Jewish-Christian Superiority in II Corinthians* [1967], p. 83 and passim.
    This is also the conclusion reached by C. K. Barrett in a number of closely reasoned studies: "ψευδαπόστολοι (2 Cor. 11, 13)" in *Mélanges B. Rigaux* [1970], pp. 377–396 (especially p. 365) and "Paul's Opponents in II Corinthians," NTS 17 [1970–71], pp. 233–54.
[42] The introductory term "if" should not be pressed to denote contingency, for Paul "is not likely to cherish real fears on the ground of imaginary suppositions" (R. H. Strachan, *Second Corinthians* [MNTC, 1935], *ad loc.*
[43] See the latest monograph by D. W. Oostendorp, *op. cit.* [1967].
[44] Assuming, as I think we must, that the text is accurately reported and has not been scribally emended, as W. F. Albright and C. S. Mann, "Two Texts in 1 Corinthians" NTS 16 [1969–70], pp. 271–6 have recently suggested.
[45] So W. Schmithals, *Die Gnosis in Korinth* (ET, *Gnosticism in Corinth*. [1971], pp. 124–135). He goes on to interpret the meaning of "any who preaches another Jesus" (2 Cor. 11:4) in the sense of "a rejection of the human Jesus" (*op. cit.*, p. 134). (Cont'd. on p. 158)

already (1 Cor. 4:8) with a tacit denial of a future resurrection made in
1 Corinthians 15:12 (cf. 2 Tim. 2:18). This experience of sharing in the
heavenly world evidently gave them the right to claim exemption from
moral restrictions (1 Cor. 5:1, 2, 9, 10; 6:12–20; 10:1–22) and to indulge
in some strange sexual and marital practices (1 Cor. 7; cf. 1 Tim. 4:3).
For our purpose we note particularly the concentration on the risen,
heavenly Lord and on an association with him in his exalted state which
led to the practice of ecstatic communion and glossolalic speech, interpreted as marks of the new age of which they were already members.
So no longer did they submit to moral discipline and were claiming
exemption from a life of suffering. The latter point comes out clearly in
Paul's defence of his apostleship in 2 Corinthians 10–13 where he has to
justify his own sufferings in the light of the claims being made by the
"false apostles"[46] of 2 Corinthians 11:13, who were charismatic figures
and claimed superiority to Paul on that account.

It is true that D. Georgi has offered a slightly different presentation of
the false ideas mooted at Corinth.[47] He considers the opponents of Paul
to be adherents of a θεῖος ἀνήρ-type of christology. They emphasized the
earthly life of Jesus as that of a miracle-worker and a Spirit-filled charismatic, and Paul has them in mind in 2 Corinthians 11:4. The value of
this reconstruction is that it does not require us to introduce a problematic
verse (1 Cor. 12:3) into the total picture, and perhaps we should hesitate
before committing ourselves too firmly to an exact description of the
christological heresy at Corinth and the nature of the opposition Paul
encountered. Even so, at a minimum, some summary statement can be
constructed. Whether it was a turning away from the earthly Jesus in
favour of interest in the spiritual Christ, or an appeal to Jesus as a wonder-
worker and man of the Spirit, it seems plain that the Corinthian deviation-
ists from Paul's teaching were basing their belief and practice on the

Cont'd. from previous page:
The ground of this argument is the parallel between what Schmithals envisages to be the
type of Christianity accepted by the Corinthian errorists and later gnosticism. Origen speaks
of the Ophite sect of gnostics as requiring an anathematizing of the earthly Jesus in the interest
of giving a central place in their system to the heavenly aeon, Christ.

This has been challenged by B. A. Pearson, "Did the Gnostics curse Jesus?" JBL 86 [1967],
pp. 301–5; but Schmithals's position and appeal to the later gnostic heresy as providing a
parallel to the situation in 1–2 Corinthians with its features of gnostic piety is maintained by
N. Brox, "ANATHEMA IESOUS (1 Kor. 12, 3)," Biblische Zeitschrift 12 [1968], pp. 103–111.

W. Marxsen, Introduction to the New Testament [ET, 1966], p. 75 reduces all the problems at
Corinth to one need on Paul's part—" to repel the Gnostic influence that has penetrated the
church" there. He lists the features of church problems at Corinth under this single rubric. In
particular, we draw attention to the belief—evidently current coin at Corinth—that the bap-
tized were already raised with Christ the heavenly Lord and made sharers of his pneumatic
spirit. They were thus placed beyond the range of temptation which afflicts mortal men, and
they took up an attitude of indifference to moral demands.

[46] W. Schmithals, The Office of Apostle in the Early Church [ET, 1969], pp. 222ff., discusses
the different ways suffering was understood in gnostic circles, though his attempt to interpret
Paul's self-understanding as apostle in gnostic categories is very dubious.

[47] D. Georgi, Die Gegner . . . pp. 282ff.

assumption that *Christians were united with a Lord who was remote from human rejection, failure and suffering.*

For that solid reason, Paul found it incumbent to argue and to illustrate the fact that this is an essentially false understanding of both the Lord's person and the nature of the Christian life. He leads off (in 1 Cor. 1–2) with a long exposition of the kerygma of the cross (1:18ff.) which has an obviously polemic slant. It is calculated to direct the readers' attention to the "cross" of Jesus which is a shorthand expression for all that was earthly, in terms of suffering, rejection and humiliation, in the life of Jesus. The reason why he does not utilize the Jesus-tradition is not clear; it may be that he had no knowledge of it, as Schulz argued (see earlier p. 147), or probably it was that this mass of tradition which centred on Jesus as an earthly figure had already been pre-empted by the Jewish-Christian opponents of Paul's party at Corinth because it favoured a θεῖος ἀνήρ assessment of Jesus.

More specifically, Paul emphasizes the centrality of the cross (1:18) because this was *the* issue at Corinth. Both Paul and the Corinthian teachers (of whom there may have been many, 4:15) agree on the importance of the resurrection—though they seriously mistake its significance as an event already realized and as having no future significance. Hence chapter 15 had to be written. But they have overlooked the cross-"side" of the kerygma, as J. M. Robinson names it,[48] and because of their lop-sided emphasis on the resurrection, Paul must show how the risen one is the crucified[49]; and that means "crucified in weakness" (2 Cor. 13:4).

At the same time, the figure of the crucified Christ (2:2: Χριστὸν ἐσταυρωμένον—perfect tense, denoting a continuing reality which began with the historical crucifixion of Jesus) sets the determinative pattern for the Christian way of life. Paul himself is the model for this, for he always carries in his human existence the dying of Jesus (2 Cor. 4:10). He shares in Christ's sufferings (1:3–7); he faces constant threats of death (6:4–10) and boasts of his hardships (11:21–29), even his affliction (12:11). And much of the apostle's teaching in the Corinthian correspondence has a single purpose, viz. to establish a "link between his founding mission and the current crisis, for he rejects the Corinthian assumption that the mature Christian has been glorified out of an existence determined by the word of the cross. The basis for their continued existence as Christians is the same as the basis of their conversion."[50]

[48] J. M. Robinson, "The Recent Debate on the 'New Quest,'" *Journal of Bible and Religion*, 30 [1962], p. 203.

[49] H. Conzelmann, *Der erste Brief an die Korinther* [KEK, 1969], p. 55, p. 71, note 16.

[50] W. Childs Robinson, Jr., "Word and Power (1 Corinthians 1:17–2:5)," *Soli Deo Gloria*, William Childs Robinson Festschrift, ed. J. McDowell Richards [1968], p. 73. The basis of this assertion rests on an understanding of 2:2, which means that "though Christ did not remain dead, but is alive, he remains—as the risen Christ—the crucified one" (*loc. cit.*, p. 71). Cf. Revelation 5:1–14 as well as Paul's use of the same participle in Galatians 3:1.

The practical application of his doctrine of the cross touches the Christian life as a call to *mimesis*, an acting upon the historical reality of Christ's salvation in such a way that the believer reproduces by his obedience in concrete life-situations a quality of life which is patterned on the humiliation of the cross (2 Cor. 4:7–12; 13:3, 4). Throughout Paul builds upon the historical elements in Jesus' own earthly life, though he couches this appeal in a theological frame of language, and does not embody the gospel tradition in explicit form by appeal to the Jesus of history, even in 2 Corinthians 8:9.[51]

This ambiguity in Paul's presentation conferred a dubious legacy on the later church. We know that his teaching was open to distortion and misunderstanding even when he was alive and exercising his ministry (Rom. 3:8; 6:1ff.; Gal. 2:17). The emergence of a situation after his death and the consequent withdrawal of his personal presence from the churches is a postulated step we take on the basis of the above considera- tion. We imagine an over-compensating stress on Paul's kerygmatic theology which placed all emphasis on Christ as a heavenly figure, remote from empirical history and out of touch with earthly reality. The end-result of this attempt to carry Paul's transcendental christology to extreme limits (a trend already visible in Ephesians), possibly in the interests of a wisdom-theology[52] or by too close an association of a Christ-figure with contemporary saviours and mediators in hellenistic religion,[53] was the gnostic version of Christianity in the second century.

[51] See W. C. Robinson, Jr., *loc. cit.*, pp. 81f., with reference to H. D. Betz, *Nachfolge und Nachahmung Jesu Christi im Neuen Testament* [1967], p. 168.

[52] This is the way Schmithals, *Die Gnosis in Korinth*,[2] p. 130 (ET, pp. 137f.) explains Paul's polemic against wisdom in 1 Corinthians 1–2. He hypothesizes a wisdom-teaching which replaced the cross, followed by a denial of any saving significance of Jesus' death on the part of the Corinthian false teachers. W. C. Robinson, Jr., (*loc. cit.*, p. 72) is critical of this deduction.

[53] The epistle to the Colossians may be mentioned in this context. If the Colossian heretics had arisen from within the church, it is likely that they were using some of Paul's own concepts and pushing them to an extent which Paul disavowed. In particular, the rôle of the cosmic Christ was interpreted by them in conjunction with a gnosticizing world-view and seen as only part of the answer to the question of the knowledge of God and access to him. Paul *both* agreed with their cosmological concerns *and* rejected their solutions—a factor which accounts for many of the problem verses in the epistle. See R. P. Martin, *Colossians: The Church's Lord and the Christian's Liberty* [1972].

The issue turns on whether (i) the Colossian heresy was "home-grown" and produced within the ranks of the church, or imported from outside the church, as W. Foerster, "Die Irrlehrer des Kolosserbriefes," *Studia Biblica et Semitica*, T. C. Vriezen Festschrift [1966], p. 72, has argued. See my commentary for the former view; and (ii) whether Paul finds the Colossian error to include a docetic element. This could be affirmed in the light of his insist- ence on a physical side to Christ's becoming man (1:22; 2:11), his death on the cross (1:20) and his afflictions (1:24).

If these two interpretations are sound, already in the Pauline churches of Asia Minor there is evidence of a denial of Jesus' full humanity and an incipient trend to turn him into a cos- mological cipher.

Whether there is any closer connection between the situation of a false christology at Colossae and the publication of Mark's gospel in view of what we have in Colossians 4:10 (Mark's name and a possible visit to the scene of error), is too speculative a question to pursue, except only incidentally. If Paul was in Rome at the time of writing the epistle and Mark was

(2) *Paul's kerygma and Mark's supplement*

It remains in this section to indicate briefly the proposed occasion for
the timely publication of Mark's Gospel. We suggest that it should be
traced to this situation which arose after Paul's death or, at least, in areas
where the influence of Paul's kerygmatic theology had sufficiently been
diluted as to suggest a loss of grip on the historical events underlying his
kerygma.

Mark's book puts together just those individual sections of the pre-
canonical tradition which emphasize the paradox of Jesus' earthly life in
which suffering and vindication form a two-beat rhythm. His christology
is *that of a teacher who has caught the essence of Paul's thought yet expressed*
it by use of language and terminology to which Paul had no access (the Jesus-
tradition) *and did so in order to compensate for what he believed to be a serious*
distortion of his master's thought as apostle par excellence.

At the same time, Mark has an intensely practical interest. The nature
of the Christian life, as he understands it, carries the same pattern as his
christology. The disciple is bidden to take up his cross and then follow
the Lord who entered his glory by way of suffering and outward defeat.
Mark's record of Jesus' teaching conforms to that purpose. He has a
limited object in view, which is to give an epitome of Jesus' call to follow
him and of the cost of discipleship. Both places where he gives extended
reporting of his teaching (ch. 4 and ch. 13) are written to convey this, and
distinctive notes are sounded elsewhere, namely, "He who loses his life
for my sake and the gospel's [on this Markan phrase, see earlier, pp. 24ff.]
will save it" (8:35); "The Son of man did not come to be served but to
serve, and to give his life a ransom for many" (10:45).

In sum, the evangelist is offering a dramatization in the life of Jesus,
by a selective use of the materials at his disposal and by his innovative
joining of a Jesus-tradition and a Passion narrative, of the twin elements
which made up the Pauline preaching. These are the humiliation and
enthronement of the church's Lord. Mark is no speculative thinker, and
can afford to bypass the question of Jesus' existence prior to his earthly
life, just as Romans 1:3, 4; 4:25; 1 Corinthians 15:3ff. do. His purpose is
directed to other issues, which speculative christological thinking will only
confuse. Indeed, it may have been just the effort of Pauline Christians
working overtime in weaving their speculative ideas about Christ' person
which led to a loss of contact with a Jesus whose feet touched the ground
in Galilee and Jerusalem.

The evangelist, therefore, is content simply to stress the twin factors
of Jesus' mundane existence and acceptance of the way to the cross, and
his ultimate vindication as his promised word of triumph is made good

his companion then, there might be room for the hypothesis that what impelled Mark to
write his gospel was the emergence and strength of a christological error, whose danger his
gospel of a *suffering Messiah* was designed to repel.

(14:28; 16:7). Further enquiry either about the pre-ministry period or the post-resurrection appearances falls outside his province. Jesus' acceptance by God at his baptism (1:11) and the believing confession (15:39) are the terminal points, with the promise of victory and hope fulfilled in veiled fashion beyond death (16:6, 7).

The way of the servant is to be the route taken by those who follow him; so Mark has interwoven strands of teaching about the nature of discipleship, the prospect of persecution and martyrdom, the reward of sharing his glory by drinking his cup of woe and the final pledge of his presence to those who are loyal members of God's kingdom. For Mark christology and discipleship are the two ingredients; and by boldly appropriating the technical term "gospel" which in his day had acquired the nuance of kerygma or saving proclamation, he makes his bid to express that Pauline message in a language which unmistakably "grounds" it in the historical ministry, rejection and death of the divine Son. He also inextricably weds it to the Christian's allegiance to a suffering Master in whose footsteps the church is bound to tread, and it should not be surprised when the road of the cross is a hard way through persecution and privation to final vindication.

VII

A THEORY TESTED

Exegetical studies on the twin Markan motifs concerning the ministry of Jesus: (a) a refusal to give demonstrable proofs; (b) a ready consent to suffer and to taste the bitterness of death in utter desolation.

I F OUR FOREGOING DISCUSSION IS ANY WAY NEAR THE TRUTH OF THE matter, it should be possible to see something of the evidence for it in particular details as well as in the overall impression of Mark's purpose. We address our enquiry in this chapter to such an examination.

It is our theorem that Mark wrote his gospel-book as a theological and practical exercise related to a specific and pressing need. In order to offset what he believed to be a dangerous trend in the church of his day he wished to set out the character of Jesus' life, death and triumph with a view to dispelling the doubt that he was truly human as well as fully divine. He also has provided a rationale for his death on the cross, which the Greek mind (inured to the idea that the divine cannot by definition endure suffering) was underplaying, possibly by an over-emphasis on Jesus as a glorious, other-worldly figure. Part of this total picture involved, on Mark's part, a concern to show how faith marked out the true response to Jesus' ministry as the most appropriate reaction to his wonderful deeds. Faith becomes the opposite of amazement and incredulity, which can only stare in bewilderment and be momentarily impressed at his mighty powers. Consistently Jesus opposed this attitude—hence the restrictions and warnings which go to make up the "Messianic secret" doctrine—and inevitably his path led him to a cross beyond which there was for his followers only the promise of his vindication.

For the evangelist this presentation has a practical application. He is no theoretician, dealing only with ideas and concepts. Nor is he only a theologian who is concerned to refute false teaching and to establish the church in its correct beliefs about its Lord. His rôle as evangelist relates to a practical interest he evinces in showing the bearing of his teaching on a community which faces trial, persecution and loss of meaning. If the two pillars of the church (as they are called in 1 Clement 5:2), Peter and Paul, had recently been taken away in death to receive a martyr's crown, it was only to be anticipated that some theodicy would be needed to justify these events as part of the divine purpose and to show that they did not contradict that purpose.

And if the church at Rome was meeting the prospect of further outbreaks of opposition—the same document, known as 1 Clement goes on to speak of "a great number of the elect" (6:1) as victims of Nero's pogrom and its aftermath—with trepidation and questioning, it would be entirely to the point for a Christian writer to issue a tract of encouragement and explanation in the light of these searing events. The novelty is that he chose, and was moved, to do so by setting the church's affliction and his call to fidelity within the framework of a story of Jesus' suffering Messiahship and his teaching that only by the disciples' taking up the cross and following him can they attain his glory.

For Mark, theology—or, more precisely, christology—and Christian living are intimately connected, since the way of the church is to follow the path of suffering already taken by the Lord. And the finest incentive to faithfulness and courage under duress is the presentation of the Markan Jesus whose profile sharply stands out in two clear lineaments:

(A) He refuses to give demonstrable proofs of his claims.

(B) He readily consents to suffer and to taste the bitterness of death.

These two parts of Mark's picture of Jesus and his witness to him may now be considered into some detail.

(A) There are three passages which fall to be treated under this heading.

(i) *The Refusal of a Sign from Heaven*

> The Pharisees came and began to argue with him, seeking from him a sign from heaven, to test him. And he sighed deeply in his spirit, and said, "Why does this generation seek a sign? Truly, I say to you, no sign shall be given to this generation. And he left them, and getting into the boat again he departed to the other side (8:11–13).

Preliminary Observations

These verses (8:11–13) clearly form an isolated section. The subject-matter is unrelated to what has preceded it, and there is some justification for Bultmann's proposal that the term "Pharisees" is introduced to provide an example of "typical participants in debate."[1] In the reply Jesus gives (v. 12) he speaks of the unbelief of "this generation" with no reference to the Pharisees since the description (ἡ γενεὰ αὕτη represents the Rabbinic *ha-dôr ha-zeh*) shows that he has in mind a comprehensive view. "He is aiming at the whole people and not at individuals."[2]

---

[1] R. Bultmann, *The History of the Synoptic Tradition* [ET, 1963], p. 52. He draws attention to the way in which Mark has described Jesus as being in another territory and "must in consequence bring the Pharisees out to him."

[2] F. Büchsel, TDNT i, p. 663.

Yet the "Pharisees" do play a significant rôle, Mark has by design introduced this brief *pericope*, which is better classified as a Pronouncement story than a Controversy story, in order to forge a link between the Feeding of the Four thousand (8:1-10) and the teaching on the "leaven" of the Pharisees (8:15). As Jesus is the dispenser of the true bread in the miracle story, he proceeds to warn against the false teaching of his opponents under the imagery of "leaven." Leaven was introduced into the making of bread in Palestinian homes but given a symbolic value as meaning an evil influence (as in 1 Cor. 5:6-8; Gal. 5:9, etc.). The disciples' lack of perception is the point at issue (8:17, 21), which suggests that they too are victims of false notions and guilty of cherishing the same spirit as that which prompted the request for a sign. They no less than the ostensible and traditional enemies of Jesus (the Pharisees of 8:11) need to be warned and put right.

A comparison of the synoptic tradition (Matt. 12:38, 39; 16:1-4; Mark 8:11-13; Luke 11:16, 29-32; 12:54-56) shows that this saying of Jesus contained in the punch-line of the *pericope*: "Truly I say to you, no sign shall be given to this generation" (Mark 8:12) has been handed down in different ways. We may suggest that a line of development can be traced.

Mark's version, which forbids absolutely the granting of a sign, stands at the furthest recoverable point of the tradition.[3] Indeed, it may be claimed that we hear a true accent of *ipsissima vox Jesu*. The chief reason for affirming this confidence is the most probable interpretation to be given to verse 12. It is introduced by the authorizing formula ἀμὴν λέγω ὑμῖν: "Indeed I say to you," a form of statement which J. Jeremias has claimed to go back to Jesus himself.[4]

Then, the Greek sentence εἰ δοθήσεται τῇ γενεᾷ ταύτῃ σημεῖον is incomplete and represents a type of construction which is borrowed clearly from Hebrew. The first word εἰ (corresponding to the Hebrew *'im*) introduces an oath and strong asseveration, meaning "Certainly not."[5] Using a phrase drawn from the Hebrew idiom, Mark conveys the sense of Jesus' uncompromising refusal to give a sign. But his Greek obviously reflects his faithfulness to a very unusual type of wording which asserts a strong denial.

---

[3] For a contrary view, see A. E. J. Rawlinson, *Commentary* [1925]: Additional note (5) The demand for a Sign (Mk. viii. 11 sqq.), pp. 257f.; N. Perrin, *Rediscovering the Teaching of Jesus* [1967], pp. 191-195.

[4] J. Jeremias, "Kennzeichen der ipsissima vox Jesu," in *Synoptische Studien*. Festschrift A. Wikenhauser [1953], pp. 86-93 [ET *The Prayers of Jesus* (1967), pp. 108-115]. In the same volume, A. Vögtle, "Der Spruch von Jonaszeichen," pp. 230-277, similarly concludes on the ground of the semitic peculiarities of Mark 8:12 that this text may be directly traceable to Jesus (p. 239).

[5] Blass-Debrunner-Funk, *Grammar*, sect. 372. The exact form is seen in Psalm 7:3ff. (4ff. LXX) with the implicit imprecation made familiar to us in the language of 2 Kings 6:31: "May God do so to me, and more also, *if* . . ."

The passive form of this verb ("shall be given") may suggest a periphrasis for the divine name, as obviously in Matthew 7:7. Then, the denial is made even more emphatic, "God will most certainly not give a sign to this generation." And we are drawn back to Jesus' attested way of expressing himself by this use of a reverential circumlocution.

As a final pointer to Mark's originality in the stream of the tradition, we consider the question why Mark would wish to eliminate the addition "except the sign of Jonah" if it stood before him. Perrin argues[6] that he has in fact done so since he elsewhere places "great emphasis upon the mighty deeds of Jesus as the only, but complete, demonstration of his messiahship, and it would be natural for him to omit the reference to some other sign, however that reference was to be understood."

This conclusion overlooks the distinction which Mark makes between "mighty deeds" ($\delta v v \acute{\alpha} \mu \epsilon \iota \varsigma$) and a sign ($\sigma \eta \mu \epsilon \tilde{\iota} o v$); and we will contend shortly that this distinction is the crux of the Markan teaching. Further, if the Q form (given in Matt. 12:39 = Luke 11:29) is original with its allusion to the sign of Jonah, it is hard to see why Mark has omitted the epithet "evil" (in both Matthew and Luke, but omitted in Perrin's translation, in dependence on C. Colpe). Compare 9:19: "O faithless generation." The conflate reading which Perrin manufactures by running Mark and Q together succeeds only in making a nonsense statement out of Jesus' words. He is made both to deny a sign and then to give one!

The Q version, attested in Luke 11:29 = Matthew 12:39, adds "except the sign of Jonah," which is an expansion found also in Matthew 16:4. Exactly what is meant by this sign is not clear. It has been proposed that originally the sign of Jonah was his preaching (as in Luke 11:32), and Jesus' word refers to the effectiveness of the spoken ministry of both the prophet and himself. Subsequently, extended applications of the sign were made, one in reference to the parousia of the Son of man (Luke 11:30; cf. 17:22ff.)[7] and another in reference to the passion, entombment and resurrection of the Son of man which are likened to Jonah's descent into the fish and release (Matt. 12:40).

The Teaching of Mark 8:11–13

Mark's version may be claimed, therefore, as the original form of the saying of Jesus in regard to the refusal of a sign. But the important questions are still to be faced; and they are two in number.

(a) What was intended by the request for a sign "from heaven"?

---

[6] N. Perrin, op. cit., pp. 192ff.

[7] So Bultmann, The History of the Synoptic Tradition, p. 118: "The meaning of the saying (in the Luke version) seems to me to be: Just as Jonah came to the Ninevites from a distant country, so will the Son of man come to this generation from heaven."

Various answers are possible.[8] The usually accepted view is that the sign requested was for a miracle of a higher order than those which Jesus had performed up to that point in his ministry. The Pharisees were asking for something which would clearly substantiate his Messianic authority and be an obvious revelation in undoubted form (e.g., a sign in the sky or a voice from heaven). The latter idea is unconsciously reflected on to the Markan version from Matthew 16:1 which reads "*to show them* a sign from heaven," as though a visible or audible interposition of God were in question.

O. Linton has shown that the notion of an extraordinary wonder is not necessarily involved in this context. The real point at issue is that of Jesus' authority and what is being sought is some authorization from God ("from heaven," as in Mark 12:30: "Was the baptism of John from heaven or from men?") that Jesus was trustworthy, not that he had supernatural powers at his disposal.

Alternatively, E. Schweizer[9] thinks that what was sought was the performing of a stupendous miracle which could not be imitated by other miracle-workers of the day. "From heaven" means "a cosmic miracle of an apocalyptic nature," which by its nature would be recognized as *sui generis* and so beyond dispute. We may compare Matthew 12:27; Luke 11:19 for exorcisms which were duplicated by Jewish healers.

There is still another possibility, which commends itself. Clearly "from heaven" means in this context "with divine authorization," and it is likely that the demand in Mark 8:11 was for a legitimating sign granted by God which would attest Jesus' claim to be one sent from God.[10] What the Pharisees wanted was not a miracle performed by Jesus' own power with the help of God, but an attesting sign which would validate his claim. The evidence is that the Jews expected the eschatological prophet to certify his mission as authorized by God and to accredit himself as the proclaimer of good news in the tradition of the herald in Isaiah 40–66 (especially 61:1).[11] Mark has already used this idea in his announcement of Jesus' preaching in 1:15 and it is fundamental to his entire work that he aims to write a "gospel," i.e. good news, which Jesus Christ came to bring and embody (1:1). Mark consciously portrays Jesus as God's special Messenger and divine Agent—Messiah is not a title that concerns

[8] They are discussed in O. Linton's article, "The Demand for a Sign from Heaven," *Studia Theologica* 19 [1965], pp. 112–129; and K. Kertelge, *Die Wunder Jesu im Markusevangelium* [1970], pp. 23–27.

[9] E. Schweizer, *Commentary, p.* 159.

[10] So F. Hahn, *The Titles of Jesus in Christology* [ET, 1969], p. 378; K. H. Rengstorf, TDNT vii, p. 235 and K. Kertelge, *op. cit.,* p.26.

[11] For the Messianic prophet and his people "who expected a miracle of accreditation whereby the legitimacy of the prophet will be demonstrated and the age of salvation will open," see R. Meyer, TDNT vi, pp. 826ff.; and Hahn, *op. cit.,* p. 380. The counterpart of σημεῖον is the Hebrew 'ôt. This Hebrew term, especially in Isaiah 7:10ff., Deut. 13:1-2, and the Rabbinic literature has an important function. It serves to ensure the trustworthiness or otherwise of a prophetic oracle or messenger. So Linton, *loc. cit.,* pp. 123ff.

him greatly—and in this *pericope* the issue is to settle the question of what authority Jesus lays claim to possessing. If he grants a sign, his enemies will be convinced that he is what Mark claims for him, and his title to be eschatological proclaimer of God's good news in the final sense will be authenticated. But is this a genuine demand and a valid test? Apparently not, for Mark. We turn to see why.

(*b*) Why did Jesus refuse absolutely (in Mark)? The evangelist intends to show that the demand for a sign was a temptation which Jesus had to refuse without compromise. Several indications in the text drive home this sharp point.

Mark's use of the verb "to seek" ($\zeta\eta\tau\epsilon\tilde{\iota}\nu$) is part of his purpose. Wherever the verb is found it is used either with a plainly hostile reference, of Jesus' enemies seeking to arrest and kill him (11:18; 12:12; 14:1, 11, 55) or in the bad sense of attempting to distract Jesus from his true mission. Peter appears in the first of his many parts as the devil's advocate in his attempted persuasion of Jesus to stay in a Galilean town and to confine his ministry to a settled place. "Every one is searching for ($\zeta\eta\tau o\tilde{\upsilon}\sigma\iota\nu$) you" (1:37). The family of Jesus have heard that Jesus is in danger of losing his mental balance, and appear on the scene. "Your mother and your brothers are outside, asking for ($\zeta\eta\tau o\tilde{\upsilon}\sigma\iota\nu$) you" (3:32). They wanted to restrain him. The word of the young man to the women at the tomb may be no exception (16:6): "You seek ($\zeta\eta\tau\epsilon\tilde{\iota}\tau\epsilon$) Jesus of Nazareth, who was crucified. He is risen, he is not here." It suggests that the women did wrong in coming to the now empty grave when they should have recalled and believed his promise, and gone off to meet him in Galilee (verse 7). So they are reproached for a misguided seeking just as Peter and the family of Jesus are rebuked by Jesus' responses to their plea. He diverts attention from their request to the true nature of his mission. So it is with the seeking of the Pharisees. They are misguided in what they ask.

The reference to "tempting" ($\pi\epsilon\iota\rho\acute{\alpha}\zeta\epsilon\iota\nu$) in the phrase "to test him" (8:11) speaks for itself. It is found in 1:13 where Jesus is in the desert "tempted ($\pi\epsilon\iota\rho\alpha\zeta\acute{o}\mu\epsilon\nu o\varsigma$) by Satan." No further elaboration of the content of the temptation or even of his success in overcoming the satanic opposition is given in Mark. We may suspect that Mark has a reason for this. If this is so, we may seek the purpose in what the subsequent drama of controversy narratives and debates contains. Jesus does not cease to be tempted in the wilderness by winning a decisive victory there (cf. Luke 4:13), nor does he vanquish Satan who is driven away (Matt. 4:11). "The whole Gospel is an explanation of how Jesus was tempted,"[12] as the theme recurs and Jesus is faced repeatedly with the issues which provocatively and summarily are presented in the Q version of Matthew

---

[12] U. W. Mauser, *Christ in the Wilderness* [1963], p. 100. See, however, the critique in E. Best, *The Temptation and the Passion* [1965], pp. 25ff., where other part of Mauser's thesis are closely scrutinized.

4:1–11 = Luke 4:1–13. Whether the temptation is directly satanic[13] or derived from human sources,[14] it is Mark's purpose to show how Jesus' entire ministry was a facing of the issues which constituted a "temptation," i.e. a solicitation to evil. Choices were presented to him and he was called upon to range himself behind one course of action or another by what he said and did (so in 10:2 and 12:15). And the same is true in Mark 8:11. The Pharisees approach him with a proposal which superficially looks to be attractive. But Jesus sees through to the implications as in the questions on divorce and the tribute-money and recognizes the evil design of what is proposed. Therefore the translation "test"[15] is to be rejected; a stronger term is needed. Their demand for a sign was an enticement to evil. And as such he must reject it out of hand.

The suggestion is countered by an emotional response on Jesus' part. "He sighed deeply in his spirit" (8:12) renders a verb, which in its compound form is found only here. It is not certain if we should take the Markan text to refer to the Holy Spirit, as in Romans 8:23. If so, there would be a parallel with 14:38, but it is very doubtful if the Gethsemane episode is to be so interpreted.[16] And the use of $\pi\nu\varepsilon\tilde{\upsilon}\mu a$ to denote the human spirit of Jesus in 2:8 rather confirms that this is how the text (8:12) is to be understood. Nevertheless, the verb in 8:12 is emphatic and stresses the disappointment and frustration of Jesus that such a demand should have been made. For a similar emotional ejaculation see 9:19. The conversation is abruptly broken off as Jesus leaves the scene (verse 13).

Mark's Purpose in 8:11–13

The evangelist has inserted this short section in order to accomplish several objectives.

(a) Primarily, he wishes to distinguish in this way between the meaning of Jesus' mighty works ($\delta\upsilon\nu\acute{a}\mu\varepsilon\iota\varsigma$) and the value of a sign ($\sigma\eta\mu\varepsilon\tilde{\iota}o\nu$).

The "mighty works" of Jesus in this gospel are intended to play several rôles. There are sixteen separate stories, and both in form and purpose they are not uniform.[17] K. Kertelge[18] has recently classified the miracle-stories and has argued that the term *dynameis* belongs most appropriately to the group of narratives in chapters 6–8. It is in this section of the gospel (6:6a–8:26) that the contrast between the Pharisees' demand for a sign

[13] So J. M. Robinson, *The Problem of History in Mark* [1957], p. 46.

[14] So E. Best, *op. cit.*, pp. 31ff.

[15] In RSV and in H. Seesemann, TDNT vi, p. 28, who renders the verb (classified so as to be taken in a secular way) "to prove."

[16] So E. Best, *op. cit.*, p. 32.

[17] As V. Taylor, *St. Mark*, p. 364 observes: "It is mistaken to assume that the Markan narratives are of one stamp. Further, narratives must be studied, not only in themselves, but in relation to the groups in which they appear, for the groups differ according as historical, topical, or doctrinal interests are uppermost."

[18] K. Kertelge, *Die Wunder Jesu im Markusevangelium* [1970], p. 165.

and Jesus' mighty deeds is set out most prominently. Here, if anywhere, we should seek an answer to the question of Mark's purpose in marking off the miracle-stories (of which he approves by his inclusion of these accounts in his gospel) from the illegitimate appeal for a sign (which has his plain disapproval).

Of the various stories in the section of chapters 6–8 the one factor in common to all of them is the centrality of Jesus as himself embodying a present salvation. Whatever the original structure and tradition of the story, Mark's redaction has brought out clearly the christological meaning and emphasized the accent of God's offer of salvation in him. By so doing Mark has adapted the miracles to fit in with his purpose in writing a gospel.[19]

On a positive side, he has drawn out the relevance of Jesus in the miracle-story. The feedings of the multitude are signs of Jesus' present salvation for both the Jews (6:34–44) and Gentiles (8:1–10). His walking on the sea (6:45–52) speaks not only of the amazement which the disciples show at such a feat (6:51) but more of the promise that Jesus is a very present help in trouble (v. 50). The universal offer of God's salvation in Jesus is the clear message in the healing of the Syrophoenician woman's daughter (7:24–30). The cures performed on the deaf-mute (7:32–37) and the blind man in Bethsaida (8:22–26) are so shaped by Mark's editorial comments, either at the conclusion of the first story (7:37) or at an earlier place in his narrative (8:18) that the full christological significance is drawn out of the historical narration. In the first place, he has appended the words, "He has done all things well" in recall of Genesis 1:31 (LXX) and thus he had made it clear that Jesus' acts are such as God only can do. Furthermore, it is a token of the new age of God's rule, spoken of in Isaiah 35:5f., that the deaf are made to hear and the dumb to speak. So Jesus is God's pledge that the new era has arrived and in him God's age-old promises of deliverance are made good. The healing of the blind man in 8:22–26 is evidently intended to show how the incapacity of the disciples (in 8:18) will be cured; and if there is hope for these men in their blindness and insensibility (8:17, 21) there is hope for all men.

These *dynameis* were intended by Mark to be tokens of God's presence and activity in Jesus. But they are not outward demonstrations by which the claim of Jesus is legitimated. They are not for Mark Messianic proof-texts, nor are they works such as the hellenistic "divine man" might have performed to draw attention to himself or to parade his credentials. As K. Kertelge[20] has correctly noted in what is the thesis of his book, the miracles of Jesus make clear his mission, though who he is in reality is *not*

[19] Kertelge, *op. cit.*, p. 125: "Only under the rubric of εὐαγγέλιον do the δυνάμεις of Jesus receive their true significance."

[20] K. Kertelge, *op. cit.*, pp. 89, 170f. This opposes T. A. Burkill's view (*Mysterious Revelation* [1963], p. 41), that "the Messiahship [of Jesus] is made manifest in the wonders which Jesus performs."

directly revealed through these wonderful events. Rather, it is Mark's way of an indirect presentation of Jesus as the hidden Son of God on earth. The miracles have no value in attesting directly Jesus' messianic status. They are ambiguous, and so are liable to misunderstanding. Indeed, in the classic case of Jesus' rejection at Nazareth (6:1–6) this is precisely what happens.[21] The neighbours and kinsfolk of Jesus' family are compelled to admit that he is the author of a supernatural power (verse 2). They freely attribute a more-than-human wisdom to him. Yet their attitude is one of astonished incredulity (verse 2a) and stark unbelief (verses 3, 6) since they are openly scandalized by his fame and success; and behind that they are shocked that "the carpenter" (verse 3) can act in this way.

There are further indications in Mark that he proposed to set a firm line of demarcation between Jesus' mighty works and his true authority.

(*b*) The Transfiguration story (9:2–8) is another example of the evangelist's deliberate denial of Jesus' recourse to signs. Recent study of this passage[22] has drawn attention to the way in which Mark's account emphasizes the part played by Elijah and Moses. There is some reference to these figures in five out of the seven verses. It is also a correct procedure to enquire why this should be and to postulate that Mark was writing to counter some form of misunderstanding or unbelief in his day. One answer is given (by M. E. Thrall, *loc. cit.*) in terms of an erroneous understanding of Jesus who was being reduced to the level of the Old Testament figures. Peter's words in verse 5 are held to imply an attitude which treats all three characters in the story on a level as equals. This prompts the false deduction (which Mark is anxious to remove), Perhaps Jesus, like them, was simply a great prophet, or a very holy man, or an outstanding interpreter of God's Law? And Mark's reply is to stress the uniqueness of Jesus as God's beloved Son (verse 7) and Messiah.

As an alternative view, we may propose that Elijah and Moses are brought on to the stage in the Markan drama as characters who, in the Jewish tradition, were believed not to have died but to have been translated directly to heaven in glory.[23] The next step in the chain of reasoning which would make Jesus stand in this succession is that he is the eschatological prophet of the last days, who would follow the example of his predecessors and be taken up into heaven, to return at the End-time.[24]

---

[21] Cf. now E. Grässer, "Jesus in Nazareth (Mark vi, 1–6a)," NTS 16 [1969–70], pp. 1–23.

[22] Especially the article, "Elijah and Moses in Mark's Account of the Transfiguration" by M. E. Thrall, NTS 16 [1969–70], pp. 305–317.

[23] For Elijah, see 2 Kings 2:11 and Ecclus. 48:9, 12; Eth. Enoch 89:52. 93:8: Josephus, Ant, 9:28. The idea of Moses' assumption (different from the biblical witness of Deut. 34:5) is given in the rabbinic literature, See J. Jeremias, TDNT ii, p. 939; iv, pp. 854ff. The rabbinic attestation (though limited) is given in these articles: "Some say Moses did not die but stands and discharges above the (priestly) service" and "Three went up alive into heaven: Enoch, Moses and Elijah."

[24] For this expectation of the eschatological prophet, see F. Hahn, *op. cit.*, p. 382; cf. p. 336.

Peter's association of Jesus within this category of prophetic, now heavenly, figures is disowned both by the editorial comment: "For he did not know what to say" (verse 6) and more emphatically by the sudden recession of Elijah and Moses from the disciples' view so that Jesus is left alone. The point about verse 8 is that Jesus is still there with his feet on the mountain. He has not been raptured to heaven, as would have been most natural if he had asserted his rightful claim to belong to the heavenly world. Instead, in an almost unbelievable contrast, he proceeds to descend from the mountain and to speak plainly about the rejection and death of the Son of man (9:9–13). No change of setting could be greater. From the mountain-top whence it was a short step into the cloud from which the legitimating voice had spoken, he comes down into the world which will treat him with contempt and kill him. No sign is given, as he prepares for the final march on Jerusalem.

(c) It is not surprising that when "false Christs and false prophets" arise, according to the Markan apocalypse (13:21–23), they will claim to be accredited in a way which Jesus had refused. "They will show signs and wonders," but the effect will be only to confuse Christians and to cause consternation and doubt.

These charismatic persons lay claim to the possession of special powers as a means by which their teaching may be legitimated. The background is Deuteronomy 13:1–2, which shows that the working of "signs and wonders" was a concomitant of the false prophet.[25]

For Mark, the picture of Jesus as true Son and God's ultimate revelation is set on a canvas where "signs and wonders" are refused since there is no way of legitimating his mission as the hidden Son of God. An appeal to oracular signs and audible tokens would be *illegitimate*, because they would effectively block the way to true faith, as well as convey a wrong impression of the true character of Jesus himself. These two aspects may be considered separately, though they merge into a total picture.

The motive which inspired Mark's Jesus to heal the sick and cure disease and infirmity is at the heart of our discussion. He is spoken of as "moved with pity" (1:41 [if this is the true reading]; 6:34; 8:2; 9:22; 10:47f.[26]) and on one occasion he assures the sufferer that his healing is accomplished because the Lord "has had pity on you" (5:19). The essence of such acts of compassion is that they are unforced by personal desire on Jesus' part to draw attention to himself or to provide an object-lesson. They are, on the contrary, spontaneous outgoings of his heart of love and not occasioned by any need on his part to use such miracles to attest his authority or support his claims. These mighty works are not recorded in Mark's use of the stories to stress Jesus' talents as a wonder-worker,

---

[25] S. V. McCasland, "Signs and Wonders," JBL 76 [1957], pp. 149–52.
[26] H. Köster, TDNT vii, p. 554.

exercising extraordinary ability, and there was nothing self-conscious in the way he worked—witness 5:30 where Jesus "knew in himself that power ($\delta\acute{v}\nu\alpha\mu\iota\varsigma$) had gone out of him" though others did not know this, except the woman who was cured of her haemorrhage—so it is not unexpected that Mark boldly records Jesus' inability to perform miracles in an unsympathetic atmosphere.

Where the folk at Nazareth (6:1–6) were hostile and critical, Jesus' power was restrained by unbelief (verse 6). Verse 5 with its two parts presents a puzzle. The denial of his ability to perform any mighty work there is modified by the additional statement "except that he laid his hands upon a few sick people and healed them." It looked as though Mark discriminates between Jesus' mighty works (*dynameis*) and acts of healing which are not to be reckoned as *dynameis* in the strict sense.[27] If so, this distinction serves to stress again the fact that the correlative of *dynameis* is *pistis* (faith). Only in the responsiveness of appeal to him and trust in his power do Jesus' mighty works take on the character of revelation. The mighty works *as such* are neutral and ambivalent. Mark goes further. He makes it clear that they are so capable of misinterpretation that where there is no perception of who the healer is and no sensitivity to his person in the deed, the only result is blank astonishment leading to sheer unbelief, as is clear from the sequence in chapter 6. Verse 2: "Those who heard him were amazed" is quickly followed by verse 3: "They took offence at him."

A recognition of Jesus as the bringer of God's salvation waits on the understanding of faith. Where there is no faith, those who see Jesus' mighty works are impressed but not changed. Rather there is the possibility that their hearts will be further hardened and their minds will be closed to God's truth. Hence the disciples are rebuked for precisely this reason (8:17). Yet faith links the person in need directly to Jesus and unites that need to the supply of God's power in him. For a description of faith in this context, we can do no better than quote the following statement. "Faith, as illustrated in Mark's Gospel, may be defined as a painstaking and concentrated effort to obtain blessing for oneself or for others, material or spiritual, inspired by a confident belief that God in Jesus can supply all human need."[28]

This double insistence by Mark that Jesus' earthly ministry is sufficiently ambiguous to call forth opposite attitudes of either rejection or acceptance and that faith is needed to penetrate the secret of his person means that a demand for a sign is an irresponsible request. For one thing, faith by its very nature can never be satisfied with a tangible proof of Jesus' authority. E. Schweizer has recognized this quality in Mark's understanding of faith.

[27] So. J. Weiss, *Schriften des NT* i³ [1917], p. 125, quoted by Kertelge, *op. cit.*, p. 123 note.
[28] J. A. Findlay, *Jesus as they saw Him* [1934], p. 107, quoted by V. Taylor, *The Gospels*⁵ [1945], p. 55 note.

> He knows . . . that everything becomes false as soon as a sign is demanded—
> as soon as faith becomes dependent upon visible proof. For then faith would
> be nothing more than a logical conclusion which anyone ultimately might
> draw without becoming involved.[29]

Jesus' person is at risk too, if he can be understood and hailed as God's Son in direct response to a sign. Then he would be no more than a false leader, a messianic pretender or pseudo-Christ who endeavoured to gain a popular following in obedience to his miracle-working powers. For Mark, such a possibility is unthinkable, since at every turn of events where this possibility is presented to him he resolutely sets his face against it—and climbs the steep road to Jerusalem and his Passion.

(d) This brings our discussion to a head. Are we to infer that Jesus' ministry in this gospel is unattested? The answer is No, since Mark takes us to those special occasions when his sonship was divinely certified (1:11; 9:7) and humanly recognized (15:39). In each instance, as we shall try to show in the next section, the proclamation of Jesus' true stature is set in the framework of his mission of filial obedience freely rendered and suffering freely accepted. This leads us to conclude that for Mark the only true sign is the cross which paradoxically is both a tragedy of outward defeat and a revelation of who Jesus really is. It is the centurion who pierces the veil which hides the latter as he sees beyond what his eyes look at (15:39). And his confession is that of a suffering figure of the Son of God.

This is Paul's teaching couched in a theological language-form in 1 Corinthians 1–2. The purport of that extended discussion is that God's weakness and hiddenness in the cross of Christ reveal his power and grace, but only to the eye of faith. To seek for signs (1 Cor. 1:22) is to miss the point and to require the very oracular demonstration that "this generation" were demanding.

For Mark and Paul the answer to this wrongful insistence is the same. There is no legitimating sign—save the ambiguity of the humiliated and crucified Lord; and to see in his cross the power and wisdom of God is to be shut up to the exercise of faith, which by definition can never rest in proofs and external signs, or else its character would be lost.

The setting of Mark's Teaching

If we may put the teaching here into a suggested first-century setting, Mark's first need was to show that the Christian message needs no other authentication than what it is in itself. The evangelist no doubt was facing here the pressures of a Jewish objection that Jesus' life ended in dismal defeat and a public execution at the hands of the Roman authority. For the Jews the scandal of the cross was a major obstacle—as Paul knew

[29] E. Schweizer, *Commentary*, p. 159.

well (Rom. 9:32; 1 Cor. 1:23; Gal. 5:11). To offer an explanation of Jewish unbelief was conceivably part of Mark's purpose.

But the Greek mind too would be puzzled at Jesus' failure. There were these stories of Jesus as a wonder-worker which superficially looked impressive and authenticating. Mark has edited these wonder-stories by showing that Jesus' mighty power often led only to momentary admiration and hardened incredulity. The deepest meaning of Jesus' deeds was hidden from public view since they would only really be appreciated as men saw through the miracle to the revelation of God in Jesus. Moreover, unbelief effectively checked that power and Jesus did not parade his claims or draw attention directly to himself by what he did. Mark is at pains, it seems, to set Jesus apart from the θεῖος ἀνήρ type of hellenistic thaumaturge and folk-hero who dispensed his favours at will and sought to gain a popular hearing and following by his reputation as a magician-healer.

Therefore, the cross takes on a meaning, since even the closest friends of Jesus and his family failed to recognize him and in spite of his fame as miracle-worker his life ended in his rejection and death. To the Greek enquirer this rationale would have some intelligibility, though he would have needed to come a long way to embrace the Markan suffering Son-of-God doctrine.

The chief interest in Mark's purpose is, as we have claimed, a domestic one. His apologetic concern is more immediately understood as his addressing his gospel message to his church. Possibly there were charismatic figures (like the false apostles in 2 Cor. 10–11) who had appeared, making pretentious claims and purporting to be Jesus-figures in the churches.[30]

The delay of the parousia may have contributed to the desire to see "signs and wonders" in expectation that the end was not far away. Especially for a persecuted church this yearning for some spectacle in the sky may have attained fever pitch; and we know how in days of stress and trial Christians have expressed a fervent desire to hasten the end of the world, and so the termination of their suffering. "How long, O Lord?" (cf. Rev. 6:10) is an instinctive reaction to the church's tribulation; and the "call for the endurance and faith of the saints" (Rev. 13:10) includes a damping down of the fires of apocalyptic eagerness to see signs which presage the end.[31]

Whatever the precise historical circumstance, there can be no doubt that Mark wished to tone down the appeal of a sign-bearing Christ and to assert the true meaning of faith. M. E. Glasswell has noticed the close relation between these two facets of Mark's intention. For the evangelist "Jesus himself is the sole sign of the Gospel as well as of the kingdom of

---

[30] So T. J. Weeden supposes. See earlier pp. 151f.

[31] Such are described in Didache 16:6, as "signs of the truth" in contrast to the signs wrought by the deceiver of the world, a bogus Son of God (Didache 16:4).

God . . . The miracle-stories belong to the earliest tradition but cannot take the place of the one to whom they witness. We are not to ask for a miracle or a sign apart from Jesus himself, grasped and met by faith."[32]

Yet he does have something positive to contribute to his church's pastoral need. If his church was in the grip of fear and isolation (especially since the recent death of the chief apostolic figures), it needed the one consolation available: the assurance of Jesus' living presence with them. This is perhaps the chief value of the miracle-stories as they passed through Mark's hands. He has imprinted on them a christological significance and used them as a way to preach Christ in his present availability. He is Lord of the waves, conqueror of death, controller of evil powers, restorer of human dignity—and dispenser of true bread.

It is significant that 8:14 follows directly on the refusal of a sign. The disciples are chided for their mutual recriminations because they had no bread with them in the boat (verses 16, 17). "Why do you discuss the fact that you have no bread? Do you not yet perceive or understand?" The point under debate was their blindness to the fact that they already had "one loaf with them in the boat" (verse 14).

While this verse 14 does not easily fit in with the subsequent story,[33] it evidently is intended to convey a single theme: Christ is the one loaf, and in having him with them in the boat they have the provider of all they need (verses 19, 20). Some scholars[34] have sought to give a eucharistic meaning to this phrase and to find herein Mark's message. "The true 'sign' is the Sign of the Broken Bread, the spiritual significance of which had become dear to the Church for which St. Mark was writing in the Eucharist, itself the weekly memorial or 'sign' of the Lord's death and resurrection" (Richardson, *loc. cit.*). In support of this view we may compare the identical phrase in 1 Corinthians 10:17: "Because there is *one loaf*, we who are many are one body, for we all partake of the same loaf"; and we may proceed to claim a further link in the points of connection between Mark and Paul. But it cannot be asserted too confidently that Mark means the spiritual presence of Christ conveyed at the Lord's table as the assurance offered to his church.

A more cautious interpretation is that Christ himself is the true sign, yet hidden in his mighty works and refusing to yield to the temptation to display his power openly. His works are seen by men but, as with his parables, the profound meaning lies under the surface to be uncovered by perceptive understanding, sympathetic appreciation and faith. It is faith which opens the eyes of those who see the *dynameis*, otherwise the

---

[32] M. E. Glasswell, "The Use of Miracles in the Markan Gospel" in *Miracles*, ed. C. F. D. Moule [1965], pp. 161f.

[33] The commentaries discuss the textual problems and form-critical issues of how Mark may have stitched the separate parts of the story together.

[34] A. Richardson, *The Miracle Stories of the Gospels* [1941], pp. 47f.; K. Kertelge, *op. cit.*, p. 172.

judgment is true, "Having eyes do you not see? Do you not yet understand?" Then, and only then, do they see the sign within the mighty works, and Christ becomes greater than his wonderful works.

(ii) *The Silence of Jesus*

The section in Mark 14:55–64 has been the subject of repeated investigation. Details of the form-analysis of the verses with a view to separating two strands of material, the exact nature of the allegation brought against Jesus at this trial scene, and the competence of the Sanhedrin at the time have been extensively sifted from both Jewish and Christian points of view.[35]

Objections of a legal and historical nature have been raised against accepting this trial as grounded in history. But it is not our concern to enter into this discussion.[36] Our immediate interest is to take note of this report as material which Mark has utilized to make certain theological emphases within the overall frame of his witness to Jesus as Son of God. Clearly the section has a pre-Markan base which can be identified by its Semitic colouring; and the evangelist has brought together some disparate *pericopae* by inserting the Trial pericope within the framework of two parts of Peter's denial (14:54; 14:66–72). This "sandwich-structure" as Catchpole calls it is (as he observes[37]) a Markan literary device but it says nothing on the question of the historicity of the events so joined together. Verses 55–64 (with which verse 65 should be connected since it continues the story, though there are problems in relating it to the scene of the mockery in Luke 22:63–65) evidently are an independent unit of tradition or possibly units of tradition, which Mark has utilized to portray important aspects of his understanding of Jesus and his mission. We call attention to one aspect in particular, viz. Jesus' refusal to speak and to give a sign by the spoken word by way of either direct confirmation or a compliance with a demand to declare himself. These are the two elements in the scene in which Mark conveys far more by his notice that Jesus did not speak than by his denial that he was willing to vindicate himself.

A Refusal to Speak

Jesus' silences in the Passion narrative in Mark are noteworthy. From the time of his arrest, the Markan Jesus speaks only three times (14:62;

[35] On the form-analytical approach, see E. Linnemann, *Studien zur Passionsgeschichte* [1970], especially pp. 127–131; for the other issues see the representative works of P. Winter, *On the Trial of Jesus* [1961]; and S. G. F. Brandon, *Jesus and the Zealots* [1967], and *The Trial of Jesus of Nazareth* [1968], ch. 4. There is a summary of the issues involved in E. Schweizer, *Commentary*, pp. 321–328.

[36] Reference may be given to a lucid summary and positive evaluation of the evidence by D. R. Catchpole, "The Problem of the Historicity of the Sanhedrin Trial," *The Trial of Jesus* (ed. E. Bammel) [1970], pp. 47–65.

[37] Following W. G. Kümmel, *Introduction to the New Testament* [ET, 1965], p. 64; and E. Schweizer, *Commentary*, p. 321.

15:2, 34). The third text is the cry of desolation, addressed to God. The
other two references are more in the form of acquiescence and an attitude
of "let-be" than of positive affirmation. This is clear in 15:2 where to
Pilate's question, Are you the King of the Jews? Jesus replied, "You have
said so." The Greek σὺ λέγεις is intentionally enigmatic. The reply is not
vai (yes), for as Dibelius observed,[38] this affirmative declaration would
have brought the scene immediately to a close and have issued directly
in Pilate's sentence of condemnation. Nor is it quite satisfactory to place
undue weight on the pronouns, as though the sense ran, "*I* do not say
so, but *you* do." The best translation lies in a paraphrase, "You do well
to ask," (Dibelius translates "Du hast recht mit deiner Frage") a reply
which deflects the thrust of Pilate's interrogation and makes possible a
continuation of the dialogue in the Trial scenario.

14:62 represents a more difficult type of reply, at least in the received
text. It states a full acceptance of Jesus' Messianic claim. V. Taylor, however, holds that the original version (well-attested by some reputable
textual traditions[39]) ran (in translation form): You say that I am. This
longer reply would then explain the versions in Matthew 27:11 = Luke
23:3, and cohere with the note of reserve regarding Messiahship which is
found elsewhere in this gospel. The reply is affirmative. That much is clear
from the verdict pronounced upon it (in verse 64) as tantamount to
blasphemy.[40] But it leaves open a difference of nuance to be read into
the nature of Messiahship, as though Jesus responded, "Yes, if you will"
or "It is your word, not mine."

These texts are sufficiently vague to lead us to conclude that Jesus made
no startling, unequivocal assertion of his claims, even when given the
opportunity and pressed to do so. "He was silent" (verse 61) in the face of a
situation of extreme provocation.[41] Mark used the historical tradition
to draw attention to Jesus' further reluctance to commit himself in a
public manner when any such declaration would give only a wrong
impression or lead to mistaken conclusions. He reserves his silence in
keeping with the entire presentation of the evangelist (contrast the
apocryphal gospels in which long speeches are placed into his mouth, and

[38] M. Dibelius, "Herodes und Pilatus," ZNTW 16 [1915], p. 117, note 2.
[39] See V. Taylor, *The Text of the New Testament* [1961], pp. 88f. And before him B. H.
Streeter, *The Four Gospels* [1926], p. 322, thought that the view of Mark's longer text explains
the language of Matthew and Luke and had claim to being original, "a genuine utterance
of our Lord." But D. R. Catchpole ("Jesus' Answer to Caiaphas [Matt. xxvi, 64])," NTS 17
[1970], pp. 213–26) opts for the shorter Markan reading partly on the ground that the note
of reserve concerning Messiahship disappears in the Passion narrative (p. 221) and that Jesus
is crucified as Messiah. But this leaves open the question whether Jesus does declare himself
by an unequivocal acceptance of the title, so liable to misunderstanding.
[40] For the meaning of blasphemy in this context, we may compare J. C. O'Neill, "The
Charge of Blasphemy at Jesus' Trial before the Sanhedrin," *The Trial of Jesus* (ed. E. Bammel)
[1970], pp. 72–77; and more briefly my contribution in *New Bible Dictionary*, ed. J. D. Douglas
[1962], p. 1295.
[41] See J. C. O'Neill, "The Silence of Jesus," NTS 15 [1968–69], pp. 153–167.

Jesus and the apostle John and Jesus and Pilate hold theological debate at extended length[42]). He refuses to make an overt claim in the presence of unbelief and hostility. This is part and parcel of Mark's doctrine of Messianic veiledness—a theme which runs through his parables, his re-telling of the miracle-stories and his narration of the crucifixion.

The background of this description of Jesus as silent in Caiaphas' presence is sometimes traced to the fulfilment of Isaiah 53:7. Then, this background is made use of in two diverse ways. For E. Best, it is enough to be able to show that the prophecy was not fulfilled since "Isa. liii. 7 would demand a total silence,"[43] and he concludes that with "the silence in Mark . . . dramatically rather than biblically determined . . . Mark does not emphasize Jesus as the Isaianic Servant." But this conclusion does not necessarily follow since the Isaiah verse refers to a dumb sheep as the point of the comparison, and is more an effective way of stressing the Servant's submission (verse 11) than imposing a ban of total silence. The Servant "makes intercession" (verse 12), presumably by what he *says* as some part of his representative work.

Eta Linnemann takes another tack.[44] She concludes that the only correct place for the silence of Jesus to be set is at the conclusion of the *pericope*, viz. at 15:5. But since the ruling motive of the Trial before the Sanhedrin is the silence of Jesus, foretold in Isaiah 53:7 and Psalm 38:13–16, it must follow that Mark 14:57–60 is a doublet of Mark 15:1, 3–5. But this line of reasoning overlooks the use of the imperfect (= continuous) tense in the verb (verse 61: ἐσιώπα: He kept silent) and with the omission of the dialogue in 15:2, it becomes difficult to know how to render the adverb in 15:5: But Jesus *still* answered nothing. Why would Mark wish to say that Jesus *again* retained his silence if, on Linnemann's showing, there has been only one question posed at him?

A Refusal to Act

A second element appears in verse 65: "And some began to spit on him and to cover his face, and to strike him, saying to him, 'Prophesy!' And the guards received him with blows."

The mockery of Jesus has no doubt been written in conscious dependence on Isaiah 50:5f. (LXX). Lohmeyer[45] makes quite a point of the close resemblance in language between the two passages; and the intention to portray Jesus in the rôle of the suffering servant may be taken as part of Mark's task. Other scholars find a background to this passage in the hellenistic setting of the mock insults heaped on slaves or the custom of

[42] See V. Taylor, *The Formation of the Gospel Tradition* [1933], pp. 46.
[43] E. Best, *The Temptation and the Passion* [1965], p. 151.
[44] E. Linnemann, *op. cit.*, p. 127, 131.
[45] E. Lohmeyer, *Kommentar*, p. 330.

mockery drawn from a contemporary children's charade, a sort of blindman's buff.[46]

The more immediate purpose of the brief incident is related to Jesus' claim to be the destroyer of the temple (14:58). In the report of this claim, he was acting in the tradition of the Old Testament prophets such as Jeremiah and before him Micah (see Jer. 26:16–19) who foretold the destruction of Jerusalem.[47] To be sure, the claim registered in verse 58 goes far beyond what the prophets predicted. They spoke of an invasion of foreign armies which would demolish the city; he laid claim to be the personal agent in the act of destroying the Temple sanctuary. It is an even more astounding bid to be the one who was to establish the new Temple (cf. 1 Enoch 90:29—"a new house greater and loftier than that first, and set it up in the place of the first which had been folded up") in place of the old. The full force of this claim is seen in John 2:19, and it forms a bedrock tradition in the gospels' passion story, as we see from Mark 15:29. Its authenticity is defensible on the ground of its wide use in the early church and the difficulty in imagining how it would be invented by anyone in the post-Easter church.[48]

If Jesus' Temple-prophecy was thought of as an utterance of a prophet, adjudged a false prophet in Jewish eyes, it throws light on the nature of the horse-play in verse 65. The unnamed spectators indulge in ironic mockery by inviting him to play the part of a prophet and favour them with some further oracles, in addition to his reported utterance about the Temple's fate. We may contrast Matthew's (Matt. 26:68) and Luke's version (22:64) which directs the call to prophesy to a more direct naming of the man who struck the blindfolded Jesus. Mark touches a deeper note and concentrates on the humiliation of the prisoner who has to endure the added insult of having his prophetic mission the subject of a rude jest. And appropriately the evangelist casts the story in the language of the rejected prophet of Isaiah 50:5f.[49]

[46] See G. Rudberg, "Die Verhöhnung Jesu vor dem Hohenpriester," ZNTW 24 [1925], pp. 307ff.; W. C. van Unnik, "Jesu Verhöhnung vor dem Synedrium (Mc 14, 65 par)," ZNTW 29 [1930], pp. 310f. A more serious intent in the blindfolding and mockery is seen by D. L. Miller, "EMPAIZEN: Playing the Mock Game (Luke 22:63–64), JBL 90 [1971], pp. 309–313.

[47] On this Temple prophecy in 14:58 see L. Gaston, No Stone upon Another [1970] who regards the first half of the threat of destruction as anti-Jewish polemic and the second half, "in three days I will build it" (the new temple) as a genuine saying of Jesus (pp. 242f.).

[48] "The first half of the saying was embarrassing so long as the church was still a part of the Jewish community, while the second half could have caused problems after the church separated from Judaism" (E. Schweizer, op. cit., p. 327). But there is a critique of this line of reasoning in E. Linnemann, op. cit., pp. 120f.

[49] The conclusion that Mark took over the call "Prophesy" from a tradition different from Luke's, which was parallel but independent, is reached by P. Benoit, "Les outrages à Jésus prophète," Neotestamentica et Patristica, O. Cullmann Festschrift [1962], pp. 92–110 (p. 105). Mark thereby ignores the element of horse-play and concentrates on the allusion to the suffering Servant.

The proposal to accept the longer reading in 14:65: Prophesy, O Christ, who is it who struck you? (cf. Matt. 26:68) is discussed by B. H. Streeter (The Four Gospels [1926], pp. 325–28),

Mark's Teaching

These two scenes of the trial and the mockery are part of Mark's narrative of the last days of Jesus' life.[50] They are of a piece with his general way of presenting Jesus as the patient sufferer who, having submitted his will to God's purpose in the garden (14:32–42) goes forward to his fate as something inevitable and predetermined in the scripture (14:49). The twin notions of conscious submission to the divine purpose and the inevitability that what was written of the Son of man must be fulfilled (14:41, cf. 9:12) govern the story-telling of the evangelist. Therefore, it is not a different motive which inspires him to place emphasis on Jesus' silence and his yielding to events without protestation or demur. It is even contributory to his deliberate design to have Jesus defenceless and unprotected by any sign which would make his tragic death meaningful. Rather he goes to that death in a way which carries no surface meaning, save only that he is obedient to God and hopeful that somehow he will be vindicated and restored to his own in Galilee (14:28).

The lessons of this presentation, intended for a church under duress—an *ecclesia pressa et militans*—would not be lost, and the apparent hopelessness of Jesus' situation in which there is no vindicating sign of God's approval nor relief offered to a tragic ending caused by the blindness and hatred of those who should have perceived who Jesus was and is would match the church's experience in the Empire when persecution broke out. The Lord spoke no word to gain his release or to summon a sign at his behest. The most that the church can hope for is the Holy Spirit's aid (13:11) to utter the good confession of Christ (cf. 1 Tim. 6:13). But Mark offers no will-'o-the-wisp expedient for escaping suffering. If the road Jesus took led to his cross, the church must expect no less (8:34–38; 10:39; 13:9).

(iii) *Come down from the cross* (15:30–32)

The foregoing account of the lonely Son of God reaches its climax in the crucifixion. Even then, in Mark's grim picture which is unbroken by sympathetic interludes (cf. Luke 23:27) and unpunctuated by any kindly word or gesture (cf. Luke 23:42), the mockery is still unfinished. After the sufferer has become the crucified, two sets of taunts[51] are levelled at him. Repeating the claim he made to be the destroyer of the Temple and the builder of a new shrine, they mock him:

and supported by G. D. Kilpatrick, "Western Text and Original Text in the Gospels and Acts," JTS 44 o.s. [1943], pp. 29f. But the difficulties are noted by Benoit, *loc. cit.*, p. 100.

[50] And linked on to the denial incident, as P. Winter notes in interpreting Mark's theological purpose. *Op. cit.*, p. 24.

[51] Mockery of Jesus is the dominant theme of the entire crucifixion narrative, as nearly one-fifth of the verses is devoted to the taunts directed at him. The reason for this heavy build-up of texts is given by J. Pobee (see footnote 53), viz. "to indicate the apparent powerlessness of the sufferer against the authorities and their associates. Jesus stands *contra mundum* and is apparently powerless as he faces the world" (p. 94).

Save yourself, and come down from the cross (15:30).

This mocking invitation for Jesus to show himself by a descent from the cross is renewed by the leaders of official Judaism:

Let Christ, the King of Israel, come down now from the cross, that *we may see* and believe (15:32).

The Markan emphasis is placed on the verb "that we may see" which is peculiar to his version (cf. Matt. 27:42: Luke 23:35–38 which is somewhat different). The point which is made is that official Judaism, like the Pharisees in 8:11–13, is still hankering after a sign. This demand for a legitimating miracle has pursued Jesus right up to the end, and even on the cross the insistence is made that he should do something, or appeal to God to do something, by which his authority will be declared valid. Then—and apparently only then—will they believe, after they have seen.

For the evangelist the *leitmotif* of his entire gospel holds intact right to the conclusion. No sign will be given to a generation which lacks faith (9:19). If faith were present, there would be no need for signs. Or rather, "signs" would play a different rôle. They would not legitimate Jesus; they would confirm faith which already has trusted Jesus as the Son of God. A "faith" which seeks to be supported by outward display or external proof is no better than unbelief; for Jesus is no "divine man" who might perform a crowning miracle and step down from the cross to the astonishment of all who saw him. The attitude to him which needs to be bolstered by such a convincing demonstration lacks the main ingredient of faith. It has destroyed the trust which sees Jesus as the hidden Son of God and fails to penetrate the veil of his incognito in order to see God at work in him—even on the cross of utter defeat and shame.

E. Schweizer helps our understanding in his summary:[52]

It would be an astonishing miracle indeed if Jesus were to come down from the cross, but this would prove only that he was a superman—not that he was "Messiah and King of Israel." This is how God differs from any man or superman—he does not have to assert himself, nor is it necessary for him to prove that he is right or to crush his enemies. This is the message of Jesus' Passion.

The enemies of Jesus failed to grasp all this. Nor were Jesus' disciples any more percipient, since they are repeatedly chided for their blindness and unbelief. There is one character of the Markan *dramatis personae* who does, however, pierce the veil of Jesus' secret and come to faith in him as God's Son. This is the Roman centurion (15:39). The sign which the Jews were agitating to see is the very event by which he is won over.

[52] E. Schweizer, *Commentary*, p. 350.

In full view of the crucified and overhearing his expiring cry (verse 37), this man utters the Christian confession.[53]

In order to drive home this message of God's presence in his crucified Son, Mark has done an unexpected piece of literary stitching. He has inserted between Jesus' cry and the centurion's response to that cry the unusual notice that "the curtain of the temple was torn in two, from top to bottom" (verse 38). We do well to ask the reason for this strange intermission.

Mark is presumably intending to add a theological comment on Jesus' death. But what is the nature of the comment in terms of the tear in the curtain which divided the Holy place and the Holy of holies (Ex. 26:31–35; 27:21; 30:6; 2 Chron. 3:14) or the curtain which covered the entrance to the Holy place (Ex. 26:36, 37; Num. 3:26)? The Greek word is used of the former in Hebrews 6:19; 9:3; 10:20.

On the basis of these references to the Temple furnishings, it is possible that Mark's meaning relates to the opening of a new access to God's presence. The close parallel will be Hebrews 10:19f. with its assurance of an entry into the sanctuary and a consequent drawing near to God (10:22). The Gentile centurion is the first man of non-Jewish religion and racial descent to be admitted, as the way is opened by Christ's death.

An alternative view, stated by G. Lindeskog,[54] is to draw out the analogy still further and make the pattern of Mark 15:38 one of Jesus' high-priestly entry into heaven and ministry in the heavenly Temple. Indeed, in this view, he is called the high-priest of the heavenly sanctuary and immediately fulfils the promise of 14:48; 15:29. But this cultic pattern seems far removed from the historical narrative of Mark, who does not show any interest in cultic matters.[55]

A criticism brought against the traditional view, expressed above, needs to be noted. Eta Linnemann[56] has rightly urged that the function of the curtain in the Levitical Temple was not to impede access to God but to veil the appearance of the divine majesty so that sinful men should not be destroyed by the vision of his splendour. To apply this idea to the Temple veil of Mark 15:38 gives excellent sense. The sequence then runs: Jesus dies as his expiring cry echoes from the cross; the veil which hitherto had hidden God's glory from human view now collapses since its function is at an end, and that glory shines forth from the crucified, not to overwhelm and destroy the beholder but to lead him to faith and to the confession, Truly this man was God's Son!

[53] We prefer to regard the centurion's cry in this way rather than follow J. Pobee's latest proposal ("The Cry of the Centurion—A Cry of Defeat") in *The Trial of Jesus* (ed. E. Bammel) [1970], pp. 91–102, that Mark inserts the cry as an admission of defeat on the part of the Roman persecutor.

[54] G. Lindeskog, "The Veil of the Temple," *Coniectanea Neotestamentica* xi [1947], pp. 132–137.

[55] Cf. L. Gaston, *op. cit.*, pp. 480f.

[56] E. Linnemann, *Studien zur Passionsgeschichte*, pp. 162f.

The cross from which Jesus refused to come down has become the locus of divine revelation. It is the sign by which Jesus' Sonship *is* legitimated, but only in humiliation and suffering. And only after his death can this be seen and acknowledged. So the Roman soldier responds to that which up to that point had been a scandal at Nazareth and in Galilee and Jerusalem; and the cross remained a scandal of God's hiddenness and weakness in Jesus in Mark's day.

(B) Under the heading of Jesus' ready consent to suffer and to taste the bitterness of death, several passages fall to be considered; to these we now direct attention.

(i) *The Removal of the Bridegroom*

And Jesus said to them, "Can the wedding guests fast while the bridegroom is with them?

As long as they have the bridegroom with them, they cannot fast. The days will come, when the bridegroom is taken away from them, and then they will fast in that day" (2:19–20).

"This saying of Jesus is of great interest since it is the earliest recorded reference to his death in the Markan story."[57] So writes Vincent Taylor, in the opening section of his study which has proved to be *grundlegend* for the present section. Not all his discussions of the Markan Passion sayings are accepted by more recent scholars, and we shall have occasion to place a question-mark against some of his conclusions. But for a comprehensive survey of the texts which bear upon the way in which Mark's Jesus anticipated his fate and strove to prepare his disciples for it Taylor's long chapter proves to be a most useful starting-point.

On form-critical grounds, verses 19b–20 have been regarded as suspect. The argument is that this part of the *pericope* is a later addition, supplied as an interpretative comment on the sayings of Jesus who defends his disciples against Pharisaic criticism. The basic form of the Pronouncement story is given in verses 18–19a, set in an indeterminate context yet descriptive of an encounter between "people" and Jesus. They raise the question about fasting, and want to know why it is that Jesus' followers do not practise a familiar Jewish custom. Up to verse 19a, the record of Jesus' reply is given as a gnomic saying, Can wedding guests fast while the bridegroom is with them?[58] This statement is intended to say no more than that Jesus justifies his disciples' abstinence from fasting on the single ground that his ministry brings a time of joy, not sadness, comparable with that of a wedding celebration.

[57] V. Taylor, *Jesus and His Sacrifice* [1937], p. 83.
[58] W. Bousset, *Kyrios Christos* [ET 1970], p. 78, wishes to abbreviate this proverb by deleting the words "while the bridegroom is still with them" and by regarding them as a Christian addition. But, if the reference to the bridegroom was intended to be non-christological, this procedure is unrequired. Compare D. E. Nineham, *Commentary*, pp. 103f.

The further reasons offered for this minimal conclusion are as follows: (i) the allusion to the bridegroom as a title for Jesus suggests the presence of allegory, which otherwise is believed to be excluded from Jesus' authentic sayings;[59] (ii) the insertion of verses 19-20 is meant to delimit the restriction on fasting to the period of Jesus' life-time. Thereafter (covered by the future reference "The days will come," meaning the time of the apostolic church) fasting will be in order. And this addition is a piece of self-justification as the early church sought endorsement and explanation of its cultic practice;[60] (iii) the prediction of Jesus' violent end (the bridegroom will be *taken away*) is held to be too premature in Mark's record, and to suggest a "prophecy after the event" read back into a setting which needed some indication that fasting would be an appropriate practice in commemoration of Jesus' death.

The counter-arguments offered by V. Taylor and others[61] need also to be recorded, with positive assertions that the use of allegory is not to be excluded from Jesus' parabolic speech; that other parts of the synoptic tradition show interest in the subject of fasting as a debated issue between Jesus and the rabbis (cf. Matt. 6:16); and that this *logion* may conceivably belong to a later phase of the ministry, e.g. after John the Baptist's death when a hint of the outcome of Jesus' ministry is more understandable in the light of that event.[62] Even on more strictly form-critical grounds there is much to be said for keeping the verses together as an independent and self-contained unit,[63] since the entire *logion* is a good example of semitic antithetic parallelism, which would be destroyed if verses 19b-20 were excised as a later addition. The argument that the idea of the removal of the bridegroom in verse 20 is already implied in verse 19a requires that all the references to the term should be taken as Jesus' self-identification; and this is perhaps the chief contextual reason why doubt is cast on the verses as authentic. It is maintained that the secondary character of verses 19b, 20 is shown by the self-description of Jesus as bridegroom, for "the allegorical representation of the Messiah as a bridegroom is completely foreign to the whole of the Old Testament and to the literature of late Judaism."[64] J. Jeremias also wishes to expunge the plain meaning of "while the bridegroom is with them" in verse 19a by treating this clause as a circumlocution for "during the wedding." As a corollary to this view, the designation of Jesus as bridegroom is a Markan interpretation, possibly supplied under Pauline influence since Paul gives clear teaching of his use

---

[59] This conclusion is reached by C. H. Dodd, *The Parables of the Kingdom*[4] [1938], pp. 116f.
[60] So E. Klostermann, *Das Markusevangelium*[4] [1950], p. 27.
[61] V. Taylor, *Commentary*, pp. 211f.; C. E. B. Cranfield, *Commentary*, pp. 109ff.; E. J. Mally in *The Jerome Biblical Commentary* [1968], p. 27.
[62] So A. E. J. Rawlinson, *Commentary*, p. 31, believes.
[63] So K. Th. Schäfer, "'Und dann werden sie fasten, an jenem Tage' (Mk. 2, 20 und Paralleln)," in *Synoptische Studien* Festschrift A. Wikenhauser [1953], p. 145.
[64] J. Jeremias, *The Parables of Jesus* [ET 1954], p. 41; and TDNT iv, pp. 1101, 1103.

of the bride-bridegroom association to enforce his ecclesiological teaching (2 Cor. 11:2; cf. Eph. 5:22–33). But the case for regarding verses 19b–20 as additions on the ground that Jesus could not have used "bridegroom" as a self-designation is not foolproof. The most that can be alleged is that there is no precedent for this title as a messianic description and that Jesus would not have publicly confessed his Messiahship prior to the climax of his ministry (so Jeremias apparently contends). But this overlooks the possibility that he was using the term as an indirect way of expressing himself, comparable with his use of "Son of man."[65]

For our purposes the weight of this saying lies in the use Mark makes of it, for it is incontestable that he intended to draw attention to the implicit claim which the teaching here registers. That claim is in terms of Jesus' authority as the one who presumed to override the Mosaic ordinance of fasting.[66] Furthermore, as the Markan saying stands, Jesus equated his own presence with the joy of God's rule over men likened to a wedding celebration, anticipated in such Old Testament hopes as Isaiah 54:5, 6; 62:4, 5; Ezekiel 16:8; Hosea 2:16–20. Set in an eschatological context, these verses look forward to a renewal of God's covenant dealings with Israel, his bride, and express the unbounded joy at the prospect of a new age to begin. Jesus' declaration is that the new age has begun, and in token of its inception there is a feast now to be enjoyed and everyone is to be happy.

But he is under no illusion that everyone will share that joy, and darkly hints that an ominous future awaits him and his own (they will fast in that day) before God's kingdom is fulfilled. This is because his proclamation of God's rule and official Judaism are scarcely compatible, and must affect each other in one of two ways. Either Jesus will revitalize the ancestral faith, or (more probably) there will be a distinct break and a new beginning. "New wine calls for fresh wineskins" (2:22).

With that prospect dimly glimpsed Jesus here talks of the bridegroom as destined to be "taken away from the wedding guests" (verse 20) at some future time. How clear a vision do these words give of his fate?

Mark is capitalizing on two ideas in his sentence with its verb ἀπαρθῇ. The verb is reminiscent of Isaiah 53:8: His life is taken away from (αἴρεται ἀπὸ) the earth. A violent end is clearly and grimly in view in the prophecy of the suffering Servant;[67] and the meaning of the saying on

---

[65] See *The New Bible Dictionary*, ed. J. D. Douglas [1962], p. 169, referring to V. Taylor, *Commentary*, p. 211. Cf. W. G. Kümmel, *Promise and Fulfilment* [ET 1957], p. 57, note 123.

[66] On fasting as Jewish religious exercise and its importance in later Judaism, see G. F. Moore, *Judaism* [1927–30] vol. ii, pp. 257–266; I. Abrahams, *Studies in Pharisaism and the Gospels* [1917], vol. ii, pp. 121–28.

[67] E. Lohmeyer, *Kommentar*, p. 60. This allusion to Isaiah 53 is overlooked by M. D. Hooker, *Jesus and the Servant* [1959], p. 92; and K. Th. Schäfer, *loc. cit.*, pp. 132f., who maintains that the absence of Jesus from the disciples says nothing about his *violent* death. His argument that Mark does not make the announcements of the Passion begin until 8:27–31 (v. 31: He *began* to teach them) and that therefore 2:20 is no prophecy of the Passion ignores

Jesus' lips is pressed to the extreme limit by O. Cullmann when he remarks that "in saying that as such (i.e. the bridegroom) he must be taken
away from men by death, he assumes that this death belongs to his
messianic mission,"[68] as suffering Servant of God.

If the implicit sense of the verb is "taken away *by death*"—as Isaiah
53:8 makes probable—this would dispose of the objection[69] that verse 20
"spoils the verisimilitude" of the scene by interrupting the guests' enjoy-
ment. Even that is only momentary since when the bridegroom leaves
the wedding party "it is no special cause for mourning and fasting."
But if he is taken away *never to return*, then there is ample cause for sorrow;
and this is the unhappy prospect in view in verse 20. The fact that Jesus
did return to his own after death and that the early church did not fast in
memory of a dead leader (except in the interval between Good Friday
and Easter day, if we give to the verb "fast" a metaphorical significance
of "being afflicted with grief" and place full emphasis on the adverbial
phrase "in that day") would be strong indications of the authenticity of
verse 20.[70]

The second idea exploited by the evangelist is the intermingling of joy
and grief. The paradox is heightened by the use of two terms which stand
at opposite ends of the spectrum of human experience and emotion: the
gladness of a wedding feast with the bridegroom at the centre, and the
summons to fasting once he is removed, with no hope of returning. Yet
these are not mutually exclusive ideas, since Jewish literature knows the
theme of joy through suffering.[71] For Jesus the pattern of his ministry is
already being set, as he foresees the inevitable opposition and the outworking of events. The twin vocations of God's messenger and Son and the
vicarious sufferer are joined in a way which recalls the baptismal scene in
1:11. It is true that the titles and nomenclature are different but the motifs
underlying the two parts of the narrative may well have seemed to Mark
to be the same. He intended to show how Jesus combined in his person
the high honour of one called by God as leader of his people (Son of
God/bridegroom) and the servant of God whose pathway lay inevitably
across a terrain in which he would encounter opposition and rejection,
even to the point of ultimate sacrifice. The royal Son of Psalm 2:7 and
the suffering servant of Isaiah's prophecy (Isa. 42:1) are transposed in this
later *pericope* to become the heavenly bridegroom who gains his bride
only by accepting a rôle of suffering and rejection. Yet he is willing for

the qualifying verse in 8:32. "And he said this *plainly*" in contrast to what he had said
cryptically and allusively earlier in his ministry.

[68] O. Cullmann, *The Christology of the New Testament*, [ET 1959], pp. 61f.

[69] Voiced by D. E. Nineham, *Commentary*, p. 102.

[70] So Cullmann, *op. cit.*, p. 62; cf. Kümmel, *op. cit.*, pp. 75f. for other possibilities of
interpretation.

[71] As W. Nauck indicates in his article entitled "Freude im Leiden," ZNTW 46 [1955],
pp. 68–80, on I Peter. He finds the same connection in many places of both the New Testament literature and Jewish sources.

this mission as God's obedient emissary, sent to gather the true Israel and to restore the nuptial harmony and bliss promised in the new age. "The Drama of the victorious Bridegroom"[72] may here receive its adumbration, with the Markan picture of the church's true Head who captivates his people only first by suffering on their behalf.

(ii) *The Passion Sayings of the Son of Man*

These sayings are in a section of the gospel which occupies a central position. By common consent, the incident at Caesarea Philippi (8:27—9:1) marks the watershed of the Markan narrative. Up to that point the story has been preparatory; thereafter it moves inexorably to its climax. And the central issue in the reported dialogue between Jesus and the Twelve is the warning that the Son of man must suffer. That prospect is repeated at 9:31 as part of his prolonged instruction of the disciples ("for he was teaching them": ἐδίδασκεν, a continuous tense of the verb). The third prediction of the rejected and humiliated Son of man is the fullest, and prepares for the climactic point of his teaching on the way in which authority is exercised (10:45). It speaks of a Son of man who will undergo indignity and shame before his death. In each case (except 10:45) there is hope; for beyond defeat and death is the assurance that the Son of man will rise.

The text of the sayings runs as follows:

> And he began to teach them that the Son of man must suffer many things, and be rejected by the elders and the chief priests and the scribes, and be killed, and after three days rise again (8:31).

> The Son of man will be delivered into the hands of men, and they will kill him; and when he is killed, after three days he will rise (9:31).

> Behold, we are going up to Jerusalem, and the Son of man will be delivered to the chief priests and the scribes, and they will condemn him to death, and deliver him to the Gentiles; and they will mock him, and spit upon him, and scourge him, and kill him: and after three days he will rise (10:33–34).

> For the Son of man also came not to be served but to serve, and to give his life as a ransom for many (10:45).

The Setting of the Sayings

Before we examine the contents and meaning of these statements, it will be well to observe some points about their place in Mark's outline.

(i) The deliberate prediction that the fate of the Son of man includes that of suffering and death is first made in the context of Peter's confession

---

[72] To use a chapter-title of C. Chavasse's *The Bride of Christ* [1939].

at Caesarea Philippi (8:27ff.), i.e. in the second part of the gospel. The earlier allusions to an ominous destiny of rejection in 2:20 (the bridegroom will be taken away); 3:6 (the Pharisees and the Herodians conspire to put him out of the way); 6:1–6 (the rejection of Jesus in his patris), and above all, the fate of John the Baptist (1:14; 6:14–29) are all important in their way, and serve the evangelist's purpose to prepare the reader for what lies ahead. But there is no way of minimizing the explicitness and pointedness of the statements recorded as Jesus' utterances which begin with 8:31. The proof of this lies more in the plain content of the sayings than in the wording of the verse. "And he *began* to teach them" cannot be used to indicate that there had been no earlier preparation for or allusion to Jesus' death, for the verb (ἤρξατο: he began) often plays no more than an auxiliary rôle in Mark, and is to be classified as part of his exceptional style, whether or not this pleonasm is due to Aramaic influence.[73]

The force of the adverb in 8:32a should not be overlooked. "And he said this *plainly*" (παρρησίᾳ), meaning an explicit declaration, in contrast to what had earlier been suggestive and expressed cryptically in his private instruction of the Twelve (4:11, 33, 34).

(ii) Within the section, 8:27—10:52, that is, from Caesarea Philippi to the beginning of the Entry into Jerusalem, the centre of gravity is located in these three passion sayings, as Bultmann recognized, "To a restricted degree it is also true to say that 8:27–52 [sic, i.e. 8:27–10:52] occupies a special place in Mark: here Christian dogma has attained its point of greatest influence on the presentation."[74]

Mark has achieved this result by several ways. It is in this section that there are other references to suffering, both the disciples' (8:34ff.) and Jesus' own (9:12; 10:35ff.). Indeed the two sets of prediction that both he and they will have to undergo trial and hardship to the point of losing life and drinking a cup of woe merge together and are closely interwoven. The theme of messianic affliction, affecting both Jesus and the community, may be said to run prominently through these chapters.

Then, the positioning of the sayings seems intentionally to be made in the course of a journey. This is seen most obviously in 10:32 with its vivid colours of Jesus striding on ahead of the Twelve as they foot the road from Galilee to Jerusalem. The third *logion* opens with the note: "Behold, we are going up to Jerusalem . . ." (10:33). From Caesarea Philippi, at the northerly point of the Markan Jesus' travels (8:31), he moves to Galilee (9:30), and thence on to the road southwards to the holy city (10:32ff.). This is Mark's travel section, which though not so pronounced as in the Lukan schema (Lk. 9:51; 13:22; 17:11), is just as

---

[73] See V. Taylor, *Commentary*, pp. 48, 63f. for a discussion of this question.
[74] R. Bultmann, *The History of the Synoptic Tradition* [ET, 1963], p. 350.

identifiable. E. Lohmeyer can even speak about "three stages of the journey" to Jerusalem, corresponding to the three sayings, but this seems forced.[75]

(iii) It cannot again be fortuitous that each prediction is followed directly by a negative response on the part of the disciples. The most infamous is in 8:32 as Peter drew Jesus aside, and presumed to contradict the prediction by rebuking him.[76]

We concur, therefore, with H. E. Tödt's judgment that Mark has consciously grouped these sayings into his central block of narrative in order to lead to the heart of the gospel, and to prepare for the ensuing Passion narrative.

The Meaning of the Sayings

Again, we are indebted to Tödt[77] for his analysis of the material which forms what he aptly calls a discernible "train of terms." He isolates the basic form of these passion *logia* and shows that in their simplest form the key-terms have attracted explanatory or cognate ideas to them.

The basic structure of the announcements is: The Son of man will be delivered to the chief priests and scribes and be killed and will rise in three days. The sentence incorporates the terms which are common to all the sayings:

(a) The Son of man (8:31; 9:31; 10:45).

(b) Kill [be killed] (8:31; 9:31; 10:34).

(c) After three days he will rise (8:31; 9:31; 10:34).

It is an open question whether even this sentence is an expansion of an abbreviated original. Lohmeyer argued that 8:31 was the original form, containing only the double statement that the "Son of man must suffer many things and be rejected"[78] We may compare Luke 17:25 and Mark 9:12 where "be treated with contempt" is a synonym for "be rejected" in 8:31, especially in view of the close connection of both Markan verses with Isaiah 53.

It is our thesis that the simplest form of the Markan passion predictions is found in the contrast between suffering and vindication. That contrast

---

[75] E. Lohmeyer, *Kommentar*, p. 160. Lohmeyer's proclivity for seeing a triadic structure in many of the biblical materials is well-known. Cf. R. P. Martin, *Carmen Christi* [1967], p. 40. See, too, H. E. Tödt, *The Son of Man in the Synoptic Tradition* [ET, 1965], p. 145, who cites Wellhausen's apposite remark that Mark 8:27—10:52 is the evangelist's *theologia crucis*.

[76] The verb is ἐπιτιμᾶν which can mean not only "rebuke, reprove, censure," but to "*warn* in order to prevent an action," so Arndt-Gingrich, *Lexicon*, sub voc. p. 303.

[77] H. E. Tödt, *op. cit.*, pp. 152ff.

[78] E. Lohmeyer, *Kommentar*, p. 165. He is followed by W. Michaelis, *TDNT* v, p. 915 who submits that the two verbs "suffer many things" and "be rejected" constituted an ancient two-member expression, signifying that on God's side the fate of Jesus is to suffer much, on man's side to be rejected.

is expressed in various ways and by the use of differing expressions, but throughout (and the data from Mark 9:12; 14:21, 41, 49 must be included to form the total picture) the emphasis falls on Jesus' deliberately chosen destiny in obedience to God's will in the scripture, which entails personal risk and involvement in suffering, on the one hand, and his expectation that he will triumph beyond death, on the other hand. It is our purpose to set down the lines of this argument.

(i) *The Son of Man and the sons of men*

If our starting-point is made at 9:31a[79] it becomes evident that a contrast is drawn between Jesus and his enemies into whose hands he expects to be delivered. They are termed, in a common Old Testament mode of expression, "sons of men," i.e. human beings. But what is the point of the self-designation, Son of man, which is found in all the passion texts, both in 8:27–10:52 and in chapter 14?

There is a distinct possibility that out of a welter of much discussion on this Son of man title in the Synoptic gospels something like a settled opinion is emerging.[80] This is that Jesus' use of the semitic phrase *bar nasha*, rendered woodenly into Greek as "the son of the man" is primarily a circumlocution for "I" and takes on its appropriate sense from the contexts in which it is found. The underlying sense is *Jesus' tacit claim to authority* on the strength of which he does those things in his ministry which only God can do (Mark 2:1–12; 2:23–28; 8:38; 13:26; 14:62). Thus Jesus as Son of man, equipped as God's Son and servant with full authority ($\dot{\epsilon}\xi o \upsilon \sigma i \alpha$), forgives men's sins, overrides the sabbath-laws, will be the assessor at the final Judgment as he comes in power, and in the interim he is exalted to occupy the throne of God.

The distinctive point is that the Son of man is a figure whom men recognize as divinely accredited and clothed with God's authority. Yet the ministry of Jesus seems to contradict this, for God appears to have changed sides and to have ranged himself on the side of the men who are about to kill Jesus. Mark's problem is to establish the authority of the Son of man in spite of seeming denials of it. So "the Son of man delivered into the hands of men" is a statement extending from one extreme to the other, viz. the all-powerful one, chosen and commissioned by God and authorized to act in his name, *consents* by voluntary choice to be surrendered to the

---

[79] Recently J. Jeremias, *New Testament Theology* [1971], pp. 276ff., has found the most elemental form of the Markan Passion prediction in this part-verse. It is in its form a riddle (Hebrew *mašal*) expressing simply the single idea: "God will (soon) deliver up the Son of man to men."

[80] Convenient summaries of the recent debate are given by I. H. Marshall, "The Synoptic Son of man Sayings in Recent Discussion," *NTS* 12 [1965–6], pp. 327–51 and R. Maddox, "The Function of the Son of Man according to the Synoptic Gospels," *NTS* 15 [1968], pp. 45–74; idem, "The Quest for Valid Methods in 'Son of Man' Research," *Theological Students' Fellowship Bulletin* 61 [1971], pp. 14–21. See also M. D. Hooker, *The Son of Man in Mark* [1967].

hands of his rejecters. "For the disciples this is the enigma of the passion"[81] (Tödt); and for Mark this is the rationale he gives of the cross and triumph of Jesus.

(ii) The destiny of the Son of man

There are several indications in these texts that the fate to befall the Son of man carries with it the note of *inevitability*. Thus:

The Son of man must suffer ($\delta \varepsilon \tilde{\iota} \ldots \pi \alpha \theta \varepsilon \tilde{\iota} \nu$) (8:31).

The Son of man will be delivered (10:33) or is being delivered ($\pi \alpha \rho \alpha \delta i \delta o \tau \alpha \iota$) (9:31).

The Son of man is betrayed into the hands of sinners ($\pi \alpha \rho \alpha \delta i \delta o \tau \alpha \iota$) (14:31).

It is possible to read these statements as concessions to a necessary fate from which Jesus found no escape. It was laid upon him by some external compulsion to take the path of suffering and rejection and no other course was viable. The two verbs of these verses can be read in this light. The Son of man *must* suffer, i.e. he has no choice but to accept his destiny; and he is delivered by God to his fate against which he utters no complaint.

Both verbs might conceivably mean this, if we take their background to be strictly one of Old Testament prophecy which Jesus came inevitably to fulfil.

E. Lohmeyer takes the impersonal verb, rendered "must" ($\delta \varepsilon \tilde{\iota}$), to be an example of the "apocalyptic law of suffering," by which the necessity of suffering is laid upon the godly in Israel in preparation for the end-time and the final vindication of God's elect. Daniel 2:28 (LXX) is appealed to for this use of the verb; and the idea is one which Lohmeyer finds elsewhere in his exegesis of passages in which the destiny of God's servant is one of suffering, followed by exaltation (e.g. Phil. 2:6–11).[82]

But there is little support for this view;[83] the most that can be affirmed is that Jesus saw that his mission according to the scripture was one which could only be fulfilled in suffering. This means that Jesus' understanding of the "necessity" imposed upon him was far more likely to derive from his awareness of a prophetic destiny than from his tame acceptance of any apocalyptic law, as E. Fascher[84] notes in his criticism of Lohmeyer for his failure to make clear the distinction between these two ways of regarding obedience to the divine will. Furthermore, it was not the record

---

[81] H. E. Tödt, *op. cit.*, p. 178.

[82] I may refer to my discussion of Lohmeyer's *Kyrios Jesus* [1928] in *Carmen Christi*, pp. 233f. He writes: "In Christ's martyrdom the law becomes apparent, according to which humiliation and exaltation are inseparably bound together": and this principle is traced to an apocalyptic time-scheme in which the afflictions of the righteous in this age prepare for their triumph in the age to come.

[83] Tödt, *op. cit.*, pp. 167, 188–193.

[84] E. Fascher, "Theologische Beobachtungen zu $\delta \varepsilon \tilde{\iota}$," *Neutestamentliche Studien für R. Bultmann* [1954], p. 251.

of past history which dictated to Jesus the way he should go—as the plan of Daniel 2 suggests—but rather an immediate awareness of God's will for his life, read off from what the scripture said of him.[85] We may therefore conclude that the "must" of Mark 8:31 means that he knew that his mission was only to be fulfilled in conformity with what the scripture said of him; and, as Tödt remarks, the verb says the same thing as the utterance of Mark 9:12b: it is written of the Son of man that he should suffer many things and be treated with contempt. Or, as V. Taylor puts it, "He did not see his death as a catastrophe, but as an essential part of his Messianic achievement. He had to suffer and to rise again; such was the Divine purpose he had made his own."[86]

The second verb, "to be delivered" is one at which we may look in a search for the type of Old Testament prophecy which Jesus embraced as his own. The Greek παραδιδόναι suggests at first glance a direct allusion to the Septuagint of Isaiah 53.[87] This link with the Suffering Servant figure would provide a definite point of reference in regard to Jesus' self-chosen destiny and throw light on what Cullmann calls "the secret of his self-consciousness." He proceeds, "In this respect it would be even more correct to speak of a *Pais* [servant]-consciousness of Jesus than of his messianic-consciousness."[88] But even those scholars who are willing to grant that Jesus saw in the Isaianic servant figure a prophecy or prefiguration of his own destiny as a sufferer concede that the precise use of παραδίδωμι is not found in Isaiah 53 and so is not derivable from that source.[89] And the propriety of calling the verb παραδίδοσθαι a formula has been questioned because it does not have a uniform meaning and the exact sense of "being delivered into the hands of someone" is not attested in Isaiah 53.[90]

An alternative suggestion has been made that the descriptions of the Son of man in the Markan predictions fit rather the scriptural pattern of the humiliated and vindicated messenger of God referred to in Psalm 118:22. In this passage the fate of the Psalmist (v. 21) has dramatically changed by some interposition of Yahweh. At one time he was overwhelmed by his enemies (vv. 10–13) and in great distress (v. 5). In his plight he summoned the aid of God who responded by not permitting his

[85] Cf. Tödt, *op. cit.*, p. 190.

[86] V. Taylor, *Jesus and His Sacrifice*, p. 90.

[87] So J. Jeremias, *The Servant of God* [ET, 1957], p. 96 (not in *TDNT* v, 710f.); C. Maurer, "Knecht Gottes und Sohn Gottes im Passionsbericht des Markusevangeliums," ZThK 50 [1953], pp. 1ff.

[88] O. Cullmann, *The Christology of the New Testament* [ET, 1959], pp. 81f.

[89] So R. H. Fuller, *The Mission and Achievement of Jesus* [1954], p. 58. And now for a similar judgment see N. Perrin, "The Use of (παρα) διδόναι, in connection with the Passion of Jesus in the New Testament," *Der Ruf Jesu und die Antwort der Gemeinde*. Festschrift J. Jeremias [1970], pp. 204–212 (208).

[90] Tödt, *op. cit.*, p. 160 against C. Maurer, *loc. cit.*, pp. 1ff.

servant to be destroyed (v. 18). The dramatic reversal of fortune is described in the following way:

> "The stone which the builders rejected has become the chief cornerstone."
> (v.22)

It is an event which is wholly ascribed to God's mercy and intervention
(v. 23), and an occasion of rejoicing (v. 24).[91]

Several factors enter into the picture which, we may agree, forms a
convincing background of the language chosen to depict the destiny of
Jesus in Mark and the concepts used in that description. For one thing,
the Targum on the text (Ps. 118:22 = 117, LXX) makes mention of the
"masterbuilders" in a special sense corresponding to the "learned," who
are the scribes who build up Israel through the Law. They reject the
"young man" (Heb. talyā', which may mean either "son" or "lamb,"
according to context); nevertheless he will not be defeated but will be
considered as king and ruler. This documentary evidence provides substance for the view that a messianic interpretation of the text was already
available in Judaism.[92]

Then, we must take note of the use made in early Christian apologetic
of this Psalm verse. In Mark 12:10, the text is employed in the punch-
line to Jesus' parable of the Tenants in the Vineyard, with the same
Greek verb employed (ἀποδοκιμασθῆναι = be rejected) as in Psalm 117:
22 (LXX). The verb used in the citation given at Acts 4:11 (ἐξουθενηθῆναι)
is a variant in Psalm 117:22, and shown to be a virtual synonym from the
parallel usages in Mark 8:31, 9:12.[93]

At their minimal value, then, these Passion sayings expressed the notion
of Jesus' self-awareness as the messenger of God who must accept humiliation but who will be vindicated and exalted beyond the bitter experience
of his rejection.

We can state the case for this thesis in another way, by the following
summary.[94]

(a) Jesus must certainly have anticipated a violent end to his ministry.
At the critical points at which he clashed with the Jewish authorities—
Mark has collected these episodes into a bracket, suitably labelled by M.
Albertz, "Controversy Stories,"[95] in chapters 2:1–3:6—the issues stated
are his claim to offer forgiveness in his own right (2:1–12), his overriding
of the laws of fasting (2:18–22) and especially his violation of the Sabbath

---

[91] A place in the Enthronement ritual in which the anointed priest-king takes his position
as Yahweh's viceregent has been given to the Psalm by A. Bentzen, *King and Messiah* [ET,
1955], ch. 2.
[92] So B. Gärtner, *Studia Theologica*, 8 [1955], pp. 23ff.
[93] Tödt, *op. cit.*, pp. 164ff.; R. H. Fuller, *The Foundations of New Testament Christology*
[1965], p. 118. See also B. Lindars, *New Testament Apologetic* [1961], pp. 169ff.
[94] I draw now upon Jeremias' provocative section, *New Testament Theology*, pp. 278ff.
[95] M. Albertz, *Die synoptischen Streitgespräche* [1921].

rules (2:23–3:6). These concerted claims were tantamount to a deliberate offence and an infraction of the Jewish law for which, as a repeated transgressor, Jesus had invited the death-sentence upon himself, since his transgressions were committed in Galilee where the Roman law which forbade the Jews the right to execute a capital sentence (John 18:31) did not apply.

As a final indictment against him, he was not only open to the suspicion of being in league with Beelzebub (Mark 3:22) as well as blaspheming God (2:7), he was branded as a false prophet (14:65) at his trial—a charge which he had brought down upon his own head since he had given cause for the rumour that he was a destroyer of the Temple (14:57, 58). Behind that charge, which Mark calls "false," lies undoubtedly the tradition associated with his final entry into Jerusalem, and his cleansing of the Temple court. Though not specified as such in Mark's gospel, this incident was the immediate occasion of the mounting tide of political opposition which bore him away to his trial and death. The Fourth Evangelist may well preserve the Passion prediction taken from Psalm 69:10: "Zeal for thy house will consume me" (John 2:17). "He means that Jesus' zeal will lead him to his death."[96]

(b) At an obviously central point in Mark's portrayal in Jesus' self-revelation to his disciples (10:45) he announces for himself an inalienable place in God's salvation-history.

The setting of the verse is important. The minds of the disciples are filled with thoughts of earthly greatness and prestige. James and John vocalize this desire to share in the coming glory which they confidently expect in Jerusalem (10:37). The ten disciples are indignant (v. 41)—because these two sons of Zebedee have got in first with their request, and "jumped the queue" ahead of them. It is time for Jesus to give all of them a sharp rebuke and to read them a lesson (vv. 42ff.).

Greatness in the Roman world is understood in terms of exercising control over men (cf. Matt. 8:9, par.) and so putting them in their place and letting them see who is the rightful master. In Jesus' tiny fellowship a new ordering of authority takes over. The master is the servant of all and his title to lordship is written in terms of his intention to serve, not play the boss with heavy hand. So the solemn announcement is made: For the Son of man also came not to be served but to serve, and to give his life as a ransom for many.

The problematic issues which centre on this *logion* are several. They have mainly to do with (a) authenticity. How can this verse be related to a verse which expresses in simpler fashion the claim of Jesus the servant, Luke 22:27? Is it not the case that Mark's version represents a late theologizing expansion of the more direct statement, I am among you as one who serves? Then (b) background. In spite of the formidable case

[96] R. Bultmann, *The Gospel of John* [ET, 1971], p. 124.

presented by R. H. Fuller in his earlier work[97] for regarding this verse as a restatement of the Isaianic picture of the suffering servant, who fulfils his servant rôle by obedience unto death and becoming an offering for sin (Isa. 53:10) on behalf of the "many",[98] later study has raised objections chiefly to do with the propriety of invoking Isaiah 53 and partly with a suggestion of a more immediate background in the Maccabean martyrs whose lives constituted a ransom-price for Israel.[99] For our immediate purpose we need not settle the issues thus provoked, except to say somewhat dogmatically that there do not seem to be sufficient grounds for raising doubt as to the authenticity of the *logion*[100] and that the precise contextual background of the language of the verse is perhaps less important a consideration than its overall insistence as a self-testimony to Jesus. On that score, it clearly speaks of Jesus' own awareness of his unique mission as divinely commissioned Son of man who has come into the world to do for men what they could never do for themselves. This is plain from the statement in Psalm 49:7, 8:

> "Truly no man can ransom himself, or give to God the price of his life, for the ransom of his life is costly and can never suffice."

The prevalence of the metaphor of ransom/redemption (Greek λυτρ-) is clear from the LXX (48:8, 9). Also emphasized is the costliness of this ransom, and the surrender of human life (Greek ψυχή).

Above all, this willing self-sacrifice on behalf of those who are otherwise hopeless and powerless to effect their own deliverance is construed by Jesus as the motif of his mission of service. He has received from God a commission to set men free. To accomplish this he must accept a life which puts him alongside them as "slave of all" (v. 44) and give his most costly possession in fulfilment of his task. This will entail the willing surrender of his life, offered as the ransom price on men's behalf and in their name. And that surely spells out the inevitability of his death and the laying down of his life in sacrifice. In this way and only in this way will he fulfil his rôle in God's purpose and execute the divine mission for which he has come into the world.

(c) He foresaw that the violent end of his life would not overtake him unwillingly or be thrust upon him as a cruel fate. He chose his destiny in obedience to the Father's will and scripture's dictates. The "necessity" which urged him on towards Jerusalem was not something impersonal or mechanical, as we have observed. Jesus' foreknowledge of his destiny was read in the scriptural predictions concerning John (9:13) and himself

---

[97] *The Mission and Achievement of Jesus* [1954], pp. 56ff.

[98] See J. Jeremias, TDNT, vi, pp. 543ff., for the sense of πολλοί (many) derived from Isaiah 53. And now cf. Perrin, *loc. cit.*, p. 211.

[99] C. K. Barrett, "The Background of Mark x. 45" in *New Testament Essays*, ed. A. J. B. Higgins [1959], pp. 1–18.

[100] See E. Best's discussion, *The Temptation and the Passion* [1965], pp. 140–144.

(9:12; 12:10; 14:49), and gladly embraced as part of his chosen portion. The ultimate acceptance of God's will was made in Gethsemane (14:32–42) and to this episode we will devote a separate section. It is sufficient here to note the climax of the incident as he rises to meet his enemies and summons his followers to join him: "The hour has come; the Son of man is betrayed into the hands of sinners. Rise, let us be going; see, my betrayer is at hand" (14:41, 42). No clearer sign could be given than this that he knew what was unfolding before him, and he rallied his disciples to meet it as he led the way forward, as in 10:32. Two prospects seem plausibly to be read into this acceptance of his suffering. First, he knows that what is to befall him is not unprepared and fortuitous; rather it is part of the Father's will, declared in scripture, and may so be welcomed, even though it entails bitter rejection and loss. Then, he looks beyond the strain of the present and the suffering which immediately awaits him to a more distant time when he will be vindicated by God and his confidence owned by him. That much he sees in prospect: in a little while ("after three days," 8:31; 9:31; 10:34) he will be raised.

(iii) *The Last Supper Words*

The eucharistic tradition found in the words of Jesus in Mark 14:22–25 has been the subject of much critical scrutiny in recent years. Part of the problem is how to relate these "words of institution" in the Markan version to the variant tradition represented in Paul and Luke (in the longer Text). For our purpose, the question of priority and authenticity is not vitally important, except that we should take note of the impressive case put forward by J. Jeremias.[101] He argues for the primitiveness of Mark's account, partly on the score that Mark's version is replete with semitisms which have been smoothed out in Paul's re-wording and partly on the ground of the stark statements attributed to Jesus in Mark's version. Those statements are the substance of Jesus' words of interpretation, which may be reconstructed in their elemental form as follows:

Take; this [is] my body (= my flesh).

This [wine] [is] my blood of the covenant [blood which is being poured out] for many.

The first saying is related to the sacrificial terminology of the Old Testament; the second statement clearly identifies the cup with its own contents of red wine (a Passover feature) with the blood of Jesus which he indicates will be poured out (again, in sacrifice) in the near future. To Jews the thought of being invited to drink human blood would be regarded with horror and revulsion, associated with "a dark animistic

---

[101] J. Jeremias, *The Eucharistic Words of Jesus*[2] [ET, 1966], pp. 160ff.

abomination."[102] This looks in every way as though it represents the *ipsissima vox* of Jesus. Paul's adaptation to read "This cup is the new covenant in my blood" (1 Cor. 11:25) is then to be regarded as secondary, explained as Paul's endeavour to avoid any suspicion that the cup contained real blood, and to deny any parallel which might be awakened in the minds of Gentile Christians who were familiar with the rites of the mystery cults. One feels that the bare   "This [is] my blood" would be as unintelligible to Gentiles as it would be shocking to Jews. Besides, the concept of "*new* covenant" is a favourite one with Paul, as we can see from his discussion in 2 Corinthians 3.

Mark's version may be regarded as original on the ground that "exactly that which seems scandalous will be historical."[103] There is no linguistic objection to be brought against the entire Markan phrase "my blood of the covenant" which represents a fair translation into its Graecized form of the Aramaic *adam qeyami* ("my covenant blood").[104]

As to the meaning of these interpretative words, it will suffice to observe how Jesus foresaw his impending death in sacrificial categories. The Passover meal, as explained in the Haggadah, invited the opportunity for words of interpretation to be spoken. Jesus, therefore, as *paterfamilias* or host at the meal, was adopting no strange custom in adding his commentary to the actions of distributing the bread and the wine. The novelty came in the way in which he identified both parts of the Passover ritual with himself as a sacrificial victim.

(a) The bread is compared with his body, soon to be surrendered in death. The token of his body (or flesh, which equally can represent the original word which he presumably spoke) is offered to the disciples who are bidden to eat the bread now broken. The purport of this action has been understood by several writers in the following way. "He meant their action to be a means whereby they might share in the power of his self-offering and the virtue of his approaching death."[105] On this understanding Jesus had in mind his body soon to be broken on the cross, and used the bread analogically to suggest to his disciples that in that meal they were being invited to share in and receive the benefit of that redeeming sacrifice. However true this view may be in a general sense, its validity

---

[102] Jeremias, *op. cit.*, p. 170, who gives the Old Testament evidence of prohibitions against consuming human or animal blood. Cf. J. Klausner, *Jesus of Nazareth* [1925], p. 329: "The drinking of blood, even if it were meant symbolically, would only have aroused horror in the minds of such simple Galilean Jews." On the other hand, 1 Chron. 11:19 records David's contemplating just such an action, although only in symbolic fashion.

[103] G. Dalman, *Jesus-Jeschua*[2] [1930], p. 143, as cited in Jeremias, *op. cit.*, p. 171, note 1.

[104] So Jeremias' latest discussion, *op. cit.*, pp. 194f.

[105] V. Taylor, *The Gospel according to St. Mark* [1957], p. 544. Cf. R. Otto, *The Kingdom of God and the Son of Man* [ET, 1943], p. 304: "Christ's action was, therefore, more than mere prediction; it was an acted, anticipatory prediction by representation; even more was it the gift of a share in the power of the thing represented, viz. in the atoning power of the broken Christ."

as an interpretation of the Eucharistic saying is open to question, for the interpreting word was spoken not at the breaking of the bread but at its distribution.[106]

Much more probable is the idea that Paschal overtones are to be seen in the actions of Jesus. The function of the bread offered to the disciples was the same as that of the Passover loaf; it carried a representative meaning. The immediate background is the use made of Deuteronomy 16:3 in the Haggadah: "Behold the bread of suffering of which our ancestors partook in the land of Egypt."[107] As the faithful Jew ate the bread, so he was linked representatively with his forefathers whom the Lord delivered from bondage in Egypt; and he was encouraged, on the principle, A man must so regard himself as though he had personally been delivered from Egypt,[108] to enjoy personal participation in the national liberation. So Jesus hands the bread to these men, who stand in the Israelite tradition, and invests the action with a new significance. They are to share in his freely-willed death as a sacrifice soon to be completed on the cross. He is soon to offer his life in this way, and now he grants them an antedonation[109] of all that the sacrifice will secure as redemption for the new Israel.

(b) It is not otherwise with the offer of the Paschal cup. The wine seals the covenant, in whose scope all (i.e. πολλοί = many, understood as a semitic expression of inclusiveness, all who are a large company) are embraced. The most likely contextual reference to "my blood of the covenant" is Exodus 24.[110] Moses inaugurated the covenant between God and Israel with blood, partly put on the altar and partly sprinkled on the people after the hearing of the book of the covenant. "And Moses took the blood and threw it upon the people, and said: 'Behold the blood of the covenant which the Lord has made with you according to all these words'" (Ex. 24:8). Now at the instigation of Jesus' purpose to offer his blood and to ratify the covenant of eternal redemption, he too took the token of the sacrifice shortly to be offered on the cross and announced to those who sat down at table as a nucleus of a new, universal community of believers, that the cup holds the blood, in symbolic fashion, which will inaugurate God's covenant relationship.

The Last Supper sayings are flanked by two important statements which Mark records. During the meal, Jesus had solemnly warned the company that there was a betrayer in their midst (14:17–21). The traitor's offence was aggravated by the fact that he chose to remain and to share the meal

---

[106] A. J. B. Higgins, *The Lord's Supper in the New Testament* [1952], p. 51; cf. F.-J. Leenhardt, *Le sacrement de la sainte Cène* [1948], pp. 36–38: "Neither the breaking nor the distribution of pieces of bread can represent a man's death" (p. 37).

[107] See *The Haggadah for Passover*, ed. S. M. Lehrman [1954], p. 11.

[108] R. Gamaliel, according to the Mishnah, tractate *Pesachim*, 10:5.

[109] J. Jeremias' expressive term, *New Testament Theology*, i, p. 290.

[110] V. Taylor, *The Gospel according to St. Mark*, p. 545; idem, *Jesus and His Sacrifice* [1937], p. 138.

as though he intended no harm to Jesus. Further, part of the Passover celebration included a sharing in a menu consisting of green herbs, bitter herbs and fruit sauce (haroseth) made from dried fruits, spices and sour wine. This dish was to precede the breaking of bread;[111] and it is the dish referred to in Mark 14:20. Jesus permitted the betrayer to remain and to take his portion from this relish—or even, if we have regard to John 13:26, to receive a piece of bread or meat dipped in the sauce as a mark of honour. He made no effort to unmask him, according to the Markan narrative, and consented to tolerate his presence incognito simply on the ground that "the Son of man goes as it is written of him" (v. 21) by whomsoever he is to be handed over to his enemies.

The other indication that Jesus, at the supper meal, set his face to betrayal, judgment and death is seen in his vow of abstinence in 14:25. The negative form of the verse is clarified by Luke 22:18. There it is clear that Jesus did not in fact share the bread and the cup with his own.[112] He fasted on that occasion, possibly as an action which carried the meaning of an intercessory prayer for his enemies and (on Jeremias' understanding) as a part of his representative office as servant of God who makes intercession for the transgressors (Isa. 53:12). His vow of abstinence is yet another sign of his willingness to be identified with sinners and to be committed to their hands as an essential part of his obedience to God. Yet he knows that out of that bitter experience and grim ordeal will come deliverance. God will vindicate his chosen one, and crown him with gladness when he rejoins his own and presides over another meal in God's kingdom at the consummation. Beyond the dark valley of humiliation and death, he sees his vindication-scene and the messianic banquet spread on God's holy hill. He will then play the part as *paterfamilias* and his vow of abstinence will be at an end.

(iv) The Consent to Suffer

There are miscellaneous incidents and *logia* of Jesus, set into the Markan story, which point forward to the cross. While each episode may not say a great deal on its own, and indeed be capable of alternative explanation, there is a cumulative force in the way in which those actions and words are grouped in the evangelist's narrative. Taken together, they seem to endorse the general verdict that Jesus freely accepted suffering as part of his messianic vocation and embraced God's will in a series of acts of obedience and faith.

(a) The Parable of the Tenants and the Son (12: 1-12)

As Mark has transmitted this parable, its place comes at a juncture where Jesus' authority is in question (11:28ff.). To the direct challenge, Who

---

[111] In the Mishnah, tractate *Pesachim* 10:3.

[112] Again we draw on J. Jeremias' illuminating discussion, *Eucharistic Words*, pp. 210ff.

gave you this authority to do these things?[113] he gives no straight affirmative or negative answer. His way of replying is to pose his own question, which in turn is not directly answered.

However, the matter of his authority is not completely evaded. He does obliquely declare himself in a parable, the point of which is taken by those to whom it was given (12:1, 12). Based on Isaiah 5:1-7, the story of 12:1-9 has allegorical features which are intended to show the identity of the chief actors, and in particular the character of his enemies who would shortly encompass his death.[114] The heart of the story is found in verse 6 in which the identity of "beloved son" who is the landlord's final appeal and gesture to the rebellious farmers seems obvious, as Mark so phrases the description (cf. 1:1, 11; 9:7; 15:39). Jesus is presented here clearly as the Father's Son who comes as God's ultimate expression of demand and succour, yet receives in the very place where his authority as God's heir ought to have been acknowledged the outrageous treatment of murderous hatred and total rejection (vv. 7, 8). In contrast to Matthew's (21:39) and Luke's (20:51) version of the same parable, Mark emphasizes that the rejection and murder took place *within* the vineyard as though to stress painfully that the very scene which should have awakened reminders of responsibility and devotion to this son who came with the owner's full authority has become the place of the deliberate crime. Jesus is depicted as the last in a succession of rejected and martyred prophets; and his presence in God's holy city carries no immunity to bodily danger. Rather, he is even then surrounded by evil men, who acting in God's name as religious leaders, will nonetheless conspire to bring about his death.

Jesus, as he appears in the dramatic rôle of this parable, is under no illusion as to how his fate would be decided. Nevertheless, he looked beyond rejection to a vindication-scene, borrowed from Psalm 118:22, 23.

(b) The Anointing at Bethany (14:3-9)

The Markan passion narrative opens with the frontispiece of this story. A woman intrudes on to the scene of a meal Jesus is taking in the home of Simon and performs an action which the disciples construe as wasteful and unnecessary. A flask of costly unguent is broken and its contents poured

---

[113] "These things" meaning the actions of Jesus in cleansing the Temple court (11:15ff.). Conceivably, if 11:27-33 is a pericope detachable from its immediate context, the issue may turn upon Jesus' authority in endorsing baptismal practices (cf. John 3:22-25). So Bultmann, *The History of the Synoptic Tradition* [ET, 1963], p. 20, note 1. This setting would at least give point to Jesus' reply in his counter-question regarding the Baptist.

[114] Cf. C. H. Dodd, *The Parables of the Kingdom* [1935], pp. 124-132. Dodd's interpretation is opposed by W. G. Kümmel, "Das Gleichnis von den bösen Weingärtnern (Mark xii, 1-9)" in *Aux sources de la tradition chrétienne* [1950] Festschrift M. Goguel, pp. 120ff. But the process of allegorization has been traced to the pre-Markan tradition by J. Jeremias, *The Parables of Jesus* [ET, 1954], pp. 55-60.

over his head as he reclines at table. In defence of this action Jesus commends the woman and her deed (v. 6). Our interest focuses on the important saying recorded as verse 8:

> She has done what she could; she has anointed my body beforehand for burying.

J. Jeremias[115] has illuminated the significance of this incident in the light of Jewish practices. He rebuts Bultmann's suggestion that the anticipation of the passion (in v. 8) is a secondary appendix to the story of the anointing[116] by drawing attention to the distinction the Rabbis made between a *gift* of love and a *work* of love. She offered her act as a gift, i.e. for her an expression of affection and sympathy apparently, though the phrase "poured it over his head" may be intended to recall 2 Kings 9:6 where Jehu is proclaimed king following his anointing in this way. Then she may be described as glimpsing Jesus' messianic claim and responding to it. If so, Mark is using the episode as a further evidence in his overall purpose of showing how unlikely persons recognized his Messiahship. It was interpreted more superficially by the disciples who then criticized her for it on the score that the worth of the ointment could more properly have been channelled into an almsgiving to the poor (v. 5). Jesus came to her rescue by interpreting the action in a different way. For him it is a *work* of love which stands higher as a duty than as an emotional display. He viewed it as part of the requirement that his dead body should receive the funeral rites in advance. So it becomes clear that Jesus expected to die by violent hands in the near future and to share a common grave. He would be buried unceremoniously and without funeral preparations, in fulfilment of his anticipation of a criminal's fate and possibly the prophecy of Isaiah 53:9. Hence his praise of the woman's act. She has (unwittingly?) taken steps to prevent this by anointing him in preparation for his death.

Against the objection that this announcement in verse 8 may well be a prophecy after the event is the simple fact that events did not turn out exactly as predicted here. In fact, Jesus did not suffer total rejection nor was his body consigned to a criminal's grave (15:46). Other women were ready to perform the funeral obsequies (16:1) and the prophecy of Isaiah 53:9 was only partly fulfilled. It seems evident that this saying in 14:8 could not have been invented later and read back when Mark goes on to record a different sequel to his story. Rather we may perceive a genuine anticipation by Jesus that he expected to suffer a terrible fate and to meet his end by dying a criminal's death.

[115] J. Jeremias, *New Testament Theology*, i [1971], p. 284. See too his essay, "Die Salbungsgeschichte Mc 14.3–9," ZNTW 35 [1936], pp. 75–82.
[116] R. Bultmann, *The History of the Synoptic Tradition*, pp. 36f.

(c) The involvement of the disciples

The same line of reasoning may be applied to the expected fate of the disciples. According to 10:35-40; 14:27, 28 Jesus foresaw that his immediate followers would be implicated in his fate. They were known to be his friends and disciples, so it seemed only natural that as he prepared himself for what lay ahead, he must forewarn them that they should be ready to suffer and die. As early as 8:34, 35 in Mark's narrative this ominous note is sounded, and the immediate call to loyalty and steadfastness under trial is given in the warning of 8:38.

In fact, the course of events ran otherwise and in spite of the loud protestations of James and John (10:39) they did not rise to the challenge of his need of them or of their professed loyalty. At 10:39 he evidently expected them to remain faithful unto death. By the time of 14:27 he contemplates their desertion, though the wording of 14:42 suggests that he will go forward to meet his enemies with the three chosen disciples at his side. The final abandonment of Jesus by his disciples is reached in 14:50; and it may well have overtaken him as a rude surprise. Mark's insertion on the little pericope (14:51, 52) adds dramatic point to the wholesale defection, in possible reminiscence of Amos 2:16: "He who is stout of heart among the mighty shall flee away naked in that day" and so he accentuates the sombre eschatological meaning of Jesus' committal to the hands of his enemies.

Yet desertion and disloyalty are not to be the end. Looking beyond the prospect of his own death and the dispersal of the disciples, Jesus sees a re-grouping of his own and his hope is that he will again take up his leadership of them (14:28; 16:7). He will lead them forth to Galilee—again, so far as Mark's story goes, this is an unfulfilled prediction, and the narrative in ch. 16 breaks off abruptly with the simple pledge that this is the hope that Jesus had as he faced his Passion and in the assurance which the messenger conveyed to the disciples through the bewildered women. There is nothing resembling a neatly composed and constructed "promise-fulfilment" demonstration. Only the hint that whatever their fate, he will see them again and be re-united with them. There may, however, be a theological undertone in Mark's language if we are correct in assuming that the dispersing of the flock (Greek $\delta\iota\alpha\sigma\kappa\rho\pi\iota\sigma\theta\tilde{\eta}\nu\alpha\iota$ in 14:27) indicates a time of tribulation before the end of the age.[117] Then the promised gathering of the scattered flock will be the sign for the inauguration of the new age, with its promise of redemption for all the Gentiles.

(d) Gethsemane (14:32-42)

The pericope which describes the scene in the garden is one fraught with

[117] So J. Jeremias, *Jesus' Promise to the Nations* [ET, 1958], p. 64.

several weighty problems.[118] What emerges from the modern discussion of this episode is that the entire framework is eschatological. Jesus' petition to have the cup removed (v. 36) is not primarily a desire to escape from his situation which closes in around him as though human fear gripped him.[119] It is quite out of harmony with all that Mark has previously shown in the Passion sayings to conclude that now Jesus' obedience faltered and he began to doubt his mission. Also, it is not quite satisfactory to interpret[120] the prayer: "Abba, Father, all things are possible to thee; remove this cup from me; yet not what I will, but what thou wilt" as a final questioning on the part of Jesus as to whether his mission would necessarily entail the suffering which he knew to be preliminary to the coming of God's kingdom. "All things are possible to thee"[121] points to his conviction that God's kingdom will come in his own way. If his own suffering is to precede the establishing of God's reign, he is prepared for it, though now at the final stage of his destined course to Jerusalem he contemplates "the possibility that the wished-for future, the establishing of the kingdom of God, might come without the necessity of preliminary suffering" (C. K. Barrett). Even when expressed in this guarded way, this interpretation suggests that at the last Jesus envisaged some other issue to his life and mission than one involving his own sacrifice on the cross.

Another possibility is to be considered. This turns upon the precise meaning to be given to the metaphor of the cup.[122] Usually the metaphor is taken to be one of God's wrath or Jesus' human suffering; it could conceivably be a vivid expression of his experience of satanic temptation.[123] Gethsemane, on this view, is indeed the scene of conflict as Jesus for the final time wrestles with the demonic insinuation that he can tread God's path and still avoid the cross. Throughout his ministry he has been tempted to fulfil his mission in a way which would have gained him an immediate and positive response. He could have offered an accrediting sign from heaven (8:11–13); he might have capitalized on his wonderful works and commanded a following among people who were impressed with his supernatural powers; he would have received the plaudits of his own disciples if he had promised them thrones (10:37) and good seats in the spectacle of an imminent kingdom. Instead, he consistently set his face against these false choices and easy roads to success and acclaim. God's

[118] See for some of these K. G. Kuhn, "Jesus in Gethsemane," *Evangelische Theologie* 12 [1952–3], pp. 260–85; E. Linnemann, *Studien zur Passionsgeschichte* [1960], pp. 11–40 and especially R. S. Barbour, "Gethsemane in the Tradition of the Passion," NTS 16 [1969–70], pp. 231–51.
[119] O. Cullmann, *The Christology of the New Testament* [ET, 1959], p. 96, emphasizes the anti-Docetic motif in the Gethsemane incident, in the light of Hebrews 5:7f.
[120] So C. K. Barrett, *Jesus and the Gospel Tradition* [1967], pp. 46f.
[121] On this sentence, see W. C. van Unnik, "Alles ist dir möglich," *Verborum Veritas* Festschrift G. Stählin [1970], pp. 27–36.
[122] For a recent discusson see M. Black, "The Cup Metaphor in Mark xiv.36," ExpT, lix [1947–48[, p. 195.
[123] R. S. Barbour, *loc. cit.*, p. 247.

kingdom must be served in God's way; and in a mystery he knows that this *will* entail his obedience unto death. Now, within the shadow of the cross, he faces his ultimate trial. The pressure to turn back is at its strongest as the hour of his final obedience comes. He prays that the temptation to be unfaithful to his calling may indeed pass as the cup is removed. His testing is real; and the disciples too are involved (v. 38), for in a real sense they would choose, if they could, an easy road for him which by-passed the cross (8:32). He must, therefore, overcome in his trial and encourage them not to dissuade him from his goal any further.

Jesus wins through to a final oblation of his will to God, and in an ultimate submission yielded his life to God as his obedient servant and trustful Son. "Rise, let us be going" is his rousing call, as he marches forward to meet his betrayer, his enemies and his freely embraced fate.

Conclusion

At the close of this lengthy and somewhat discursive chapter, we can announce a conclusion in few words. The data point inevitably to Mark's intention in portraying the mission and purpose of Jesus. It was his consistent and undeviating purpose not to give any proof of this messianic authority which could be construed as demonstrating who he was. Right up to the last he refused to accede to the request that he should so declare himself. Then, as a direct consequence of this determination, he freely accepted his commitment to rejection, humiliation and suffering as part of his destiny. His obedience to the Father and his acceptance of a scriptural pattern for his life were decisive—even where there was no immediate response from God (15:34). Nonetheless he entered upon his mission in the full knowledge of what would befall him. He trod a single path, refusing to be side-tracked or deflected from the purpose which gripped him. He entered upon the final phase of his obedience with confidence that he was responding to God's will for his life. And even if that obedience entailed his own sacrifice and death he believed that, after defeat and suffering and the final self-giving of himself there would come triumph for him and his own and validation of his authority as Son of man. "God will raise me up" (from Hosea 6:2) was his hope and conviction.

Our next chapter will investigate what Mark does with this christology of obedience, suffering, and subsequent vindication.

VIII

MARK'S GOSPEL IN TODAY'S. WORLD

The place of the Markan historical Jesus in the post-Pauline situation and contemporary criticism and church-life. The message of the cross and triumph of Jesus as God's way in his world. The form of a servant as a paradigm for the persecuted church. Mark's missionary motifs. Mark's message for the church, then and now.

BECAUSE OUR STUDY IS NOT SIMPLY AN ACADEMIC EXERCISE OR A STRICTLY historical enquiry, we may pass on to ask about its results for our contemporary situation. But lest we should be unwittingly guilty of importing our own ideas into the text and discovering a relevance about Mark's Gospel which it does not in fact possess, it is imperative that we pause first to sum up the conclusions we have so far reached. And this (hopefully) is a re-statement of an objective nature, though a novel interpretation is bound to contain an individualizing motif as well.

The chief emphases of this Gospel are at the same time the data we need to examine in order to ascertain Mark's purpose. If it is true that before Mark wrote there existed only a loose collection of traditions and that it was this evangelist who first conceived the idea of putting the traditions together into a connected and coherent sequence, then clearly Mark had a purpose in view. And that purpose (or those purposes) may be judged from the use he makes of the material at his disposal, whether by selective emphasis of intentional arrangement or passing over material which he might have included if he had so chosen.

Once we frame our enquiry in this way, it becomes clear that Mark's Gospel is concerned to place maximum emphasis on the following ideas.

(a) *The humanity of Jesus.* Such an affirmation is made by the various methods open to the evangelist. Obviously he does not state the belief in credal form (as in Ignatius' use of the adverb "truly" [Trallians 9] or the later *vere homo*). Rather his "life of Jesus" is a dramatization in real life situations of what that credal confession means. And Mark does this in at least three ways.

First, there is Jesus' consistent refusal to give demonstrable proof of his claims. As we have observed, the Jesus of Mark rejects every petition which is directed to him that he should declare himself and show his hand. Both by peremptory refusal and by a willingness to remain silent when he could have spoken or acted in self-defence, he refused to declare himself in the way that his enemies, accusers and friends would have desired. It is small wonder, therefore, that all turn against him—and Mark records painfully the total rejection of Jesus as a *leitmotif* of his passion story—and that at the last Jesus died in solitary anguish, uncomforted and misunderstood by all the central characters in the drama of the trial and crucifixion. The pathetic cry of forsakenness (15:34) touches the nadir of this desolation by which the rejected Jesus is engulfed.

Then, Jesus actively consented to suffer and to taste the bitterness of death. From the beginning of his narrative, Mark has the end of his life in view and prepares the reader for it. First with allusive hints and suggestions (1:14; 2:20), then by more forthcoming declarations (3:6) he indicates that the ministry will end in rejection, hostility and loss. The watershed comes with the incident at Caesarea Philippi (8:27ff.) after which Jesus speaks openly about his fate and the need to follow him along a path of suffering discipleship. He sets his face towards Jerusalem in the full consciousness that a violent end will await him, and for this he is prepared since he has come to surrender his life on behalf of his people (10:45). The final engagement with temptation comes in Gethsemane (14:32–42) after which he goes forward to his judges in the consciousness that he can expect no favourable verdict from their court. Rather the scripture has decreed that he must die and he maintains a passivity and non-co-operation (seen in his almost total silence before his accusers) until the end.

Thirdly, this gospel record goes out of its way to place undisputed emphasis on a frank admission of Jesus' fully human character. He is limited in his ability (6:5, 6); he confesses to an area of knowledge to which he has no access (13:32); his last cry is one of astonished grief that even his Father has deserted him (15:34). Mark relates all these items with no apology offered to mitigate the harshness of the descriptions. He is content simply to state the facts with a simplicity and starkness which does not expect to cause a scandal or to provoke embarrassing questions. For him it is just a matter of factual detail and part of the bedrock of humanity on which his gospel rests.

(b) *The importance of faith* is stressed as the atmosphere in which Jesus' mighty works were performed. It is true that there are stories of Jesus' healing work which *could* be taken as examples of his divine power displayed as a wonder-worker (e.g. 7:31–37), but the characteristic feature which Mark brings out in the bulk of his miracle-stories is that Jesus worked most successfully only when expectant or embryonic faith was present (5:25–34; 7:24–30; 9:14–29). The unique Markan statement in 6:5, 6 bears this out.

Mark, by this token, seems to be saying emphatically that there is no substitute for human confidence in Jesus' power. Just as his hands were tied in the presence of unbelief (6:1–6), he was most able to minister to human need when men and women approached him in an awareness of that need and a trustful attitude which turned away from doubt and fear (the great enemies of faith) and placed confidence in his ability. Sayings of Jesus, such as 5:34 and 9:23 and 11:22, were evidently highly regarded in the Markan community and the lesson was drawn to the Christians' edification that Jesus was both the exemplar of faith (9:19–24) and the miracle-worker whose power was controlled by a moral purpose, which meant that he responded to an unself-regarding faith. He was *not* a magician performing conjuring tricks to enhance his own reputation—or else he would have worked a miracle to save himself and to confute unbelief (15:32) as well as have dazzled people in Galilee by a pyrotechnic display. Instead he looked for faith and like the patient farmer (in a parable unique in Mark, 4:26–29) he taught and was himself prepared to accept that God's kingdom comes in God's good time and without any feverish attempt to promote it.

(c) *The cost of discipleship* is underlined and driven home to Mark's readers through the warnings given to the disciples themselves. They are called by Jesus to follow him along a road which he has chosen. Inevitably it is a pathway across a rugged terrain of misunderstanding and calculated enmity.

Ties of family life are severed as his kinsfolk prove hostile (3:21, 31–35) and his own people show themselves unresponsive to the sort of leader he wants to be (6:1–6). Official Judaism is declared to be irreconcilably at odds with his publication of the kingdom (2:21, 22), since the scribal interpreters of the law are insistent on maintaining their iron-clad system and on refusing to change (7:7–9). In the end they will compass his death and have the Roman authority carry out the sentence of judicial execution, death by crucifixion.[1]

It is a remarkable sequence to note that Mark spells out the parallel between the destiny of Jesus as a faithful Servant of God and the expected sufferings of his own. As he met with opposition from his kinsfolk in his *patris* (6:1–6), so they must anticipate a forsaking of all earthly ties (10:28–30) and it is in this context that "persecutions" are spoken of. Disloyalty and fratricidal strife will be the painful experience of his followers (13:12); and they will be hated as he was.

The Jewish authorities will prove unsympathetic to their witness, and disciples must expect a time of arraignment and interrogation on account of their faith (13:9–11).

Following Jesus entails an acceptance of the call to active suffering, since the imagery used in 8:34ff. makes it clear that the disciples voluntarily

---

[1] The verb "to crucify" occurs in Mark only in connection with the passion-story in ch. 15. But the inference leading to the fate of a Roman death is given in such statement as "delivered into the hands of [sinners] men" (9:31; 14:41) and "delivered to the Gentiles" (10:33).

and deliberately assume the cause of their Lord and follow him who carried his cross to the place of death (15:21, 22). All the indignity and horror of death by impaling (interpreted in the light of Deut. 21:23: He who is hanged on a tree is accursed by God) is to be read into these words, both on the Jewish side, for which the Old Testament rubric would have profound meaning (as we know from Gal. 3:13) but also on the hellenistic side.[2] And there is the well-known evidence of Roman writers who express disgust at the sight of the crucifixion and counsel all good Romans to turn away from it.[3] To the Roman mind there could be no greater object of shame and scorn than the picture of a God upon a cross.[4] And to believe that Jesus actually forewarned that his followers would suffer this horrific death was to recognize that the cost of discipleship was indeed a heavy one.

The minds of the disciples are, however, filled with contrary thoughts, and not only does Peter play the part of the devil's advocate in seeking to turn Jesus aside from his purpose (8:32) and to reject his fore-shadowing of what must befall him, the disciples as a body are expecting that Jesus' march on Jerusalem will be crowned with glory (10:35ff.). Though there is a hint that at least some of Jesus' warnings may have struck home (10:32). At all events, the costliness of following Jesus is reviewed at the close of the ministry both in explicit statements (14:27) and by the prospect which awaits the disciples in the future (13:9ff.). The greatest object-lesson of all is given in the desolation which engulfs Jesus himself as he goes forward to his death and offers his life in a willing submission to God but not without the disturbing admission that he died in abject misery (15:34) with none to console and apparently none to confide in.

(*d*) *The true messiahship of Jesus* is for Mark essentially an incognito one. It is misunderstood by the representatives of official Judaism (3:20–30), hidden from the inattentive onlooker and unrecognized by the disciples who fill the term apparently with a political or worldly content (8:27–9:1). The evidence for this inference is in Jesus' corrective teaching in 10:42ff. which begins with the important statement, "You know . . ." and goes on to expose the baseness of what they considered real power, which was patterned after models in the Graeco-Roman world.

But the truth is glimpsed by unlikely characters in the Markan drama, and *in the three special cases* which Mark describes in some detail attention

---

[2] In hellenistic stories to carry the cross is a disgraceful act. So E. Percy, *Die Botschaft Jesu* [1953], p. 172.
[3] Cicero, *Pro Rabirio* v. 10: "Far be the very name of a cross not only from the body, but even from the thought, the eyes, the ears of Roman citizens!" Cf. *In Verrem* v. 66: "How shall I describe crucifixion? No adequate word can be found to represent so execrable an enormity."
[4] Cf. the satirical inscription, "Alexamenos worships his god" found on the Palatine hill in Rome as the caption of a graffito and used to depict a Christian who is reverencing a crucified figure with an ass's head.

is drawn to an aspect of Jesus' mission which the disciples failed to appreciate.

There is first of all the incident of the Syrophoenician woman (7:24–30), with its immediate sequel in the healing of the deaf-mute in Decapolis (7:31–37). Both healings are set on Gentile territory—so apparently in 7:24 which speaks of "the territories of Tyre and Sidon," and 7:31 which reads "He went by way of Sidon to the sea of Galilee through the middle of the territory of Decapolis." Both verses have caused perplexity, both on the grounds of textual criticism (in verse 24 where the words "and Sidon" are thought to be added by assimilation with Matthew 15:21) and geography (in verse 31[5]).

Further, even if visits to the district of Tyre are envisaged, it is still feasible that he was concerned with outposts of Jewish people living in these predominantly Gentile regions, as Albrecht Alt supposes[6] in the thesis where he proposes, on topographical grounds, that Jesus never ventured beyond the boundaries of the Jewish population.

This may indeed be so, and it would be in line with the early tradition recorded in Matthew 15:24: "I was sent only to the lost sheep of the house of Israel."[7] The important question which we should address to Mark's gospel is rather the one of whether Mark himself believed that Jesus encountered non-Jews and *his* attitude to the material which came into his hands. Mark omits the *logion* recorded in Matthew 15:24, as does Luke. When the question is put in this fashion, it becomes evident that Jesus in this gospel does deal directly with Gentiles and holds out some hope for them. Exactly what that hope entailed is the subject of our enquiry.

We may observe the topography to begin with. "Tyre (and Sidon)" in 7:24 are included in the general reference in 3:7f. where Mark describes a great concourse of people flocking to meet Jesus. They came from the main divisions of Israelite territory (Galilee, Judaea, Jerusalem), but also from Idumaea, Transjordan and the territories of the coastal cities of Tyre and Sidon. Evidently Mark wished to show the wide compass of Jesus' reputation, leading to this assembly of a "vast crowd"($\pi o \lambda \grave{v} \varsigma \ \mathring{o} \chi \lambda o \varsigma$) stretching beyond Israelite territories, and including the inhabitants of the coastal plain.

It is the same idea which governs his setting of the healing story (in 7:31–37) in Decapolis. He intended his readers to recall that the Gerasene demoniac lived here (5:1, 20); the herd of pigs (5:11) shows that it was a Gentile environment, and the report of the miracle is told in order to

---

[5] See A. E. J. Rawlinson, *Commentary*, p. 101, who refers to Wellhausen's suggestion of a textual emendation, reading "to Bethsaida" for "by way of Sidon." On the larger issues of this verse, see V. Taylor, *Commentary*, pp. 632–6.

[6] So A. Alt, *Where Jesus Worked* [ET, 1961], pp. 27–29.

[7] See J. Jeremias, *Jesus' Promise to the Nations* [ET, 1958], pp. 26ff.

show "how Jesus won fame in a foreign land."[8] It is true that in the story of 7:31–37, the indications are that Jesus cured the deaf-mute at his command which was expressed in the Aramaic injunction, "Ephphatha" (Aram. *'etpattaḥ*), "Be opened" (v. 34). The crowd's reaction to this miracle is again conveyed in a sentence, "He has done all things well: he makes both the deaf hear and the dumb speak" (v. 37) which recalls Genesis 1:31 (LXX).[9] It is the same in Mark's use of the extremely rare adjective rendered "stammerer" ($\mu o \gamma \iota \lambda \acute{a} \lambda o \varsigma$) in verse 32 which seems to be taken directly from the Greek version of Isaiah 35:6 in which it is a sign of the new age that the tongue of those unable to speak clearly (Heb. *'illem*: Greek $\mu o \gamma \iota \lambda \acute{a} \lambda o \varsigma$) will be made distinct.[10] This is part of the Jewish messianic hope that Messiah will open blind eyes and release dumb lips.[11]

Yet, in spite of these unmistakable Jewish features of the story in its original formulation, it seems that Mark has intended to portray the healing of a Gentile by the geographical detail with which he introduces it. The Markan "seam" of verse 31 betrays the hand of the evangelist and consequently the purport he wished to attach to the story.

What is inferential in the later story is borne out positively by the evangelist's description of the appellant in the earlier narrative (7:26). She is called "a Greek, a Syrophoenician by race," and this description is far more positive in its assertion of her foreign-ness in the eyes of a Jew than in Matthew's version (15:22). It is in Matthew's account that she approaches with a Jewish title of address on her lips (15:22: "O Lord, Son of David").

The main thrust of the story concerning the woman is that Jesus is made at first to refuse her plea for her daughter's healing. Food on the table is for the children of the house (= Jews) not for the dogs (= Gentiles). That term "dog" is one of grave insult and it cannot be denied that an extremely harsh refusal of her request is implied.[12] She is reproached for what she is, by birth and religion.

However, there is a ray of hope, once this line of demarcation between Jews and Gentiles is recognized. The woman perceives the divine ordering which gives precedence to Israel (v. 27), yet she bases her renewed appeal on the ground that Jesus will be ready to help her in a way which knows

---

[8] So T. A. Burkill, "Concerning Mark 5, 7 and 5, 18–20," *Studia Theologica* 11 [1957], pp. 159–166 (166).

[9] A. Richardson, *The Miracle Stories of the Gospels* [1941], p. 54n.

[10] E. C. Hoskyns, "Jesus, the Messiah," *Mysterium Christi*, ed. Bell and Deissmann [1930], pp. 72ff.

[11] C. K. Barrett, *The Holy Spirit and the Gospel Tradition* [1947], pp. 70f.

[12] The diminutive $\kappa \upsilon \nu \acute{a} \rho \iota o \nu$ in place of the normal word for dog ($\kappa \acute{\upsilon} \omega \nu$) may not be significant (so J. Jeremias, *op. cit.*, p. 29 n.2 against O. Michel, *TDNT* iii, p.1104). If the choice of the Greek term to render a semitic word for "dog" (Heb. *keleb*, Aram. *kalba'*) does have meaning, the emphasis is made by the Greek translator, for semitic has no diminutive form (Jeremias).

no frontiers (Michel). She places herself under Messiah's lordship, yet recognizes that his office cannot be limited to one people but must embrace the Gentiles in its scope.

The evangelist has clarified this lesson by recording the important word "first" ($\pi\rho\tilde{\omega}\tau o\nu$) in his report of Jesus' saying (it is absent from Matt. 15:26). The implication is that Israel's prerogative is only temporary and that "later" the divine purpose will explicitly be widened to provide the messianic food for the Gentiles. Mark's missionary purpose here seizes an important lever and rejoices that already in his dealing with the Gentiles Jesus looked forward to a universal ministry as the exclusive privilege of Israel passed into a deeper understanding of God's will for a worldwide church in the wake of Paul's Gentile mission. This woman already benefits from what will come to pass, since she prefigures, by her perceptiveness and persistence, the body of Gentiles who will share in Messiah's banquet spread for all nations (cf. Isa. 25:6, 7).

Then, there stands as the frontispiece of the Markan passion narrative the account of the woman's anointing at Bethany (14:1–9). We have already observed the symbolic nature of her act, how by the use of anointing oil poured over the head of Jesus as he sat at table Mark intends the reader to see an action of proclaiming him as Messiah, the anointed of God (cf. 1 Sam. 10:1; 2 Kings 9:1–13). Other motifs are intertwined in the story (for example, a prophecy of the burial); but it would appear *at least* that the purpose is to place on record a woman's confession (however dimly seen) of Jesus as Israel's Messiah. Then, it stands in stark contrast to the failure of others to see even a glimmer of this truth. The disciples can only murmur their complaints (vv. 4, 5) and take her to task for an act which they woefully misconstrue. But Mark is doing something else here, for by placing this episode at the opening of his passion narrative he is tacitly calling attention to the nation's unbelief which shortly will show itself in the rejection and crucifixion of the Messiah (14:1, 2). The very people who should have recognized and welcomed their Lord as the rightful heir of God's inheritance (12:6–8) are strangely blind and perversely opposed to Jesus, so that they in the person of their leaders plot his death. From the beginning the Galilean leaders have opposed him (3:6) and the Jerusalem scribes have attributed his success to a liaison with Satan (3:22). Now it is the final rejection as the Jewish ecclesiastical leaders devise a way to rid themselves of him. So little do they perceive who he is.

But an unnamed woman does. And in so piercing the veil which surrounds Jesus' true person as Israel's hidden Messiah she receives his encomium (v. 8) and equally Mark's approbation as part of a story which gains for itself an inalienable place in his gospel book (v. 9).[13]

---

[13] Hardly with a futuristic reference to the last Judgment, which is the way Jeremias interprets verse 9 (*op. cit.*, p. 22). He renders: "Amen, I say unto you, when the triumphal news is proclaimed (by God's angel) to all the world, then will her act be remembered (before

The third revelation of a hidden dignity which Jesus properly possesses comes at the cross. Again it is Mark's artistry which has brought together scenes of indescribable horror and total rejection, and a momentous insight. The heavenly Lord, hidden in his common humanity, has suffered the indignities of a mock trial and a barbarous punishment. Insult is heaped upon injury, as the Jewish leaders mock (15:31, 32) and the by-standers mishear his cry (15:35). A final utterance from Jesus brings his life to a close.

Two incidents are placed next and side by side, with no apparent con-nection uniting them. But Mark's symbolism is masterful. For he is obviously setting down in these verses (15:37-39) the direct consequences of Messiah's mission and death. The religious privileges of Judaism appar-ently did not include a recognition of the Messiah—and now the time has come to close that chapter of God's dealings with his people. So "the curtain of the Temple was rent in two from top to bottom" (v. 38).

In a previous section (pp. 182ff.) we have considered some of the implications of this part of the Markan drama. The destruction of the Temple veil is intended to proclaim that access to the divine presence is now open to all, since the destruction of the Temple is meant to imply the abolition of all Jewish privileges and the universalizing of the Christian gospel.

The Gentile soldier has therefore the freedom to enter the divine sanc-tuary, and he does so by means of the Christian confession. In a sense this is the climax of Mark's story, for he consciously set out in his title-verse to relate the gospel of Jesus Christ, the Son of God (1:1). Now he brings his work to a close on that same note as he registers the first beneficiary of Jesus' redeeming mission and achievement. The signal point, however, is that this first confessor of Christ crucified as Son of God is a non-Jew, and so a token of the success which will attend the church's evangelistic mission to the Graeco-Roman world. Once more, the lesson is writ large in Mark's own fashion. The truth which has met with little or no under-standing response in the body of the gospel—that Jesus is both divine Son and suffering servant, who reveals his divinity on the cross by a humble submission to God's purpose—now breaks out and is immediately accepted by this pagan centurion. In some way which is unexplained, it is the manner of Jesus' death and his cry of desolation which arrests the man and calls him to faith. Perhaps Mark is again underscoring the missionary message of Paul's gospel of him who was crucified in weakness (2 Cor. 13:4) and who died under divine judgment. Yet he is the Saviour of the world and the appointed Lord of the non-Jews who lives by the divine power (2 Cor. 13:4 again) to call men to his side. What the men and

God), so that he may be gracious to her (at the last judgment)." This is a terribly complicated exegesis, which is justly criticized by A. L. Moore, *The Parousia in the New Testament* [1966], pp. 203ff.

women of Jesus' earthly life failed to see is now the saving revelation by which the Gentiles are blessed (Gal. 3:6–9).

Conclusions

From this analysis of the main Markan features, it becomes possible to draw certain conclusions regarding his purpose. At an earlier point in this book (pp. 157ff.) I envisaged a situation in the post-Pauline mission churches in which Paulinist Gentile Christians had carried the apostle's teaching to the extreme of denying Jesus' true humanity and thereby they were reposing their confidence in a heavenly Redeemer figure, remote from empirical history.

I. The occasion for the timely publication of Mark's Gospel may be traced to this situation. His gospel book represents the first attempt of which we have knowledge to put together just those individual sections (*pericopae*) which emphasize the paradox of Jesus' earthly life in which suffering and vindication are set side-by-side as a two-beat rhythm. To an already existing Passion narrative, Mark has appended a lengthy prolegomenon with the same purpose in view, viz. to show that the earthly Jesus prepared himself as part of his total obedience to God and sought to prepare his disciples for what he knew to be the divine outworking of that obedience.

Moreover, a further piece of Mark's editorial enterprise has been to revise the setting of a hypothetical Book of miracles (notably the section 4:35–6:56 which *The New English Bible* entitles "Miracles of Christ") so that Jesus' mighty deeds take on a different character. The evangelist is concerned to show that Jesus was no "divine man" thaumaturge nor did he accredit himself by his wonderful deeds nor overpower onlookers by compelling their acceptance of his powers. Mark's teaching on the importance of faith is the safeguard he uses in conjunction with his stress on the hiddenness of Jesus' claims and the ambiguity of his person.

Furthermore, the nature of the Christian's life, as Mark unfolds it by his use of teaching which centres on Jesus' mission and his call to the disciples to share that mission with him, carries the same pattern. The disciple is bidden to take up his cross and then follow the Lord who entered his glory by a way of suffering and outward defeat.[14] Just as Jesus trod a path which awaited God's vindication after he had pursued it to the bitter end of a sacrificial obedience and voluntary humiliation, so the Markan disciple is intended to get the message from which the contemporary disciples of Jesus shrank back. A crucified Messiah was

---

[14] The term "way" (ὁδός) carries in Mark a specialized sense of discipleship and following a road of suffering (see 2:23; 6:8; 8:27; 9:33f.; 10:17 and especially 10:32). The story of Bartimaeus with its climax in 10:52c is therefore significant. Mark has interpreted the cure as a commitment to discipleship involving suffering.

abhorrent to the Jewish mind; and a divine figure who underwent physical suffering repelled the Greeks. On both counts Jesus was a scandal, as Paul found in his mission preaching (1 Cor. 1:23). ·

Yet the scandalous nature of this gospel did not stop there, to judge from what we know of Paul's Christian opponents at Corinth. They entertained notions of power which by-passed the cross and focused all their interest on the heavenly Lord, even to the point (apparently) of anathematizing the human figure of Jesus.[15] This was a perversion of Paul's teaching, but it was an understandable mis-step for it simply carried to an extreme the cautiously framed language of the apostle.

We take for granted the full acceptance by Paul of the Lord's human person; and rightly so, since we judge the apostolic teaching within the framework of the total New Testament picture. Moreover, Paul re-iterates the Jewish-ness of his Lord and his intimate connections with God's salvation-history purposes which stem from the Old Testament. Romans 9:1–5; 15:8 are specimen passages which could be multiplied.

However, there are isolated expressions which could very well be taken in the opposite direction. Romans 8:3 is a case in point: God sent forth his Son in the likeness of sin-dominated flesh. The language is deliberately ambiguous, since the composite phrase (literally "in the like-ness of the flesh of sin") guards against two false notions. One is a denial of a real taking of our human life by the incarnate Son of God, for one sense of "likeness" stresses a similarity which borders on identity (as in Rom. 5:14). But Paul found it needful to insert the qualifying (yet ambiguous) term "likeness" lest the impression should be drawn, on the opposite view, that there was too close an identity of the incarnate Lord with our fallen nature, which would incapacitate him from being sinful man's Redeemer. So he appends the qualifying "sinful" to the term "flesh" to show that he did not share our sin, else he would not have been "without sin." Sanday and Headlam put it neatly. "The flesh of Christ is 'like' ours inasmuch as it is flesh; 'like' and only 'like,' because it is not sinful."[16]

The expression is so finely constructed that it is not inevitable that it should not be misunderstood; and this was precisely what happened in later Docetism, a heresy which cast doubt on the reality of Jesus' true humanity. The same ambiguity of language is present in Philippians 2:7 where the hymnic line runs: he was born in the likeness of men. Much controversy has surrounded this line in conjunction with its comple-mentary line (in the stichos, v. 8a).[17] For our immediate purpose it is

---

[15] So W. Schmithals in his seminal discussion of 1 Corinthians 12:3 in the light of 2 Corinthians 11:4. See *Gnosticism in Corinth* [ET, 1971], pp. 124ff.

[16] W. Sanday and A. C. Headlam, *The Epistle to the Romans* [ICC, 1911], p. 193.

[17] I have endeavoured to survey these problems in *Carmen Christi: Philippians ii, 5–11* [1967], pp. 197ff.

enough to call attention to J. Weiss's exposition.[18] For him Paul is consciously avoiding an expression of the complete humanity of Christ in view of his doctrine of human nature which he believed to be in the grip of the demonic power of sin. Yet he did appear on earth in what seemed to human observation as an earthly form which enveloped his divine form. But, in reality, says Weiss, this appearance was only a "disguise, appropriate to the role which he played here"; and therefore, "in this, Paul grazes the later heresy of 'Docetism.'"[19]

This interpretation is open to doubt in the total context of Pauline thought, but the point I wish to emphasize is that it is not unthinkable that some of Paul's immoderately ardent followers may well have drawn just such a corollary from the teaching of these verses. And in this way they may have paved the road for the later, full-blown heresy of Docetism, just as some other of Paul's over-enthusiastic friends perverted his moral teaching into an antinomian licence (Rom. 3:8, 31; 6:1ff.).

When we can point to a plausible exegesis of the texts which address a situation at Corinth where it seems that a denial of the Lord's humanity had been made, our position is further buttressed. Now the probability of an excess leading to a docetic view becomes substantially confirmed by the existence of such a teaching—if our acceptance of Schmithals's interpretation is correct.[20]

Our thesis may be stated thus. In Pauline Gentile churches a dangerous exaggeration of Paul's christology had developed leading to a tacit denial (or glossing over) of Jesus' true humanity. In churches on a Gentile foundation this denial is very likely to have been caused by a misplaced understanding of the earthly figure of Jesus as a heavenly visitant, an epiphany of the divine, and a revealer-figure who wielded charismatic power. The pre-Markan miracle-stories may well have emphasized these qualities.

Mark is the inheritor of these traditions. As he takes them over as the necessary frontispiece of his new "gospel" and as he fits the sections into the historical framework of Jesus' life with a view to demonstrating how it was that the Lord of glory came to end his earthly life on a cross, he drastically changes their purport. In the alembic of his creative mind and under the pressure of a disturbing situation which he wishes to rectify, the pre-canonical material takes on a different shape. Jesus is shown still in the rôle of a miracle-worker but it is made clear that (a) he worked

---

[18] J. Weiss, *The Earliest Christianity* [ET, 1959], vol. ii, pp. 488ff.; idem, *Christ: the Beginnings of Dogma* [ET, 1911], pp. 110ff. For a recent discussion, see J. Knox, *The Humanity and Divinity of Christ* [1967], p. 44.

[19] J. Weiss, *The Earliest Christianity*, vol. ii, p. 490; idem *Christ*, p. 115. 1 Corinthians 2:8 is a text which is laid under tribute in this discussion.

[20] See a full defence of it by N. Brox, "ANATHEMA IESOUS (1 Kor. 12, 3)" *Biblische Zeitschrift* n.f. 12 [1968], pp. 103ff., as well as a reply offered to his critics by Schmithals, *Gnosticism in Corinth* [ET, 1971], pp. 349f.

only in response to human faith and so his mighty deeds were morally conditioned; (b) he did not advertise his reputation; (c) and he was rejected by those who should have been impressed by a display of divine power because there was an ambiguity about his person. This, says the evangelist, is why and how he came to be condemned and crucified. He would not declare himself on his enemies' terms; nor would he parade his messianic status as he evidently expected bogus leaders to do (13:5, 6, 21, 22). In fact, these false Messiahs and their followers are the very people whom Mark is writing to oppose.

This interest in the earthly career of Jesus may be termed "biographical" —provided we give to that description a specific meaning. It is *not* intended to say that Mark wished to compose a life of Jesus; rather his concern is with the kerygma or public preaching of the gospel. But, though he utilizes the expression "gospel" as characteristic of his work in its entirety, he senses the danger that a declaration of Christ may lose contact with the human figure of Jesus who lived in Galilee and died at Jerusalem.

The death of Jesus is the datum which Mark has inherited in the Pauline tradition; his innovative task is to clothe that figure with flesh-and-blood in such a way as to show how he came to be put to death at the hands of the Romans because he was first rejected by Israel. This is the inestimable worth of Mark's controversy stories (2:23–28; 3:1–6 in particular). They show how Jesus made claims (e.g. to forgive sins, to override the Sabbath-laws) which set him at odds with rabbinic Judaism; and they point irresistibly to his fate as the outcome of that conflict (3:6).

The Palestinian origin of these accounts is unquestioned as is their pre-Markan formation. The evangelist, however, uses the stories as part of his purpose, viz. to give illustrative point to this contention that because of conflicts such as these Jesus was rejected by Israel; and so Mark is raising an appropriate question for the Christian faith to ask, How do the conflict stories which show Jesus in debate with his enemies explain the reason for his being crucified at the end?[21]

II. The inconclusiveness of Jesus' claims, meaning that either they may be refused and attributed to his being in league with the devil or accepted as the gift of insight, obedience and trust is acted upon, may have still another application to Mark's situation.

We have already shown cause for agreeing with the church tradition that Mark's Gospel is best set on the historical background of a persecuted community which the evangelist wished to console. Part of his *raison*

---

[21] This is how J. Roloff, *Das Kerygma und der irdische Jesus* [1970], pp. 73f., has recently framed the reason for Mark's "biographical interest." It is put more simply by W. L. Knox, *The Sources of the Synoptic Gospels* I–II [1953–57], p. 8: "For the stories as a group would seem intended to meet the question, familiar to anyone who has ever tried to teach the Gospel story to children or simple people: 'Why if Jesus was the Messiah, did his own people want to kill him?'"

d'être in composing a gospel is to illustrate the inevitability of suffering in obedience to and in fellowship with the suffering Messiah. He writes to offer a theodicy to a beleaguered church, surrounded by a hostile and menacing world and afraid of its destiny as a church under the cross. Mark is seen to be a faithful minister to such a community since he offered no easy way out. He prescribed no simple placebo to Christians needing a stiff tonic to brace their spirits and strengthen their faith. All he could do is to show how vital that constant dependence on God really is (11:22); how prayer is efficacious even when faith grows dim (9:23); how God's kingdom is his care (4:26–29) and how Jesus foretold that all these bitter times were the inevitable concomitant of fidelity to him (8:34ff.; 13:9ff.). But two other factors enter in to the picture, and it is not gratuitous to hold that Mark's pastoral concern is reflected in them.

One is his vivid narrative of Jesus as active in his help, both in his Galilean ministry and beyond death. The episode of 4:35–41 has been carefully composed so as to make the story of his presence and control of the elements a vivid reality *in the present*. The historic present tense of the verbs is a Markan feature often found in his Gospel; but the present tense in the "punch-line" of verse 41, "who then is this, that even wind and sea *obey* him?" seems intentional. Mark is contemporizing the finale of the story as though to make it clear that winds and waves of the church's oppression are powerless to harm the little ship in which Christ's disciples travel. There is still a great calm once he who is with them in the boat arises to speak peace (only Mark reports the words of Jesus in v. 39 in *oratio recta*).

The other essentially Markan *paraclesis* offered to comfort the church is his model of the incarnate Lord himself. Nothing comes through the Markan narrative more clearly than Jesus' divine authority and numinous presence. Yet he goes to his death without remonstrance and offers his life an oblation to God on the altar of sacrifice. The reader may well have expected some divine response to this sacrificial act—some last-minute averting of the fate of Jesus as though a *deus ex machina* might dramatically show that all is right in the end. Or, if there is not to be such a histrionic ending, then there might be expected some assurance from Jesus that his work is ended and his mission complete—some cry of victory (John 19:30), some trustful resignation to the Father's care (Luke 23:46) or else some phenomenon to attest that God hears and understands his Son's anguish (Matt. 27:51b–53). In Mark there is nothing but silence.

Only a desolating cry (15:34) followed by an unspecified call (15:37) and he dies: that is how Mark concludes his account of Jesus' earthly life in which misunderstanding, hardness of heart and bitter animosity against the Lord's anointed have been its chief landmarks. Nor does Mark go on to redeem the tragedy by showing a full reversal in the resurrection. It is true that he does proclaim the message (16:6), but there is no tangible proof to demonstrate that the risen Lord did encounter his own disciples. There are no visions of the appearing Lord who came to certify his risen reality (as all three of the other gospels record; and the apocryphal gospels are even more detailed in their descriptions of what the risen Christ said and did). There is simply the promise of his presence, the validation of his word and the assurance that he will lead them on as before (16:7; cf. 14:28).

This is Mark's way of encouraging the church. He provides no props for a weak faith and extends no crutch on which the persecuted believers may lean. He is realistic in admitting that Christians may have to tread a lonely path in darkness, with no last-minute dénouement to save them from death. Some Christians may even die in the anguish of God's withdrawn face, when he fails to comfort and cheer his own. The sole support the Markan church is offered is Jesus' own promise to return to them after death. He faced the end as one supported only by God's pledge to raise him up in the near future (8:31, etc.), this is all they can hope for, that beyond defeat and death God will care for his church and vindicate his people in his own way.[22]

III. Mark's missionary interest shines through in several places. This line of teaching suggests that the evangelist also felt urged to press home upon his readers' minds and consciences the duty of promoting the evangelization of the Gentiles.

It is necessary now to gather the scattered references into a coherent statement. The data for our investigation and use are seen in those places where Mark's gospel adds its unique contribution. This is not an easy task to accomplish with certainty because all the gospels have a missionary purpose which is more or less explicit in them. What can we detect about Mark's peculiar concern?

Mark's Jesus is seen to have a conscious mission (1:38) which is intimately related to his ministry of preaching (1:14). The initial announcement of his message is couched in Pauline terms (1:15) and matches the evangelist's purpose set down as the title of his work (1:1).

He is shown to embody a teaching which is irreconcilably opposed to the ethos and practice of Judaism (2:21–22), though it is clear that Jesus is no iconoclastic reformer who opposed his ancestral faith with no respect at all (cf. 1:40–44 where Jesus recognizes the claim of Moses' law). The underlying issue is brought to the surface in the debate recorded in 7:1–13.

The gravamen of the charge the scribes brought against Jesus was that he disregarded "the tradition of the elders" (7:5, 8, 9). The debate centres

[22] This confession of God's strange silence and inactivity in the face of his people's woe is not new in the biblical story (e.g. the fall of Jerusalem in 586 B.C.). It is raised in acute ways in the Maccabean struggle and in Rabbi Aqiba's martyrdom as well as in events known by such place-names (sacred to Jewish memory) as Masada and Auschwitz. See L. E. Keck, *A Future for the Historical Jesus* [1971], pp. 228ff.

on the matter of ritual washings, a custom to which the Jews attached great importance, as we know from the detail given in the sixth division of the Mishnah which is entitled *Tohoroth* ("cleannesses") especially the first tractate, *Kelim* ("vessels"). Jesus, with sovereign freedom, overrode these rules and regulations with his insistence on the inwardness and heart-sincerity of worship (vv. 6–8). The issue under discussion was the binding authority of the Torah and its scribal interpretation which later became codified in the Mishnah. Mark does not explicitly draw the conclusion but leaves it as an inference that Jesus as Messiah brings in a new age in which Torah's authority is at an end.

On a second matter, closely related to the first, Jesus again joined battle with the scribes. This has to do with the law of vows. The details are given in the Mishnaic tractate *Nedarim* ("vows") which distinguishes between solemn vows taken deliberately, and rash vows undertaken in error. The former are regarded as irrevocable and have the effect of making the property "offered to God" (Heb. *qôrbān*[23]) sacrosanct, even where the plainest human obligations are neglected. Jesus (in vv. 10–13) recalls the discussion on the legitimacy of vows (a debated question among the rabbis[24]) to a consideration of simple human rights and duties, in the light of the paradise-will of God. In a similar vein, ritual lustrations cannot displace the prime importance of a pure inner life (vv. 15, 20–23). Mark's editorial note in verse 19b: "Thus he declared all foods clean" clearly has its eye on a situation such as developed in the Pauline mission churches in which questions of clean and unclean foods (cf. Acts 10:9–16; 11:5–10 and see Rom. 14:13ff.) and idol-meats became live issues (as we know from 1 Cor. 8, 10).[25] This chapter in Mark 7 is perhaps the most obvious declaration of Mark's purpose as a Christian living in the Graeco-Roman world who wishes to publicize the charter of Gentile freedom by recording in the plainest terms Jesus' detachment from Jewish ceremonial and to spell out in clear tones the application of this to his readers. It is part of his plan to show how from the days of Jesus' ministry a universalistic emphasis in his activity was found. No room is given for any circumscribing of the gospel which would keep it within its Jewish context.

This interest in Gentile freedom leads Mark to emphasize the mission of Jews to non-Jews (7:24–37) who respond to his message and applaud his success. The feeding of a crowd, numbered at "about four thousand" (8:9) is sometimes taken to be a doublet of the earlier *pericope* (6:30–44) in which the feeding of the five thousand is recorded. But more probably it is to be regarded as an intentional insertion of a story, set in a non-Jewish *milieu* which is designed to portray Jesus as the bread of life to the

[23] For the rule here see the Mishnah, *Maaser Sheni* ("Second Tithe") 4:10, 11. Cf. J. D. M. Derrett, "Korban, Ho Estin Doron," NTS 16.4 [1970], pp. 364–68.

[24] See the Detached Note by T. W. Manson, *The Teaching of Jesus*[2] [1935], pp. 315–319.

[25] For some discussion of this burning question in the early church see NBD "Idols, Meats offered to" (pp. 554f.).

Gentiles. There are striking differences in the vocabulary used in the two stories.[26] And it cannot be accidental that the feeding of 8:1–10 is set at the close of a section in which Gentile interest has predominated, and the next *pericope* (8:11–13) brings to a head the conflict with the Pharisees in Galilee, issuing in Jesus' abandonment of them (v. 13) since he has nothing to say to a generation which demands his credentials (see earlier pp. 165ff.) on its own terms.

Parallel with 8:11–13 is the scene in 10:1–9. This *pericope* removes the public ministry of Jesus from Galilee to Judaea and Transjordan, and it is the evangelist's stage-setting for the final drama of the crucifixion. As soon as Jesus set foot in Judaea, conflict breaks out. The point at issue was the vexed question of marriage and divorce (10:2–12). Jewish law at that time gave an unshared right of divorce to the husband, a right which could be exercised in a most arbitrary way by serving a written notice of the marriage's dissolution. No redress was possible for the wife, nor did she enjoy any corresponding right of divorce. Her sole method of obtaining a divorce was to persuade her husband to take the initiative and to offer her release from the marriage vow.

According to Mark, Jesus challenged this situation in his concern to uphold the ideal of the indissolubility of marriage and to base his teaching on God's primal intention, declared in his paradise-will (Gen. 2:24), that marriage is an equal partnership and expresses a life-long commitment on both sides (vv. 6, 7, 9). In so interpreting the Lord's mind, Mark has assumed (in v. 12) that a woman can institute divorce action against her husband. This is a hall-mark of Mark's own situation in which he writes for a non-Jewish community, just as Matthew (in Matt. 5:32; 19:9 which includes the exceptive clause, based on Deut. 24:1 which implied that a man could divorce his wife on the ground of her immodest behaviour[27]) writes with his eye on a church situation in which this rabbinic dispute was a live issue. From this comparison we may deduce that Mark's intention is to address the teaching of Jesus to an audience in a Gentile church background as part of his missionary concern.[28]

The evangelist's missionary motifs are to be seen in those parts of his gospel at which he adapts the tradition. There are three specific cases to be considered.

(a) 7:24–10: *The Syrophoenician woman*

We have already drawn attention to this story which is plainly intended to show the appeal of a Gentile woman to Jesus and her reward. At verse 27 there is a Markan insertion to which appropriate importance should be

[26] Noted by A. Richardson, *The Miracle Stories of the Gospels* [1941], p. 98.
[27] Cf. Mishnah, *Gittin* ("Bills of divorce") 9:10.
[28] Cf. A. Isaksson, *Marriage and Ministry in the New Temple* [1965], pp. 127–141.

given. Jesus' reported words run: "Let the children first be satisfied, for it is not good to take the children's food and throw it to the dogs." The contrast "children-dogs" is clearly an allusion to the division between Jews and Gentiles in ancient society. The interesting addition in Mark lies in his insertion of "first" ($\pi\rho\tilde{\omega}\tau ov$); cf. Matthew 15:26. As F. Hahn remarks, "The $\pi\rho\tilde{\omega}\tau ov$ quite clearly assumes a $\delta\varepsilon\dot{v}\tau\varepsilon\rho ov$ in this passage, and thus the precedence of the 'children' is determined by the already established fact of the Gentile mission."[29] This is taken by Hahn to mean that the mission to Israel has priority, as in Romans 1:16; and on this understanding it apparently says that missionary work among the Jews has a continuing validity alongside the Gentile mission. But even if that is possible for the period up to A.D. 70 when the Jerusalem Temple fell, the teaching of 7:27a stands to be corrected by 13:10 which announces the proclaiming of the gospel "first to all the Gentiles" as a prelude to the End. "Thus Mark understood the $\pi\rho\tilde{\omega}\tau ov$ 'Ιουδαίοις (first to the Jews, in Rom. 1:16) in the sense of two sequential periods, one of which already belonged to the past."[30] Hahn thus reaches his conclusion that, with the judgment on Israel already having taken place, the way for the offer of the gospel to the Gentiles is open, and Mark is expressing by this part of the Jesus-tradition the same conviction as that stated by Paul in 1 Thessalonians 2:15f. in terms of the final abandonment of Israel's salvation.

The gospel of Mark is seen in this way as a gospel of Gentile freedom—a statement with which we may concur, while at the same time reserving our judgment on Hahn's exegesis of Mark 7:27a. A more plausible view is to attach an eschatological sense to this verse as to 13:10, and to treat the insertion of a $\pi\rho\tilde{\omega}\tau ov$ as a note required to indicate the passing of the exclusive privilege of Israel. The period immediately following the birth of the Jerusalem church saw the time of Israel's opportunity when the children "first" would be fed; but this is no exclusive right belonging to the Jews. Later ($\ddot{v}\sigma\tau\varepsilon\rho ov$) there would be provision for the (Gentile) dogs, and this is the justification for the Pauline mission, already envisaged in Jesus' ministry to non-Jews.[31] Mark stands in that Pauline tradition as he records the endorsement of the woman's claim which, by a proleptic anticipation of what the Gentile mission was to offer her people, grasped the promise as available in her present situation (v. 28). She is spokeswoman for the non-Jewish world which will become beneficiaries of Messiah's bounty after Israel has been offered the divine mercy.[32]

(b) 13:10 and 14:9: *A worldwide preaching of the Gospel*

On 13:10 there is a widespread agreement among expositors that this

[29] F. Hahn, *Mission in the New Testament* [ET, 1965], p. 75.
[30] F. Hahn, *op. cit.*, p. 119.
[31] So J. Jeremias, *Jesus' Promise to the Nations* [ET, 1958], p. 29.
[32] Cf. J. C. Fenton, "Paul and Mark," *Studies in the Gospels*. Essays in memory of R. H. Lightfoot [1955], p. 110.

verse fits only awkwardly into the framework of Jesus' admonition. The whole section is a warning addressed to the disciples that they must expect opposition from the (Jewish) authorities. The main thought is that when Christians stand up "on account of me" (ἕνεκεν ἐμοῦ) they must anticipate trouble. Their action is further described as "for a testimony to them." Then comes the statement which fits only loosely with the foregoing, "And the gospel must first be proclaimed to [or among] all nations."

The Matthean parallel (24:14) is found at the different point in his tradition of the discourse, and it is a reasonable suggestion that Mark has "borrowed" the *logion* from its place in the tradition and inserted it in the context of his verses 9ff. in order to amplify the meaning of the phrase "on my account." Witness to Christ is then explained in terms of a preaching of the gospel to the Gentiles. This view comports with Markan editorial practice elsewhere in his writing where his use of the term "gospel" plays an interpretative rôle, in terms meaningful to both his own understanding as a gospel-writer and the situation of his own day (see pp. 24ff.). In both ways he is self-confessedly speaking to the church of his own time. By his use of the dominical sayings he is consciously setting up a framework of encouragement to aid a persecuted community with a call to fidelity, and also of exhortation as he renews Jesus' call to a missionary task. That task is as wide as the Gentile world, represented by the terms "governors" and "kings" (v. 9: cf. Paul's detentions and arraignments in the Acts); and it is part of the Lord's will that witness should be borne "among all the nations."[33]

Two matters remain for consideration. First, is the purpose of this testimony exclusively negative and judgmental? This is H. Strathmann's opinion which argues that the construction of the Greek allows no other sense than "for an evidence against."[34] So "the goal of this witness is to make opponents guilty."[35] It is doubtful if this strictly negative rendering of the phrase can be pressed, but if it is accepted we could go on to take note of Strathmann's other argument that in the phrase "as an [incriminating] witness against *them*," the final pronoun refers to the Jewish authorities. Then, Mark's purpose would be to contrast the judgment on Israel as setting the church free to offer the gospel to all the Gentiles. In this view the last three words of verse 9 pave the way for the Markan insertion of verse 10 and are thought to be included to establish a connection of cause and effect.

The other exegetical problem is to ask whether G. D. Kilpatrick's transposing of the sense of "to all the nations" (in v. 9) makes for a better

---

[33] Or "as far as the entire Gentile world" see Acts 22:21 (as in Acts 1:8), giving to the preposition εἰς + accusative the meaning of extent of space.
[34] H. Strathmann, *TDNT* iv, pp. 502ff.
[35] Or, "to prove the opponents' guilt" (cf. Cranfield, "Mark 13," SJT 6 [1953], p. 291).

understanding.[36] According to him a revised punctuation of verses 9, 10f. better accords with Mark's usage and the sense of his purpose. This makes the text run: "You will be set for my sake for a testimony to them, and among all nations. First, the gospel must be preached, and when they arrest you and bring you into court," etc. The direct upshot of this redistribution of the words is to lead to the conviction that "there is, strictly speaking, no mention of preaching the Gospel to all nations" (loc. cit., p. 149).

While there is some support for this view in the ancient versions and it accords with some data of Mark's usage, the evidence is by no means conclusive.[37] It would leave the statement of verse 10 (now read as "First the gospel must be proclaimed") unrelated to what precedes and what follows it, and so largely meaningless. Some sense could be given if the adverb πρῶτον ("first") were taken to mean "above all," with a consequent denial of a temporal significance. Then the chief duty of the apostles is to proclaim the good news, and there is no necessary correlation between the preaching and the End.[38] But this is countered by W. G. Kümmel[39] who rightly insists that πρῶτον never has this non-temporal meaning in the synoptic gospels and that the preaching of the gospel is set within an eschatological framework. And it is the human proclamation of the gospel to all nations which must precede the End-time.[40]

(c) The justification for the cleansing of the Temple

The third text in Mark which looks in a universalistic direction is 11:17: My house shall be called a house of prayer for all the nations. This citation of Isaiah 56:7 in its full form, corresponding to the LXX,[41] is intended to justify Jesus' action in cleansing the Temple and is a veiled messianic claim on his part to be Lord of the Temple. He exercises his authority in administering God's judgment against the abuses of his house (cf. Hos. 9:15; Mal. 3:1, Zech. 14:21). According to the context of the Isaiah oracle from which verse 17 of Mark's chapter is taken, part of the post-exilic hope was that Yahweh's house would be a centre of attraction for "foreigners" (Isa.56:6) and "others" beyond the pale of the covenant community (Isa. 56:8). The universalistic scope of this promise means that Yahweh's shrine will be accessible to "all nations." This is not a

[36] G. D. Kilpatrick, "The Gentile Mission in Mark and Mark 13:9-11," Studies in the Gospels, Essays in memory of R. H. Lightfoot [1955], pp. 145-158.
[37] So Cranfield, St. Mark, p. 398.
[38] Cf. G. R. Beasley-Murray, Commentary on Mark Thirteen [1957], p. 41, for a discussion. He supports W. G. Kümmel's view (see next footnote).
[39] W. G. Kümmel, Promise and Fulfilment [ET, 1957], p. 84.
[40] Against J. Jeremias' attempt to give to the preaching an exclusively apocalyptic reference: Jesus' Promise to the Nations [ET, 1958], p. 23. Equally unpersuasive is his treatment of 14:9, on which see pp. 212f.
[41] Matthew (21:13) and Luke (19:46) close the quotation with the words"house of prayer," omitting the phrase πᾶσιν τοῖς ἔθνεσιν from the LXX version.

statement of present reality, but holds out a prospect which belongs to the messianic era.

The existence of the court of the Gentiles in Herod's Temple is a witness to this promise. Jesus' action is to ensure that the provision did not go by default. But, as R. H. Lightfoot remarks,[42] from Mark's standpoint, the record of Jesus' action is full of profound Christian significance, for it is a tacit claim that with Messiah's advent he seeks to make available to the Gentiles the privileges which belonged to the new age and thereby he proclaims that the time of universal worship, uninhibited by Jewish restrictions, has come. Mark enforces the point by his citation of the prophetic verse which underlines the scope of the worship of God's house to include "all the Gentiles". His readers were to see the divine judgment visited on the Temple in the dramatic events of the Jewish war of A.D. 66–70, with the tragic finale in the demolition of the Temple in A.D. 70. The evangelist is recalling to them by his incorporation of this section of his gospel the Lord's authority for the new order which came into full realization after A.D. 70. Indeed, even with the Temple still standing, Jesus had claimed the full text of Isaiah's prophecy and had sanctioned the belief that, with his presence as Messiah and Lord of the Temple, Gentile privileges were freely offered, and the particularism of Jewish worship was at an end.

The total impact of Mark's recorded teaching of Jesus is unmistakable. By narrative material (7:27a), by his transmission of sayings of Jesus within a missionary framework (13:10; 14:9) and by his use of an Old Testament testimony (11:17), the evangelist has placed Jesus' universalistic appeal in the forefront of what he desires the reader to learn about Jesus' mission in the world. This is true even if Jesus never made a direct approach to the Gentile peoples. Yet implicit in his actions and attitudes was a breadth and range of appeal which transcended the ancestral faith. And it is this missionary message which Mark is concerned to get across to his own generation.

Application

If these indications of Mark's purpose are on the right lines, it is not too difficult a task to see their abiding relevance for the church.

As we today cannot remain content with a version of Christianity which is simply that of a mystery religion attached to Christ's name—and a concentration on the simple "that-ness" of his earthly existence is a danger signal that the fatal heresy of Docetism is around the corner—so we tacitly express our need of the human Jesus. This needs to be said against a kerygmatic theology which would dispense with him or give him only a minimal value. Equally, it is said against any form of evangelism which

[42] R. H. Lightfoot, *The Gospel Message of St. Mark* [1950], p. 64.

professes to call men to "decision" without a basis being laid in the historical facts of gospel history and a knowledge of Jesus in his real life-situations. On both counts the road back to Jesus as a historical person is needed as a quest to be resumed.[43]

This is, however, not an invitation to put the clock back to the mid-19th century, forgetful of all that gospel criticism has taught us in the intervening century. Rather our reconstruction of Jesus takes on new meaning as it submits to the control of the kerygma and so is delivered from pious sentimentality, idle speculation and psychologizing fancy. That would be to fall victim to the peril of modernizing Jesus.[44]

But some clothing of the kerygma is needed to avoid the other pitfall of docetic Christianity. Mark's gospel was written to assert just this, and to say emphatically that Paul's dying-with-Christ mysticism needed to be fleshed out in the gospel story of a human person in touch with our concrete existence.

From this statement of the Servant Jesus, it is a short step—but how hard to take—to the servant church, which lives under the cross and in the ambiguities of our human condition, with no claim to pretensions of power and no guarantees of exemption from suffering. The cost of discipleship and the life of faith are common and current phrases to describe how our Christianity should function in the modern world. In Mark's gospel we see what the modern slogans meant, not as catch-phrases but as a serious call to a life of discipleship to Jesus Christ which entailed the acceptance of his cross in persecution and a following of him in the darkness of unexplained and unrelieved suffering.

The Markan church also expected its vindication, already promised to its Lord who, true to his pledge, had re-gathered his own and was leading them forth. With this presence, they needed to face the tasks of missionary service with courage and confidence. For the gospel which Jesus Christ brought into the world was still their inalienable possession and challenge. He had told them to proclaim it by verbal communication and by the quality of their lives and service. Now Mark, by his writing, ensures that the same gospel shall present its claim upon us who read it today.

---

[43] W. D. Davies has pleaded for this: "A Quest to be resumed in New Testament Studies," reprinted in *Christian Origins and Judaism* [1962], pp. 1–17; cf. E. Schweizer, "Mark's Contribution to the Quest of a Historical Jesus," NTS 10 [1963–64], pp. 421–32, or, best of all, T. W. Manson, "The Quest of the Historical Jesus-Continued," *Studies in the Gospels and Epistles*, ed. M. Black [1962], pp. 3–12.

[44] H. J. Cadbury's title, published first in 1937.

BIBLIOGRAPHY

Achtemeier, P. J. "Person and Deed. Jesus and the Storm Tossed Sea," Interpretation 16 [1962], pp. 169–76. "Toward the Isolation of pre-Markan Miracle Catenae," JBL 89 [1970], pp. 265–91.

Allen, W. C. *The Gospel according to Saint Mark*, London [1915].

Alt, A. *Where Jesus Worked*, ET, London [1961].

Aune, D. E. "The Problem of the Messianic Secret," NovT xi [1969], pp. 1–31.

Bacon, B. W. *The Beginnings of Gospel Story*, New Haven [1925]. *Is Mark a Roman Gospel?* Cambridge, Mass. [1919].

Bahr, G. J. "The Seder of Passover and the Eucharistic Words," NovT xii [1970], pp. 181–202.

Barclay, W. "A Comparison of Paul's Missionary Preaching and Preaching to the Church," *Apostolic History and the Gospel*. Essays Presented to F. F. Bruce, eds. W. Ward Gasque and Ralph P. Martin, Exeter [1970], pp. 165–175.

Barbour, R. S. "Recent Study of the Gospel according to St. Mark," ExpT 79 [1967–68], pp. 324–329. "Gethsemane in the Tradition of the Passion," NTS 16 [1969–70], pp. 231–251.

Barrett, C. K. "The Background of Mark 10:45," *New Testament Essays*. Studies in Memory of T.W. Manson, ed. A. J. B. Higgins, Manchester [1959], pp. 1–18. *Jesus and the Gospel Tradition*, London [1967]. "ψευδαπόστολοι (2 Cor. 11:13")," *Mélanges B. Rigaux* [1970], pp. 377–396. "Paul's Opponents in II Corinthians," NTS 17 [1970–71], pp. 233–254.

Bartlet, J. V. *St. Mark* (Century Bible), Edinburgh [1922].

Bartsch H.-W. "Die 'Verfluchung' des Feigenbaums," ZNTW 53 [1962], pp. 256–60.

Beasley-Murray, G. R. *Jesus and the Future*, London [1954]. *Commentary on Mark 13*, London [1957].

Benoit, P. "Les Outrages à Jésus Prophète," *Neotestamentica et Patristica*. Festschrift O. Cullmann, Leiden [1962], pp. 92–110.

Best, E. *The Temptation and the Passion*, Cambridge [1965].

Betz, H. D. "Jesus as Divine Man," *Jesus and the Historian*. Festschrift E. C. Colwell, Philadelphia [1968], pp. 114–33.

Betz, O. *What Do we Know about Jesus?* ET, London [1968].

Black, M. "The Cup Metaphor in Mark xiv, 36," ExpT 59 [1947], p. 195.

Bonnard, P. *L'évangile selon Saint Matthieu*, Neuchâtel [1963]. "Matthieu Educateur du peuple chrétien," *Mélanges B. Rigaux* [1970], pp. 1–7.

Bornkamm, G. "The Stilling of the Storm in Matthew," *Tradition and Interpretation in Matthew*, London [1963], pp. 52–57.

Bowman, J. *The Gospel of Mark: The New Christian Jewish Passover Haggadah*, Leiden [1965].

Brandon, S. G. F. *The Fall of Jerusalem and the Christian Church*, London [1957]. "The Apologetical Factor in the Markan Gospel" Studia Evangelica ii, 1 [1964], pp. 34–46. *Jesus and the Zealots*, Manchester [1967]. "Jesus and the Zealots," Studia Evangelica iv, 1 [1968], pp. 8–20. "The Date of the Markan Gospel," NTS 7 [1960–61]. pp. 126–41. *The Trial of Jesus of Nazareth*, London [1968]. "Jesus and the Zealots: Aftermath," BJRL 54, 1 [1971], pp. 47–66.

Brox, N. "ANATHEMA IESOUS (1 Kor. 12, 3)," Biblische Zeitschrift n.f. 12 [1968], pp. 103–111.

Bruce, F. F. "'Our God and Saviour': A Recurring Biblical Pattern." *The Saviour God*. Festschrift E. O. James, ed. S. G. F. Brandon, London [1963], pp. 51–66. "When is a Gospel not a Gospel?" BJRL 45 [1963], pp. 325. "History and the Gospel," *Jesus of Nazareth: Saviour and Lord*, ed. C. F. H. Henry, London [1966], pp. 89–107. *New Testament History*, London [1969].

Burkitt, F. C. *The Gospel History and its Transmission*, Edinburgh [1911]. *The Earliest Sources for the Life of Jesus*, London [1922].

Burkill, T. A. "Concerning Mark 5, 7 and 5, 18–20," Studia Theologica 11 [1957], pp. 159–166. "Anti-Semitism in St. Mark's Gospel," NovT iii [1959], pp. 34–53. *Mysterious Revelation: An Examination of the Philosophy of St. Mark's Gospel*, New York [1963].

Burney, C. F. *The Poetry of our Lord*, Oxford [1925].

Buse, I. "The Markan Account of the Baptism of Jesus and Isaiah LXIII," JTS 7 n.s. [1956], pp 74–75.

Butler, B. C. *The Originality of St. Matthew*, London [1951].

Bultmann, R. *Theology of the New Testament*, i ET, London [1952]. *The History of the Synoptic Tradition*, ET [1963], Oxford. "The Relationship of the Primitive Christian Kerygma to the Historical Jesus" in *The Historical Jesus and the Kerygmatic Christ*, eds. C. E. Braaten and R. A. Harrisville, Nashville [1964]. *The Gospel of John*, ET, Oxford [1971].

Carrington, P. *The Primitive Christian Calendar: A Study in the Making of the Markan Gospel*, Cambridge [1952]. "The Calendrical Hypothesis of the Origin of Mark," ExpT 67 [1956], pp. 100–103.

Casey, R. P. "St. Mark's Gospel," Theology 55 [1952], pp. 362–370.

Catchpole, D. R. "Jesus' Answer to Caiaphas [Matt xxvi, 64]," NTS 17 [1970–71], pp. 213–226. "The Problem of the Historicity of the Sanhedrin Trial," in *The Trial of Jesus*, ed. E. Bammel, London [1970].

Clarke, W. K. L. *Divine Humanity*, London [1936].

Cranfield, C. E. B. "St. Mark 13," SJT 6 [1953], pp. 189–196, 287–303, 7 [1954], pp. 284–303. *The Gospel according to St. Mark* (The Cambridge Greek Testament), Cambridge [1963].

Colwell, E. C. "A Definite Rule for the Use of the Article in the Greek New Testament," JBL 52 [1933], pp 12–21.

Conzelmann, H. "Present and Future in the Synoptic Tradition," in *God and Christ: Existence and Province* (Journal for Theology and the Church, 5), Tübingen/New York [1968]. "Historie und Theologie in den synoptischen Passionsberichten," in *Zur Bedeutung des Todes Jesu*, ed. F. Viering, Gütersloh [1968]. Der erste Korintherbrief (KEK), Göttingen [1969]. *An Outline of the Theology of the New Testament*, ET, London [1969].

Cullmann, O. *The Christology of the New Testament*, ET, London [1959]. *Jesus and the Revolutionaries*, ET, New York [1970].

Davies, W. D. "Reflections on Archbishop Carrington's 'The Primitive Christian Calendar'" in *The Background of the New Testament and its Eschatology*, eds. W. D. Davies and D. Daube, Cambridge [1956], pp. 124–152. "A Quest to be Resumed in New Testament Studies", reprinted in *Christian Origins and Judasim*, London [1962].

Derrett, J. D. M. "Korban, Ho Estin Doron," NTS 16, 4 [1970], pp. 364–68.

Dibelius, M. "Herodes und Pilatus," ZNTW 16 [1915], pp. 113–126. *From Tradition to Gospel*, ET, London [1934].

Dinkler, E. "Peter's Confession and the 'Satan' Saying: The Problem of Jesus' Messiahship," in *The Future of our Religious Past*. Essays in honour of Rudolf Bultmann, ed. J. M. Robinson, ET, London [1971], pp. 169–202.

Dodd, C. H. "The Framework of the Gospel Narrative," ExpT 43 [1930–31], pp. 396–400. *The Parables of the Kingdom*, London [1935].

Dunn, J. D. G. "The Messianic Secret in Mark," Tyndale Bulletin 21 [1970], pp. 92–117.

Dupont, J. "The Conversion of Paul and its Influence on his Understanding of Salvation by Faith," in *Apostolic History and the Gospel*. Essays presented to F. F. Bruce, eds. W. W. Gasque and Ralph P. Martin, Exeter [1970], pp. 176–194.

Ebeling, G. *Word and Faith*, ET, London [1963].

Ebeling, H. J. *Das Messiasgeheimnis und die Botschaft des Marcus-Evangelisten*, Göttingen [1939].

Elliott-Binns, L. E. *Galilean Christianity*, London [1956].

Evans, C. F. "What kind of a book is a gospel?" in *The New Testament Gospels*, London [1965]. *The Beginning of the Gospel . . .* London [1968].

Farmer, W. R. *Maccabees, Zealots and Josephus*, New York [1956]. *The Synoptic Problem*, New York [1964].

Farrer, A. M. *A Study in St. Mark*, London [1951]. *St. Matthew and St. Mark*, London [1954].

Fascher, E. "Theologische Beobachtungen zu δεῖ," in *Neutestamentliche Studien für R. Bultmann*, Berlin [1954], pp. 228–54.

Fenton, J. C. "Paul and Mark," in *Studies in the Gospels:* Essays in Memory of R. H. Lightfoot, ed. D. E. Nineham, Oxford [1955].

Fuller, R. H. *The Mission and Achievement of Jesus*, London [1954]. *The Foundations of New Testament Christology*, London [1965].

Gardner, H. *The Limits of Literary Criticism*, London [1956].

Gärtner, B. "The Habakkuk Commentary (DSH) and the Gospel of Matthew," Studia Theologica 8 [1955], pp. 1–24.

Gaston, L. *No Stone upon Another*, Leiden [1970].

Georgi, D. *Die Gegner des Paulus im 2. Korintherbrief*, Neukirchen-Vluyn [1964].

Gerhardsson, B. *The Testing of God's Son: (Matt. 4:1–11 and par.)*, ET, Lund [1966].

Glasswell, M. E. "The Use of Miracles in the Markan Gospel," in *Miracles*, ed. C. F. D. Moule, Oxford [1965].

Goppelt, L. "The Freedom to Pay the Imperial Tax (Mark 12, 17)," Studia Evangelica ii [1964], pp. 183–194.

Grant, F. C. *The Earliest Gospel*, Nashville [1943].

Grant, R. M. "The Oldest Gospel Prologues," Anglican Theological Review 23 [1941], pp. 231–45.

Grässer, E. "Jesus in Nazareth (Mark vi, 1–6a)," NTS 16 [1969], pp. 1–23.

Grundmann, W. Das Evangelium nach Markus (Theologischer Handkommentar zum Neuen Testament, 2), Berlin [1971].

Guy, H. A. The Origin of the Gospel of Mark, London [1954].

Hahn, F. The Titles of Jesus in Christology, ET, London [1969].

Harnack, A. What is Christianity? ET, New York [1901].

Harrison, E. F. "Gemeindetheologie: The Bane of Gospel Criticism," in Jesus of Nazareth: Saviour and Lord, ed. C. F. H. Henry, London [1966], pp. 159–173.

Harrisville, R. A. The Miracle of Mark, Minneapolis [1967].

Hartmann, L. Prophecy Interpreted, ET, Lund [1966].

Héring, J. Le Royaume de Dieu et sa venue, Paris/Neuchâtel [1959].

Higgins, A. J. B. The Lord's Supper in the New Testament, London [1952].

Hillyer, N. "The Servant of God," EQ 41 [1969] pp. 143–160.

Hooker, M. D. Jesus and the Servant, London [1959]. The Son of Man in Mark, London [1967]

Hoskyns, E. C. (with Davey, F. N.) The Riddle of the New Testament,[3] London [1947].

Howard, W. F. "The Anti-Marcionite Prologues to the Gospels," Exp. T 47 [1936], pp. 534–38.

Isaksson, A. Marriage and Ministry in the New Temple, Lund [1965].

Jeremias, J. "Die Salbungsgeschichte Mc 14, 3–9," ZNTW 35 [1936], pp. 75–82. Jesus' Promise to the Nations, ET, London [1958]. The Servant of God, ET, London [1958]. The Parables of Jesus,[2] ET, London [1963]. The Eucharistic Words of Jesus,[2] ET, London [1966]. Ἡλ(ε)ίας TDNT ii, Grand Rapids [1964], pp.928–41. παῖς θεοῦ v. Grand Rapids [1967], pp. 654–717. πολλοί TDNT v, Grand Rapids [1968], pp. 536–545. "Kennzeichen der ipsissima vox Jesu." Synoptische Studien. Festschrift A. Wikenhauser, München [1953], pp. 86–93. New Testament Theology, i, ET, London [1971].

Johnson, S. E. Commentary on the Gospel according to St. Mark (Black-Harper), London [1960].

Kähler, M. The So-Called Historical Jesus and the Historic Biblical Christ, ET, Philadelphia [1964].

Käsemann, E. "The Problem of the Historical Jesus," Essays on New Testament Themes, ET, London [1964].

Karnetzki, M. "Die galiläische Redaktion im Markusevangelium." ZNTW 52 [1961], pp. 238–272.

Keck, L. E. "The Introduction to Mark's Gospel," NTA 12 [1966–67], pp. 352–70. "Mark 3: 7–12 and Mark's Christology," JBL 84 [1965], pp. 341–58. A Future for the Historical Jesus, Nashville [1971].

Kennard, J. S. "'Hosanna' and the Purpose of Jesus," JBL 67 [1948], pp. 171–76.

Kertelge, K. Die Wunder Jesu im Markusevangelium, München [1970].

Kilpatrick, G. D. "The Western Text and the Original Text in the Gospels and Acts," JTS 44, o.s. [1943], pp. 24–36. "The Gentile Mission in Mark and Mark 13, 9–11," in Studies in the Gospels: Essays in Memory of R. H. Lightfoot, ed. D. E. Nineham, Oxford [1955].

Kittel, G. ἀκολουθέω TDNT i, Grand Rapids [1964], pp. 210–16.

Klostermann, E. *Das Markusevangelium* (Handbuch zum NT, 3), Tübingen [1950].

Knigge, H.-D. "The Meaning of Mark," Interpretation 22, 1 [1968], pp. 53–70.

Knox, W. L. *The Sources in the Synoptic Gospels*, i, St. Mark, London [1953].

Köster, H. *Synoptische Überlieferung bei den apostolischen Vätern*, Tübingen [1957]. "The Purpose of the Polemic of a Pauline Fragment," NTS 8 [1961–62], pp. 317–332. σπλάγχνον, TDNT vii, Grand Rapids [1971], pp. 548–559.

Kuby, A. "Zur Konzeption des Markus-Evangeliums," ZNTW 49 [1958], pp. 52–64.

Kümmel, W. G. "Das Gleichnis von den bösen Weingärtnern (Mark 12, 1–9)" in *Aux sources de la tradition chrétienne*. Festschrift M. Goguel [1950], pp. 120ff. *Promise and Fulfilment*, ET, London [1957]. *Introduction to the New Testament*, ET, London [1965]. "Eschatology and Expectation in the Proclamation of Jesus," in *The Future of our Religious Past*. Essays in honour of Rudolf Bultmann, ed. J. M. Robinson, London [1971].

Leenhardt, F.-J. *Le sacrement de la sainte Cène*, Paris/Neuchâtel [1948].

Lightfoot, R. H. *History and Interpretation in the Gospels*, London [1934]. *The Gospel Message of St. Mark*, Oxford [1950].

Lindars, B. *New Testament Apologetic*, London [1961].

Lindeskog, G. "The Veil of the Temple," Coniectanea Neotestamentica, xi [1947], pp. 132–137.

Linnemann, E. *Studien zur Passionsgeschichte*, Göttingen [1970].

Linton, O. "The Demand for a Sign from Heaven," Studia Theologica 19 [1965], pp. 112–129.

Lohmeyer, E. *Lord of the Temple*, ET, Edinburgh [1961]. *Das Evangelium des Markus*[17] (KEK), Göttingen [1967].

Lohse, E. "Hosianna," NovT vi [1963], pp. 113–19.

Longenecker, R. N. *The Christology of Early Jewish Christianity*, London [1971].

Luz, U. "Das Geheimnismotiv und die markinische Christologie," ZNTW 56 [1965], pp. 9–30.

Maddox, R. "The Function of the Son of man according to the Synoptic Gospels," NTS 15 [1968], pp. 45–74. "The Quest for Valid Methods in 'Son of Man Research,'" Theological Students' Fellowship Bulletin, 61 [1971], pp. 14–21.

Maier, P. L. "The Episode of the Golden Roman Shields at Jerusalem," Harvard Theological Review, 62 [1969], pp. 109–21.

Manson, T. W. *The Teaching of Jesus*, Cambridge [1931]. "The Failure of Liberalism to interpret the Bible as the Word of God," in *The Interpretation of the Bible*, ed. C. W. Dugmore, London [1944]. *Studies in the Gospels and Epistles*, ed. M. Black, Manchester [1962]. *The Beginning of the Gospel*, Cambridge [1950].

Martin, R. P. "The New Quest of the Historical Jesus," in *Jesus of Nazareth: Saviour and Lord*, ed. C. F. H. Henry, London [1966], pp. 25–45. *Carmen Christi: Philippians ii, 5–11 in Recent Interpretation and in the setting of early Christian Worship*, Cambridge [1967].

Mally, E. J. "The Gospel according to Mark," in *The Jerome Biblical Commentary*, London [1968].

Marshall, I. H. "The Synoptic Son of Man Sayings in Recent Discussion," NTS 12 [1965–66], pp. 327–51. "Son of God or Servant of Yahweh? A Reconsideration of Mark i, 11," NTS 15 [1969], pp. 326–36. "The Divine Sonship of Jesus," Interpretation 21 [1967], pp. 87–103.

Marxsen, W. *Mark the Evangelist*, ET, Nashville [1969]. *Introduction to the New Testament*, ET, Oxford [1968].

Maurer, C. "Knecht Gottes und Sohn Gottes im Passionsbericht des Markusevangelium," ZThK 50 [1953], pp. 1–38.

Mauser, U. W. *Christ in the Wilderness*, London [1963].

McCasland, S. V. "Signs and Wonders," JBL 76 [1957], pp. 149–52.

McIntyre, J. *The Shape of Christology*, London 1966.

Meye, R. P. "Messianic Secret and Messianic Didache in Mark's Gospel," in *Oikonomia*. Festschrift O. Cullmann ed. F. Christ, Hamburg [1967], pp. 57–68. *Jesus and the Twelve*, Grand Rapids [1968].

Meyer, R. προφήτης TDNT vi, Grand Rapids [1968], pp. 812–28.

Michaelis, W. *Einleitung in das neue Testament*, Bern [1954]. πάσχω TDNT v, Grand Rapids [1967], pp. 904–39.

Miller, D. L. "EMPAIZEIN: Playing the Mock Game (Luke 22: 63–64)," JBL 90 [1971], pp. 309–13.

Moule, C. F. D. "The Intention of the Evangelists," in *New Testament Essays*, in memory of T. W. Manson, ed. A. J. B. Higgins, Manchester [1959], pp. 165–179. "Jesus in New Testament Kerygma," in *Verborum Veritas*. Festschrift G. Stählin, Wuppertal [1970], pp. 15–26.

O'Neill, J. C. "The Silence of Jesus," NTS 15 [1968–69], pp. 153–167. "The Charge of Blasphemy at Jesus' Trial before the Sanhedrin," in *The Trial of Jesus*, ed. E. Bammel, London [1970].

Oostendrop, D. W. *Another Jesus: A Gospel of Jewish-Christian Superiority in II Corinthians*, Kampen [1967].

Otto, R. *The Kingdom of God and the Son of Man*, ET, London [1943].

Neill, S. *The Interpretation of the New Testament, 1861–1961*, Oxford [1964].

Niederwimmer, K. "Johannes Markus und die Frage nach dem Verfasser des zweiten Evangeliums," ZNTW 58 [1967], pp. 172–88.

Nineham, D. E. "The Order of Events in St. Mark's Gospel—An Examination of Dr. Dodd's Hypothesis," in *Studies in the Gospels*. Essays in memory of R. H. Lightfoot, ed. D. E. Nineham, Oxford [1955], pp. 223–39. *Saint Mark* (Pelican Gospel Commentaries), London [1963]. "Eye-witness Testimony and the Gospel Tradition," JTS ix, 1 [1958], pp. 13–25, ix, 2 [1958], pp. 243–252, xi, 2 [1960], pp. 253–64.

Percy, E. *Die Botschaft Jesu*, Lund [1953].

Perrin, N. *The Kingdom of God in the Teaching of Jesus*, London [1963]. "The Creative Use of the Son of Man Traditions by Mark," Union Seminary Quarterly Review 23 [1968], pp. 357–65. *Rediscovering the Teaching of Jesus*, London [1967]. *What is Redaction Criticism?* Philadelphia [1969]. "The Literary Gattung 'Gospel'—Some Observations," ExpT 82 [1970], pp. 4–7. "The Use of (παρα) διδόναι in connection with the Passion of Jesus in the New Testament," in *Der Ruf Jesu und die Antwort der Gemeinde*. Festschrift J. Jeremias, [1970], pp. 202–12.

Pesch, R. *Naherwartungen*, Düsseldorf [1968]. *Jesu ureigene Taten?* Freiburg [1970].

Pobee, J. "The Cry of the Centurion—a Cry of Defeat?" *The Trial of Jesus*, ed. E. Bammel, London [1970].

Popkes, W. *Christus Traditus*. Eine Untersuchung zum Begriff der Dahingabe im Neuen Testament, Zürich/Stuttgart [1967].

Powley, B. "The Purpose of the Messianic Secret: A Brief Survey," ExpT 80 [1968–69], pp. 308–10.

Quesnell, Q. *The Mind of Mark*, Rome [1969].

Rattey, B. K. *The Making of the Synoptic Gospels*, London [1942].

Rawlinson, A. E. J. *The Gospel according to St. Mark*, London [1925].

Rengstorf, K. H. σημεῖον TDNT vii, Grand Rapids [1971], pp. 200–60.

Reploh, K.-G. *Markus: Lehrer der Gemeinde*, Stuttgart [1969].

Richardson, A. *The Miracle Stories of the Gospels*, London [1941].

Riesenfeld, H. "Tradition und Redaktion im Markusevangelium," *Neutestamentliche Studien für R. Bultmann*, Berlin [1954], pp. 157–164. "On the Composition of the Gospel of Mark," *The Gospel Tradition*, ET, Philadelphia [1970].

Roberts, T. A. *History and Christian Apologetic*, London [1960].

Robinson, J. M. *The Problem of History in Mark*, London [1957]. *A New Quest of the Historical Jesus*, London [1959]. *Kerygma und historische Jesus*, Zürich [1960]. "The Problem of History in Mark Reconsidered," Union Seminary Quarterly Review 20 [1965], pp. 131–147. "On the *Gattung* of Mark (and John)" in *Jesus and Man's Hope*, ed. D. G. Buttrick, Philadelphia [1970]. "The Recent Debate on the 'New Quest,'" Journal of Bible and Religion 30 [1962], pp. 198–218.

Robinson, W. C. Jr. "Word and Power (1 Corinthians 1:17–2:5)," *Soli Deo Gloria*. W. C. Robinson. Festschrift ed. J. M. Richards, Richmond [1968], pp. 68–82.

Rohde, J. *Rediscovering the Teaching of the Evangelists*, ET, London [1968].

Roloff, J. *Das Kerygma und der irdische Jesus*, Göttingen [1970].

Ropes, J. H. *The Synoptic Gospels*, London [1934].

Sahlin, H. "Die Perikope vom gerasenischen Besessenen und der Plan des Markusevangeliums," Studia Theologica 18 [1964], pp. 159–172.

Sanday, W. "A Survey of the Synoptic Problem." Expositor iii, 4th series [1891], pp. 88–91. *The Life of Christ in Recent Research*, Oxford [1907].

Sawyer, H. "The Marcan Framework," SJT 14 [1961], pp. 279–294.

Schäfer, K. Th. "Und dann werden sie fasten, an jenem Tage (Mk. 2, 20 und Paralleln)", in *Synoptische Studien*. Festschrift A. Wikenhauser [1953], pp. 124–147.

Schille, G. "Bermerkungen zur Formgeschichte des Evangeliums. Rahmen und Aufbau des Markus-Evangelium," NTS 4 [1957–58], pp. 1–24.

Schmid, J. *The Gospel according to Mark*, ET, Cork [1968].

Schmidt, K. L. *Der Rahmen der Geschichte Jesus*, Berlin [1919].

Schmithals, W. *Gnosticism in Corinth*, ET, Nashville [1971]. *The office of Apostle in the early Church*, ET, Nashville [1969]. *Paul and the Gnostics*, ET, Nashville [1972].

Schneider, C. κάθημαι TDNT iii, Grand Rapids [1965], pp. 440–44.

Schniewind, J. *Euangelion. Ursprung und erste Gestalt des Begriffes Euangelion*.

Schrenk, G. ἱερός TDNT iii, Grand Rapids [1965], pp. 221–47.

Schulz, S. "Die Bedeutung des Markus für die Theologiegeschichte des Urchristentums," Studia Evangelica ii [1964], pp. 134–145. *Die Stunde der Botschaft*, Hamburg [1967] (²1970).

Schreiber, J. "Die Christologie des Markusevangeliums," ZThK 58 [1961], pp. 154–183.

Schweizer, E. "Anmerkungen zur Theologie des Markus," in *Neotestamentica et Patristica*. Festschrift O. Cullmann, Leiden [1962], pp. 35–46. *Lordship and Discipleship*, ET, London [1960]. "Mark's Contribution to the Quest of the Historical Jesus," NTS 10 [1963–64], pp. 421–32. "Die theologische Leistung des Markus," Evangelische Theologie 24 [1964], pp. 337–55. πνεῦμα TDNT v, Grand Rapids [1968], pp. 396–415. *The Good News according to Mark*, Richmond [1970]. ET of *Das Evangelium nach Markus* (Neue Testament Deutsch), Göttingen [1967].

Schweitzer, A. *The Quest of the Historical Jesus*, ET, London [1910] (New York, 1968, ed.).

Sowers, S. "The Circumstances and Recollection of the Pella Flight," Theologische Zeitschrift 26.5 [1970], pp. 305–20.

Stauffer, E. "Der Methurgeman des Petrus," in *Neutestamentliche Aufsätze: Festschrift J. Schmid*, Regensburg [1963], pp. 283–293.

Stein, R. H. "What is *Redaktionsgeschichte?*" JBL 88 [1969], pp. 45–56.

Stonehouse, N. B. *Origins of the Synoptic Gospels*, London [1963].

Strathamann, H. μάρτυς TDNT iv, Grand Rapids [1967], pp. 489–508.

Strecker, G. *Das Judenchristentum in den Pseudoklementinen*, Berlin [1958]. "Besprechung von W. Marxsen Der Evangelist Markus," Zeitschrift für Kirchengeschichte 72 [1961], pp. 145. "Zur Messiasgeheimnistheorie im Markusevangelium," Studia Evangelica ii [1964], pp. 87–104. "The Passion and Resurrection Predictions in Mark's Gospel," Interpretation 22 [1968], pp. 421–42.

Streeter, B. H. *The Four Gospels*, London [1924].

Talbert, C. H. *Reimarus: Fragments*, Philadelphia [1970].

Taylor, V. "The Messianic Secret in Mark," ExpT 59 [1947–48], pp. 146–51. "W. Wrede's The Messianic Secret in the Gospels," ExpT 65 [1953–54], pp. 248–50. *The Formation of the Gospel Tradition*, London [1935]. *Jesus and His Sacrifice*, London [1955]. *The Gospel according to St. Mark*, London [1959]. *The Text of the New Testament*, London [1961].

Thrall, M. E. "Elijah and Moses in Mark's Account of the Transfiguration," NTS 16 [1969–70], pp. 305–17.

Tillesse, G. Minette de, *Le secret messianique dans l'évangile de Marc*, Paris [1968].

Trocmé, E. *La formation de l'évangile de Marc*, Paris [1963].

Tödt, H.-E. *The Son of Man in the Synoptic Tradition*, ET, London [1965].

Turner, H. E. W. "The Tradition of Mark's Dependence upon Peter," ExpT 71 [1960], pp. 260–63.

Unnik, W. C. van. "Jesu Verhöhnung vor dem Synedrium (Mc. 14, 65 par)," ZNTW 29 [1930], pp. 310–311. "Zur Papias-Notiz über Markus (Eusebius H.E., III. 39.15)," ZNTW 54 [1963], pp. 276–77. "Alles ist dir möglich" in *Verborum Veritas*. Festschrift G. Stählin, Wuppertal [1970], pp. 27–36.

Vermès, G. *Scripture and Tradition*, Leiden [1961].

Vielhauer, Ph. "Erwägungen zur Christologie des Markusevangeliums," in *Zeit und Geschichte*. Festschrift R. Bultmann, ed. E. Dinkler, Tübingen [1964].

Vögtle, A. "Der Spruch vom Jonaszeichen," *Synoptische Studien*. Festschrift A. Wikenhauser, München [1953], pp. 230–77.

Votaw, C. W. *The Gospels and Contemporary Biographies in the Greco-Roman World*, Philadelphia [1970].

Walls, A. F. "Papias and Oral Tradition," Vigiliae Christianae 21 [1967], pp. 137–40.

Weeden, T. J. "The Heresy that Necessitated Mark's Gospel," ZNTW 59 [1968], pp. 145–58. *Mark: Traditions in Conflict*, Philadelphia [1971].

Williams, C. S. C. *Alterations to the Text of the Synoptic Gospels and Acts*, Oxford [1951].

Wilson, R. McL. "Gnostics—in Galatia?" Studia Evangelica iv [1968], pp. 358–67.

Wink, W. *John the Baptist in the Gospel Tradition*, Cambridge [1968]. "Jesus and Revolution: Reflections on S. G. F. Brandon's *Jesus and the Zealots*," Union Seminary Quarterly Review 25.1 [1969], pp. 37–59.

Wrede, W. *Das Messiasgeheimnis in den Evangelien*, Göttingen (3rd. ed.) [1963].

Zahrnt, H. *The Historical Jesus*, ET, London [1963].

ABBREVIATIONS

Arndt-Gingrich	W. F. Arndt and F. W. Gingrich, *A Greek-English Lexicon of the New Testament and Other Early Christian Literature*, Cambridge, 1957 (English Translation of W. Bauer, *Griechisch-Deutsches Wörterbuch zu Schriften des neuen Testaments*, Berlin, 1952⁴).
Blass-Debrunner-Funk	F. Blass and A. Debrunner, *A Greek Grammar of the New Testament and Other Early Christian Literature*, Cambridge, 1961 (English Translation and Edition by R. W. Funk of *Grammatik der neutestamentlichen Griechisch*, Göttingen, 1959¹⁰).
BJRL	*Bulletin of the John Rylands Library.*
EQ	*The Evangelical Quarterly.*
ExpT	*The Expository Times.*
HTR	*Harvard Theological Review*
JBL	*Journal of Biblical Literature.*
JTS	*Journal of Theological Studies.*
KEK	*Kritisch-Exegetischer Kommentar über das NT.* Edited by H. A. W. Meyer.
NBD	*The New Bible Dictionary*, ed. J. D. Douglas, 1962.
NovT	*Novum Testamentum.*
NTS	*New Testament Studies.*
SJT	*Scottish Journal of Theology.*
TDNT	*Theological Dictionary of the New Testament.* English translation by G. W. Bromiley of
TWNT	*Theologisches Wörterbuch zum neuen Testament*, Stuttgart, 1933ff. Edited by G. Kittel and G. Friedrich.
ZKG	*Zeitschrift für Kirchengeschichte*
ZNTW	*Zeitschrift für die neutestamentliche Wissenschaft.*
ZThK	*Zeitschrift für Theologie und Kirche.*

INDEX OF MAIN SUBJECTS TREATED

CHIEF VERSES IN MARK TREATED

INDEX OF MODERN AUTHORS